Statecraft and Nation Building in Africa: A Post-colonial Study

Godfrey Mwakikagile

Statecraft and Nation Building in Africa:
A Post-colonial Study

First Edition

ISBN 978-9987-16-039-6

New Africa Press
Dar es Salaam, Tanzania

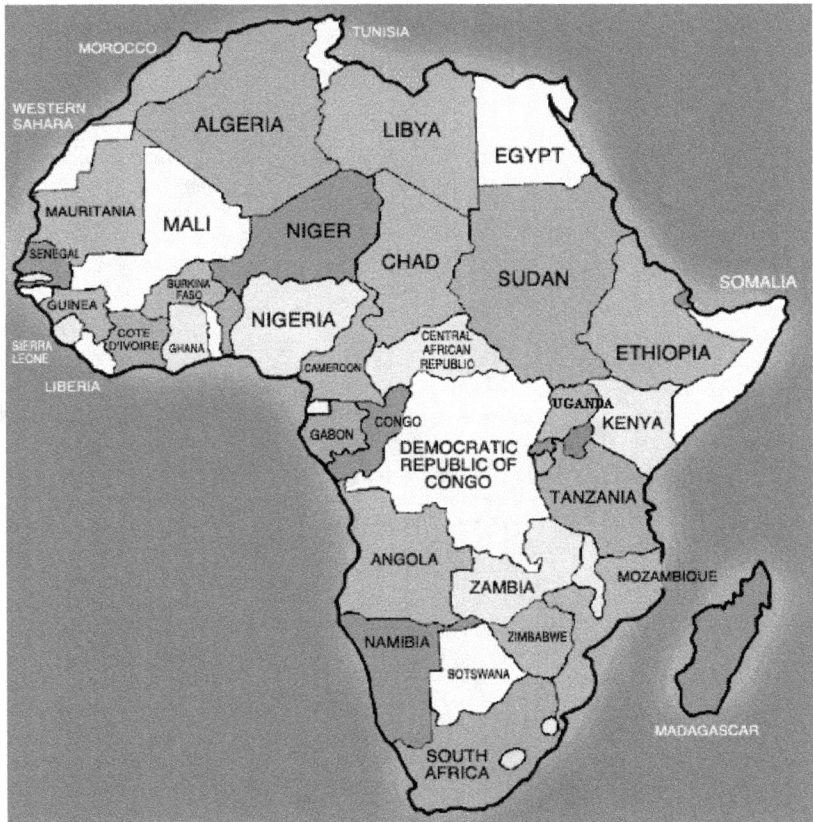

Contents

Chapter Five
Post-colonial Uganda:
National consolidation

Chapter Six
Amin's regime

Chapter Seven
Obote returns to power

Chapter Eight
Uganda under Museveni

Part III:

Conclusion

Introduction

THIS IS a study of statecraft and nation building in Africa in the post-colonial era.

Subjects covered include the early years of independence, the legitimacy of the state, institutional transformation, autocracy, quest for democracy, national integration, and consolidation of the state among others.

It focuses on case studies whose relevance is continental in scope.

The work has focused extensively on Uganda as one of the major case studies in the examination of Africa's transformation during the post-colonial period.

The country has gone through transitional phases characteristic of many countries on the continent: attainment of sovereign status under a democratic constitution, emergence of autocracy shortly after independence, ethno-regional rivalries, military coups, civil wars, and attempts to establish democratic institutions under very difficult conditions because of the refusal by the leaders to relinquish power.

As the highly centralised state continued to exercise hegemonic control over the people across the continent through the decades, a number of countries faced the prospect of disintegration. Civil strife ensued as a result of such mass regimentation.

Some countries descended into chaos. Many became highly unstable as the people continued to demand meaningful participation in the political process without which nation building is virtually impossible since its foundation is laid at the grassroots level requiring mass participation.

It was not until the 1990s that many African countries started to enjoy some form of democracy. But even that has been very limited in many cases.

Uganda provides a classic example of an African country that has gone through fundamental change since independence, including attempts to institutionalise democracy. And it continues to grapple with problems of democratic transformation and nation building just like other African countries do, providing an excellent case study that can help to provide some insights into the problems other countries on the continent face in their quest for peace, unity and development.

Part I

Chapter One:

One-Party System and National Unity: Consolidation of the Nation-State

SOON AFTER INDEPENDENCE, African countries faced the formidable task of nation-building, an undertaking which in most cases proved to be more difficult than the struggle for independence itself; except in a few countries where Africans had to resort to armed struggle to win their freedom.

But the Mau Mau phenomenon, if all the liberation wars in Africa may be collectively identified that way, was not continental in scope, although it had the potential to develop into one if the colonial authorities continued to ignore the demands of Africans. In the majority of cases, the colonial rulers transferred power to the nationalist leaders on peaceful terms; not because they wanted to, but because that was better than the alternative.

The prospect for mass insurrection in the colonies was real, and the colonial powers knew they would not have been able to contain it forever, as was clearly demonstrated in Angola, Mozambique, Guinea-Bissau, Zimbabwe, Namibia, and finally South Africa itself, the bastion of white minority rule on the continent.

But nation-building – which meant forging a common national identity by uniting the people in a given territory by appealing to nationalist sentiments and fostering and propagating shared values as well as invoking a common historical experience including suffering and humiliation at the hands of the colonial rulers; overcoming ethnic and regional rivalries and hostilities in pursuit of unity and stability on the basis of a common African identity and values; pursuing economic development and modernization – all that could not be done in countries which were not quite nations yet, although they identified themselves as such. It is true that Africans in the colonies fought for independence as one people.

However, that does not mean that they really considered themselves as one. As the premier of Northern Nigeria, Sir Ahmadu Bello, said during the Nigerian civil war (1967 - 1970) which threatened to split the country along ethnic lines:

"Politicians always delight in talking loosely about the unity of Nigeria. Sixty years ago there was no country called Nigeria. What is now Nigeria consisted of a number of large and small communities all of which were different in their outlooks and beliefs. The advent of British and Western education has not materially altered the situation and these many and varied communities have not knit themselves into a complete unit."[1]

It is a sentiment that was echoed by the Northern Nigerian delegation to the Ad Hoc Conference on the

Nigerian Constitution in Lagos in September 1966:

"We have pretended for too long that there are no differences between the people of Nigeria. The hard fact which we must honestly accept as of permanent importance in the Nigerian experiment especially for the future is that we are different peoples brought together by recent accidents of history. To pretend otherwise will be folly."[2]

But it was not just the Northern Nigerians who felt that way. The leaders of all the three massive regions which then constituted the Federation of Nigeria – formed in 1946 – expressed the same sentiment, only in varying degrees. In the midst of the civil war itself, the Biafran leader Colonel Odumegwu Ojukwu made an impassioned plea before the Organization of African Unity (OAU) in Addis Ababa, Ethiopia, on August 5, 1968, for recognition of his secessionist region as an independent state on grounds of incompatibility:

"The former Federation encompassed peoples of such vast political, economic, religious and cultural differences as could hardly ever have co-existed peacefully as one independent political entity."[3]

And as far back as 1947, the leader of Western Nigeria, Chief Obafemi Awolowo, stated in his book *Path to Nigerian Freedom*: "Nigeria is not a nation. It is a mere geographical expression. There are no Nigerians."[4] And in the 1950s, the decade preceding independence, Northern Nigerians talked seriously about pulling out of the federation and establishing their own independent state, as did Awolowo in 1953 when the British Colonial Secretary Oliver Lyttelton ruled that Lagos shall remain federal territory as capital of the federation.

Awolowo wanted Lagos to be incorporated into the Western Region under his jurisdiction, since it was located in Western Nigeria, his tribal homeland of the Yoruba. When the British colonial secretary ruled against that at the constitutional talks on the future of Nigeria attended by all Nigerian leaders in London in August 1953, Awolowo stormed out of the conference and threatened to pull the Western Region out of the federation. Only Eastern Nigeria did not threaten to secede. Ironically, it was also the first to secede, but only after it was compelled to do so by the massacres of tens of thousands of its people – 30,000 to 50,000 – in Northern Nigeria in 1966, and by the unwillingness of the northern and the federal authorities to intervene and stop the pogroms.

But such secessionist sentiments were not peculiar to Nigeria. The history of the former Belgian Congo during the turbulent sixties is well-known when Katanga Province, led by Moise Tshombe, seceded only 11 days after Congo won independence on 30 June 1960. South Kasai Province, home of the Baluba tribe, also seceded in December 1961 under the leadership of Albert Kalonji who declared himself king of Kasai. And the remaining four provinces also tried to establish themselves as independent states in the early sixties.

In Ghana, the Ashanti were resolutely opposed to a unitary state established by Dr. Kwame Nkrumah, and made unsuccessful attempts to have a federal constitution which would have enabled them to retain their independence through extensive devolution of power short of sovereign status. For centuries before the advent of colonial rule, Ashanti, also known as Asante, had existed as an independent nation ruled by the Asantehene (king).

It was also one of the most powerful kingdoms in pre-colonial Africa before it was finally conquered by the British in one of the bloodiest wars in colonial history.

Uganda was also seriously threatened by the attempted

secession of the Buganda kingdom. Like Ashanti, Buganda was also an independent nation before the imposition of colonial rule, and was ruled by a king known as *kabaka* in the local Kiganda language. Even after independence, the kingdom considered itself to be a separate nation. On 20 May 1966 almost four years after independence, the kingdom's parliament known as Lukiiko demanded Uganda's expulsion from Buganda by May 30th because it did not fully recognize the national government's jurisdiction over the kingdom. And it did not relent until Ugandan Prime Minister Milton Obote, in a swift military move, took over Kabaka Edward Frederick Mutesa's palace.

The *kabaka* went into self-imposed exile in Britain where he continued to rail against Ugandan authority over his kingdom until his death in November 1969.

Other kingdoms in Uganda – Toro, Bunyoro, Ankole, and the princedom of Busoga – were also opposed to the national government. They considered themselves to be autonomous entities with their own political systems and institutions independent of central authority, as had been the case before the conquest of Africa and imposition of colonial rule by Europeans.

Zambia also had to contend with secessionist threats, especially by Barotse Province also known as Barotseland, home of the Lozi people, ruled by its own king known as *litunga* in the Lozi language. Other provinces and different tribes were also embroiled in ethnoregional rivalries. But the greatest threat to national integrity came from Barotseland. However, they all posed great danger to national unity and, for a short period in February 1968, President Kenneth Kaunda resigned as head of state. As he put it, he was "upset by a terrible provincial and tribal approach to our national problems."[5]

It was true elsewhere across the continent, and such ethnoregional loyalties caused a lot of problems for the young nations which had just won independence as "one people," yet had to contend with tribalism – hence secession in a number of cases – as the biggest threat to national unity. Compounding the problem was the fact that, contrary to what many people had expected, independence did not bring immediate relief to millions of Africans trapped in poverty and suffering from disease and ignorance; even decades after the end of colonial rule, millions across the continent have yet to enjoy the fruits of independence.

Such rising expectations only fuelled resentment against central authority, as Africans grappled with the problems of nation-building with only scant resources in countries which are the poorest of the poor in the world. And they could not expect to survive as nations if they were structured along tribal lines. Therefore, even before nation-building in terms of economic development could be seriously considered, every African country had to contend with another formidable task: forging a sense of common identity and loyalty to the nation composed of different tribes, many of which were suspicious and jealous of each other or one another, and sometimes outright hostile towards each other.

So, tribes "had to go." They could no longer exist as autonomous entities for one simple reason. Tribalism is incompatible with nationalism, and nation-building is impossible without nationhood. And you can't have nationhood without a genuine feeling of common citizenship and identity which goes beyond saluting the same flag and travelling on the same passport.

Therefore, right from the beginning, consolidation of the nation-state – institutions of authority over national territory – went hand-in-hand with nation-building. One could not be given priority over the other, and the state could not be consolidated without containing or neutralizing tribalism. Tribalism was, and still is, a constant threat to the existence of African countries, almost all of which were artificially created during the partition of Africa by the European powers about 130 years ago at the Berlin Conference which lasted from November 1884 - February 1885.

With the exception of the Arab countries in North Africa, and Somalia which is almost entirely composed of ethnic Somalis except for a small number of people from Bantu tribes in Kenya, Tanzania and Mozambique who were taken there as slaves by the Arabs during the slave trade more than 300 years ago, none of the countries on the continent are ethnically homogeneous entities, as is the case in most countries around the world.

Even Botswana is not entirely Tswana, although it is about 80 percent; nor is Swaziland entirely Swazi, although it is in overwhelming numbers in black Africa's last kingdom.

After the partition of Africa, the countries created were no more than a collection – not even an amalgamation – of different, often antagonistic, tribes just lumped together by the colonial powers to satisfy their imperial ambitions. The colonial boundaries were arbitrarily drawn without the slightest concern for the interests and well-being of Africans. All the tribes, not just some, saw themselves as independent entities or nations – even if held captive by other tribes – and would secede anytime if they got the chance to do so. Besides their skin colour and hair texture, they saw themselves as different from each other, and the nation-state a mere imposition by alien intruders from Europe, thus making the task of nation-building a very complicated one. As Obafemi Awolowo said, the people who are called Nigerians – a collection of more than 250 different ethnic groups – are as different from each other as much as the people of different European countries are. 6

But African countries have survived as political entities despite the odds against them through the decades since independence. Therefore, just holding them together, preventing them from falling apart, is a great achievement even though they have survived as weak nations. But Africa would have been even weaker, much weaker, had the countries broken up along tribal lines, with each tribe ruling itself as was the case in precolonial times, except for conquered tribes which were ruled by others.

Yet African countries are not given credit for that. Keeping the tribes together is an enormous task even today. And maintaining the countries as functional units where members of different tribes and races work together and even identify themselves as one people, is an even greater achievement, considering the fact that the disruptive forces inherent in such complex multi-ethnic societies are beyond the capacity of the state to contain them without using a skillful combination of persuasive and coercive power. There is no army that can stop all the tribes in a country from tearing it apart if they decide to go their own way. Only a few can be destructive enough, wreaking havoc nationwide.

Therefore in fairness, if African leaders are considered to be a failure in many areas, which they are, frankly speaking, they should at least be given credit for keeping their countries united and, in some cases, for creating a sense of common identity among different tribes within their national boundaries. As Julius Nyerere said many years after he stepped down as president of Tanzania, his greatest failure was that although he managed to unite Tanganyika and Zanzibar to create Tanzania in 1964, he was never able to persuade the leaders of neighbouring countries to form a larger federation, a move he believed would have made the region a powerhouse:

"I felt that these little countries in Africa were really too small, they would not be viable – the Tanganyikas, the Rwandas, the Burundis, the Kenyas. My ambition in East Africa was really never to build a Tanganyika. I wanted an

East African federation. So what did I do in succeeding? My success is building a nation out of this collection of tribes."[7]

He also went on to say: "A new leadership is developing in Africa....The military phase is out. I think the single-party phase is out."[8]

A few years after independence, the one-party state was introduced in most African countries and was justified by the leaders on the grounds that it was the most effective apparatus for mobilizing different tribes under one leadership to achieve national unity. And it proved to be a potent weapon, although in more than one way, including suffocation of legitimate dissent in most cases. But, in spite of its shortcomings, the one-party system did eliminate one danger which threatened practically all African countries during the early years of independence when peoples of different tribes did not identify with each other as one people: formation of political parties along ethnic and regional lines in the name of democracy under a multi-party system, despite constitutional bans against formation of such parties. There would always have been ways to circumvent that, including formation of ethnoregional alliances to the exclusion of others.

That would have been the end of African countries. Besides Nkrumah, Nyerere was probably the most articulate exponent of the one-party state on the continent, and its most successful practitioner for two decades; Tanzania became a *de jure* one-party state in 1965, and Nyerere stepped down from the presidency in 1985, although he continued to be chairman of the ruling party (Chama Cha Mapinduzi - CCM - Party of the Revolution) until 1990, two years before multi-party politics was introduced with his full support. As he said in an interview not long before he died:

17

"I really think that I ran the most successful single-party system on the continent. You might not even call it a party. It was a single, huge nationalist movement....I don't believe that our country would be where it is now if we had a multiplicity of parties, which would have become tribal and caused us a lot of problems. But when you govern for such a long time, unless you are gods, you become corrupt and bureaucratic.... So I started calling for a multiparty system."[9]

Few would say it would have better for African countries to have split up along tribal lines, plunging them into chaos and civil wars, than to have peace and unity under one-party rule that guaranteed their survival as nations even if that meant curtailed freedom, suffocating dissent. There was not one African country that was safe then, or is safe today, from the danger of tribalism. And that includes those composed of small tribes, such as Tanzania whose 126 tribes – except one or two – are too small, weak and poor to survive as viable entities even if they wanted to secede. But if tribalism is widespread, even small tribes can be just as disruptive. Aware of the danger of tribalism, President Nyerere addressed the subject in his annual radio broadcast to the nation on the seventh independence anniversary on 9 December 1968. He spoke in Kiswahili, the national language:

"I have begun to hear whispers about tribalism. Just after independence, we got complaints that people were being appointed to government positions on the basis of tribalism, and we immediately appointed a commission to look into the allegations. The commission proved without any doubt that there was no tribalism in the allocation of jobs in government.

But just recently, I began to hear this complaint again. I did not treat it lightly. We called some of these people who were saying there is tribalism, and told them to give their evidence either to me or to Chief Mang'enya (the ombudsman). We promised to investigate immediately. But they have not given us one shred of evidence....

Tanzanians who had the opportunity for higher education during colonial rule were mostly Wahaya, Wachaga, and Wanyakyusa. And because most of the education was provided by missionaries, most of these people are also Christians. And when we replace Europeans who hold responsible jobs, and give those jobs to Tanzanians, the people who get them come mostly from these three tribes. Therefore, if you ask me why Wahaya, Wachaga, and Wanyakyusa have most of the jobs which require higher education, the answer is very obvious. They are the ones who got higher education during colonial times.

I would say, look at the positions in politics, where a person is not asked about his educational qualifications. Look at Parliament, the National Executive, the Central Committee of TANU (ruling party), and at the Cabinet. How many Wanyakyusa, Wahaya, or Wachaga are members? You will find that perhaps there aren't any, or there is one or two....

It is the job of the government to help, even favour, the more backward parts of the country, especially regarding education. We are doing this and will continue to do so. But if a Mchaga, a Mhaya or a Mnyakyusa young man were denied a job because of his tribe – when he is capable and there is no other Tanzanian with the necessary qualifications – then we would be practising a very stupid and very evil kind of tribalism which led to the establishment of Biafra."[10]

It would have been very easy for such people, who were complaining about tribalism yet could not prove it was a factor in the allocation of jobs as President Nyerere said, to form their own political parties on tribal and ethnoregional basis – and even forge alliances with other "victimized" tribes – under the multiparty system and ignite tribal conflict; a potential catastrophe the one-party system, which embraced and accommodated all the tribes under the same political tent, was able to contain and neutralize in many African countries, especially in the early years of independence when the countries were in their formative stage trying to forge a true sense of national identity among the different ethnic groups.

This should not, in any way, be misconstrued as a defence of dictatorship but an objective appraisal of the functional utility of the one-party system and the positive role it played in saving African countries from splitting along tribal lines. And that entailed curtailment of freedom in many cases; a sad necessity, not in all but in some cases, when it was critical to avert the catastrophe of national disintegration. In most cases, it was sheer abuse of power, with many leaders invoking the specter of national disintegration to perpetuate themselves in office.

But that does not mean that the positive role played by the one-party system as a unifying force during those critical years should be ignored; a positive contribution even some African leaders don't want to acknowledge simply because they are so much opposed to one-party rule, although for good reasons, mostly abuse of power. As Nicephore Soglo, former president of Benin, stated after losing the election in 1996:

"The West African country of Benin held elections in March (1996). I lost the presidency....

While former President Mathieu Kerekou has returned to power, there is a difference now. Twenty-four years ago, he came to power by the barrel of the gun. This year it was by way of the ballot box....

Many claim that Africa is different, that it is not ready for democracy. Ethnic tensions are pointed to as poisoning democracy. We have ethnic tensions in Benin. We have managed them. Sadly, many African leaders of the early independence years used these same arguments to justify their repressive rule."[11]

Yet Benin itself, then known as Dahomey, was almost torn apart by ethnic strife during the early years of independence, something Soglo conveniently overlooks. It is a subject I have also addressed in one of my books, *Military Coups in West Africa since the Sixties.*[12]

Would a multiparty system, with several parties formed on ethnic and regional basis as was the case in Dahomey in the sixties, have served the country better? Or would it have made things worse, exacerbating ethnoregional rivalries and hostilities? It is true that Nicephore Soglo conceded ethnic tensions still exist in Dahomey today, as they do in other African countries. And Benin has survived under those tensions in a democratic environment of multiparty politics. But that is today.

African countries are stronger today as political entities than they were during their early years of independence, although all are still vulnerable to ethnic conflicts; but not as vulnerable as they were when they emerged from colonial rule. They were very young then, newly born. They did not have strong governments. They did not command full allegiance from different tribes which regarded central authority as an alien institution imposed on them to destroy their tribal and traditional values and leadership. And all their political institutions, inherited from the departing colonial masters, were not restructured to reflect African realities and accommodate or harmonise conflicting ethnoregional interests.

They were not firmly established and could have collapsed any time from the slightest push by tribalists if these tribal chauvinists had the opportunity to form opposition parties to promote their agenda. And being tribalists and regionalists, they naturally would have appealed to tribal sentiments to achieve their goals which would have been at variance with national aspirations.

The situation is different today across Africa. African countries are more mature. They have survived an entire generation since independence; most of them half a century. And they don't need one-party rule as they did before, except – and that's may be – in some cases such as Rwanda and Burundi where the one-party system embracing both the Hutu and the Tutsi may be the only way to guarantee justice and equality for all. The Tutsi will never win an election against the Hutu majority under a multiparty system.

Political parties in both countries have always been structured along ethnic lines, excluding the Hutu majority from power, except in Rwanda from 1962 to 1994 when the Hutu were in control. Both Rwanda and Burundi have historically been dominated by the Tutsi for about 400 years since they came from the northeastern part of Africa and conquered the Hutu.

The one-party system may also be a temporary safeguard against national disintegration when a country faces total collapse, requiring the need for a united or coalition government under strong leadership.

Although it is true that African countries today are ready for multiparty democracy, Soglo's contention that such a system would have been appropriate for Africa even in the sixties after independence, does not correspond to reality even in his own country. How could it have contained tribalism and ethnoregional rivalries in Dahomey, as Benin was then called, during those early years of independence?

Dahomey won independence on 1 August 1960, under the leadership of Hubert Maga, a northerner. His main support came from the north because the country was plagued by ethnic rivalries, especially between northerners and southerners. Because of such ethnoregional rivalries,

President Maga did not have clear mandate to rule the country, since he hardly had any support in the south. And as expected, southerners also had their own leaders who enjoyed little support in the north, President Maga's ethnoregional stronghold. Justin Ahomadegbe had solid support in the south, while another leader, Migan Apithy, commanded allegiance in the central part of the country and in some parts of the south. Such divisions made it virtually impossible for the national leaders to govern effectively. In October 1963, President Hubert Maga was overthrown in a military coup led by Colonel Christophe Soglo, a southerner.

But the coup did not end ethnic and regional rivalries. Democracy was tried but thwarted by ethnic rivals. When Dahomey tried to hold elections in 1970 after the results of the 1968 electoral contest were annulled, northern and southern politicians were so bitterly divided that the elections were cancelled. It would, of course, be an oversimplification to blame all of Dahomey's problems on ethnic rivalries. Economic problems and social unrest across the country caused by a number of factors also played a significant role and made it it difficult for the government to exercise effective control. They were one of the main reasons why President Hubert Maga's government was overthrown.

But all those problems were exacerbated by ethnic rivalries which have always plagued African countries since independence, even in times of economic prosperity and political stability rarely enjoyed on this troubled continent.

Contending that the multiparty system would have served African countries better than the one-party system in the early years of independence when they were most vulnerable to ethnic and regional rivalries, is to ignore the destructive nature of ethno-nationalism; the most potent force in the world even today, as much as it has been throughout history. It is also to ignore the potential for disruption unscrupulous politicians always exploit in multiparty politics, a term synonymous with multi-tribal politics in the African context. Because of its tolerance of dissent, the multiparty system enables – even if it does not legally allow – almost anybody, including tribalists and regionalists and other disruptive elements, in the name of democracy to form political parties with a hidden partisan agenda while professing national unity. And Africa has already suffered and continues to suffer from some of the worst excesses of this ethno-nationalist impulse.

In the sixties, ethnic hatred of the Igbos in Nigeria exploded with such unconstrained fury that it almost destroyed Africa's largest nation at a cost of more than one million lives, mostly Igbo. It also exploded in Rwanda where almost one million Tutsis were slaughtered in only three months, and in neighbouring Burundi where hundreds of thousands of Hutus – at least 300,000 – were massacred by the Tutsi in the 1990s alone. And the massacres continued as the Tutsi refused to share power with the Hutu on meaningful basis. Where was the multiparty system to avert such catastrophe? Instead, it fanned flames in all three countries.

When Nigeria exploded during the sixties, it was a multiparty state. But all the parties were regionally entrenched with a strong ethnic bias. Even the National Convention of Nigerian Citizens (NCNC) – until 1960 known as the National Council of Nigeria and the Cameroons – which was led by Dr. Nnamdi Azikiwe and had supporters in all three regions of Nigeria, was strongest in the Eastern Region dominated by the Igbos. The Action Group led by Chief Obafemi Awolowo enjoyed overwhelming support among the Yorubas who dominate the Western Region. And the Northern People's Congress (NPC) led by Sir Ahmadu Bello, the Sardauna of Sokoto, was firmly entrenched in the Northern Region dominated by the Hausa-Fulani; Bello was Fulani.

Would a one-party state, under a single party of

national unity, have helped Nigeria in its turbulent times through the years? No one knows, given its size and complexity as a multi-polity of more than 250 ethnic groups and religious differences especially between the predominantly Muslim north and Christian as well as animist south. But one thing is certain, however controversial it may be. Militocracy – or military rule also known as stratocracy – as a kind of "one-party state," at least kept the country united, through coercion, and prevented the genocidal rampage that took place during the sixties and which was triggered by tribalism.

This is not to justify military rule – soldiers do not have the mandate to rule, they should stay in the barracks, and obey the rule of law under democratically elected leaders; it is simply to point out that an ethnically diverse population with a history of tribal conflicts needs strong leadership under one central government that is capable of accommodating all groups on equal basis but which also should be willing to decentralise power to diffuse tensions.

The alternative is national disintegration, or a weak federal system – or confederation – under which different ethnic groups become autonomous entities with the right to secede; a subject I have addressed in the last part of the book. A weak federal system is better than total disintegration of African countries into hundreds of independent ethnostates. But most lleaders across the continent chose one-party and authoritarian rule to contain tribalism and maintain national unity. And it worked.

Even today, when most African countries are trying to experiment with multiparty politics, a case can still be made for one-party rule. If the multiparty system is going to enable people to form political parties on ethnic or regional basis and even form alliances to prevent members of some ethnic groups from winning public office, then one-party rule is justified to maintain national unity and guarantee equality for all. Or let some people go, if they are excluded from power by their fellow countrymen. They have the right to establish their own independent state and rule themselves, as the Igbos did in the late sixties.

It is true that one-party rule has been a tragedy in most African countries for decades. But when you have ethnoregional rivalries accentuated by multiparty politics, one-party rule may be a better alternative. It may be the only way members of all tribes and all regions can compete for office on equal basis because the single party is open to everybody, as was the case in Tanzania under President Julius Nyerere. In fact, Tanzania's ruling party was more than just a political party. It was a national movement.

In defence of multiparty politics, an argument can be made that the constitution prohibits formation of tribal or regionally entrenched parties. And it can. But in practice, how effective is it? Tribal and regional parties – or parties with a hidden agenda to promote tribal and regional interests – have ways of legally qualifying for the ballot under the constitution by merging with other ethnoregional parties to win national mandate. They may seem to be nationally representative. But they will continue to be tribalist if their purpose of forming a coalition is to exclude members of some regions or tribes from winning elections. And such alliances have been formed in the past, although in the case of Azikiwe's NCNC, its decision to form an alliance with the Northern People's Congress (NPC) at independence in 1960 was not in pursuit of a tribal agenda.

Dr. Azikiwe's NCNC and the Northern People's Congress (NPC) led by Sir Abubakar Tafawa Balewa but dominated by Sir Ahmadu Bello, formed an alliance which excluded Awolowo's Action Group from the first African federal government formed at independence in October 1960. It would, of course, be wrong to characterize the alliance as tribalist deliberately intended to exclude

26

Yorubas from power. It was a marriage of convenience for political expediency. Azikiwe's party, the NCNC, was not ethnic but national in character. It was the only party which had members in all three regions and even won seats in the Northern and Western Regional Assemblies, the regional strongholds of the Hausa-Fulani and the Yoruba, respectively.

Therefore Azikiwe's move was a tactical alliance with a party – the Northern People's Congress – which had the largest number of representatives in the federal legislature, although it represented only one region: Northern Nigeria. It was also the most tribalistic, and most conservative, of all the Nigerian political parties dominated by northern Muslim traditional rulers who brooked no dissent. Even the Action Group, led by Awolowo, an uncompromising Yoruba bigot who died in 1986 at the age of 76, had some members in the Eastern Region, although not many.

But in spite of its virulently ethnoregional bias, the Northern People's Congress emerged as Nigeria's ruling party, since it dominated the federal legislature because of the structural imbalance of the federation favouring the north.

The British colonial rulers formed a structurally flawed federation of three massive regions – instead of several – dominated by the country's three largest ethnic groups. The smaller ones were left out of the equation and never became a factor in determining the future of the country. They were frozen out of power.

The Northern Region had the largest population, officially, although the other two regions disputed the 1956 census figures taken just four years before independence. The census was deeply flawed.

And because of the numerical preponderance enjoyed by the north, based on those census figures, the region also produced the largest number of representatives in the national legislature.

An entire half of the members of the Nigerian

parliament were northerners who, by simple majority rule, were legally entitled under the constitution to form the federal government. And that meant a national government dominated by the Northern People's Congress whose dominant figure was the Sardauna of Sokoto, Sir Ahmadu Bello. The federal prime minister, Tafawa Balewa, also a northerner and titular head of the Northern People's Congress and the Nigerian Federal Government, was no more than a puppet manipulated at will by the Northern Premier Ahmadu Bello.

Nigeria emerged from colonial rule with a federal constitution which theoretically guaranteed justice and equality for all. But its future looked bleak because of the lopsided nature of the federation favouring the north at the expense of the other regions, and excluding minority groups from the centre. And it had catastrophic consequences, plunging the country into civil war only a few years later, a conflict that almost destroyed the nation.

The flawed structure of the federation continued to be a source of many problems and instability even after the federation was restructured several times; it now has 39 states, the last added by democratically elected President Olusegun Obasanjo, a southerner.

And because of historical inequalities in the allocation of power, northerners dominated the federation for almost 40 years since independence. Most of the rulers were soldiers from Northern Nigeria. Tribalism and regional biases continue to be some of the major problems Nigeria faces, and northern military rulers only made the situation much worse. As Professor Crawford Young stated in his article, "The Impossible Necessity of Nigeria: A Struggle for Nationhood," in *Foreign Affairs:*

"During most of Nigeria's 27 years (almost 30 years until May 1999 when Olusegun Obasanjo took over as elected president) of military rule, the senior autocrat has been from the north. The two civilian prime ministers (one

28

was actually a president, Shehu Shagari, 1979 – 83) – from 1960 to 1966, and 1979 to 1983 – (the only civilian rulers the country had since independence in 1960 before Obasanjo, a former military head of state, was elected as a civilian president in 1999) were both Hausa-Fulani, the politically and demographically dominant ethnic category in the north. Even though Generals Yakubu Gowon (1966 – 1975), Ibrahim Babangida (1983 – 1993), and Sani Abacha (1993 –1998) are not themselves Hausa-Fulani, (they are all northerners and) Nigerians view them as integral parts of what Wole Soyinka terms 'a self-perpetuating clique from the yet feudally oriented part of the country.'"[13]

Soyinka goes on to denounce this ruling clique in his book, *The Open Sore of A Continent: A Personal Narrative of the Nigerian Crisis:*

"(It is an) infinitesimal but well-positioned minority....In denouncing the activities of this minority, described variously as the Sokoto Caliphate, the Northern Elite, the Kaduna Mafia, the Hausa-Fulani oligarchy, the Sardauna Legacy, the Dan Fodio Jihadists, et cetera, what is largely lost in the passion and outrage is that they do constitute a minority – a dangerous, conspiratorial, and reactionary clique, but a minority just the same. Their tentacles reach deep, however, and their fanaticism is the secular face of religious fundamentalism."[14]

And when Sani Abacha, a demented Kanuri – not Hausa-Fulani – from Kano, annulled the results of the June 1993 presidential election won by Moshood Abiola, a Yoruba from the southwest but who was able to garner impressive support in the eastern and northern parts of Nigeria as well, in addition to overwhelming backing in his native Yorubaland in the west, he only confirmed fears among many Nigerians that he was determined to perpetuate northern domination of the federation and pushed the country to the brink of disaster. The country almost split along ethnic lines, and would probably have, had he not suddenly died of a heart attack in July 1998, reportedly after being poisoned by a prostitute.

The results of the June 1993 elections had actually been annulled by his predecessor, Ibrahim Babangida, but Abacha sealed the annulment instead of reversing it after he seized power and imprisoned Abiola when he claimed office the following June as the legitimate president of Nigeria. Abacha had the chance to rectify the situation. But he chose not to, and made the annulment final. And as Soyinka said about this betrayal and denial of the people's mandate: "(It was) the most treasonable act of larceny of all time: It violently robbed the Nigerian people of their nationhood."[15]

Soyinka is not alone in doubting that Nigeria will continue to exist as a single political entity. Many other Nigerians share the same sentiment. They include a significant number of Yorubas, Igbos, Ogonis, Ijaws and others in the Niger Delta who have been marginalised, especially under northern military rulers who dominated the federation for decades. Even the three titans of the Nigerian independence movement – Nnamdi Azikiwe, Obafemi Awolowo, and Ahmadu Bello – did, at different times, question the viability of the structurally flawed federation, and even the wisdom of preserving Nigeria as one country.

Ethnic rivalry and mistrust was, and still is – together with religious fanaticism among some Muslims such as Boko Haram and others in the north – the fundamental problem threatening the existence of Nigeria.

Soyinka, like many Nigerians and other Africans including this writer, still would like to see Nigeria remain united, but admits: "I...frankly could not advance an invulnerable reason for my preference for a solution that did not involve disintegration."[16]

Even more tragic for Africa is the fact that Nigeria is not the only country facing this bleak prospect. The Democratic Republic of Congo, the giant nation that has become the bleeding heart of Africa right in the middle of the continent, was virtually partitioned into fiefdoms dominated by rebel groups in the east and by an inept and powerless central government that exercised virtually no control over the remaining parts of the country since 1998 when the insurgents launched a rebellion – ignited by Rwanda and Uganda, with Burundi's involvement – to overthrow President Laurent Kabila.

The rebellion continued after his son Joseph Kabila took over, following his assassination in January 2001. This former Belgian colony, which lost at least 10 million people under the brutal imperial rule of King Leopold II, has been the scene of carnage for more than a century. Between August 1998, when the rebellion started, and June 2001, about 3 million people died in eastern Congo as a result of the war. And the carnage continued. The Congo should never have been one country. And as Professor Crawford Young wrote about another giant African nation: "Nigeria has little cultural logic; its peoples would never have chosen to live together."[17]

Most of the tribes in other African countries would never have chosen to live together either. Before the advent of colonial rule, each had its own leaders. And had it not been for the European colonial rulers who partitioned Africa and lumped different tribes together, they would have continued to live the same way as independent micro-nations or ethnostates. The secessionist attempts by all three regions in Nigeria dominated by three main ethnic groups is instructive in this context.

Yet, in Nigeria like everywhere else across the

continent, attempts were made by African leaders to transcend tribalism and regionalism for the sake of national unity. When Dr. Nnamdi Azikiwe formed an alliance with Federal Prime Minister Tafawa Balewa, a northerner, it was with the hope that although Nigerians "would never have chosen to live together," they could at least try to contain or even submerge their tribal and regional differences in order to live together. Therefore this alliance was different from many others in one fundamental respect: It was not formed to promote tribal interests or deliberately exclude Yorubas from power but to save Nigeria as a collective entity, with the predominantly Yoruba party, the Action Group, forming the official opposition.

However, there have been other alliances in Nigeria and other African countries that have been formed deliberately to promote tribal interests and exclude members of some ethnic groups from holding public office; for example the Igbo in Nigeria. Tribal and regional parties forming such alliances in order to technically qualify as "national parties" under the constitution which expressly forbids formation of such parties are not complying with the constitution – they are circumventing and subverting the constitution.

And if there is no other way members of excluded groups can be protected and qualify for office, then – short of secession – the one-party system is totally justified under those circumstances, since it is capable of accommodating members of all tribes and regions on equal footing. It is in this context that the one-party system should be viewed as a very effective weapon against tribalism in African countries. And that was especially the case when they were just new nations trying to establish themselves shortly after independence.

Even as late as the 1990s and beyond, many people in Tanzania questioned the functional utility of the multiparty system because of the divisions and the violence it caused in what had been one of the most peaceful and stable countries in Africa for decades when it was under one-party rule. Tanzania was a one-party state for almost 30 years under the leadership of President Julius Nyerere. And not once in those years was the country rocked by violence caused by political factions pursuing partisan interests as happened after the introduction of multiparty democracy which has even provided an opportunity for many tribalists to form tribal associations; a phenomenon unheard of under Nyerere.

Even students at the University of Dar es Salaam, who are supposed to be liberal-minded, have formed tribal organizations. As one student from Tanga complained in an interview with one of Tanzania's leading newspapers, *The Guardian,* on 20 July, 2002, the situation on campus was so bad that even a sick student could not count on getting help from a roommate who was not a member of the same tribe. Help had to come from his or her fellow tribesmen and their organization.

And that is tragic, posing great danger to national unity that was carefully nurtured by the nation's founding father Mwalimu Julius Nyerere for almost half a century.

If Tanzania is to remain a strong, stable, and united nation, then tribal associations should be banned, and should not enjoy legal protection from the government in the name of pluralism. People of different tribes should belong to the same civic organizations, which may be called the Tanzania Brotherhood Associations, or whatever other names they choose, in place of tribal associations. Otherwise Tanzania may be headed towards catastrophe, with prospects for tribal conflict and national disintegration being a distinct possibility.

That is the main reason why, in a national survey conducted before the introduction of multiparty politics in the early 1990s, the majority of Tanzanians who participated in it were resolutely opposed to the adoption of the multiparty system. They feared it would divide the country and threaten national stability and were vindicated a few years later when violence erupted following the general election in 2000 which resulted in a number of deaths, prompting President Benjamin Mkapa to publicly wonder if the people were not wiser than the leaders when they rejected the multipatry system in the early nineties.

But the multiparty system was introduced, anyway, against prevailing national sentiment and in defiance of the people's will. Yet the people, popularly known as *wananchi* in Kiswahili meaning citizens or owners of the country or the land, were vindicated by subsequent events, including the irresponsible conduct of some opposition parties such as the Democratic Party under the leadership of a fiery fundamentalist minister, Christopher Mtikila, inciting violence and preaching racial and religious intolerance.

The people of Tanzania should have voted in a referendum to determine their wish, although the national survey conducted in the early 1990s was comprehensive enough as a statistical tool to gauge collective national sentiment towards divisive politics legitimized by multiparty democracy. And they should have been allowed to continue living under a one-party state if that is what the majority wanted. The electoral mandate won by the ruling Chama Cha Mapinduzi (CCM) – Party of the Revolution or Revolutionary Party – which virtually constitutes a *de facto* one-party state, seems to indicate that. It is the same party that has ruled Tanzania since independence: Tanganyika African National Union (TANU) on the mainland, and Afro-Shirazi Party (ASP) on the isles, until the two parties merged in 1977 to form CCM, as urged by Nyerere.

But there is really no need for one-party rule in any African country, except in extreme cases when nations are in danger of collapsing because of ethnic conflicts or violence between political parties pursuing partisan interests at the expense of national unity and stability. That is an emergency involving national survival and can not be dismissed lightly. Even Western multiparty democracies submerge their differences in times of national crisis.

Therefore African countries should be not be expected to act differently when their survival is at stake. And when opposition parties are so weak, unable to win national mandate because of rivalry and lack of direction within the opposition camp, they lose the rationale for their existence and even resort to subversive tactics to win power. They also do everything they can to weaken or frustrate the government in order to make it look bad before the electorate from whom it won the mandate to rule. And incumbents also invoke this to stifle legitimate dissent and justify repressive rule and a return to the status quo ante in order to re-institute one-party rule, mostly *de facto*, in this era of multiparty democracy.

There are, of course, exceptions to this common trend towards multiparty democracy sweeping across the continent. Rwanda and Burundi are prime examples. The Hutu and the Tutsi in both countries may be beyond the point where they could have genuinely tried to resolve and submerge their differences amicably, if they ever took that route. Even one-party rule intended to forge national unity and guarantee peace and security for all, is not going to work in these two countries.

The hostility between the Hutu and the Tutsi runs so deep, and has been going on for so long, that partition of Rwanda and Burundi along ethnic lines seems to be the only solution to this problem; although it is going to be a Herculean task, given the integrated nature and interwoven structure of both societies, if it is ever attempted; which is highly unlikely.

And it is impossible for slaves and masters to live together as equals. The Tutsi have been holding the Hutu in feudal subjugation for 400 years in spite of the fact that they are a small minority who comprise about 14 percent of Burundi's population, and only about 9 percent of

Rwanda's; while the Hutu constitute a formidable 90 percent of Rwanda's population, and 85 percent of Burundi's, with the Twa (pygmies) making up 1 percent of the population in each of the two countries. Ultimately, numbers will determine the fate of these twin states, with dire consequences for the Tutsi minority if they continue to subjugate the Hutu majority.

However, the solution of partition suggested here in the case of Rwanda and Burundi is not appropriate in all contexts where African countries are torn by ethnic conflicts, as many of them have been since independence in the sixties; nor does it mean that the solution is viable today, as ethnic strife continues to threaten the integrity of African nations.

Like secession, partition should only be the ultimate solution, as a last resort, if nothing else works; for example in the case of Sudan where the Arabs in the north want to perpetually dominate and enslave blacks in the south and forcibly convert them to Islam in order to transform the country into a fundamentalist theocratic state based on a radical interpretation of the Koran.

Had such a solution been implemented in the past, it would have split up African countries along tribal and regional lines, creating non-viable mini-ethnostates. It was avoided because of the one-party system and the coercive power of the state which helped to forge national unity on the anvil of uniformity. And such uniformity was possible only under the one-party system because of its monolithic nature, contrasted with the multiparty system which many politicians and their supporters unscrupulously exploit to pursue ethnoregional interests at the expense of national unity.

Therefore, in spite of its shortcomings, and there are many, there is no question that the one-party system saved African countries from falling apart and, indeed, saved Africa. And history is highly instructive in this context when we look at some cases involving multiparty politics

36

across Africa soon after independence in the sixties. The relevance of these cases is continental in scope.

Immediately after independence, Ghana's leader Dr. Kwame Nkrumah faced strong opposition from political parties which were regionally entrenched. He was the founder of the Convention People's Party (CPP) which led the country to independence. The strongest opposition during the 1950s and after independence came from the Ashanti region spearheaded by Dr. Kofi A. Busia and Dr. J.B. Danquah of the United Gold Coast Convention (UGCC), the first party to campaign for independence before the CPP was formed by Nkrumah in 1949.

Compounding the problem was the fact that there were strong secessionist tendencies among the Ashanti. The secessionist threats were particularly strong in the late fifties, and when Ghana won independence, celebration among the Ashanti was muted. The Ewe in eastern Ghana also threatened to secede and unite with their fellow tribesmen across the border in Togo. This irredentist movement started even before Ghana won independence and continued thereafter. Also in northern Ghana, separatist tendencies threatened to break up the nation. And different political parties capitalized on all those secessionist sentiments in the name of multiparty democracy.

But Nkrumah suppressed the secessionist movements by instituting a unitary state under one-party rule. Otherwise, there probably would be no Ghana today. In 1964, the people of Ghana voted in a referendum – although the results were controversial – and gave President Nkrumah the mandate to establish a one-party socialist state, effectively ending multiparty politics which encouraged secessionist and irredentist movements.

In Dahomey (renamed Benin in 1975) in the sixties, three major leaders represented various ethnic groups and regions as we learned earlier: President Hubert Maga in the north, Migan Apithy in the central and parts of the south, and Justin Ahomadegbe in other southern areas. Without solid support in the north, Maga would not have become Dahomey's president when the country won independence from France in 1960. And the other two leaders, Apithy and Ahomadegbe both of whom briefly served as president at one time or another, would not have served in that post had it not been for the overwhelming support of their tribal members and allies in their respective regions.

In fact, tribal and regional divisions were so strong that the three leaders were forced to form a coalition government – triumvirate – to prevent civil war from breaking out, due to resentment among the tribes and regions which would have felt, and rightly so, that they had been left out of power if one of the regionally-entrenched parties or two in alliance ruled the country. The political parties led by the three leaders were strongly ethnic and regional in character under a multiparty system which was supposed to promote democracy for the sake of national unity. Instead, it ended up dividing the nation purely on tribal and regional basis.

In The Gambia, Prime Minister – later President – Sir Dawda Jawara's ruling People's Progressive Party (PPP), which ruled for 32 years until 1994 when Jawara was overthrown, was predominantly Malinke, the largest ethnic group in the country, and could not even be voted out of office because of the numerical superiority of its supporters who belonged to the dominant ethnic group and allied tribes.

By contrast, opposition parties drew most of their support from smaller ethnic groups. Gambia was said to be democratic, yet elections became useless when the smaller parties, hence tribes, could not dislodge the main party – read, Malinke – from power by electoral means. It was said to have a multiparty system, yet, in practice, it was a *de facto* one-party state because of the dominant position of the Malinke-backed People's Progressive Party.

In Sierra Leone, the Sierra Leone People's Party (SLPP) led by Dr. Milton Margai, the country's first prime minister, and next by his brother Sir Albert Margai who succeeded him as the nation's leader, was primarily composed of members of their ethnic group, the Mende, one of the two largest constituting at least 30 percent of the country's population. In the same way, Dr. Siaka Stevens' All People's Congress (APC) was mostly supported by members of the Temne tribe (although his father was a Limba and his mother a Mende), which also makes up about 30 percent of the population.

Hostility and rivalry between the two ethnic groups and their allies continued through the decades and was a major factor in the ouster of President Ahmad Tejan Kabbah, although a Mandingo but staunch member of the Mende-dominated SLPP, in 1997, and subsequent persecution of the Mende by the military junta of Major Johnny Paul Koromah, a member of the Limba tribe. The mutliparty system has not been able to contain or defuse such tension between members of different tribes in Sierra Leone but has, instead, thrived on it.

In Nigeria, before and after independence, all of the country's major political parties owed their existence to solid regional and ethnic allegiance as we learned earlier. Even after years of military rule, and after political parties were again allowed to operate and explicitly prohibited by the constitution from appealing to regional and tribal sentiments, Nigerians still overwhelmingly voted for candidates from their own tribes and regions in national elections, clearly demonstrated by the 1979, 1983 and 1993 general elections.

The Hausa-Fulani voted for their own kind for president, as did the Yoruba and the Igbo, the country's dominant groups which constitute a triad that virtually props up the Nigerian federation. The same pattern was repeated in the 1998 - 1999 general elections because of the toxic politics of ethnic loyalties.

In the Belgian Congo before independence, Joseph Kasavubu – who became the country's first president when the country won independence in 1960 – drew his strongest support from members of his own ethnic group, the Bakongo. And the political party he led, ABAKO - *Alliance des Bakongo* - was solidly Bakongo, yet claimed to be nationally representative in a country of more than 200 ethnic groups which were not Bakongo. In fact, Kasavubu, who was partly Chinese, dreamt of reuniting the Bakongo people who had been split up by the colonial borders of the French Congo (now Congo-Brazzaville), the Belgian Congo, and Portuguese Angola, and rebuilding the old Kongo kingdom. And under his leadership, ABAKO became a militant organization which advocated secession for the Bakongo more than it fought for Congolese independence as one country.

Moise Tshombe also mobilized his supporters into a powerful tribalistic and secessionist party known as CONAKAT – *Confederation des Associations Tribales du Katanga* – which had its strongest support in southern Katanga, the copper mining area which produced the country's most valuable export. The secessionist leader, who was related to the royal family of the Lunda ethnic group in his home province of Katanga, was solidly supported by members of his tribe, the Lunda. And his party, CONAKAT, dominated Katanga Province which he led into secession on 11 July 1960, only 11 days after Congo won independence on June 30th under the leadership of Patrice Lumumba. Tshombe's secessionist move plunged the country into chaos and anarchy and claimed more than 100,000 lives.

Neither Tshombe nor Kasavubu was interested in transforming his party into a truly national party transcending ethnic and regional loyalties. The multiparty system encouraged the two leaders and their parties to exploit and fortify regional allegiances to the detriment of national unity. In fact, every political party in Congo had been formed to protect and promote tribal interests, with the exception of Patrice Lumumba's Congo National Movement – *Movement National Congolais* – which campaigned from a Congolese nationalist and Pan-Africanist platform.

But even the highly popular Lumumba himself, the only Congolese leader of national stature with significant support in different parts of the country, could not overcome or suppress regional sentiments among his supporters in his home province. He had no control over that. Among all the country's six provinces, he drew his strongest support from Orientale Province in the east whose capital was Stanleyville (renamed Kisangani), his political base, and from members of his own tribe, the Batetela, although he did not encourage such ethno-regional loyalties like the other Congolese leaders did. But he could not make his regional and ethnic supporters overcome their biases, or stop them from throwing their weight behind him purely on the basis of regional and ethnic loyalties, because of the tremendous influence of ethnoregional allegiances in Africa's highly volatile cauldron of ethnic politics.

However, Lumumba's politics was examplary and transcendent. He led the Congo National Movement, the most nationalist and Pan-African-oriented political party in the history of the country, and became Congo's first prime minister and minister of defence when the country won independence.

But the multiparty system which fuelled ethnic and regional rivalries thwarted his efforts to unite the country, weaknesses outside powers exploited during the turbulent sixties to try and break up the country.

In Uganda, Dr. Milton Obote, a northerner from Lango district, drew his strongest and biggest support from fellow northerners: the Langi, the Acholi and other ethnic groups including Idi Amin's small Kakwa tribe. However, his ruling party, the Uganda People's Congress (UPC) he

41

formed in 1960, was the only party which had the largest number of supporters in other parts of the country embracing all ethnic groups and championed nationalist causes.

By contrast the official opposition, the Democratic Party led by Benedicto Kiwanuka, was mostly supported by members of his tribe the Baganda and was regionally entrenched in the Buganda kingdom. In addition to being tribal and regional, the opposition party was divisive in another respect. It deliberately appealed to Catholic voters across Uganda and exploited religious sentiments to the detriment of national unity.

The other party in Uganda was the Kabaka Yekka, meaning Kabaka Only. It was led by the Kabaka (King) Edward Frederick Mutesa II and was unabashedly tribalistic, composed almost exclusively of members of the Baganda ethnic group who constituted the Buganda kingdom. And it was secessionst, demanding full independence for the kingdom. Although the two opposition parties – the Democratic Party and the Kabaka Yekka – both entrenched in the Buganda kingdom were intentionally divisive and therefore a threat to national unity, they were able to continue their activities in the name of multiparty democracy. The multiparty system clearly fostered and thrived on tribalism despite professions to the contrary.

In Rwanda, after centuries of subjugation and oppression by the Tutsi, the Hutu majority rose against their minority oppressors and deposed the Tutsi aristocrats in the mass uprising of July 1959. More than 100,000 Tutsis were massacred, and at least just as many fled to Burundi, Uganda, and Tanganyika (now Tanzania).

Just two years earlier in 1957, the Hutu had formed two political parties demanding a voice in the country's affairs commensurate with their numerical strength: the Association for the Social Improvement of the Masses led by Joseph Gitera, and the Party of the Hutu Emancipation

Movement (Parmehutu) led by Gregoire Kayibanda who became Rwanda's first president when the country won independence from Belgium on January 1, 1962.

Automatically, the dethroned Tutsi constituted the opposition in the national legislature, a case of unmistakable ethnic rivalry and hostility sanctioned by by the multiparty system in the name of democracy at whatever cost to peace and security and national integrity. It is an almost identical situation in neighbouring Burundi where the same ethnic groups, the Hutu and the Tutsi, have locked horns. And multiparty politics has fuelled ethnic hostilities in Rwanda and Burundi because the Hutu and the Tutsi vote strictly along tribal lines, threatening national unity, already fragile.

In Zambia also, like in many other African countries, the multiparty system proved to be divisive soon after the country won independence from Britain on 24 October 1964. President Kenneth Kaunda's United National Independence Party (UNIP) was national in scope, while the opposition African National Congress (ANC) led by Harry Nkumbula, and the United Party (UP) led by Maluniko Mundia, were based on regional loyalties with strong separatist tendencies, and appealed to tribal and regional alliances.

The two opposition parties were strongest in the south and in the west, respectively, where separatist tendencies were also strongest. Secessionist sentiments were strongest in Barotse Province, also known as Barotseland, in the west dominated by members of the Lozi tribe. Nkumbula was the favourite son of the Tonga and the Ila tribes in the south, and Mundia of the Lozi in the west.

And they organized their parties on that basis under the multiparty system, hardly a basis for national unity, yet one that acquires legitimacy in the name of multiparty democracy.

In Zimbabwe, the Shona and the Ndebele, traditional rivals and the country's largest ethnic groups, were neatly split along ethnic lines even during the struggle for independence. Their support for the two nationalist movements which waged guerrilla warfare for 15 years against white minority rule in the former British colony of Rhodesia was solidly ethnic, yet in pursuit of a nationalist cause. The Zimbabwe African National Union (ZANU) led by Robert Mugabe was and still is mostly Shona. And the Zimbabwe African People's Union (ZAPU) was overwhelmingly Ndebele and entrenched in the southwestern part of the country, Matebeleland.

ZAPU became the official opposition after the country won independence in 1980, and the two parties even fought in the early 1980s, with Matebeleland being the bloodiest battleground where more than 20,000 people, mostly Ndebele, were killed by government soldiers and security forces in a brutal campaign launched by the Shona-dominated government to crush the opposition.

The conflict erupted mainly because of ZAPU's refusal to accept ZANU as the legitimate government of Zimbabwe in spite of the fact that its leader Robert Mugabe won the general election just before independence. But it is also true that ZANU won because of overwhelming support from the Shona, the country's largest ethnic group constituting a formidable 70 percent of the total population, and the Ndebele about 20 percent; a case of clear ethnic rivalry exacerbated by the multiparty system.

The two parties merged in 1987 to form one ruling party, ZANU-PF (Patriotic Front). But the unity remained fragile at best because of the hostility between the two ethnic groups, much of it rooted in history when the Ndebele, who came from what is now Kwazulu-Natal Province in South Africa, emigrated north and conquered the Shona in the 1830s, forcing them to pay tribute. The Shona were not only subjugated but also humiliated. Many of them have not forgotten that.

In Kenya, ethnic loyalties were so strong in the 1992

and 1997 general elections that the opposition parties failed to defeat President Daniel arap Moi who won only about 40 percent of the vote in both elections. They failed to unite behind a single candidate because they were split along tribal lines; a lesson they remembered well during the 2002 elections when they formed a coalition and united behind a single candidate, Mwai Kibaki, to defeat Uhuru Kenyatta, Jomo Kenyatta's son, who was the KANU (Kenya African National Union) candidate, a party that had ruled the country for almost 40 years since independence in December 1963.

Yet, the parties which formed the coalition, NARC, were *still* tribal and regional in orientation and in pursuit of ethnoregional agendas in their quest for the national pie. It was essentially a coalition of the main tribal parties, representing the largest ethnic groups in the country, although smaller ones were also represented.

The coalition collapsed within three years, and tribalism again reared its ugly head when Kenya exploded during the December 2007 general elections which were rigged by President Mwai Kibaki and his fellow Kikuyus to deny Raila Odinga, a Luo, victory and perpetuate Kikuyu hegemonic control of the country. About 2,000 people were killed in the violence which tore the country apart along ethnic and regional lines and more than 600,000 people ended up homeless, refugees in their own homeland: Kenyans refugees in Kenya.

National unity has been an elusive goal in Kenya's history since independence and even before then.

In fact, the quest for national unity was clearly evident during the struggle for independence when KANU was formed. It was formed in May 1960 as a merger of three major parties: the Kenya African Union (KAU) formed in 1944 and led by Jomo Kenyatta; the National People's Convention Party (NPCP) formed in 1957 and led by Tom Mboya; and the Kenya Independence Movement (KIM) formed in 1959 and led by Oginga Odinga and Dr.

Gikonyo Kiano.

KAU was founded by James Gichuru. He stepped down from the party's leadership in favour of Jomo Kenyatta who returned to Kenya in 1946 from 15 years of self-imposed exile in Britain campaigning for independence. Kenyatta became the leader of KAU the following year in 1947.

But because KANU was dominated by the Kikuyu, and to a smaller degree by the other major tribes such as the Luo and the Kamba, smaller tribes feared that they would be left out of the equation as one of the determining factors in the country's future. This led to the formation of the Kenya African Democratic Union (KADU) in 1960, under the leadership of Ronald Ngala, which favoured a federal system of government with a weak central government as opposed to a strong unitary state advocated by KANU under Kenyatta.

KADU was preceded by the formation of another party for smaller tribes, the multiracial Kenya National Party (KNP), in 1959, with the support of European settlers apprehensive of the rise of African nationalism spearheaded by the major tribes which also had the largest population in a country of 42 tribes. The Kalenjins – an alliance of different small tribes in the Rift Valley Province – in the KNP were led by Daniel arap Moi and Taita Towett; the Baluhya-Bukusu by Masinde Muliro, and the smaller tribes in the Coast Province by Ronald Ngala. The KNP evolved into KADU the following year, led by Ngala.

However, in the 1963 general elections a few months before independence, KADU lost and, in the following year, its leader Ronald Ngala announced the voluntary dissolution of his party. This paved the way for the establishment of one-party rule by KANU which lasted until 1990 when the Kenyan constitution was amended to allow the re-introduction of multiparty politics.

The tragedy is that such liberalisation of the political

system only led to a return to the status quo ante of tribal politics reminiscent of the pre-independence era, tragically demonstrated by the prominence of ethnoregional loyalties and rivalries as well as violence in the general elections of the 1990s.

In the 1992 and 1997 presidential elections in Kenya, each major tribe – except the Kisii who did not field a presidential candidate – voted for its own candidate. The Kikuyu, Kenya's largest, overwhelmingly voted for Mwai Kibaki; the Luo for Raila Odinga, son of former Vice President Oginga Odinga under Jomo Kenyatta; the Luhya for Kijana Wamalwa; and the Kamba for Mrs. Charity Ngilu. They all lost, of course, because of tribalism among themselves and kept in power an unabashedly tribalistic president, Daniel arap Moi of KANU, whose government was dominated by his fellow Kalenjin tribesmen.

Those are just some of the countries whose political parties were split along ethnic and regional lines under the multiparty system despite professions of national unity, and despite a constitutional ban explicitly forbidding tribal politics and appeal to regional sentiments.

Yet ethnoregional alliances prevailed, and the multiparty system failed to transcend such sectarianism. In fact, it accomplished exactly the opposite. And little has changed.

Still, uncompromising proponents of the multiparty system contend that it is the only system which can maintain national unity and sustain robust democracy, despite evidence to the contrary, especially with regard to national unity. For example in Ghana, Dr. Kofi Busia, the opposition leader in parliament during Nkrumah's tenure, railed against Nkrumah's "one-party dictatorship" and presented himself as the embodiment of democratic ideals and the best alternative to despotic rule.

Yet, he not only ended up being a dictator himself – like Frederick Chiluba in Zambia in the 1990s, and other African leaders – under the multiparty system, of all systems, when he became prime minister in 1969, but led a party, the Progress Party, whose strongest support came from his ethnic group (and home region), the Ashanti, which is also the nation's largest.

That is something Dr. Nkrumah fought against, ethnoregional allegiances, when he led Ghana. Still, the multiparty system under which Dr. Busia won the election in 1969 did little to neutralise such ethnic and regional loyalties in national politics like Nkrumah did.

That is a significant number of countries where the multiparty system has played such a divisive role by thriving on tribal and regional sentiments in the name of national unity and democracy. And that is still the case today in a number of countries across the continent which have adopted multiparty democracy, thus putting the whole matter in its proper perspective necessary for one to understand *why* African leaders instituted one-party rule soon after independence in the sixties.

And the tragedy is that we Africans don't seem to have learned much from all this, as our countries continue to fan flames of ethnic hatred fuelled by multiparty politics.

Contemporary cases where ethnically-based political parties have caused conflict, sometimes leading to catastrophe, include Somalia, whose clan-based political interests and quest for power plunged the country into civil war after the fall of dictator Siad Barre in 1991, leaving it without a national government; Ethiopia, whose government was dominated by the Tigrean People's Liberation Front, an ethnically-based group representing only 10 percent of Ethiopia's population (Tigreans in Tigre Province in the north), since the ouster of dictator Mengistu Haile Mariam in 1991.

There is also Kenya, where – even after the coalition government was formed following the 2002 general elections – the Kikuyu mostly supported the Democratic Party. The Luhya, now the second-largest ethnic group after surpassing the Luo, were solidly behind FORD (the

Forum for the Restoration of Democracy); the Luo fiercely loyal to the National Development Party, and the Kamba to the Social Democratic Party; and Tanzania, where the Civic United Front (CUF) is mostly supported by opponents of the union of Tanganyika and Zanzibar and by a large number of Muslims who see it, rightly or wrongly, as a party fighting for the interests of Muslims.

There are other political parties in Tanzania which get their strongest support from specific regions where their leaders come from, thus tainting them with regional bias regardless of the positions they articulate as truly national parties. They include the United Democratic Party, the Tanzania Labour Party, and CHADEMA (Chama cha Demokrasia na Maendeleo - the Party of Democracy and Progess or Development).

Compounding the problem, and the felony, of ethnoregional biases of different political parties in different African countries is the fact that the governments themselves – with very few exceptions – have been dominated by a few ethnic groups through the years at the expense of others who end up playing a peripheral role in national affairs because of their marginal status.

In Zaire under Mobutu, the government was dominated by members of his tribe, the Gbande, from Equateur Province, as was the ruling party which for all practical purposes was the government across the spectrum.

In Congo-Brazzaville, also known as the Congo Republic, you have the Bembe and the Bakongo ethnic groups and their political parties in the southern part of the country competing with the Mbochi, the Sanga and other ethnic groups from the north. Gabon is dominated by the Mbochi, President Bongo's tribe. They have dominated the ruling party and the government since November 1967 when the then 32-year-old Bernard (renamed Omar) Bongo became president.

Across the border in Congo-Brazzaville President

Denis Sassou-Nguesso – who overthrew democratically elected President Pascal Lissouba (a member of the Bakongo tribe in the south) in October 1997 after a four-month civil war in which more than 10,000 people were killed and the capital Brazzaville destroyed – is a member of the Sanga tribe and has a daughter who was married to the late President Omar Bongo. Thus, you had two oil-rich countries ruled by a father-in-law and a son-in-law, also with strong ethnic ties. The Sanga and the Mbochi are strong allies, an alliance that has proved critical to the assumption of power by the northerners in Congo-Brazzaville through the years.

In Angola, the opposition party UNITA was compromised in its claim as a national party because it was supported almost entirely by the Ovimbundu tribe against the democratically elected government of the MPLA, the party which also fought for independence more than any other in the country. In Mozambique, RENAMO, the opposition party, draws its largest support from ethnic groups and regions opposed to the democratically elected government of FRELIMO.

In South Africa, the Inkatha Freedom Party (IFP) is supported almost entirely by the Zulu and rules Kwazulu-Natal Province, one of only two provinces where the governing African National Congress (ANC) had not been able to win elections before winning in the Western Cape. By contrast, the ANC, once led by President Nelson Mandela and next by President Thabo, enjoys enormous support across the country. Yet it is also worth remembering that ethnic loyalty is clearly evident even in the ruling ANC itself despite its stature as a truly multi-ethnic and multi-racial party. The vast majority of the Xhosa, the second largest ethnic group in South Africa after the Zulu, support the African National Congress. Also both Mandela and Mbeki were Xhosa.

But the first president of the African National Congress when the party was founded in 1912 was a Zulu,

Dr. John Dube. And the man who presided over the conference at the founding of the party, Dr. P. ka Seme, also belonged to a group closely related to the Zulu; in fact even the Xhosa themselves are closely related to the Zulu.

Therefore the ANC has never been an exclusively or even remotely a Xhosa party, unlike the Inkatha Freedom Party which is Zulu and openly advoctes Zulu interests, especially in Kwazulu-Natal Province.

In Malawi during Dr. Kamuzu Banda's life presidency, the ruling Malawi Congress Party (MCP), hence the government, was dominated by the Chewa, his tribe. In Kenya, when Mzee Jomo Kenyatta was in power, his tribe the Kikuyu dominated the ruling party, KANU, and the government. After he died and was succeeded by Daniel arap Moi, it was Moi's tribesmen the Kalenjin who became dominant in the government and in the ruling party KANU. In Cameroon, it is the Beti, President Paul Biya's tribe, which is dominant both in the ruling party and in the government; in the Ivory Coast, it was the Baoule, of which President Felix Houphouet-Boigny was a member. He ruled from 1960 until his death in December 1963, only to be succeeded by another Baoule, Henri Konan Bedie.

After a brief tenure of General Robert Guei who overthrew Bedie on Christmas eve in 1999, another Baoule, Lawrence Gbagbo became president. The Baoule is a predominantly Christian and southern tribe which treated the government of the Ivory Coast as its exclusive domain since independence, incurring the wrath of northern tribes who are also mostly Muslim; an injustice which led to civil war in 2000 and beyond and which virtually split the country into two: Muslim north versus Christian south.

In Liberia, after a military coup in 1980 by some of the country's indigenous tribesmen overthrew the Americo-Liberian oligarchy which dominated the country for 150 years since its founding, the Krahn, the tribe of military ruler Samuel Doe, came to dominate the government during his tenure which eventually plunged the country into civil war from which it has not fully recovered, just as Somalia has not, and may not for decades to come.

In Togo, the Kabye, a northern tribe to which the late President Gnassingbe Eyadema belonged, as does his son who succeeded him, dominates the country and the army, versus the Ewe most of whom live in the southern part of the country, as well as other groups.

That is the depraved nature of ethnic politics in Africa on which the multiparty system thrives.

It is true that under the multiparty system, groups that have been excluded from power also get the chance to form their own political parties; which is good, since they get the opportunity to ventilate their grievances from political platforms and speak up for their rights. But tribalism also becomes legitimized and institutionalized as an integral part of multiparty democracy.

Even when political candidates rise above tribal politics, they are still constrained by the partisanship of their parties and supporters. For example, in the 1996 general election in Ghana, which was also the last for him, Jerry Rawlings again won the presidency in a free and fair election, although his victory in 1992 was controversial. And most Ghanaians voted across ethnic lines. But still, Rawlings' National Democratic Convention (NDC) ruling party also drew massive support from the Ewe, his mother's ethnic group in the Volta Region, his home in the eastern part of the country; while his leading opponent John Kufuor of the New Patriotic Front (NPF) also got support from different parts of the country but mostly from the Ashanti Region, his stronghold fortified by ethnic loyalty.

So, regardless of how nationalist or Pan-African-oriented some candidates may be, ethnic and regional divisions don't only remain a prominent feature of electoral contests under the multiparty system but are, in fact, exacerbated and legitimized by the very nature of multipartyism as a contest between competing interests, be they class, tribal or regional. Tribes take advantage of that by promoting their ethnic and regional interests through political parties they form or support in the name of multiparty democracy, which really means multiparty tribalism.

It is against this background that the establishment of one-party rule in Africa must be looked at, especially in the early days of independence, in order to understand why truly nationalist and Pan-Africanist leaders such as Kwame Nkrumah and Julius Nyerere chose the one-party system and became its most articulate exponents; and why they felt it was the best system under the circumstances. It helped Tanzania to become one of the most stable, and most peaceful, countries in Africa for almost 30 years under the leadership of Nyerere.

And it is a legacy that continues today, although the country has now and then been threatened by the fractious nature of multiparty politics since it was re-introduced in 1992 and led to incidents of violence especially during the 2000 general election and thereafter, including threats by some opposition leaders that they would resort to violence to achieve their political objectives under the multiparty system.

Therefore, both systems have major pitfalls. And both must be looked at objectively. Yet, given a choice between the two, there is no question that after decades of one-party misrule in most countries, the multiparty system must be given a chance to work in Africa, now that it has been adopted across the continent. But it must be adapted to the realities of African politics characterized by ethnic and regional rivalries.

There is no better argument for forming coalition governments in all the countries riven by ethnic tensions to replace the winner-take-all system common in all African countries which only fuels ethnic hostilities when some groups are excluded from power. The result is perpetual conflict, paralyzing the nation. It can even lead to civil war, as it already has in many countries across the continent. Coalition government composed of winners and losers in general elections should be institutionalized as a permanent feature of democracy in Africa in order to contain hostilities and defuse tensions among ethnic groups competing for power.

There is no question that the multiparty system is good and, in most cases, is even better than one-party rule. But it is contextual in relevance and application, depending on local circumstances and the nature of society. Having a multiparty system just for the sake of it, even when it is going to tear the country apart along tribal and regional lines with members of different parties appealing to ethnoregional loyalties, is not very good statesmanship. In countries threatened by ethnic rivalries, as almost all African countries are including Tanzania where – despite its excellent reputation for peace and harmony – some opposition parties thrive on ethnoregional loyalties, it is utterly naive, or rank dishonesty, to discount that.

And it has been vindicated by history: the former Belgian Congo, although at the instigation of Western powers and financial interests, exploiting local rivalries; Nigeria, because of the massacre of the Igbos which forced them to secede; Uganda, Ghana, and even Zambia, are some of the countries which were seriously threatened by ethnic conflicts and rivalries in the sixties, although – especially in the case of Nigeria and may be even the Congo – the one-party system would probably not have prevented the horrendous tragedies that befell these two giant nations and almost destroyed them in the turbulent sixties.

It was with those problems in mind that most African countries adopted the one-party system soon after independence; knowing full well that if they did not submerge the tribe, the tribe would destroy the nation. The rationale was extended even to the individual level. The primacy of the community, hence the nation, was invoked over the interests of the individual; admittedly, with dire consequences in many cases.

But this approach had a perfectly rational basis. Forging a national ethos that would fuse the people of different tribes into an organic whole, and not just as a collection of antagonistic groups, entailed placing the interests of the community above those of the individual including his freedom. It was not done for political expediency but for national survival; an imperative underscored by President Sekou Toure when he said:

"We have chosen the freedom, the right, the power, the sovereignty of the people, and not of the individual. Before this people you should have no individual personality. Our personality becomes part of the personality of the nation."[18]

And anyone who was not ready to submerge his personality and freedom in the supra-entity called the nation in the interests of the people was considered to be more than just a dissenter – he was a "traitor"; although he himself, like everybody else, was one of the people constituting "We the people," without whom there would be no people. And that was one of the most tragic aspects of the one-party state, its benefits notwithstanding. Thus, the ethic of individual freedom became anathema to the nationalist ideologies of the young African countries whose existence and survival was predicated on the inculcation of the primacy of a collective ethos throughout the populace.

In a very tragic way, individual freedom was considered to be as dangerous to national integrity and survival as tribalism was. As Sekou Toure put it:

"Tribal, ethnic, and religious (as well as political) differences...have caused so much difficulty to the country and people....We are for a united people, a unitary state at the service of an indivisible nation."[19]

Therefore, it is critical to understand the context in which such nationalist sentiments were articulated across the continent before one passes judgment, condemning African leaders as dictators just lusting for power. Most of them were despotic or authoritarian rulers. But inculcation of the ideal of collective will and spirit, as opposed to individual liberty, was critical to the very survival of African countries during the early years of independence. These were countries which did not really even "exist" as countries, except on the map and as a mere collection of tribes, many of them hostile towards each other and haphazardly put together by the colonial rulers, with little in common in terms of loyalty to higher authority; each having its own princes, chiefs, and other traditional rulers. It was a herculean task to build a nation out of such an amorphous whole.

Even some ardent critics of Africa in Western countries concede that much. As Robert Greenberger wrote about Tanzania – a country the size of Texas, Oklahoma and West Virginia combined, or bigger than Nigeria in terms of area, and made up of more than 120 tribes – in *The Wall Street Journal*:

"Nyerere was a skilled nation builder. He fused Tanzania's 120 tribes into a cohesive state, preventing tribal conflicts like those plaguing so much of Africa."[20]

Jomo Kenyatta, the Grand Old Man (called Mzee in Kiswahili) of the African independence movement, accomplished the same feat in Kenya, although to a smaller degree, compared to Nyerere; so did Nkrumah in

Ghana, Sekou Toure in Guinea, Obote in Uganda, Kaunda in Zambia, and other African leaders elsewhere on the continent, but in varying degrees of success.

Yet, there was also abuse of power in most countries across the continent under the one-party state and military rule during those years of national consolidation, and all the way through the decades since independence. That is what makes the multiparty system so appealing in all African countries today, including Tanzania which was very peaceful and stable, and relatively free, under President Nyerere's one-party state for almost 30 years.

Curtailment, and in most cases total denial, of individual freedom was not always necessary to maintain national unity and stability in the fledgling states. Most African leaders invoked the specter of national disintegration just to perpetuate themselves in office and suffocate dissent, as they still do today.

Yet, without putting a premium on national interest, and inculcating the ideals of a collective national spirit, a common identity, and commitment to national unity even at the expense of individual freedom in some cases, there probably would be no African countries as we know them today.

We would have hundreds of "nations": micro-states, none of them viable, structured along tribal lines, making it impossible for Africa to survive let alone develop. Therefore, the emphasis on national survival was justified. But it did not justify dictatorship, although it justified curtailment of freedom in some cases.

The invocation of slogans such as "national survival," "national unity," "One Zambia, One Nation," "Harambee! - Let's Pull Together," "Uhuru na Umoja – Freedom and Unity," "the people, not the individual, come first," and many others, has always been an integral part of the indoctrination process for which African countries are despised in the West as a diversionary tactic to justify dictatorship.

And in many cases such criticism by Westerners and others is justified. But let us also be brutally frank: We all practice indoctrination. Western countries do, communist countries do. So do all the rest, including African countries.

Inculcation of individual and national values is indoctrination. Even glorification of a nation's practices and beliefs, values and traditions, ideals and ideology, is a form of indoctrination. When Americans are taught that capitalism is better than socialism or communism, that is indoctrination, even if it is true; which it is, in terms of producing wealth but *not* in terms of protecting the weak from exploitation since capitalism is predatory by nature and thrives on greed. When they are taught that America, the first republic since Rome, was founded on the twin ideals of liberty and equality, that is indoctrination, even if it is not true; which it isn't. America was founded on slavery, and thrived on slavery.

Millions of Americans were not taught - and are still not taught - in school and when growing up that African slaves and their descendants helped to build America more than anybody else, especially in its early years, and without being paid. As Malcolm X said, African slaves worked "from can't see in the morning to can't see in the evening without being paid a dime. Yet we built this country...and we aren't American yet. As long you and I have been here, we aren't American yet."

African slaves built America's foundation without which the country would not have survived and thrived as a nation. And it would not be what it is today, as the richest nation in history, had it not been for the forced labour extracted from African slaves and their descendants. They made America rich. Yet they were never paid one cent for it.

But a number of black American conservatives contend otherwise. One is Dr. Thomas Sowell, an economics professor and a prolific author, who argues in his book, *Race and Culture,*[21] that there is no conclusive evidence showing that America derived net economic benefits from slavery.

He and a number of other blacks, especially conservatives, are opposed to reparations for slavery for various reasons. They are mostly middle-class and upper-class blacks who are detached from their own people in a desperate attempt to be accepted by and integrated into white America. Yet, they are not accepted by whites as equals. Alienated from their own people, and rejected by white America, they are caught in a predicament similar to the situation many educated Africans were trapped in during colonial times. Western education "de-Africanized" them, mentally. Yet it did not elevate them to the same status enjoyed by their colonial masters and other whites; a subject I have addressed in one of my books, *Africa and the West.*[22] It is also a subject – in the American context – black nationalist scholar, Professor Harold Cruse, has tackled in his magnum opus, *The Crisis of the Negro Intellectual.*[23] And as he said about slavery and the myths being propagated to distort American history, in another book, *Rebellion or Revolution?*:

"America lies to itself that it was always, from the beginning, a democratic nation when its very constitution sanctioned and upheld chattel slavery. Moreover, America conveniently forgets that the first capitalist 'free enterprise' banks and stock markets in the land were made possible by accumulated capital accrued from the unpaid labor of Negro slaves. But it would be too much to expect contemporary America to go back over its own history and reassess all these racial facts."[24]

America does not want to face that because it still has a serious racial problem – although it is no longer a racist society in the legal sense – and wants to continue propagating the myth that African slaves and their descendants did not significantly, if at all, contribute to the economic growth of the United States. This myth is an integral part of America's racist ideology, and it is indoctrination. Yet, all this indoctrination which started as soon as Africans were taken to America in chains, has not always worked.

Even slaves knew better; they had to, they were the ones doing all the work on the plantations without pay. As Bailey Wyat, a former slave and although illiterate, put it poignantly in broken English when arguing for redistribution of land to former slaves not long after the Emancipation Proclamation:

"We has a right to the land where we are located. For why? I tell you. Our wives, our children, our husbands has been sold over and over again to purchase the land....And then didn't we clear the land, and raise the crops?....And then didn't them large cities in the North grow up on the cotton, on the sugars, on the rice that we made?....I say they has grown rich and my people is poor."[25]

When America denies that, to insulate itself from reality and its ugly past, it is practising indoctrination that is no better than the kind that is practised by many African leaders and their people when they blame American imperialism for all their problems; nor is it wrong for Americans to say capitalism is better than communism, just as it is *not* wrong for Africans to say Pan-Africanism is better than nationalism, and nationalism *better* than tribalism.

Indoctrination serves a purpose, good or bad. Hitler preached a racist ideology. It was even taught to the young. It was indoctrination, at its worst, with dire consequences at a cost of more than 6 million lives of people who belonged to the "wrong race," mostly Jews. But it could have served a good purpose under a different kind of leadership, with a different ideology, unlike that of Nazi Germany.

In Africa, indoctrination has also served a purpose. And it has served Africa well in many areas when it corresponds to reality. And that included justifying centralisation of power "in the name of the people" during the early years of independence under one-party rule. That is because a strong central government was vital and critical to national unity and survival, in pursuit of economic development by mobilizing resources at the national level under one leadership.

That was also the case in the United States when Alexander Hamilton argued that a strong central government was necessary for the young nation. It is doubtful that America would have survived without it. This was clearly demonstrated when the states constituting the union adopted a federal constitution at the Philadelphia convention in 1787 to replace the Articles of Confederation in order to establish a strong central government.

In addition to instituting a unitary state, most African countries also adopted a common or similar ideology to develop their economies and consolidate national unity. The approach most took towards development was socialism, and its concomitant, centralisation of power, as the most effective mechanism for rapid mobilisation of resources at the national level; and as a weapon against tribalism and regionalism. As Professor Ali Mazrui states in his book *Towards A Pax-Africana*:

"A former Labour Party Colonial Secretary, Arthur Creech Jones, once remarked that he did not consider it the duty of that office to impose socialism on the colonies. In the case of Africa it has now turned out such an imposition was not necessary.

61

No ideology commands respect so widely in Africa as the ideology of 'socialism' – though, as in Europe, it is socialism of different shades. In Guinea and Mali a Marxist framework of reasoning is evident. In Ghana Leninism was wedded to notions of traditional collectivism. In Tanzania the concept of *Ujamaa*, derived from the sense of community of tribal life, is being radicalized into an assertion of modern socialism.

In Kenya there is a dilemma between establishing socialism and Africanizing the capitalism which already exists. In Nigeria, Senegal and Uganda some kind of allegiance is being paid to the ideal of social justice in situations with a multi-party background.

There are places, of course, where no school of socialism is propagated at all. But outside the Ivory Coast there is little defiant rejection of the idea of 'socialism' in former colonial Africa.

Yet the kind of socialism which Arthur Creech Jones would have propagated was a socialism operating in the context of a multi-party system of politics. What is more common in Africa, however, is a socialism wedded to a one-party structure of government."[26]

Dr. Mazrui's book was first published in 1967, the same year Tanzania adopted its famous Arusha Declaration in February, outlining the country's socialist policies. It was a period – throughout the sixties – when interest in socialism among African leaders was at its peak, with most countries across the continent having adopted the socialist ideology in one form or another within that decade of euphoria which also marked the end of colonial rule. By 1968, most African countries had won independence.

But their war against tribalism, ignorance, disease, and poverty had just begun. African countries saw socialism as the best solution to these problems, with central planning being one of its most attractive features. And it is easy to understand why. When all tribes and regions are brought together under one leadership, there is no room for division along ethnoregional lines. If power is too decentralized, it can help strengthen tribal and regional institutions to the detriment of national unity. That is the argument African countries used to justify concentration of power at the centre. And they made a rational choice under the circumstances when they instituted the unitary state during those years when African countries were so fragile, and national unity virtually non-existent.

And their belief in socialism as the best means to achieve rapid economic development was not without foundation. There was the example of the Soviet Union, with all its faults, yet persuasive enough that development could indeed be achieved in a relatively short time – as opposed to the centuries it took the West to develop – if decision-making on the allocation of the nation's resources, which include people, was centralised.

Even some of those who criticized African leaders for taking the socialist path felt that the leaders were vindicated in their belief because of the rapid industrialization the Soviet Union was able to achieve within 40 years under socialism; although the foundations of the future great nation had largely been built by Peter the Great in the preceding years.

There was another equally compelling argument why African leaders chose socialism over capitalism: equitable distribution of wealth to achieve social justice. They saw capitalism as a predatory system for survival of "the fittest" under which people sought to accumulate wealth without the slightest concern for the poor and for the well-being of others. "I got mine, you get yours. Each to his own," is the underlying logic of capitalism.

Although it is true that capitalism capitalizes on greed, there is no question that it provides incentives to production more than socialism does, much as some of us may hate its predatory instincts. But that is part of its nature. If you like its virtues, be prepared to accept its vices.

By contrast, socialism emphasizes sharing. Therefore, with its redistributive ethic, it was seen as morally superior to capitalism which nurtures and nourishes predatory instincts in man; pursuit of profit being incompatible with social justice, since people exploit others to accumulate wealth. In short, capitalism is based on inequality, and is therefore the very antithesis not only of social justice but of human equality.

But probably the biggest attraction to socialism among African African leaders was that – as the only ones who "knew what was best" for the people and the nation – it enabled them to control all the nation's resources in order to plan and direct economic development; something that is impossible under capitalism where economic development of the whole country is mostly left to the invisible hand of the free market. Under socialism, they were not only able to choose development targets and allocate resources to achieve national goals; they even used coercive means to achieve these goals. All this was seen as necessary to achieve economic development. As Dr. Kwame Nkrumah put it:

"The economic independence that should follow and maintain political independence demands every effort from the people, a total mobilization of brain and manpower resources. What other countries have taken three hundred years to achieve, a once dependent territory must try to accomplish in a generation if it is to survive....

Capitalism is too complicated a system for a newly independent nation. Hence the need for a socialistic society. But even a system based on social justice and a democratic constitution may need backing up, during the period following independence, by emergency measures of a totalitarian kind. Without discipline, true freedom cannot survive."[27]

Most African leaders did not explicitly say they were going to employ "measures of a totalitarian kind," as Nkrumah bluntly stated. But they ruled that way, and still do. And besides saying "capitalism is too complicated a system for a newly independent nation," Nkrumah, like most African leaders, also believed that the capitalist system would only perpetuate exploitation of their countries by the metropolitan powers.

Capitalism was not only identified with colonialism; it was organically linked to their former colonial masters who were determined to continue exploiting Africa; capitalism, by nature, being an exploitative system and an integral part of colonialism and imperialism as the history of Africa clearly demonstrated since slavery and colonisation. If it was adopted by the newly independent nations as the best path towards economic development, local capitalists would continue to work with foreign capitalist interests to exploit the people. Even African leaders such as Tom Mboya found much that was desirable in socialism. As he stated:

"It might be argued that African socialism stands in a class by itself. This is not true. The basic tenets of socialism are universal and we are either socialists by these basic principles or not at all....I strongly believe that in the field of economic relations we can be guided by the traditional presence of socialist ideas and attitudes in the African mental make-up."[28]

Yet, Mboya was not a socialist, at least not in the same way Nyerere, Nkrumah, and Sekou Toure were, in terms of policy formulation and implementation. If Mboya was a socialist, then Nyerere was a capitalist. They were poles apart. And his socialism must have been shelved when he was a cabinet member in Kenya's capitalist government under Kenyatta where he held key ministerial posts including economic planning.

But articulation of his feelings on the relevance of socialism to Africa shows the kind of strong appeal the socialist ideology had across a broad spectrum of African leaders during the sixties and through the decades. Today, of course, with the collapse of the Soviet Union and its satellites, it is a discredited ideology. But that does not diminish the significant role it played in the establishment and consolidation of the African nation-state through the years under the one-party system which also has been replaced by the multiparty system in most African countries, although only in theory. Most are *de facto* one-party states.

But there is also no question that both socialism and the one-party system had a negative impact on African countries in terms of diminished freedom and retarded economic growth. There were some notable achievements in the economic arena, but not as significant as they would have been had African governments adopted a free-market approach even with limited state intervention in the economy.

However, when looked at in the context of the sixties when most African countries won independence, and even in the seventies when they were still struggling to consolidate their nation-states as much as they are still struggling to do so today, the negative impact of both socialism and the one-party system should be weighed against the fact that the African nation-state was established against overwhelming odds and would probably not exist today had African leaders taken a different path.

In Africa, unlike in Europe, nationalism preceded the establishment of the nation-state. The leaders who campaigned for independence had to appeal to nationalist sentiments of non-existent nations in order to create a sense of collective identity among different and antagonistic ethnic groups which constituted the colonies. And it was a formidable task.

Convincing members of different tribes that they were the same people – as Tanganyikans and not just Sukumas, Nyakyusas, Zanakis, Digos, Chagas, Ngonis, Gogos, Makondes, Nyamwezis, Yaos, Hayas, Pares, Hehes, Benas, Makuas or Kingas; Ghanaians and not just Ewes, Fantis, Ashantis, Gonjas, Dagombas, Nanumbas, or Konkombas; Kenyans and not just Kikuyus, Kambas, Luos, Luhyas, Samburus, Masais, Pokots, Merus, or Somalis – required strong central authority at the national level under a unitary state with no room for divisive politics and partisanship so typical of the multi-party system.

The one-party system as well as socialism, both with an instinct for mass mobilisation under one strong leadership at the national level, provided just the kind of institutional tools and mechanisms which enabled Africans to establish, build, and consolidate the nations which exist today across the continent, however fragile they may be.

This is not to gloss over the negative impact of socialism and one-party rule on African countries. Both had tragic consequences. They stifled individual initiative, lowered productivity, and curtailed freedom. But they also taught and enforced discipline, similar to army discipline, to maintain national unity which would have been impossible without mass regimentation in societies fragmented along ethnic lines.

Therefore, the positive contribution of socialism and one-party rule must also be acknowledged, at least in the African context where, instead of the 53 countries we have today, we probably would have hundreds, equal to the number of tribes or ethnic groups and racial groups on the continent.

If that is what multi-party "democracy" is going to do, weaken or split up countries, then it is recipe for disaster.

African countries should therefore not rule out a return to the status quo ante if circumstances dictate, and temporarily re-institute one-party rule before returning to multi-party democracy. But the decision to form such government of national unity must be by popular consent approved in a referendum. Otherwise, when faced with the prospect of national disintegration and bloodshed as a result of ethnic conflicts, let the people learn the hard way; if they want their countries to dissolve in anarchy under the multiparty system which thrives on divisive politics in the name of democracy even when national survival is at stake.

African nationalists of all ideological stripes have always been very much aware of the danger our countries face because of their pluralistic nature as multi-ethnic societies or multi-national states. As Dr. Nnamdi Azikiwe, who was no admirer of the one-party system, said when he warned against the Pakistanization – Balkanization – of Nigeria:

"It is essential that ill-will be not created in order to encourage a Pakistan in this country. The North and South are one, whether we wish it or not. The forces of history have made it so."[29]

Preservation of national integrity is better than the ghastly alternative of total disintegration which can also be averted by extensive devolution of power to the regions and districts, but while retaining strong central authority. One-party rule, with all its faults, has been able to maintain national unity across much of Africa.

Only time will tell whether or not its antithesis, the multiparty system, will be able to do the same. And it can, if it effectively contains tribalism and regional loyalties, as the one-party system has done, by establishing parties that are truly national in character cutting across regional and ethnic lines.

Unfortunately, few tribes in Africa have demonstrated the capacity to transcend ethnoregional loyalties for the sake of national unity. The perennial ethnic rivalries which continue to threaten the very existence of African countries is a rueful reminder of that.

Probably the best solution to this seemingly intractable problem is for African countries to limit the number of political parties, preferably to three, to broaden the base of support cutting across ethnic lines.

Members of different tribes will then have to learn to live together, and work together, as members and supporters of those few parties in order to build strong African nations without promoting tribal and regional interests at the expense of their fellow citizens. As Mrs. Charity Ngilu, the first woman to be a serious contender for Kenya's presidency, lamented after the 1997 general elections which the incumbent Daniel arap Moi won because the opposition was hopelessly divided along tribal lines and failed to rally behind a single candidate:

"Honourable Mwai Kibaki got most votes in 1997 from the Kikuyu, Honourable Raila Odinga from the Luo, Honourable Kijana Wamalwa from the Luhya and I myself from the Kamba. President Moi got most of his votes from the Rift Valley. Is this the Kenya we want?"[30]

Is this the Africa we want for the sake of multi-party politics?

The adoption of the multiparty system should not blind us to reality. And the reality in this context is that ethnic politics, and manipulation and exploitation of tribal loyalties in the quest for national office, is a dominant feature of the African political landscape. And it is going to remain that way for a long, long time in most countries across the continent.

How to address this problem is going to be one of the main challenges Africa will have to face in the twentieth-first century, which South African President Thabo Mbeki declared to be the century of the African Renaissance.

Chapter Two:

Milestones:
Africa Since the Sixties

AFRICA has come a long way since the sixties, and still has a long way to go. The tortuous journey has been marked by important milestones which can help us look at Africa in its proper historical context, as we recall some of the major events which have taken place on the continent since independence.

The year 1960 occupies a special place in the annals of the continent probably more than any other in one fundamental respect: It was the year when an unprecedented number of African countries won independence, a feat that was never duplicated in any of the following years.

A total of 17 countries won independence in 1960. The United Nations called it Africa's Year. The attainment of sovereign status by so many African countries in a single year ushered in a new era for the continent whose most celebrated decade was the euphoric sixties.

But 1960 was also a tragic year for Africa. It was a year marred by the Congo crisis, an unprecedented catastrophe at the dawn of Africa's post-colonial era. The Congo tragedy was engineered and fuelled by Western powers. Communist countries stepped in at the invitation of the nationalist forces in their desperate attempt to oust a puppet regime backed by the United States and spearheaded by the CIA. It was also supported by Belgium, the former colonial power, apartheid South Africa, France and other Western powers and financial interests. It was a coalition of forces, and a concerted effort, determined to perpetuate domination and exploitation of Africa and dismember the Congo in pursuit of Western interests.

The crisis erupted right in the middle of Africa, earning the Congo the unenviable distinction as the bleeding heart of Africa. More than 100,000 people, mostly Congolese, perished in the early sixties alone in this conflict which also had ideological dimensions involving super-power rivalry between the United States and the Soviet as well as the People's Republic of China. Among the casualties was Congo's first and popular prime minister, Patrice Lumumba. Compounding the tragedy was Africa's inability to do anything to end the conflict right on its own soil. As Julius Nyerere said about the Congo crisis in a speech in August 1961 about three months before he led Tanganyika to independence:

"I am an advocate of African unity. I believe firmly that, just as unity was necessary for the achievement of independence in Tanganyika or any other nation, unity is equally necessary to consolidate and maintain the independence which we are now achieving in different parts of Africa.

I believe that, left to ourselves, we can achieve unity on the African continent. But I don't believe we are going to be left to ourselves! I believe that the phase through which we are emerging successfully is the phase of the first scramble for Africa - and Africa's reaction to it. We are now entering a new phase. It is the phase of the second scramble for Africa....

I used the phrase 'the second scramble for Africa.' It may sound farfetched, in the context of the Africa of the 1960's....But anybody who thinks this is farfetched has been completely blind to what is happening on the African continent....

There were obvious weaknesses in the Congo situation, but those weaknesses were deliberately used in a scramble for the control of the Congo....So I believe that the second scramble for Africa has begun in real earnest. And it is going to be a much more dangerous scramble than the first one."[1]

The assassination of Lumumba, like the Congo tragedy itself as a whole, was an important milestone in the history of Africa. Much is known about the CIA's and Belgium's involvement in Lumumba's assassination which American President Dwight Eisenhower wanted carried out as soon as possible. A team of CIA agents worked on a covert operation which involved more than one assassination scheme including poisoning and shooting the Congolese leader with a high-powered telescopic rifle.

Even the CIA station chief in the Congo, Laurence Devlin conceded that much after Lumumba was killed. He also confirmed this in an interview as late as 1996 from Princeton, New Jersey, where he lived; so did Dr. Sidney Gottlieb, a CIA doctor, who went to Congo in September 1960 with a poison kit to kill Lumumba. Many people have written about the subject, which I have also addressed in one of my books, *Africa after Independence: Realities of Nationhood,*[2] in a chapter devoted to the Congo crisis. And as John Reader states in his book,

"An agent (of the CIA) was dispatched to Leopoldville. An initial assassination plan required someone to apply a dose of poison to Lumumba's toothbrush; alternatively, a high-powered rifle with telescopic scope and silencer was proposed....

In a radio broadcast on 5 September (1960), President Kasavubu, urged by American diplomats, Belgian political advisers, and Congolese supporters, announced that he had dismissed Lumumba as prime minister. When the news reached Lumumba, he in turn rushed to the radio station and announced that he had dismissed Kasavubu as president. Confusion ensued. Some parts of the Congo declared their support for Lumumba, others for Kasavubu and Ileo (the new prime minister), and parliament voted to annul both decisions.

With arrests and counter-arrests by the contending parties threatening yet another round of violent disturbance, the impasse was resolved on the evening of September 14 when the twenty-nine-year-old army chief of staff, Colonel Joseph Mobutu, announced that he was taking power in the name of the army....Then, in a move that warmed the hearts of the CIA agents who had been indoctrinating him for weeks, Mobutu ordered the Soviet and Czechoslovak embassies to get out of the Congo within forty-eight hours....

Though deposed by Mobutu on 14 September 1960, after just seventy-six days in office, Lumumba continued to live at the prime minister's residence in Leopoldville, guarded by an inner ring of UN troops in the garden to prevent his arrest and surrounded by an outer ring of Mobutu's troops on the perimeter to prevent his escape. Hence the difficulty of obtaining access to his toothbrush that the CIA agents had experienced."[3]

But his days were numbered, and he fell right into the hands of his enemies, the most powerful of whom were the Belgians and the Americans helped by their Congolese henchmen, including Mobutu:

"Meanwhile, Lumumba's supporters regrouped in Stanleyville. At the end of November Lumumba decided to join them – a fatal move. He was arrested en route and handed over to Mobutu's army.

Lumumba was consigned to a military prison, but his supporters continued to have an unsettling effect on the country at large....Kasavubu and his (American and Belgian) advisers decided that he should be sent to Elisabethville, the Katangan capital, where the errant Tshombe was in charge.

On 17 January 1961, Lumumba and two colleagues (Maurice Mpolo and Joseph Okito) were flown to Katanga, where a Swedish warrant officer with the United Nations forces witnessed their arrival:

'The first to leave the aeroplane was a smartly dressed African. He was followed by three other Africans, blind-folded and with their hands tied behind their backs. The first of the prisoners to alight had a small beard [Lumumba]. As they came down the stairs, some of the *gendarmes* ran to them, pushed them, kicked them and brutally struck them with rifle butts; one of the prisoners fell to the ground. After about one minute the three prisoners were placed in a jeep which drove off....'

Neither Lumumba nor his colleagues were ever seen again. It is believed they were taken to a farmhouse on the outskirts of Elisabethville, where they died at the hands of Katangese officials and Belgian mercenaries."[4]

It was also said that Lumumba was killed in the presence of Tshombe himself. And there was ample evidence showing that the United States and Belgium had conspired to eliminate Lumumba; further confirmed by intelligence and diplomatic messages coming from each other's capital. One was a cable from the American ambassador in Brussels, on 19 July 1960, advising Washington that Lumumba had "maneuvered himself into a position of opposition to West, resistance to United Nations and increasing dependence on Soviet Union and on Congolese supporters who are pursuing Soviet ends....Only prudent, therefore, to plan on basis that Lumumba government threatens our vital interests in Congo and Africa generally. A principle (sic) objective of political and diplomatic action must therefore be to destroy Lumumba government as now constituted, but at the same time we must find or develop another horse to back which would be acceptable in rest of Africa and defensible against Soviet political attack."[5]

That horse turned out to be Mobutu, one of the most loyal servants of the West who started working for the CIA even before he became head of the Congolese army. At the time of his appointment as head of the army, he was Lumumba's private secretary and already on the CIA payroll. And both the Americans and the Belgians – as well as others including the French, and the apartheid regime of South Africa – supported Mobutu. Therefore, they were all responsible for what happened in Congo; the Americans and the Belgians being the most culpable.

The West did not want any truly independent nationalist to lead any African country. They wanted puppets they could manipulate at will. Lumumba was not one of those stooges. On independence day, June 30, 1960, Lumumba gave a fiery response to Belgian King Baudouin's racist and patronizing speech which even Joseph Kasavubu, a conservative leader and friend of the West, found to be offensive and demeaning.

Lumumba's speech was not well-received in the West. Western governments saw Lumumba as a threat to their

76

economic, political and strategic interests in Congo and on the entire continent. A true nationalist and Pan-Africanist, he believed that political independence was meaningless without economic independence. Therefore Africa had to cease being an economic colony of Europe or a plantation for the metropolitan powers.

Yet, Western powers, especially Belgium, the United States and France, had invested heavily in Congo to exploit its vast amount of minerals and other resources. And Lumumba, because of his independent and pro-African policies, was a direct threat to this hegemonic control of the Congolese economy by the West. As Professor Adam Hochschild of the University of California-Berkeley stated about the CIA's involvement in Lumumba's assassination in his book, *King Leopold's Ghost: A Story of Greed, Terror, and Heroism in Colonial Africa*:

"An inspired orator whose voice was rapidly carrying beyond his country's borders, Lumumba was a mercurial and charismatic figure. His message, Western governments feared, was contagious. Moreover, he could not be bought. Anathema to American and European capital, he became a leader whose days were numbered.

Less than two months after being named the Congo's first democratically chosen prime minister, a U.S. National Security Council subcommittee on covert operations, which included CIA chief Allen Dulles, authorized his assassination. Richard Bissell, CIA operations chief at the time, later said, 'The President [Dwight D. Eisenhower]...regarded Lumumba as I did and a lot of other people did: a mad dog...and he wanted the problem dealt with.'

Alternatives for dealing with 'the problem' were considered, among them poison – a supply of which was sent to the CIA station chief (Laurence Devlin) in Leopoldville – a high-powered rifle, free-lance hit men.

But it proved hard to get close enough to Lumumba to use these, so, instead, the CIA supported anti-Lumumba elements within the factionalized Congo government, confident that before long they would do the job. They did. After being arrested and suffering a series of beatings, the prime minister was secretly shot in Elizabethville in January 1961. A CIA agent ended up driving around the city with Lumumba's body in his car's trunk, trying to find a place to dispose of it...

The key figure in the Congolese forces that arranged Lumumba's murder was a young man named Joseph Desire Mobutu, then chief of staff of the army and a former NCO in the old colonial *Force Publique*. Early on, the Western powers had spotted Mobutu as someone who would look out for their interests. He had received cash payments from the local CIA man and Western military attaches while Lumumba's murder was being planned."[6]

Hochschild was in the Congo during that time, and had first-hand knowledge of some of the events that went on and which had to do with Lumumba's assassination:

"I had been writing about human rights for years, and once, in the course of half a dozen trips to Africa, I had been to the Congo.

That visit was in 1961. In a Leopoldville apartment, I heard the CIA man, who had too much to drink, describe with satisfaction exactly how and where the newly independent country's first prime minister, Patrice Lumumba, had been killed a few months earlier. He assumed that any American, even a visiting student like me, would share his relief at the assassination of a man the United States government considered a dangerous leftist troublemaker."[7]

The CIA and the Belgian government not only worked

together to assassinate Lumumba; they plotted to get rid of him in the most gruesome manner. New revelations about the assassination by some of the people who were directly involved in it only add to our understanding of the sinister plot as one of the most diabolical deeds in the history of post-colonial Africa, conceived by some of Africa's worst enemies.

Some of these revelations come from a Belgian sociologist, Ludo de Witte, who quotes some of the killers in his book, *The Assassination of Lumumba*,[8] published in 1999. And they were right on target, although it took them some time to get to Lumumba. But the objective was clear. As CIA Director Allen Dulles wrote: "In high quarters here, it is the clear-cut conclusion that if [Lumumba] continues to hold high office, the inevitable result will [have] disastrous consequences...for the interests of the free world generally. Consequently, we conclude that his removal must be an urgent and prime objective."[9]

De Witte explains in detail the prominent role the Belgian government played in Lumumba's assassination. According to *U.S. News & World Report*:

"De Witte reveals a telegram from Belgium's African-affairs minister, Harold d'Aspremont Lynden, essentially ordering that Lumumba be sent to Katanga. Anyone who knew the place knew that was a death sentence.

When Lumumba arrived in Katanga, on 17 January (1961), accompanied by several Belgians, he was bleeding from a severe beating. Later that evening, Lumumba was killed by a firing squad commanded by a Belgian officer. A week earlier, he had written to his wife, 'I prefer to die with my head unbowed, my faith unshakable, and with a profound trust in the destiny of my country.' Lumumba was 35.

The next step was to destroy the evidence. Four days later, Belgian Police Commissioner Gerard Soete and his brother cut up the body with a hacksaw and dissolved it in sulfuric acid. In an interview on Belgian television last year (1999), Soete displayed a bullet and two teeth he claimed to have saved from Lumumba's body....

A Belgian official who helped engineer Lumumba's transfer to Katanga told de Witte that he kept CIA station chief Laurence Devlin (in Leopoldville) fully informed of the plan. 'The Americans were informed of the transfer because they actively discussed this thing for weeks,' says de Witte. But Devlin, now retired, denies any previous knowledge of the transfer."[10]

Other sources give similar and sometimes almost identical accounts of the assassination, thus corroborating each other. According to one such source: "A U.N. investigating commission found that Lumumba had been killed by a Belgian mercenary in the presence of Tshombe."[11]

The Belgian mercenary was said to be a CIA agent. Other CIA agents (American) were also probably at the scene, including one American agent who tried to get rid of Lumumba's body before they decided to dissolve it in acid. In addition to that were Congolese henchmen and their Belgian masters.

Also present was Godefroid Munongo, Tshombe's confidant and a member of his cabinet. Although a Congolese, Munongo was a Nyamwezi, a large ethnic indigenous to what is now western Tanzania some of whose members migrated to Congo in the latter part of the 1800s and founded the Yeke kingdom whose ruler, Msiri, was Munongo's ancestor.

Lumumba went down in history as one of the most admired political martyrs in modern times. To many people, especially in Congo and other parts of the continent, he was and still is one of the most revered political figures in the history of post-colonial Africa, together – even if not necessarily in the same league – with leaders such as Julius Nyerere, Kwame Nkrumah, and Nelson Mandela.

The Congo crisis was one of the biggest tragedies that befell Africa during the sixties. And its domino effect and devastating impact is still being felt today, as the Congo lies in ruins. It is, indeed, the bleeding heart of Africa.

The assassination of Lumumba ushered in a new era of political assassinations and military coups in sub-Saharan Africa. On 13 January 1963, almost exactly two years after Lumumba was brutally murdered, another prominent African leader, President Sylvanus Olympio of Togo, was assassinated in a military coup led by a 25-year-old sergeant, Etienne Eyadema, who became one of Africa's longest-ruling and most brutal dictators re-named Gnassingbe Eyadema.

I remember President Olympio's daughter came to live in Tanzania and taught French at our school, Tambaza High School in Dar es Salaam, when I was there from 1969 – 1970 in Form V (Standard 13) and Form VI (Standard 14). She was married to a Tanzanian, Professor Anthony Rweyemamu, now deceased, who was then head of the political science at the University of Dar es Salaam. Her father was shot at the gates of the American embassy in Togo's capital, Lome. It was the first military coup in black Africa.

Although Lumumba was ousted earlier in 1960 when another soldier, Mobutu, seized power, his ouster was not a typical military takeover – like the one in Togo in 1963 – but part of a larger conspiracy by Western powers to dominate and break up Congo and at a time when Lumumba and Kasavubu were competing for power, both claiming to be in charge. Mobutu seized power only later in November 1965 in a typical military coup.

It was Western powers who engineered and supported the secession of mineral-rich Katanga Province in July 1960, only 11 days after Congo won independence on June

81

30th under the leadership of Prime Minister Lumumba, plunging the country into chaos and full-scale civil war. And they continued to support Katanga's secessionist leader Moise Tshombe until 1963 when his forces were defeated by UN peacekeeping troops sent to Congo at the request of Lumumba and other African leaders to keep the country united.

Tshombe died in Algiers, Algeri,a on 29 June 1969 where he was held in captivity since July 1967 after his plane was forced to land, en route to Congo, to cause more mischief. He was 49. He was travelling from Spain. And he did everything he could to break up Congo. He was buried in Belgium.

Ironically, his Western masters accused him of being a racist who didn't like whites; the same people who supported him in his diabolical schemes to destroy Congo.

Had Congo disintegrated, it would have set a dangerous precedent for the rest of Africa, encouraging secession in other parts of the continent.

Tragically, another dangerous precedent was gaining prominence on the continent in the form of military coups when Eyadema assassinated President Olympio and seized power in Togo. Olympio's assassination drew swift condemnation from other African leaders. The government of Tanganyika under Julius Nyerere sent an urgent message to the UN Secretary-General, questioning the dubious credentials of Togo's new leadership:

"After the brutal murder of President Olympio, the problem of recognition of a successor government has arisen. We urge no recognition of a successor government until satisfied first that the government did not take part in Olympio's murder or second that there is a popularly elected government."[12]

At the founding of the Organization of African Unity (OAU) in May 1963 in Addis Ababa, Ethiopia, attended by African heads of state and government, the seat that would have been occupied by the late Togolese President Sylvanus Olympio was conspicuously empty in the conference hall, known as Africa Hall; sending a chilling message to the assembled leaders and future ones on how vulnerable their governments were to subversion by a mere handful of soldiers. But it was also a warning to aspiring coup makers that coups and assassinations would not be tolerated on the continent.

The new Togolese president was Nicholas Grunitzky, Olympio's brother-in-law and opposition leader who had been living in exile in neighbouring Dahomey, re-named Benin in 1975. He was invited by Eyadema to return to Togo and assume leadership; only to be ousted by Eyadema himself four years later on 13 January 1967, on the fourth anniversary of Olympio's assassination.

Unfortunately, the stern warning by African leaders at the OAU summit in May 1963 to soldiers intent on overthrowing governments fell on deaf ears. And military coups became a continental phenomenon and a ritual of African politics for almost 40 years from the sixties to the nineties.

A total of 32 independent African countries were represented at the summit and signed the OAU Charter establishing the Organization of African Unity. They were: Algeria, Burundi, Cameroon, Central African Republic, Chad, Congo-Brazzaville, Congo-Leopoldville, Dahomey, Ethiopia, Gabon, Ghana, Guinea, Ivory Coast, Liberia, Libya, Madagascar, Mali, Mauritania, Morocco, Niger, Nigeria, Rwanda, Senegal, Sierra Leone, Somalia, Sudan, Tanganyika, Togo, Tunisia, Uganda, United Arab Republic (Egypt), and Upper Volta (now Burkina Faso).

Of the 32 countries, 26 had experienced military coups by the end of the 1990s, most of them more than once and sometimes within the same year. For example, three governments were overthrown in Sierra Leone within a month, in April 1968, and two in Nigeria in January and July 1966.

Only Cameroon, Gabon, Morocco, Senegal, Tanganyika (renamed Tanzania after uniting with Zanzibar in 1964), and Egypt, among the OAU founders, escaped this scourge between the sixties and the nineties. But they all had, at one time or another, been targeted by soldiers trying to seize power. Egypt had already experienced two military coups before then: one in 1952, and another in 1954. And it was the only country represented at the 1963 OAU summit that had been under military rule.

Almost exactly a year after the assassination of President Olympio on 13 January 1963, the armies of the three East African countries of Tanganyika, Kenya, and Uganda, mutinied in January 1964. The mutiny started in Tanganyika on January 20th and spread to Kenya and then Uganda in only a matter of days. President Nyerere asked Britain for help to suppress the mutiny in Tanganyika; so did President Jomo Kenyatta of Kenya, and Prime Minister Milton Obote of Uganda. All three countries were former British colonies.

But British troops did not stay long in Tanganyika. Uncomfortable with the presence of foreign troops on African soil, and in an independent country on top of that, Nyerere called for an emergency session of the Organization of African Unity (OAU) in Addis Ababa, Ethiopia, to ask for help from fellow Africans to replace British soldiers as soon as possible. Soon thereafter, Nigeria under President Nnamdi Azikiwe sent troops to Tanganyika to replace the British. Kenya and Uganda continued to rely on British assistance until the situation return to normal.

The army mutinies in the three East African countries helped inspire military coups on the continent when soldiers in other countries saw how they could use guns to extract concessions from civilian governments and even

84

overthrow them at will. And they were some of the earliest manifestations of the intrusive power of the military in African politics as a continental phenomenon, and of what was yet to come in an even more violent way: coups and assassinations spanning four decades.

The 1964 military crisis in the three East African countries occurred around the same time when two major political developments took place in what came to be known as Tanzania. On 12 January 1964, the Zanzibar revolution ended the political dominance of the Arabs when the Arab government was overthrown in one of the bloodiest conflicts in post-colonial Africa. Thousands of people, probably no fewer than 4,000, were killed.

The revolution was supported by Tanganyika. And according to Thabit Kombo who became secretary-general of the Afro-Shirazi Party (ASP) which assumed power in Zanzibar after the revolution, President Kwame Nkrumah of Ghana also helped finance the Zanzibar revolution, as Andrew Nyerere, President Julius Nyerere's eldest son, told me when I was working on the expanded edition of one of my books, *Nyerere and Africa: End of Era*, which I discussed with him throughout the project.

Only about a month before on 10 December 1963, Zanzibar won independence from Britain. But the Arab leaders to whom power was transferred by the departing colonial masters excluded blacks from the government. Not long after the revolution, Tanganyika united with Zanzibar on 26 April 1964. The Union of Tanganyika and Zanzibar was renamed the United Republic of Tanzania on October 29 the same year.

However, some people in the region and elsewhere expressed strong reservations about the union, fearing that it was communist-inspired and would become a launching pad for communist penetration of Africa. Apprehensive of the situation, Ronald Ngala, leader of the Opposition – and of the federalist Kenya African Democratic Union (KADU) – in the Kenyan parliament, had the following to

85

say:

"I hope...that the overseas influence infiltrated into Zanzibar will not spread to Tanganyika in any malicious way."[13]

He made the comment on the same day Tanganyika united with Zanzibar, and mentioned "communist" influence on the former island nation because the Zanzibar revolution had been supported by some communists, including Fidel Castro, and some of the Zanzibari revolutionaries were communist or communist-oriented. But Ronald Ngala's fear of communist penetration of Tanzania, shared by others including the eccentric president of Malawi, Dr. Hastings Kamuzu Banda, proved to be unfounded.

Through the years, Tanzania remained non-aligned – maintaining strong ties with both the East and the West – under President Nyerere and his successors, Ali Hassan Mwinyi (1985 – 1995), and Benjamin Mkapa who became president in 1995 not long after the collapse of communism except in a few countries such as China, Cuba, and North Korea where it remained a state ideology, even if not a functional one in all aspects.

The union of Tanganyika and Zanzibar was the first between independent states on the entire continent, and the only one that has survived for decades.

Consummation of the union between Tanganyika and Zanzibar was a step towards African unity and consolidation of African independence.

But only about a year-and-a-half later, Africa suffered a reversal in its quest for freedom. In November 1965, the same year and month in which General Joseph Mobutu overthrew President Joseph Kasavubu, the white minority government of the Rhodesian Front party led by Ian Smith in the British colony of Rhodesia declared independence illegally, totally excluding the black majority from power.

The unilateral declaration of independence, which came to be known as UDI, was in outright defiance of the wishes and aspirations of not only the black majority in the colony but of the entire continent except the other white minority regimes in South Africa, South West Africa (Namibia) which was ruled by apartheid South Africa, and in the Portuguese colonies of Angola, Mozambique and Portuguese Guinea (Guinea-Bissau), and in other colonial territories. Rhodesia was on the way to becoming another state like South Africa: a bastion of white supremacy on the continent.

Since Rhodesia was a British colony, African leaders urged Britain to intervene and end Smith's rebellion. But Britain did nothing, prompting most African governments to break diplomatic relations with London, in protest. Yet the British government conceded it had jurisdiction over Rhodesia and the constitutional mandate to intervene in the rebellious colony, but still used twisted logic to justify non-intervention. It was neither impressive logic nor clever semantics, and triggered the following response from President Nyerere:

"What has Britain done since 11 November (when Rhodesia declared independence)? On that date Mr. Wilson (the British prime minister) used some strong words: he said 'it is an illegal act, ineffective in law; an act of rebellion against the crown and against the constitution as by law established.' But he then went on to instruct the civil servants of Southern Rhodesia to 'stay at their posts but not to assist in any illegal acts.' He was unable to explain how they could do that when they were serving an illegal government.

As regards the use of force Mr. Wilson repeated his stock phrase despite the changed circumstances. Britain would not use force to impose a constitutional settlement, he said, but he went on to say that the British Government 'would give full consideration to any appeal from the Governor (of Rhodesia) for help to restore law and order.' Mr. Wilson refrained from explaining how the law could be more broken than it had been by the usurpation of power, that is to say, by treason. He refrained later from explaining how the Governor was to transmit his appeal once the telephone had been taken from him as well as all the furniture of his office, his staff and his transport.",[14]

African countries continued to uphold what came to be known as the NIBMAR principle: No Independence Before Majority Rule. But rebel Prime Minister Ian Smith saw the future of Rhodesia from an entirely different perspective. He vowed, at different times, there shall be no majority rule in Rhodesia "not in my lifetime; not in one hundred years; not even in a thousand years." History proved him wrong within his own lifetime.

As the world entered the 21st century, Ian Smith was still living on his farm, but as an ordinary citizen this time, in a country he once ruled defiantly with a tight grip on the black majority. He was now living under his nemesis, Robert Mugabe, a black president, a man he once kept in prison for more than 10 years. Mugabe's crime was simple, yet profound in its implications for white minority rule. He was imprisoned for demanding independence on the basis of majority rule: one man, one vote, regardless of race, gender, class, religion, or national origin. He won, and Rhodesia became Zimbabwe. It was a crowning achievement after a long, bitter struggle, and one of the bloodiest in British colonial history. But, back in 1965, no one foresaw that realization of this goal would be many years away.

It was also in the same year that Africa witnessed another military coup. The coup was the second military takeover on the continent, after the first one in Togo only about two years earlier, and from which Africa had not yet recovered. On 24 November 1965, General Joseph Mobutu overthrew the government of President Joseph Kasavubu in Congo-Leopoldville, coincidentally only 13 days after the white minority regime of Ian Smith illegally declared independence for Rhodesia.

Among the casualties was Evariste Kimba, appointed prime minister by President Kasavubu in October 1965 to replace Moise Tshombe who was invited in 1964 to return from exile to become Congo's premier as fighting intensified in Katanga Province, hoping that his appointment would help to end the fighting in his former secessionist province. Kimba was hanged on orders from Mobutu; so were other opponents, soon after the coup.

As Africa was still grappling with the Rhodesian crisis, and with the Congo which was still in turmoil, two major developments of political and historical significance for the continent took place in 1966.

On 15 January 1966, Nigeria, Africa's most populous country, was rocked by its first military coup in which Federal Prime Minister Sir Abubakar Tafawa Balewa and two regional premiers and other top government officials were assassinated.

The coup was led by a group of young army officers from Eastern Nigeria. And it triggered a violent reaction against easterners living in Northern Nigeria after the Northern Premier Ahmadu Bello, Federal Prime Minister Abubakar Tafawa Balewa, also a northerner, and a large number of northern military officers were killed.

The other premier who was killed was Chief Samuel Ladoke Akintola of Western Nigeria.

Tens of thousands of Eastern Nigerians were massacred in retaliation, pogroms which largely contributed to the secession of the Eastern Region and subsequent civil war in the following year, as did Nigeria's second military coup only a few months later in July 1966 in which the head of the federal military government, Johnson Aguiyi Ironsi, an easterner, was assassinated.

Another major political event in Africa in 1966 was the military coup in Ghana, only about a month after the first coup in Nigeria which may have helped to inspire it. On 24 February 1966, Dr. Kwame Nkrumah was overthrown when he was in Peking on his way to Hanoi at the invitation of Ho Chin Mihn to help end the Vietnam war. The coup was masterminded by the CIA. Black American ambassador to Ghana, Franklin Williams who was Nkrumah's schoolmate at Lincoln University, a historically black college in Pennsylvania, played a critical role in facilitating the coup. The coup makers were reportedly given at least $6 million by the CIA through the American embassy in Ghana to oust Nkrumah; his ouster partly inspired by his increasingly dictatorial rule, and by a deteriorating economy drained by expensive projects and failed socialist policies.

Dr. Nkrumah's downfall was significant in a number of respects. Not only was he one of Africa's most controversial presidents because of his daring and policy initiatives; he was also one of the most influential.

Nkrumah was the first leader in sub-Saharan Africa to lead his country to independence on 6 March 1957. He was the most ardent proponent of immediate continental unification. He was the first black African head of state to institute a one-party state and adopt socialism. He was one of the strongest supporters of African independence and liberation movements. He articulated an ideology and concepts which stimulated debate and had profound impact on the course of political events on the continent. And he remains, even today, the most influential African leader besides Julius Nyerere and Nelson Mandela; with Mandela's influence mainly as a moral authority, and not as a political theorist like Nkrumah and Nyerere.

In a poll conducted by the BBC in 2002, the majority of Africans who participated in the survey voted for Nkrumah as the most influential African leader in the twentieth century.

While many people in Ghana were debating the legacy of Dr. Nkrumah and adjusting to new life under military rule for the first time in their lives, Nigeria was hurtling towards disaster, inexorably propelled by the spiraling wave of violence as a result of the two military coups in 1966.

The hour of reckoning came on 30 May 1967, when the leaders of Eastern Nigeria declared independence and renamed the secessionist region, the Republic of Biafra, "land of the rising sun." Secession of Eastern Nigeria from the rest of the federation was the biggest threat the country had faced since independence in 1960. And it had serious implications for the entire continent.

Nigeria was seen as an anchor of stability on a continent of weak states, and, because of its sheer size and enormous wealth mostly from oil, had the potential to become one of the most powerful countries in the developing world. Should it collapse, its weaker neighbours would inevitably be sucked into the vortex and suffer tremendously from the spill-over effects of the implosion.

This dreadful prospect seemed to be a distinct possibility when, not long after Eastern Nigeria declared independence, hostilities broke out between the two sides in July 1967, plunging the country into civil war. From then on, until 1970, the Nigerian conflict became the dominant story dominating headlines across the continent.

The secessionist forces capitulated to federal might on 12 January 1970, and the war officially ended three days later, on January 15, when the Biafrans finally surrendered.

More than one million people, mostly Igbo, perished in the conflict. Most of them died from starvation which the federal military government used deliberately and effectively as a weapon against the Biafrans. Chief Obafemi Awolowo, vice-chairman of the Executive Council, hence vice-president of Nigeria under General

Yakubu Gowon, unequivocally stated that starvation was a legitimate instrument of war against the secessionists to force them to surrender. Other estimates, including those of the BBC and other news organizations and relief agencies, put the death toll at 2 million.

It was, until then, the deadliest conflict in modern African history and one of the biggest humanitarian disasters the world had ever seen, evoking memories of the Jewish holocaust in Nazi Germany when 6 million Jews were exterminated.

The conflict in the Middle East also had direct bearing on Africa. When the third Arab-Israeli war broke out in June 1967, just one month before the Nigerian civil war erupted, almost all the Arab countries in North Africa became directly involved in the conflict. Egypt, the leader of the Arab world and the most powerful Arab nation, played the most dominant role, sending to the front the largest number of troops among all Arab countries comprising North Africa and the Middle East; in fact, most Arabs in the world live in Africa, not in the Middle East, and Arab countries in Africa constitute the largest percentage of Arab land in the world.

In addition to Egypt, two other North African countries, Algeria and Libya, also sent troops. And most African countries supported the Arab cause, especially at the Organization of African Unity (OAU), the United Nations and in other international forums. It was also during this period that one of the most dominant political figures in the Arab world and on the African continent, President Gamal Abdel Nasser, died. He died of a heart attack on 28 September 1970. He was 52.

The year 1971 witnessed the emergence of a new political phenomenon on the African continent: Idi Amin. Ignorant and arrogant with only a standard two education – Americans call it second grade; flamboyant and comical, he earned himself a place in history for his atrocities and buffooneries – including antics unheard of – few would envy. An eccentric and bizarre character, he admired Hitler and tried to emulate him. He even wanted to build a monument to the Fuhrer, in his likeness, in Uganda's capital Kampala.

Yet he did not have a policy of systematic ethnic cleansing involving extermination, although he initially targeted members of the Langi and Acholi ethnic groups whom he thought were loyal to deposed President Milton Obote who was a Langi.

The Acholi and the Langi constituted a disproportionately large number of enlisted men and officers in the Ugandan army whom Amin swiftly replaced with men loyal to him from his home region, West Nile Province, in the northwest. And through the years, he also targeted assorted groups, including real and perceived enemies, across the spectrum, and praised Hitler as a true nationalist for persecuting and exterminating Jews. He even expelled almost all Asians from Uganda in 1972, including Ugandan citizens of Asian – mostly Indian and Pakistani – origin, and gave them only three weeks to leave the country. About 70,000 left Uganda.

I remember the expulsions well. I was on the same flight, East African Airways (EAA), with some of the expelled Asians in November 1972 on my way to Britain, and got the chance to talk with an elderly Indian sitting next to me. He was one of those kicked out of Uganda by the burly dictator and talked about this forced exodus, about which I had known when I was a reporter at the *Daily News* in Dar es Salaam, Tanzania.

The flight originated from Dar es Salaam, Tanzania's capital, where I caught the plane on my way to the United States for the first time as a student. Our first stop was Nairobi, Kenya; next, Kampala, Uganda, where the expelled Asians boarded the plane on their way to Britain and whatever other countries would take them in.

Stripped of their possessions including financial assets, they landed in Britain, and in other countries such as

Canada and the United States, destitute. Most of them ended up in Britain, Uganda's former colonial ruler. Almost all the passengers on the flight I was on from Uganda were Asians expelled by Idi Amin, as were those on subsequent flights, booked full.

President Julius Nyerere of Tanzania publicly condemned Idi Amin for expelling the Asians and called him a racist. Two other African leaders, President Kenneth Kaunda of Zambia and President Samora Machel of Mozambique, also criticized Amin for his brutalities and eccentric behaviour in general.

But it was Nyerere who was most explicit in his condemnation of Amin, and strongly criticized other African leaders for their silence and tolerance and even their admiration of the Ugandan despot and for practising tyranny in their own countries.

He reminded them that had Idi Amin been white, and had the apartheid regime of South Africa gone on a genocidal rampage, slaughtering blacks across the country, these same leaders would have been furious. There would have been an outcry across the continent, calling for severe sanctions and even military action against the white murderers. But because Amin was black, other African leaders simply looked the other way, as they did when other atrocities were being committed across the continent by fellow Africans. Black leadership had become a license to kill fellow blacks.

Idi Amin was one of the most brutal tyrants Africa has ever produced. And he was probably the most notorious, grabbing international headlines every few days – sometimes everyday – for his antics and brutality. He went on a genocidal rampage, killing an estimated 300,000 – 500,000 people during his eight-year blood-soaked reign of terror in a relentless campaign viciously prosecuted across ethnic lines by his henchmen.

Anybody, including his wives, was fair game as he sought to eliminate all his enemies, real and imagined.

And he himself participated in many of those killings, personally delivering the final blow. He also reportedly bragged about eating the flesh of some of his opponents, although this was never confirmed. As David Lamb stated in his book, *The Africans*, Amin could be as playful as a kitten and as lethal as a lion:

"Ugandans coined a word – Aminism – to describe the terrible happenings in their country, and by the time the Aminisms ended in 1979, an estimated 300,000 Ugandans - or one Ugandan in every forty - were dead. The carnage was tantamount to murdering the entire population of Louisville, Kentucky.

It was as though Amin had studied presidential protocol in Papa Doc's Haiti or Pol Pot's Cambodia. And in the process the Ugandan people learned how to survive but forgot how to feel. 'Killing was so commonplace,' a grocer in Kampala told me, 'that if you heard your brother had been picked up by the police, you knew that was the end of him. You'd say, 'Too bad,' and you'd feel bad for a few days, then you'd just go back to work and forget about him.'

A single human beast, as playful as a kitten, as lethal as a lion, had managed almost single-handedly to destroy a nation of 13 million people." – (David Lamb, *The Africans*, Vintage Books, New York, 1987, p. 78).

After he was chased out of Uganda eight years later in April 1979 by Tanzanian troops and Ugandan exiles, he left the country in tatters; a monument to the incalculable damage he had inflicted on that beautiful land and on his fellow countrymen during his brutal reign, drenched in blood on a scale unparalleled in the history of post-colonial Africa.

Other brutal dictators who earned notoriety in the seventies included President Masie Nguema of Equatorial Guinea. During his 11-year reign from 1968 – 1969, he terrorized the entire country and left it in ruins. About one-third of the population, at least 100,000 people, fled into exile, and an estimated 40,000 were tortured and killed. His nephew, 33-year-old Colonel Teodoro Obiang Nguema overthrew him in August 1979. President Nguema tried to escape but was captured, tried for genocide and witchcraft, and executed with six aides in September 1979.

Another brutal tyrant with a knack for grabbing headlines like Idi Amin was President Jean-Bedel Bokassa of the Central African Republic. In January 1966, Colonel Bokassa overthrew President David Dacko, his cousin. He dissolved the national legislature, abolished the constitution, and banned political parties. Suspected political opponents were routinely arrested and summarily executed or tortured indefinitely. He was also said to practice cannibalism like Idi Amin, his friend.

In December 1976, Bokassa crowned himself Africa's first socialist emperor at a sports stadium in the capital Bangui in a ceremony that cost $20 million and drained the coffers of his impoverished nation. His official title was Emperor Bokassa I. His brutality knew no bounds. When school boys demonstrated against a government decree ordering them to buy uniforms from a shop partly owned by one of his three wives, the notorious dictator ordered them arrested. About 100 of them were brutally murdered in April 1979. Bokassa himself personally killed 39 of the students.

The seventies also witnessed a series of other tragedies on the African continent. In 1972, a campaign of ethnic cleansing in Burundi by the Tutsi military rulers claimed more than 200,000 Hutu lives within three months; a genocide which presaged what was to happen 22 years later in neighbouring Rwanda which has roughly the same ethnic ratio and composition and whose holocaust claimed even more lives than the massacres in Burundi. At least five times as many lives were lost in Rwanda, but of Tutsis this time, and at a rate five times faster than Hitler killed the Jews.

In 1974, one of Africa's most influential and revered leaders, Emperor Haile Selassie of Ethiopia, was deposed in a military coup. He died in 1975 in captivity, reportedly smothered with a wet pillow, and was buried in an unmarked grave, symbolically intended to shunt him into oblivion. Other reports said he was buried under a toilet in his former imperial palace in Addis Ababa where he was detained and where his remains were found in 1992. President Julius Nyerere intervened and tried to save his life but did not succeed in convincing the military rulers to free the deposed emperor and spare his life.

One of the reasons for his ouster was his unwillingness or refusal to admit that tens of thousands of his people were starving – he was ashamed, as an emperor. Also known as the Lion of Judah, and King of Kings, Haile Selassie was said to be a descendant of King Solomon and the Queen of Sheba, and the 250th king in that line of succession, although some people dispute this claim to royal lineage.

But the military regime which ended the monarchy turned out to be ruthless on a scale unheard of during Emperor Haile Selassie's reign. In June 1974, Ethiopian troops overthrew the government and declared "war on feudalism." At least 200 former cabinet members and advisers to the emperor were arrested. Haile Selassie himself was deposed in September 1974, ending his 58-year reign as Africa's only emperor and one of the most respected leaders on the continent and in the entire world.

The military junta officially abolished the Ethiopian monarchy in March 1975. After a protracted power struggle, Lieutenant-Colonel Mengistu Haile Mariam emerged as Ethiopia's ruler. A dictator, he went on to institute a reign of terror that claimed more than 5,000 lives in 1977 – 1978.

Nine assassination attempts on Mengistu were reported by his government in 1978, leading to the execution of many members of the ruling military junta. In 1981, Amnesty International estimated that 10,000 to 40,000 political prisoners remained in Ethiopian jails and prisons. Many were tortured and killed.

The famine in Ethiopia went on to claim more than one million lives through the seventies and early eighties. In 1982 – 1985, Ethiopia had one of the worst droughts in its history. More than 9 million people faced starvation.

A major international relief effort mobilized more than $700 million in government and private aid for the famine victims who received thousands of tons of grain and other supplies including medicine.

Famine in other African countries such as Niger, Mali, Chad, and Upper Volta (renamed Burkina Faso in 1984), also claimed hundreds of thousands of lives during the same period.

Civil wars also dominated headlines in Africa during that period.

In 1975, the Portuguese colonies of Angola and Mozambique won independence after 500 years of colonial rule; Portuguese Guinea, also the oldest colony on the continent, won hers as Guinea-Bissau in 1974, becoming the first Portuguese colony in Africa to emerge from colonial rule.

But immediately after that, Angola was plunged into full-scale civil war – the war actually never stopped between the three contending parties, the MPLA (Popular Movement for the Liberation of Angola), UNITA (Union for the Total Independence of Angola), and FNLA (National Front for the Liberation of Angola), which had been fighting for control of Angola while at the same fighting against the Portuguese.

The FNLA withered in the late seventies, not long after Angola won independence, but UNITA continued to fight against the ruling MPLA through the decades and into the twentieth-first century. By the end of 2000, the war had cost more than one million lives and devastated the country. It ended in April 2002 after rebel leader Dr. Jonas Savimbi was killed by government soldiers in February the same year.

While the war in Angola was raging in the seventies, another major conflict erupted between Ethiopia and Somalia in 1977 after Somalia invaded its neighbour to reclaim the Ogaden Region in the southeast – which is predominantly ethnic Somali – annexed in 1896 by Ethiopian Emperor Menelik II; he also annexed several other provinces to the west during the same period.

The two countries continued to fight intermittently through the years until 1988 when Somalia surrendered. The Somali army was devastated back in 1978 after eight months of intense warfare, but was still able to sustain a protracted conflict between the two countries through its surrogates, Somali guerrillas in the Ogaden, until 1988 when Somalia conceded defeat and signed a peace agreement with Ethiopia virtually on the victor's terms.

It was also during the same period that Tanzania and Uganda went to war after Idi Amin invaded Tanzania in October 1978 and annexed 710 square miles of its territory in the northwest Kagera Region bordering Uganda. He also had other territorial ambitions to seize and annex a corridor of Tanzanian territory and what then was the country's second largest city, Tanga on the east coast, ostensibly to have an outlet to the sea.

But his imperial ambitions didn't get very far. Tanzania drove out the invaders and, together with an army of Ugandan exiles, marched all the way to Kampala, forcing Amin to flee the country in April 1979. He sought refuge in Libya, welcomed by another mercurial leader, Muammar al-Qaddafi who earlier sent troops and weapons to Uganda to help Amin fight Tanzania.

The war, which lasted for six months and finally ended Amin's brutal dictatorship, inflicted a heavy blow on Tanzania and cost the poverty-stricken country more than $500 miilion.

Africa entered a new decade, the 1980s, with some good news. In April 1980, white minority rule in Rhodesia came to an end after a 15-year intense guerrilla war of independence in which tens of thousands of people were killed. The country was renamed Zimbabwe. But the euphoria of independence was marred by the massacre of more than 20,000 people by government troops in the early 1980s in the opposition stronghold of Matebeland in southwestern Zimbabwe; a brutal campaign that exacerbated tensions between the country's two major ethnic groups, the Shona who constitute about 70 percent of the population and dominate the government, and the Ndebele who make up about 20 percent and once ruled the Shona before the advent of colonial rule.

But more than any other country in Africa, Sudan has suffered the longest from the scourge of war. Its war began in 1955, just before the country won independence from Britain and Egypt in 1956, and cost more than 500,000 lives by 1972 when the Arab-dominated government in the north reached a cease-fire agreement with the black insurgents in the south who had been fighting against Arab domination and for autonomy.

The war re-ignited in 1983 and claimed more than two million lives by 1999 in that 15-year period alone. With about three million dead since 1955, it was the bloodiest conflict in African post-colonial history up to the end of the twentieth-century and beyond, and came to be known as the world's longest, bloodiest, and most forgotten war.

In July 2002 , the two sides signed the Machakos Agreement – in the town of Machakos, Kenya, under the auspices of Kenyan President Daniel arap Moi – and agreed to share power; allow the south to enjoy extensive autonomy; and hold an internationally supervised referendum after six years, in 2008, to enable the people of the south decide if they wanted to remain an integral part of Sudan or secede and establish their own independent state.

In a referendum that was held in January 2011, southerners overwhelmingly voted for independence. On 9 July 2011, the south became independent as the new nation of South Sudan.

The mid-eighties saw the eruption of another major civil war in Africa, besides the conflict in Sudan that was already going on. In 1986, a rebel group called RENAMO (Portuguese acronym for Mozambique National Resistance) started waging a sustained military campaign against the FRELIMO government of Mozambique; FRELIMO is an acronym for Front for the Liberation of Mozambique, an organization which waged guerrilla war and ended Portuguese colonial rule in the country.

The conflict between RENAMO and FRELIMO started earlier, before 1986, but escalated in the mid-eighties. RENAMO was created with the help of the Rhodesian security forces and was supported by apartheid South Africa, the United States, and right-wing organizations in the West. Other countries including Saudi Arabia also supported RENAMO.

The war went on for 16 years. When it ended in 1992, more than one million people had been killed and at least five million ended up as refugees mostly in Tanzania and Malawi. It was one of the most brutal wars in modern African history characterized by gruesome mutilation, chopping off limbs, ears and lips as in Sierra Leone where the rebels also chopped off buttocks and branded civilians with hot iron and steel.

Chad was also embroiled in civil war in the 1980s. Civil conflict in Chad began in the sixties between Arabs in the north, who are mostly Muslim, and blacks in the south who are predominantly Christian. In the seventies and eighties, outside powers were involved in the conflict and switched sides supporting one side and then the other whenever it suited their interests. The United States and France were allies against Libya and her clients throughout the conflict. Tens of thousands of people died in the war in the seventies and eighties alone.

The government of Hissene Habre, a northerner, killed more than 40,000 people and tortured more than 100,000 in southern Chad, his opponents' stronghold. The conflict was political as much as it was racial as has been the case since the sixties when Arabs in the north, a minority in the country, tried to secede or establish an autonomous state with the help of Libya after they failed to dominate the country following the end of French colonial rule in 1960.

Famine also continued to ravage Africa in the 1980s and many countries in a belt stretching across the north-central part of the continent from Mali to Ethiopia faced massive starvation. They were helpless and could only count on international relief efforts to alleviate their plight. Hundreds of thousands of people died. Drought was responsible for most of the famine and also wiped out livestock. But mismanagement, corruption, wrong policies and inept leadership also played a major role in aggravating the situation.

The collapse of communism in the late 1980s and early 1990s ushered in a new era round the globe. Just as the sixties saw most African countries become one-party states and socialist or socialist-oriented, the early nineties witnessed a reversal of that when almost all the countries embraced multiparty democracy and capitalism, once considered their nemesis in the quest for unity and development.

After the end of communism, free-market policies were adopted in countries – including Russia and former Soviet satellites – which had pursued socialist policies for decades even before African countries won independence. And multiparty democracy found ready acceptance where it had been reviled by leaders as a tool of the capitalist West to divide and dominate weaker countries. African countries shared this view after they attained sovereign status.

And when change came, showing that communism had

failed, Africa was no exception from this reconfiguration of the political landscape. In the early 1990s, a wave of democratisation swept across the continent which had been dominated by one-party states since the sixties, and socialism was renounced as a state ideology even by countries which had been the strongest exponents of this politico-economic philosophy.

The early nineties also witnessed the beginning of the end of apartheid in South Africa, the bastion of white supremacy on the continent. In February 1990, South Africa's most prominent political prisoner, Nelson Mandela, was released from prison after being incarcerated for more than 27 years. The apartheid regime finally collapsed in May 1994 when Mandela became president after the first multiracial democratic elections in the country's history. However, the transition to the new dispensation had also been marred by political and ethnic violence in the early nineties that cost more than 10,000 lives within three years before the April 1994 elections which were a spectacular success.

But in spite of the good news about the end of apartheid whose demise was celebrated across the continent, 1994 was also a tragic year for Africa. It was the year when about one million people, mostly Tutsi, were massacred by the Hutu in Rwanda within three months at a rate five times – some say six times – faster than Hitler killed the Jews.

The massacres took place from April to July 1994, around the same time South Africa was emerging from her nightmare of apartheid. It was a strange coincidence, "the best of times,...the worst of times," in the words of Charles Dickens. As Wole Soyinka stated in one of his articles, "The Blood-soaked Quilt of Africa," in May 1994: "Rwanda is our nightmare, South Africa is our dream." Tragically, the nightmare has not yet ended, not only in Rwanda but in many parts of Africa.

The bloodshed in Rwanda was only one of the

103

tragedies that befell Africa during the nineties. It was a decade of wars, and AIDS, and other calamities. Besides having the largest number of AIDS victims and casualties, Africa also had the largest number of civil wars in the 1990s more than in any other period since independence in the sixties. At least 25 countries were torn by civil conflicts: Algeria, Sierra Leone, Liberia, Guinea-Bissau, Sudan, Somalia, Ethiopia, Uganda, Rwanda, Burundi, Congo-Kinshasa (Zaire), Congo-Brazzaville (Congo Republic), Angola, Mozambique, Kenya, Chad, the Central African Republic, Cote d'Ivoire (Ivory Coast), Nigeria, Mali, Senegal, Niger, the Comoros, Lesotho, and South Africa during the transition from apartheid to democracy.

Some of the bloodiest conflicts which erupted in the nineties took place in Liberia and Sierra Leone. The war in Liberia started in December 1989, and in Sierra Leone in March 1991. Both countries were totally destroyed. About 200,000 were killed in Sierra Leone, more than 100,000 maimed, and tens of thousands were uprooted from their homes and ended up as refugees in neighbouring countries. In Liberia, also more than 200,000 were killed, more than 800,000 ended up as refugees, and about 6 to 8 percent of the total population perished in the seven-year conflict.

In Sierra Leone, the rebels of the Revolutionary United Front (RUF) earned international notoriety because of their gruesome tactics, chopping off limbs, ears and lips, gouging out eyes, chopping off buttocks, and other brutalities inflicted on innocent civilians including the elderly, women, and babies only a few weeks old. They all met the same fate, sometimes with both arms and legs chopped off.

As the century came to an end, the wars were still raging in both countries. The war in Sierra Leone formally ended in January 2002. But there was no guarantee that peace would be maintained after British troops, which

104

ended the war, left the country. UN peacekeeping troops, the largest force ever deployed anywhere in UN's history, also helped restore peace but were not as effective as British combat troops. In Liberia, the war formally ended in 1996 but low-intensity warfare – and sometimes pitched battles in sporadic fighting in different parts of the country – continued through the years in an attempt by rebel groups to overthrow President Charles Taylor; a brutal warlord and dictator who intimidated his fellow countrymen into voting for him in 1997, with the implied threat that he would plunge Liberia back into war if he did not win the presidency.

A thug even in office, he continued to use brutal tactics against real and perceived enemies, torturing and killing them. The brutalities helped fuel the war against his regime. In February 2002, he came perilously close to being overthrown when one of the rebel groups advanced towards the capital, Monrovia, and was within striking range – only about 20 miles – when government forces fought back.

The conflict escalated into full-scale war in different parts of the country, forcing tens of thousands of refugees to flee and seek shelter elsewhere within Liberia and in the Ivory Coast and other neighbouring countries.

Finally, rebels belonging to two groups – LURD (Liberians for Reconciliation and Democracy) and MODEL (Movement for Democracy in Liberia) – entered the capital Monrovia and forced Taylor to relinquish power in August 2003. He left Liberia and was granted political asylum in Nigeria as part of an agreement to end the civil war. But he was later arrested, handed over to the Liberian government which, in turn, sent him to a UN court in Sierra Leone to be tried for crimes against humanity. Hew was finally transferred to stand trial at The Hague in the Netherlands. On 26 September 2013, he was sentenced to 50 years in prison and was sent to Britain to serve his sentence.

The 1990s were tragic in another respect. These were also the years when Somalia died as a nation, pulverized from within, the only African country to "disappear" from the map; and the only country in the world that had no government and remained stateless from 1991 – when it first collapsed – well into the 21st century.

It was also during this period that another nation, Eritrea, was born out of Ethiopia in May 1993. Ethiopia became the first African country to break up peacefully, and Eritrea the first to be born out of another since the advent of colonial rule and in the post-colonial era, although it once was an Italian colony and was forcibly incorporated into Ethiopia in 1952 by the United Nations as a condition for its "independence." Ethiopia ended up absorbing it, turning it into one of its provinces and a virtual colony. It was, for all practical purposes, the last "colony" on the continent, colonised within the "mother country," Ethiopia, and ended that status as Africa, with all her problems, staggered towards the beginning of another century, with hope and despair.

Some of the deadliest conflicts hardly made headlines outside Africa. In Congo-Brazzaville, a four-month civil war from 5 June – 15 October 1997, devastated the capital, Brazzaville. Entire parts of the city were reduced to rubble, and more than 10,000 people were killed in the capital alone when government troops of President Pascal Lissouba fought a militia group, the Cobra, supporting former miltary dictator Denis Sassuou-Nguesso.

Lissouba, a former professor, won the presidency in a democratic election in 1992 but fled to Burkina Faso where he was granted asylum after he lost the war in 1997.

Sporadic fighting continued in different parts of the country in the following years, with the Ninja rebels and other forces loyal to former President Lissouba and to the former Brazzaville mayor Bernard Kolelas who once served as prime minister under Lissouba, trying to oust President Denis Sassou-Nguesso.

In 1998, another major civil war erupted in Guinea-Bissau between government troops loyal to President Joao Bernardo Vieira and rebel soldiers led by former army chief Ansumane Mane. The rebels seized most of the country and much of the capital, Bissau, and finally toppled the president in May 1999. Tens of thousands of people fled their homes, creating a major refugee crisis in one of the world's smallest and poorest countries. General Ansumane Mane was eventually killed by government troops in November 2000 for allegedly trying to launch a coup d'etat.

The last two years of the decade (1998 - 1999) also witnessed the bloodiest conflict on the continent since World War II when Ethiopia and Eritrea went to war over a barren piece of land. The war involved tanks, fully mechanized battalions, combat jets and other modern weapons, but was mostly fought as trench warfare like World War I.

The war cost more than 100,000 lives in a combined total of only a few weeks of intense fighting, sometimes claiming as many as 5,000 – 10,000 lives within a few days.

Although the war was fought intermittently, it drained the economies of both countries, some of the poorest in the world. Both countries spent hundreds of millions of dollars, buying expensive and highly sophisticated weapons, while their people, especially in Ethiopia, were starving.

The 1990s were also a period when the AIDS epidemic wreaked havoc across the African continent more than anywhere else and continued to do so well into the 21st century, with no cure in sight. The statistics were appalling, and AIDS became an acronym for Africa Is Dying Slowly.

Since the beginning of the epidemic in the early 1980s, more than 20 million people in sub-Saharan Africa had died of AIDS by the end of 2000; more than twice the

107

number of those who died in World War I. For example, in Zimbabwe, at least 5,000 people were dying everyday. And about half of all 15-year-olds infected with the HIV virus that causes AIDS will eventually die of the disease even if infection rates drop substantially through a combination of therapies and education on AIDS prevention.

Thus, even with the combined casualties from all the African wars since the 1950s and 1960s, including liberation wars against colonial regimes, the death-toll in those conflicts comes nowhere close to the number of people who died of AIDS in Africa by the end of the 1990s; a casualty rate that was bound to grow exponentially through the years, short of divine intervention or some miracle cure including combination therapy to stop the pandemic.

There was also another dimension to some of the African conflicts during that period. There were secessionist threats which led to skirmishes between the insurgents and government troops on the independence-prone island of Bioko in Equatorial Guinea in 1998, and in Caprivi Strip in Namibia in 1999 and beyond. However, they were not major threats.

But there were other secessionist attempts on the continent that were far more deadly and escalated into full-scale war on the separatist islands of Anjouan and Moheli in the Comoros in September 1997, while the conflict in Casamance Province in Senegal had been going on as a full-scale guerrilla war since 1983 when secessionist forces in the region resorted to violence to achieve their goal.

There were other appalling statistics in the 1990s on this embattled continent. The civil war in the Democratic Republic of Congo, formerly Zaire, which drew armies from at least nine African countries, cost almost 2 million lives in Eastern Congo alone between August 1998 when the latest round of fighting started and May 2000. By June

2001, more than 2.5 million people had died, and no fewer than 3 million by mid-2002 in the same region. By 2013, the war and ts accompanying disasters, including hunger and disease, had claimed 6 million lives.

When the war started, the countries involved were Congo itself, Zimbabwe, Angola, Namibia, Rwanda, Uganda, Burundi, Chad, and Sudan. Rwanda, Uganda and Burundi supported the rebels trying to overthrow the government of Laurent Kabila, while the rest backed up the Congolese army in its war against the insurgents; also, there were about 20 rebel groups involved in the war, with conflicting interests.

The intervention by foreign armies from other African countries internationalized the conflict which some people called "Africa's First World War"; a hyperbolic statement whose outlandish nature did not help to put the conflict in its proper historical context. Although it was an inflated statement, there was no question that the war was a major conflict and catastrophe with serious implications for the stability of the continent. And it was still going on as Africa entered the 21st century, as did other wars on the continent. Africa had declared war on itself.

Even in a continent used to wars, the casualty list is staggering. Millions of Africans have died in these conflicts: Angola, more than 1 million; Mozambique, more than 1 million; Congo, formerly Zaire, about 6 million in the Second Congo War from 1998 – 2013; Rwanda, about 1 million killed within 100 days; Burundi, between 250,000 – 500,000 killed within 5 years since the mid-1990s; Somalia, more than 500,000 dead in the 1990s; Ethiopia, tens of thousands dead; Eritrea, also tens of thousands dead in a senseless war with Ethiopia over some tiny, barren piece of land, two bald-headed men fighting over a comb; Sudan, more than 3 million dead since 1983; Sierra Leone, more than 200,000 dead, and more than 100,000 left limbless, their limbs, and even buttocks, ears and lips, chopped off by rebels in an 11-year

109

civil war from 1991 – 2002; Liberia, more than 200,000 dead, about 6 – 8 per cent of the entire population, equivalent to 16.2 million – 20.6 million Americans dead in a civil war within the same period. And this is not an exhaustive list of the number of people killed in wars in this mangled continent.

Some of the least known wars have also been some of the deadliest. Uganda has, relatively speaking, a reputation for stability in a region torn by conflict; although not like neighbouring Tanzania which is far more peaceful and more stable than all the countries in East Africa. Yet, for years, it had to contend with several rebel groups since the eighties when President Yoweri Museveni assumed power in 1986 after waging a successful guerrilla campaign against the government.

One of the bloodiest conflicts was in northern Uganda where rebels of the Lord's Resistance Army (LRA) backed by Sudan killed tens of thousands of people and abducted just as many, mostly children, forcing them to join the rebel army to work as sex slaves and as porters, in addition to fighting. The rebel group continued to wage war as late as 2007 and remained the deadliest among all the insurgents in Uganda including those waging a sporadic guerrilla campaign in the western part of the country.

In neighbouring Kenya, more than 10,000 people were killed within three weeks in a tribal war between the Pokot and Turkana tribesmen in the northern part of the country in 1998.

Earlier in 1992, ethnic cleansing in the Rift Valley Province, home of President Daniel arap Moi and his fellow Kalenjin tribesmen, claimed hundreds of Kikuyu lives, at least 1,300, and forced 300,000 others to flee for their lives, while their property was ransacked and destroyed by the Kalenjins.

Other tribal conflicts in Kenya, including those during the 1997 general elections in the Coast Province and again in the Rift Valley Province, claimed more lives in different parts of the country through the years.

In Nigeria, communal and ethnic violence threatened to tear apart Africa's biggest nation and continued to do so well into the 21st century. Within only three years since the inauguration of President Olusegun Obasanjo in May 1999, the violence claimed more than 10,000 lives in different parts of the country. The conflicts were exacerbated by the introduction of Islamic law, know as *sharia* (in Kiswahili, a language which is about 25 - 30 percent Arabic, *sheria* - not *sharia* – simply means law, any law), in the predominantly Muslim states in the north, triggering clashes between Muslims and Christians originally from the south.

Besides the religious dimension, the conflict was also ethnic. The Christians from the south living in Northern Nigeria are mostly Igbo and members of other ethnic groups, while the Muslims in the north are mostly members of the Hausa and Fulani ethnic groups which are so close to each other – ethnically, culturally, and religiously – that they are simply and collectively known as Hausa-Fulani; with the Fulani mainly constituting the ruling class.

The conflicts in Nigeria, especially in the oil-rich Niger Delta, were ignited and fuelled by government neglect, prompting some people to call for secession.

The end of the 1990s were also marked by another tragedy. Famine threatened the lives of millions of people in East Africa. About 18 million people faced starvation in Ethiopia; 13 million in Kenya faced the same dreadful prospect, prompting one elderly Kenyan photographed and quoted by *The Washington Post* to say, "It's only you white people who can save us," a searing indictment against African governments in general for their inability and unwillingness to help their people. And 13 million people in Tanzania, about 40 percent of the population, were threated by famine during the same period.

Hardest hit were the countries of southern Africa

which faced massive starvation at the dawn of the new century, especially in 2001 - 2004. Malawi, Zambia, Zimbabwe, Angola, Botswana, Mozambique, Swaziland, Lesotho, Namibia, and even South Africa, all faced famine, only in varying degrees. Malawi, Angola, and Zimbabwe whose crisis was aggravated by the seizure of white-owned farms by President Robert Mugabe's government, were the hardest hit, and an international relief effort was launched to help alleviate the plight of millions of people in the region.

But there was also a glimmer of hope, at least for future generations, when the defunct East African Community (EAC) which collapsed in 1977 was revived in 2001 and became functional in 2002 in pursuit of stronger regional integration including federation.

The original member states are Kenya, Uganda and Tanzania which, together with Rwanda and Burundi which joined the EAC in July 2009, may one day form an East African federation that has been an elusive dream since 1963 when Julius Nyerere, Jomo Kenyatta and Milton Obote tried to unite their countries.

The prospects for regional integration also gave some hope to the people of West Africa when the countries in the region decided in 2000 to institute a common currency known as the Eco by 2004; unfortunately, they did not.

It was an ambitious project whose fulfillment would have to depend on the commitment of the member states – Economic Community of West African States (ECOWAS) – to the ideal of regional integration.

The goal towards integration on a continental scale assumed another dimension in June 2001 when the Organization of African Unity (OAU) founded in May 1963 was replaced by the African Union (AU) to facilitate the establishment of a common market, a common currency - the Afro? - and other institutions including a continental parliament.

The OAU officially came to an end at an annual

summit of the African heads of state and government in Lusaka, Zambia, in June 2001 under the chairmanship of Zambian President Frederick Chiluba. It was skillfully led for an unprecedented three consecutive terms by Dr. Salim Ahmed Salim of Tanzania who served as OAU secretary-general from 1989 to 2001, the longest term ever served in that capacity.

The African Union (AU) was formally launched in Durban, South Africa, in July 2002 under the chairmanship of South African President Thabo Mbeki.

The Southern African Development Community (SADC) composed of 14 countries in East and Southern Africa, which is also the strongest economic bloc on the continent because of South Africa's membership, the continent's powerhouse, continued to grow and took further steps to achieve full economic integration in the region. Measures proposed included establishment of a common market, a common currency, and a regional parliament.

On a continent dominated by bad news, the trend towards regional integration was some of the best news to come out of Africa as the 20th century came to an end.

But there was more bad news. Africa suffered another tragic loss at the end of the 1990s that was also an important milestone in the history of Africa. Tanzania's first president, Julius Nyerere, died of leukaemia at a hospital in London, England, on 14 October 1999. He was 77.

Nyerere was one of the most prominent African leaders in the 20th century who spearheaded the independence movement across the continent. He was also one of the most articulate and ardent spokesmen for the Third World. His death marked the end of an era in the history of post-colonial Africa, and the dawn of a new one in terms of ideological orientation and leadership.

He was one of the last of the most prominent African leaders who led their countries to independence in the

113

fifties and sixties. They included Kwame Nkrumah, Jomo Kenyatta, Nnamdi Azikiwe, Patrice Lumumba, Ahmed Sekou Toure, and Modibo Keita. He outlived them all, except Kenneth Kaunda, Milton Obote, Leopold Sedar Senghor, and Ahmed Ben Bella.

His belief in socialism remained unshaken, and he died with his reputation for integrity intact.

Nyerere will be remembered for generations as one of the founding fathers of independent Africa and a staunch advocate of Pan-Africanism whose ideology and philosophy was embraced by those in the diaspora as well, comparable in stature to another uncompromising Pan-Africanist, Dr. Kwame Nkrumah. As one South African journalist wrote about Nyerere's role in the liberation of the countries of southern Africa from white minority rule:

"All these countries are now free, with their liberation sprung from Dar es Salaam."[15]

Another one stated:

"From Dr. Nyerere's commitment flowed the liberation first of Mozambique, Angola, Guinea-Bissau and Cape Verde in the early '70s, followed by Zimbabwe in 1980, Namibia in 1990 and eventually South Africa."[16]

And as Nyerere himself said about some of his achievements:

"We took over a country with 85 per cent of its adults illiterate. The British ruled us for 43 years. When they left, there were two trained engineers and 12 doctors. This is the country we inherited. When I stepped down, there was 91 per cent literacy and nearly every child was in school. We trained thousands of engineers, doctors and teachers."[17]

The death of Julius Nyerere evoked strong feelings from many people in different parts of the world, most of it positive. One of the most memorable tributes came from Ghanaian member of parliament, Hackman Owusu-Agyemang, who was also minority spokesman for foreign affairs, later minister of foreign affairs under President John Kufuor:

"Dr. Nyerere even in death at the state-owned St. Thomas Hospital in London, symbolised the humility and modesty that had come to be associated with his life-style.... That he retired from politics with nothing more than a second-hand tractor and a bicycle showed that as President he neither dipped his hands into state coffers nor private pockets. Nor were his hands covered with anyone's blood....

His Ujamaa community-based farming collective which was conceived with due acknowledgement of the African communal way of life, in spite of its failure as a concept, demonstrated his sensitivity to the plight of his people and his desire to provide the needed leadership.... Dr. Nyerere indeed personified selflessness, sincerity and sensitivity.

An avowed fighter against colonialism and apartheid, Mwalimu who played a pioneering role in the O.A.U. will forever be remembered as an African leader with his name engraved in gold.

By his retirement from the Presidency of Tanzania in 1985, Dr. Nyerere lived up to his title as Mwalimu since he not only taught but demonstrated the virtue in bowing out even when the applaud is loud....

As we mourn the loss of this gem and giant of a statesman, we take consolation in the fact that death, coming at this time, has been the crown of a historic, rich and fulfilling life for Mwalimu Julius Nyerere.... The death of Dr. Julius Nyerere has robbed Africa of a leading light, whose exploits as a politician and statesman filled the hearts of Africans with joy and inspiration.

We...recall with nostalgia the passion and zeal with which a young Dr. Julius Nyerere together with our own Dr. Kwame Nkrumah and other African nationalists, prosecuted the anti-colonist and independence struggle to liberate Africa from foreign domination. That today, the last vestige of colonialism has been routed in Africa, is to a large extent, due to the untiring efforts of Dr. Nyerere and his co-fighters in the African liberation struggle."[18]

Tragically, he died when Africa, mired in conflict, needed him most. As he himself said not long before he died: "Africa is in a mess."

But in spite of all the tragedies the continent has endured through the years, there was also some good news out of Africa at the end of the 1990s, although not much. And it inspired many people across the continent. Africa's giant nation, Nigeria, finally returned to democracy in May 1999 after 15 years of uninterrupted brutal military dictatorship.

Where Nigeria is headed, and what the future has in store for the rest of Africa, was never meant for us to know. But we know one thing. We have come a long way since the sixties. And we still have a long way to go. We will keep on going, even if we don't get there. We have no other choice. And that is Africa's only choice.

Chapter Three:

Africa After Independence: Realities of Nationhood

IT HAS BEEN almost 50 years since most African countries won independence. But their independence was and in most cases remains more apparent than real.

Attributes of sovereignty and nationhood were not and could not have been derived from a constitutional text simply because the colonial rulers transferred power to Africans at independence. They had to be given concrete expression, which was by itself a herculean task compounded by the unwillingness of the former imperial powers to totally relinquish control of their former possessions.

When most African countries won independence in the sixties, the former colonial powers wanted to maintain close ties with their former colonies for a number of reasons: economic control; political domination; strategic interests; Cold War imperatives; and national prestige. They still considered their former colonies as their

117

property and spheres of influence. Colonialism was transmuted into neocolonialism but in essence it remained the same as a system of political domination and economic exploitation through indirect rule.

The most glaring example of such hegemonic control was France. To hang on to their colonies, the French formed the French Community in 1958. That was the same year when France granted internal autonomy to all her colonies. It was also the same year in which Guinea demanded and won full independence and pulled out of the French Community.

But the Community collapsed two years later in 1960 when all the French African colonies attained sovereign status. The French Community was formed to replace the imperialist French Union formed in 1946 and which was more brazen in its operations and pursuit of its imperial goals.

The notion that the former colonies would be satisfied only with internal self-government – granted in 1958 – and let the French formally control their defence, foreign policy, finance, communication and other vital matters, was contrary to the nationalist aspirations for full independence; although that is exactly what almost all of them allowed to happen except Guinea which voted for independence in 1958, and Mali among countries which won independence in 1960, as well as Algeria which became independent in 1962.

Tunisia and Morocco, which won independence in 1956, also did not submit to the dictates of France although her influence in both countries was still substantial even after they won independence mainly because of their economic ties with the former imperial power.

But they all publicly expressed a strong desire for independence, partly to gain credibility especially among other Africans as genuinely nationalist countries and France was aware of that. The former French colonies have through the years been known for their subservience to Paris. Nkrumah called them "client states." And as Nyerere stated in an interview:

"I went to Addis (in May 1963 when the Organisation of African Unity (OAU) was formed) and it was an incredible meeting.

Here is this continent of young nations coming from colonialism and so forth and the debate is awful, and really what provoked me was the French-speaking countries, you know.

With all their French culture, training in rationalization – you can't really argue with those fellows.

And I discovered some of these fellows have their visas – *their visas* – signed by the French ambassadors in their own countries! And I said, 'Oh, but I thought you were fighting for freedom?'"

Nyerere was interviewed by Bill Sutherland and the interview is published in a book by Bill Sutherland and Matt Mayer, *Guns and Gandhi in Africa: Pan African Insight on Nonviolence, Armed Struggle and Liberation in Africa,* Africa World Press, 2000.

So when Mali, led by the militant Pan-Africanist leader Modibo Keita, demanded full independence in 1960, France, determined not to repeat the mistake she made with regard to Guinea in 1958 when that country refused to bow to her wishes, acceded to that demand. And she proceeded to dismantle the entire Community apparatus in the same year in order to grant independence to almost all her colonies.

However, the decision by France to fulfill Mali's demand for independence infuriated Felix Houphouet-Boigny, the leader of the Ivory Coast and an unabashed Francophile, who also went on to demand independence for his country, succumbing to nationalist agitation among his own people who did not want to remain under French rule, contrary to his wishes and belief that his country was not ready for independence.

Houphouet-Boigny was so subservient to France that even years after his country won independence, he refused to attend meetings of the Organization of African Unity (OAU) claiming that he was afraid of flying. Yet he did not show any fear when he flew to Paris every year.

Another leader, Dr. Hastings Kamuzu Banda of Malawi, also refused to attend OAU meetings because he saw them as useless, as did Houphouet-Boigny although he was not as blunt as Dr. Banda was on the subject. Banda went on to forge links including diplomatic ties with the apartheid regime of South Africa in defiance of OAU resolutions against any relations with the white minority government.

The Ivory Coast under Houphouet-Boigny also established ties with South Africa, although the Ivorian leader was not openly defiant as Dr. Banda was. And his capitulation to demands for independence among his people in the Ivory Coast had domino effect, as did Mali's demand for full independence. Other French African colonies followed suit.

Houphouet-Boigny's hostility to full independence demanded by Mali in 1960 was also evident two years earlier when Sekou Toure pulled Guinea out of the French Community after 95 percent of the electorate[1] endorsed his demand for total independence.

The Ivorian leader took sides with France and even fuelled her hostility towards Sekou Toure because of Guinea's demand for full independence. But the French did not need to be urged, exhorted or prompted by Houphouet-Boigny to adopt such a hostile attitude and try to destroy Guinea. They were already furious on their own because Guinea refused to be a satellite in the French orbit by remaining under the neo-colonial umbrella of the French Community.

However, that does not exonerate Houphouet-Boigny

from what he did or justify his anti-pan-African stance against Sekou Toure. As Professor Fred Greene, although he overstates his case about Houphouet-Boigny's role, states:

"In the 1958 vote all but Guinea chose to stay in the (French) Community, and the French, at the urging of Houphouet-Boigny, influential leader of the Ivory Coast, adopted a hostile attitude to that recalcitrant state."[2]

The French burned government files, severed communication links to the outside world and within the country itself, and cleaned out the treasury before leaving Guinea, not because Houphouet-Boigny urged them to do so, although he was obviously delighted; they did that, and tried to cripple Guinea, because they were infuriated by what they saw as Sekou Toure's defiance of their wishes when he refused to be subservient to the metropolitan power.

Therefore, they would have done what they did, anyway, even without Houphouet-Boigny encouraging or urging them to do so.

When Sekou Toure pulled Guinea out of the French Community, the French took that as an insult and saw it as a challenge to their authority over their empire, a dangerous precedent they feared others would follow by also withdrawing from the "French family" of nations which were no more than puppets of Paris.

The French may have been the most brazen in exercising control over their imperial possessions. But they were not the only ones who were openly determined to stay in Africa as masters of their sphere of influence.

In order to perpetuate imperial control over their possession like the French did through the French Community, the Belgians also formed a nominal, formal union with their huge colony, the Belgian Congo, which was the size of Western Europe. They also devised a network of financial and defence agreements to bind the Congo to Belgium after the country won independence in order to perpetuate their hegemonic control over this vast expanse of territory in the heart of Africa.

But all those arrangements and the union itself were disrupted when the Congo slid into anarchy immediately after independence and the two countries severed diplomatic ties. However, because of Belgian intervention during the Congo crisis ostensibly to help stabilize the situation but in reality to dismember the Congo and take full control of the country's mineral resources in Katanga Province, the weak government of Prime Minister Cyrille Adoula resumed diplomatic relations with the former colonial power in 1962.

Adoula's government had no national following; nor did Adoula himself have his own power base of loyal supporters or a strong regional backing which would have given him some clout and leverage.

His position was in sharp contrast with that of the other Congolese leaders such as President Joseph Kasavubu who had a strong backing among his people, the Bakongo who also constitute the largest ethnic group in the country; Moise Tshombe based in the mineral-rich secessionist Katanga Province and who was related to the royal family of the Lunda, one of the largest ethnic groups in the Congo; and Albert Kalonji who in 1962 declared himself King of South Kasai dominated by his people, the Luba, also one of the largest ethnic groups in the entire country.

The appeal to ethno-regional loyalties and sentiments was strong throughout the whole country. And all the leaders mentioned – with the exception of Patrice Lumumba who was assassinated on 17 January 1961 – exploited those differences and conflicting interests to pursue their partisan agendas and helped fuel the Congo debacle in the sixties.

Although the Congolese had their own problems and

122

conflicting ethnic and regional interests, the Congo crisis itself was engineered by Western powers – led by the United States and Belgium – who intervened in one of Africa's biggest and richest countries to secure their economic and geopolitical interests – vis-a-vis the Soviet Union and China – at the expense of the Congolese and other Africans in general.

Just as the Congo crisis was a significant event in the history of post-colonial Africa with far-reaching consequences for many years, the end of colonial rule in Africa from 1951 when Libya won independence from Italy until 1968 when most African countries had won independence was one of the most contentious periods during the Cold War era.

Western powers, apprehensive of their declining influence on the continent because Africans had won their freedom, did everything they could to keep the Russians and the Chinese out of there. On the other hand, the Soviet Union and her satellites in the Eastern bloc, as well as the People's Republic of China, saw in that "vacuum" – created by decolonization – opportunities for penetration and even counter-mischief against the West.

In the midst of all this were the Africans themselves who, determined to maintain their newly-won independence, forged links with both the East and the West in the areas of trade, education, diplomatic representation, and technical assistance. But whenever they tried to assert or demonstrate any degree of independence from both power blocs, they were either threatened or thwarted by one side or the other.

The greatest threat came from Western countries which, having ruled Africa, felt that they had the first and final say on what Africans were supposed to do. And that intensified the Cold War between the two ideological camps. African countries, weak and caught in the middle right on their own continent, could only remonstrate or try to play one power bloc against the other.

But their desire and determination to remain independent and keep the Cold War out of Africa was evident from the beginning as soon as they emerged from colonial rule. As one Nigerian scholar, Dr. Okon Udokang, stated:

"By the 1960s, a period that witnessed the unprecedented proliferation of independent states on the continent of Africa, there arose a powerful upsurge of pro-nonalignment sentiments in Afro-Asian countries. It is significant that this development coincided with the period when the Cold War seemed to have reached its apogee, and in certain regions of the world was already taking on an explicit and pronounced military character, as in Vietnam and the Congo.

It was indeed fashionable for the leaders of the new African states to argue that in the Cold War African states belonged to neither camp, but only to Africa. President Nyerere of Tanzania, one of the more perceptive leaders of contemporary Africa, declared that the fledgling African states 'must struggle all the time to stay out of the great power competition.' This sentiment was echoed in the capitals of nearly all the new African states, as their governments attempted to consolidate their individual domestic political base, while grappling with the taxing problem of economic and social reconstruction."[3]

And as Nyerere stated about two years earlier on December 19, 1961, just ten days after he led Tanganyika to independence from Britain, Africans wanted to be friendly with countries in both ideological camps and in the Third World: "(But) we have no desire to have a friendly country choosing our enemies for us."[4]

Nyerere's commitment to non-alignment and his determination not to submit to ideological dictates from either the East or the West was tested in 1964 when West

Germany demanded that the newly-formed United Republic of Tanzania should not allow East Germany to establish a diplomatic mission on her soil; to which Nyerere responded:

"When our people united to win independence...they wanted to have a government responsible to them, so that it would consider their interests and not the interests of people thousands of miles away who had a separate government....The case in which this principle was most openly challenged was the one relating to the recognition of East Germany....

The West Germans...put heavy pressure on the Government (of Tanzania). When diplomatic pressure failed to move Tanzania,...the West German Government unilaterally and without notice, broke a five-year training and aid agreement relating to the new air wing, and returned all their technicians overnight. They went further, and threatened to cut all their aid if we continued with our declared policies."[5]

The actions taken by West Germany because of Tanzania's determination to maintain her political independence remind us of what the French did to Guinea in 1958 when Guinea refused to be a client state and pulled out of the French Community. Had Guinea succumbed to pressure from Paris, her independence would have been compromised and rendered meaningless; so would have Tanzania's, had Tanzania bowed and capitulated to West German demands.

The Cold War had entered Africa with a big chill and the world was watching with interest if Tanzania, one of the the first test cases on the continent during the early years of independence, would be able to withstand it. As Nyerere explained:

"The choice before Tanzania was then clear; we could either accept dictation from West Germany and continue to receive economic aid until the next time we proposed to do something they did not like, or we could maintain our policies and lose the aid immediately. In effect, therefore, we had to choose whether to become a puppet state of Germany in return for any charity she cared to give us....

East Germany wanted Tanzania to give diplomatic recognition to her, and West Germany wanted us to ignore the existence of the German Democratic Republic and pretend there is no such administration over the Eastern part of Germany....As a result of our decision West Germany withdrew some types of aid and announced that other aid was under threat if Tanzania did not change her policies. Tanzania refused to do this and told the West Germans to withdraw all their federal government aid."[6]

In this diplomatic confrontation, Tanzania as the weaker country was supposed to back down, given the harsh realities of realpolitik where power means everything, and morality means nothing. Tanzania's insistence on asserting her independence was perceived by some observers and others as recklessness and not in the best interest of the nation desperately in need of help; power politics is not the kind of game weak nations play. And Nyerere was aware of such criticism. But the issue was bigger than that, more than just bread and butter. As he put it in perspective:

"It has been suggested that the Government made a mistake by telling the Germans to withdraw all their aid, without waiting for them to do this on their own. Yet even in this regard the Government had little alternative if it was to uphold the dignity of our independent country. For there is no doubt that had we simply maintained our policy and waited for the Germans to react by withdrawing aid as and when they liked, they would have been misled into believing that economic pressure would eventually make us change our minds, and there would have been a great deal of intrigue designed to undermine the unity of the country. It is also clear that only by taking this very strong stand could our determination to defend our independence be recognized - both by the Germans and by others."[7]

Guinea faced a similar situation, although the parallels are not exact. After the former French colony severed ties with France in 1958, it sought and obtained economic assistance from the Communist bloc, mainly from the Soviet Union. But gradually, Guineans became disillusioned by Communist attempts to interfere in their affairs and, in December 1961, Sekou Toure expelled the Soviet ambassador, a move which surprised those who considered Guinea to be a Soviet satellite or a strong ally of the Soviet Union.[8]

In 1964, Tanzania also expelled some diplomats from a major power, the United States. Tanzania was also involved in another diplomatic wrangle with the United States for her involvement in an attempt to overthrow the Tanzanian government. As Nyerere stated:

"We have twice quarrelled with the US Government, once when we believed it to be involved in a plot against us, and again when two of its officials misbehaved and were asked to leave Tanzania....The disagreements certainly induced an uncooperative coldness between us."[9]

Attempts by the American Central Intelligence Agency (CIA) to undermine, destabilize and overthrow the Tanzanian government in the mid-sixties were an integral part of a global strategy by the United States during the Cold War intended to install a puppet regime which would dance to the tune of Washington and the West in general;

Nyerere was fiercely independent and took an uncompromising stand on matters of principle even if such a stance offended world powers, as it always did. There were even suggestions by the American government to arm groups in Tanzania opposed to Nyerere. As John Prados states in his book, *Safe for Democracy: The Secret Wars of the CIA*:

"The Special Group (at the CIA) reportedly considered a State Department proposal to supply arms to certain groups in Tanzania, where secret-war wizards saw President Julius Nyerere as a problem, in the summer of 1964....Like Nyerere, Washington viewed Ghana's leader Kwame Nkrumah as a troublemaker." – (John Prados, *Safe for Democracy: The Secret Wars of the CIA*, Ivan R. Dee, Publisher, Chicago, Illinois, USA, 2006, p. 328).

In addition to American hostility towards Nyerere and his socialist-oriented government, the conflict between Tanzania and West Germany over East Germany's diplomatic representation also demonstrated the intensity of the rivalry between East and West and which both camps were more than prepared to wage on African soil by proxy if they could find surrogates on the continent. After all, it was on German soil that the Russians had built the Berlin Wall dividing that city in East Germany between East and West, a move that threatened to trigger a nuclear confrontation between the two super powers.

The Berlin crisis of 1961 which started when the Berlin Wall was built in August in the same year was later linked with the Cuban missile crisis of October 1962. In both cases, the rest of mankind looked with apprehension at how the two super powers were determined to secure their interests even at the risk of a major military conflict which could have escalated into a nuclear conflagration engulfing the whole world.

That Africa, the world's weakest and poorest continent

could be converted into a theatre of conflict between the two ideological camps showed not only how intense but also how reckless the competition was. Aware of the gravity of the situation, African countries and other Third World nations tried to diffuse tensions between the two super powers when the Belgrade Conference of Non-Aligned Nations in 1961 sent Modibo Keita, president of Mali, to Washington, and Dr. Kwame Nkrumah to Moscow.

But as leaders of weak countries, they could only count on moral appeal to influence the leaders of the two super powers. Their role was only peripheral because of their weakness as leaders of weak countries and both were ignored by President John F. Kennedy and Soviet Premier Nikita Khrushchev in their attempts to resolve the Berlin crisis. As President Kennedy told Modibo Keita:

"Are you finished? Well, let me tell you that I, on behalf of the people of the United States, subscribe 100 percent to the objectives of the conference (of Non-Aligned Nations) in spite of the tone of the language....I support your views. Now you have a much harder job - you go and sell this to Chairman Khrushchev in Moscow. Is there anything further you want to say?"[10]

President Modibo Keita was accompanied by President Surkano of Indonesia. As Richard Reeves states in his book *President Kennedy: Profile of Power*:

"Two of the neutrals came to Washington on September 12 (1961): President Surkano of Indonesia, short and volatile, and President Keita of Mali, a tower of dignity almost seven feet tall. Their mission was to inform Kennedy of the results of the Conference of Non-Aligned Nations, just completed in Belgrade, Yugoslavia."[11]

129

The marginal role played by Modibo Keita and Dr. Nkrumah in power politics during the Berlin crisis painfully underscored one harsh reality about power because of the weakness of Africa in the international arena: If you are weak, no one pays you any attention, and you are always wrong because might is right and morality means nothing.

Professor Oran Young also describes in similar terms the two African leaders as peripheral actors in the conduct of international diplomacy during the Berlin crisis. As he states in his book *The Politics of Force*: *Bargaining During International Crises*:

"Informal and often rather indirect means of communication appear to have played a somewhat greater, though frequently ambiguous, role during the 1961 crisis. Some contacts of this kind were largely perfunctory and therefore relatively inconsequential. This seems to be the most reasonable assessment...of the September missions of Nehru and Nkrumah to Moscow and Surkano and Keita to Washington....

The Belgrade Conference clearly demonstrated the new-found concern of the nonaligned states about the dangers of the Berlin crisis, but it also emphasized both the peripheral quality of their deliberations on the subject and the limitations on their abilities to influence the behavior of the great powers."[12]

Although Keita and Nkrumah, two of Africa's leading statesmen, played only a marginal role during the Berlin crisis, their role in the Congo crisis was different even if most of the time it was more symbolically than qualitatively substantive in terms of influencing events and the outcome of what transpired in the Congo.

The Congo crisis thrust them and other African leaders as well as the entire continent into the international spotlight precisely because they could not keep the major powers out of the Congo due to their weakness; painfully aware as they were of the danger power politics posed to the security of Africa. As Dr. Nkrumah stated in his speech to the UN General Assembly on 7 March 1961, just two months after Lumumba was assassinated, Africa had the right to know what the United Nations was doing in the Congo and demanded accountability for its actions:

"Unless at this juncture the United Nations acts in full consultation with the African states and in accordance with the needs of Africa, the same results will flow from the United Nations' intervention in the Congo as flowed from the intervention of the great powers in African affairs."[13]

To Nkrumah and other African leaders such as Nyerere, the Congo imbroglio was a chilling reminder of what the imperial powers did almost a century earlier at the Berlin conference (November 1884 - February 1885) which led to the partition of Africa. During the sixties, in the second half of the twentieth century, the big powers were competing for control of the Congo; while during the latter part of the nineteenth century, the colonial powers competed – during "the cold war of those days" as Nkrumah put it – for colonies in Africa.

The Congo during the early sixties was a tinder box which could have ignited and escalated into global warfare due to super-power competition. It was a major international crisis, demanding immediate attention and direct intervention by a large number of UN forces and was therefore more than just an African problem.

But it was during the Cuban missile crisis in October 1962 that the world came perilously close to nuclear war and went through one of its most dangerous periods in history, a debacle that was inextricably linked with the super-power rivalry over Berlin.

In their book, *The Kennedy Tapes*: *Inside the White House During the Cuban Missile Crisis*, Ernest R. May and Philip D. Zelikow, quote President Kennedy as he ominously warned his colleagues about the consequences of any conflict between the two super powers and on what would happen if the United States invaded Cuba. They would have to be ready for a forceful response from Khrushchev and his colleagues in the Kremlin:

"He'll grab Berlin, of course....I'm not so worried about the air. But the atomic bombs, they can get a couple of them over on us anyway....

If we attack Cuban missiles, or Cuba, in any way, it gives them a clear line to take Berlin....If we do nothing then they'll have these missiles and they'll be able to say any time we ever try to do anything about Cuba, they'll fire these missiles....If we go in and take them out on a quick air strike, we neutralize the chance of danger to the United States of these missiles being used....On the other hand, we increase the chance greatly, as I think - there's bound to be a reprisal from the Soviet Union, there always is - (of) their just going in and taking Berlin by force. Which leaves me only one alternative, which is to fire nuclear weapons - which is a hell of an alternative - and begin a nuclear exchange....

They can't let us just take out, after all their statements, take out their missiles, kill a lot of Russians (in Cuba) and not do anything....The problem is not really so much war against Cuba. But the problem is part of this worldwide struggle with the Soviet Communists....

If we invade Cuba, we have a chance that these missiles will be fired on us....When you talk about the invasion, the first (point), excluding the risk that these missiles will be fired, (is that) we do have the 7 or 8,000 Russians there....Ambassador Thompson (to the Soviet Union) has felt very strongly that the Soviet Union would regard, will regard the attack on these SAM sites and missile bases with the killing of 4 or 5,000 Russians as a greater provocation than the stopping of their ships. Now, who knows what?....We are going to blockade Cuba."[14]

But few people, including advisers to President Kennedy such as Defence Secretary Robert McNamara, knew how close the world came to the brink of nuclear catastrophe. And even today, most people still don't know.

After the end of the Cold War, Fidel Castro said in 1992 and later that had the Americans attacked Cuba, the Soviets would have fired the Cuban-based missiles which had already been targeted at the United States. McNamara himself was shocked when he learnt this after the collapse of the Soviet Union and when he attended a conference in Cuba on the Cold War.

Had it not been for Kennedy's and McNamara's restraint − as opposed to the hawkish attitude and the recommendation of most of his advisers including the joint chiefs of staff who favoured an air strike and an outright invasion of Cuba − the Cuban missile crisis would have ended in a nuclear exchange between the two super powers with dire consequences for the entire world.

The Americans had also − despite their intelligence capabilities and constant surveillance over Cuba − grossly underestimated Soviet strength on the Cuban island and the Russians' resolve to use nuclear weapons already on the island if the United States launched an invasion.

Had the United States known the actual number of Soviet combat troops and technicians, and Soviet nuclear capability on the island, they probably would never have contemplated an air strike against the missile sites. As Professor Jorge G. Castaneda states in his book *Companero*: *The Life and Death of Che Guevara*:

"It is now known - because Soviet participants insinuated as much at the Moscow meeting of 1989, and Fidel Castro stated so categorically at the Havana conference of January 1992 - that twenty of the forty-two Soviet missiles deployed in Cuba were armed with *nuclear warheads*. And six tactical missile launchers, loaded with nine missiles with *nuclear tips*, were ready to be used in the event of a US invasion....Arthur Schlesinger and Robert McNamara, who both attended the Havana conference, almost fell off their seats when they heard this.

Furthermore, the number of Soviet troops sent to Cuba was much larger than the Americans suspected. They estimated 4,500 in early October, 10,000 at the height of the crisis, and 12,000 to 16,000 at its end. In reality, 42,000 soldiers entered Cuba, disguised with winter clothing and even snow skis. Castro confirmed this figure, also put forth by Alexeiev and Mikoyan.

In other words, the Soviets were able to deploy missiles, atomic warheads, troops, and sophisticated antiaircraft equipment in Cuba before American intelligence caught on. So much so that Walt Rostow, then a State Department adviser, reported to President Kennedy in a 'top-secret and sensitive' memorandum dated September 3, 1962 - less than a month before the crisis - that 'on the basis of existing intelligence the Soviet military deliveries to Cuba do not constitute a substantial threat to US security'....

The problem was not keeping the missiles secret, but what the Soviets were willing to do with them once they had been introduced into Cuba....Soviet military officers in the field were authorized to launch the missiles with nuclear warheads....in the event of a US invasion; and the U-2 (American) spy plane shot down over Cuba on October 27 was attacked under instructions from the Soviet base in Cuba - not Moscow."[15]

Although Soviet prestige around the world may have suffered in what some people perceived to be capitulation to American demands to withdraw Russian missiles from

Cuba, in exchange for a pledge by the United States not to invade the island, Kremlin leaders knew that in some areas – especially in a number of Third World countries including African – their reputation was not, for historical reasons, as bad as that of the West.

Western countries were identified with colonialism. By remarkable contrast, the Soviet Union never had colonies in Africa or anywhere else in the Third World. Western countries were also identified with imperialism in developing countries which they continued to dominate even after those countries won independence. Such domination included exploitation of the Third World by Western conglomerates which has now reached its peak in this era of globalisation, with globalisation itself being dictated by Western countries which dominate the global economy under capitalism. Globalization is the new imperialism in this post-Cold War era in a unipolar world dominated by the United States.

Countries dominating Africa and other parts of the Third World included the United States, the leading Western power, which also had and still has the largest number of corporations with tentacles extended to all parts of the world. As Americans say, what is good for General Motors is good for America; and for the world, they might as well add, as some of them probably do, since the United States dominates the world economy.

But as a super power itself, the Soviet Union was not entirely blameless. Together with the United States, the Soviet Union had twice pushed the world to the brink of a nuclear holocaust: over Berlin in 1961, and during the Cuban missile crisis in 1962, the most dangerous crises since World War II. And coincidentally during the same period was the Congo crisis, which became a major international crisis right in the heart of Africa, again involving the two nuclear giants and other world powers.

While the Berlin and Cuban crises were eventually contained, although not entirely resolved (the United

States continued with its attempts to undermine Castro surreptitiously through surrogate forces and more brazenly by economic means including imposition of an embargo on the island nation), the Congo crisis continued to pose great danger to Africa and threaten world peace. The threat continued at least until the mid-sixties when the West finally gained the upper hand over the Soviets and the Chinese in that troubled African country. Because of their weakness, the other independent African countries could not do anything about Western imposition of its will on the Congo.

It was Western powers led by the United States which ousted and assassinated the popular Congolese prime minister, Patrice Lumumba, installing Colonel Joseph Mobutu in his stead. Mobutu was already on the CIA payroll when he was working under Lumumba before he became army chief.

However, the Soviets never gave up on Africa despite the setbacks they had suffered in the Congo. Western countries also, because of their history of colonialism in Africa, and even of American enslavement of millions of Africans earlier during the slave trade, all of which tarnished the West, feared that the Soviets had great advantage over them in winning friendship among Africans during the Cold War since the Soviet Union had never owned any colonies anywhere on the African continent.

Compounding the problem for Western countries was continued colonialism and white minority rule in the countries of southern Africa and Portuguese Guinea (Guinea-Bissau) in West Africa. The colonial powers were Western, and the racist minority regimes were also Western in origin and ideological orientation. All that worked to Soviet advantage, as did the intransigence of the white minorities in relinquishing control of the countries they dominated.

Not all African countries had won independence during

the sixties or even the seventies and eighties; not even the early nineties. The last African countries to win their freedom were Zimbabwe in 1980; Namibia ten years later in 1990; and finally South Africa in 1994. They all had been under white minority rule.

Even after the collapse of the Soviet Union in 1991, the West was still tarnished in the eyes of many Africans because of the continuing racist policies of its strongest ally on the continent, apartheid South Africa, which during white minority rule had always been an integral part of the Western world and the main custodian of Western values and traditions – and civilization – on a continent many Westerners considered to be "backward and uncivlized."

The Congo crisis also tarnished the West among Africans because of its involvement in the assassination of Patrice Lumumba and its support for the secession of Katanga Province which had in fact been engineered by the West. The Soviets tried to exploit that, showing that they were on the side of Africans and the nationalist forces opposed to Katanga's secession.

But Africans did not want to exchange one master for another and wanted both sides – East and West – out of the Congo. Instead, they supported UN intervention to keep the Cold War out of Africa.

Among all the colonial powers, France maintained the strongest and most pervasive influence in her former colonies not only during the early years of independence but also all the way through the years until the 1990s when that influence began to decline in a few of those countries.

One of the countries under very strong French influence – and with a presence of no fewer than 40,000 Frenchmen – was the Ivory Coast which also considered itself to be the leader of Francophone Africa; although Senegal, especially under its Francophile President Leopold Sedar Senghor, also claimed that "eminent" status and mantle of leadership.

When the Mali Federation formed in 1959 and

comprising Mali and Senegal – it collapsed the following year after Senegal pulled out – demanded and won independence in 1960, Ivorian leader Houphouet-Boigny became furious. He wanted all French African colonies to remain under French tutelage.

However, because the French had acquiesced in the Federation's decision to become independent, Houphouet-Boigny – as a protest against France but mainly because of pressure exerted on him by his own people who wanted to end colonial rule – also demanded independence for his country in the same year. And together with Dahomey, Niger, and Upper Volta – all of which also won independence in 1960 as did most of the other French African colonies – Ivory Coast formed a weak association known as *Counseil de l'Entente.*

France's enormous influence over the Ivory Coast was clearly visible even to a casual observer. For example, in 1965 and thereafter, more than 120,000 Frenchmen were living in Abidjan alone, the nation's capital. They led the army and the police, ran the country's administration and even occupied ministerial positions in the cabinet including the most influential ones. Like most of the former French African colonies, Ivory Coast was independent in name only. As Henry Tanner stated in his report from the Ivory Coast published in *The New York Times* on 25 March 1962:

"The most striking anachronism to the radical African nationalists is that M. Houphouet-Boigny has practically abdicated sovereignty in the military field. The Ivory Coast has only a small force for internal security. And even this force has French officers. The French army assures the external defense of the country. It has been asked to do so, M. Houphouet-Boigny says, because 'we wish to devote our modest means to economic and social development.'"[16]

It was that kind of subservience which prompted Dr. Nkrumah to describe the former French African colonies as "client states," with the exception of Guinea under Sekou Toure, Mali under Modibo Keita, and Algeria under Ben Bella later under Boumedienne. The former vice president of Kenya, Jaramogi Oginga Odinga, also articulated the same sentiment about his country in his book *Not Yet Uhuru* which he wrote after he fell out with Kenyatta during the late sixties. Nyerere wrote the introduction to the book.

Odinga went on to form an opposition party, the Kenya People's Union (KPU), and accused the Kenyan leadership of ignoring the interests of *wananchi* (the people) and of selling the country to the imperialists.

But he did not last long as a political force. His party, formed in March 1966, was effectively neutralized within two years and banned shortly thereafter. And that ended an illustrious political career of a leader of continental stature who was also one of the most prominent figures in the struggle for African independence and one of the strongest advocates of African unity. He was an ideological compatriot of Nyerere and Nkrumah and shared their socialist and Pan-Africanist vision.

Ironically, independence for the largest number of the African colonies came first to the least nationalistic and least pan-African-oriented countries, those of Francophone Africa, which cherished their ties with the metropolitan power, "mother" France, more than they did their natural ties with their African brethren in other African countries.

Another irony was that the French-speaking African countries which also had a reputation as the least militant in pursuit of continental unity were also among the first to forge links among themselves although they were also, individually and collectively, institutionally linked to "mother" France; thus casting serious doubt on their commitment to African unity. For example, their common currency (CFA) and airline (*Air Afrique*), were not formed

139

on their own initiative but France's in order to enable the former colonial power – which never left – to perpetuate her domination over her former colonies.

Therefore soon after independence, there was an effort, however lukewarm, by different African countries to pursue the goal of African unity even if such pursuit meant forming different regional and sub-regional groups which were mutually antagonistic; hardly a path towards continental solidarity which had to be achieved even before the idea of unity could be seriously considered. In spite of all that, they proceeded along that path nonetheless.

In 1960, the same year they won independence, twelve of the former French African colonies formed what came to be known as the Brazzaville Group. They were tied to the franc zone and received financial, technical, and military assistance from France. The group was named after Brazzaville, the capital of Congo-Brazzaville where the group was formed and had its headquarters.

The Brazzaville Group, also known as the UAM or the Union of African and Malagasy states, went on to establish – on French initiative – a common currency, the CFA; a common bank, common monetary policy, telecommunication links, and an airline, *Air Afrique*. But they refused to form a federation.

The original members were Cameroon, the Central African Republic, Chad, Congo-Brazzaville, Dahomey, Gabon, Ivory Coast, Malagasy Republic, Mauritania, Niger, Senegal, and Upper Volta. They were later joined by Rwanda, a former Belgian colony but French-speaking, which won independence in 1962.

Another Pan-African group that was formed was the Casablanca Group with a reputation as a group of radical states. It was formed in Casablanca, Morocco, in 1961 and was the most diverse in ts composition – racially, historically, linguistically, and even ideologically – among all African groups; a microcosm, in terms of diversity, of

140

what was yet to come only about two years later when the Organization of African Unity (OAU) was formed in Ethiopia's capital, Addis Ababa, in May 1963.

The Casablanca Group was composed of the most militant states with the exception of one member. The member-countries were Egypt, Ghana, Guinea, Mali, Morocco, and Algeria even before Algeria won independence from France in 1962 after one of the bloodiest liberation wars in colonial history which cost an estimated one million lives, mostly Algerian.

Morocco was the least militant member of the Casablanca Group - ironically the group was formed in Morroco's largest city – except for her support of the Algerian independence struggle, a position which made the conservative North African Arab state as "militant" as the rest of the members in the group. Ghana was, of course, also an oddity as an Anglophone member in a predominantly Francophone group and the least-Muslim country. Not only were most of them French-speaking but also overwhelmingly Muslim. Another exception was Egypt – Muslim but not Francophone.

And racially, of course, the Casablanca Group was "split" in half. Three member-countries, Ghana, Guinea and Mali were mostly black; and the other three – Egypt, then officially known as the United Arab Republic (UAR), Morocco and Algeria – were predominantly Arab with a population of Berber minorities especially in Algeria and Morocco. However, Mali also provided a bridge between the two racial groups.

Unlike the other two black members, Ghana and Guinea, Mali has a large number of its citizens, especially in the northern part of the country bordering Arab North Africa, who are Berber and Arab. About 10 percent of Malians are Tuareg and Moors; 6 percent Songhai, and a smaller percentage Arab. The first three groups are mainly Berber mixed with Arabs. Tuareg nomads alone in northern Mali constitute a substantial population of more than 700,000.

Yet, in spite of its diversity, the Casablanca Group was also one of the most cohesive. It was also one of the most influential because of its leaders such as Nkrumah and Nasser who were formidable political personalities of international stature.

Later in the same year, 1961, when the Casablanca Group was formed, the Brazzaville group joined Nigeria, Liberia and other moderate states to form the Monrovia Group, later known as the Lagos Charter Group, in order to formulate plans for the establishment of an All-African organization on continental basis.

The Casablanca Group, which was militant, refused to attend meetings of the Monrovia Group – formed in Monrovia, Liberia – and talked about continental unification, a radical proposition in pan-African rhetoric and diplomacy even today. The group even proposed formation of an African High Command for continental security. Nkrumah was the first African leader to propose that.

The Monrovia Group considered such propositions by the Casablanca group not only too radical but also too dangerous for Africa.

In reality, the Monrovia Group was politically weak. It even failed to take a firm stand on the Algerian war of independence which lasted for seven years at an enormous cost. By contrast, the Casablanca Group fully supported the Algerians in their struggle against France.

Yet, in spite of its weakness and moderate stand, it was the Monrovia Group which laid the groundwork for the establishment of the Organization of African Unity (OAU). It also proposed that African heads of state and government should meet every three years; sought to establish a permanent secretariat and headquarters for the organization, and a permanent supervisory council of ministers. The group also proposed the creation of an African common market and a permanent tribunal for conflict resolution among African countries with the mandate to settle both intra- and inter-state disputes.

The quest for African unity under one government as advocated by the Casablanca Group of radical states – all of which were in West and North Africa – got a boost from another part of the continent, East Africa, when in June 1963, Kenya, Uganda and Tanganyika agreed to form an East African federation before the end of the year. President Julius Nyerere of Tanganyika, Prime Minister Milton Obote of Uganda, and Prime Minister Jomo Kenyatta of Kenya, issued the following statement in Nairobi, Kenya, on June 5, 1963:

"We, the leaders of the people and governments of East Africa assembled in Nairobi on 5 June 1963, pledge ourselves to the political Federation of East Africa.

Our meeting today is motivated by the spirit of Pan-Africanism and not by mere selfish regional interests....Within this spirit of Pan-Africanism and following the declaration of African unity at the recent Addis Ababa conference (from May 22 - 25, which led to the establishment of the Organization of African Unity - OAU), practical steps should be taken wherever possible to accelerate the achievement of our common goal. We believe that the East African Federation can be a practical step towards the goal of Pan-African unity...and wish to make it clear that any of our other neighbours may in future join this Federation."[17]

Nyerere was the strongest proponent of an East African federation and even offered to delay independence for Tanganyika so that the three East African countries – Kenya, Uganda and Tanganyika – would attain sovereign status on the same day and unite under one government.

But the federation was never formed. Nationalism won over Pan-Africanism.

An even bigger federation including Ethiopia, Somalia,

Zanzibar, and Nyasaland, was also discussed. But it also got nowhere.

Nkrumah vehemently opposed formation of an East African federation and dismissed it as "Balkanization on a grand scale."

Nyerere responded to Nkrumah's argument by saying "those are attempts to rationalize absurdity."

Nkrumah also he did everything he could to try to block formation of the federation.

Nkrumah's interference infuriated Nyerere so much that he wrote Nkrumah directly about it:

"His meddling became so apparent that on 6th August, 1963, President Nyerere of Tanzania wrote him a very angry letter on this subject." – Donald S. Rothchild, *Politics of Integration: An East African Documentary*, Institute of Development Studies, University College of Nairobi; East African Publishing House, Nairobi, Kenya, 1968, p. 112).

Nkrumah strongly denounced attempts to form an East African federation because he would not be in a position to control it. He wanted to be the driving force behind any kind of regional integration in Africa so that if the leaders of those regional blocs eventually decided to unite, they would choose him to be the head of a continental government.

Therefore he was not really opposed to regional federations; only if he could not control them. He himself had attempted to unite his country with Guinea in 1958 to form the Ghana-Guinea Union and with Mali as well in 1960 to form the Ghana-Guinea-Mali Union. But the unions were not successful.

Had the Ghana-Guinea-Mali Union evolved into a functional entity under one government, it is inconceivable that Nkrumah would have denounced it as an obstacle to continental unification. Ghana does not even share borders with Guinea and Mali. Yet Nkrumah was willing to form a political union with them; the latter two share a common border. But when Nyerere tried to do the same thing, form a regional union in East Africa, Nkrumah denounced the move not only as an obstacle to African unity and as discriminatory; he contended it would divide Africa even further, on a grand scale. As Professor Ali Mazrui stated:

"Nkrumah pointed out that his own country could not very easily join an East African federation. This proved how discriminatory and divisive the whole of Nyerere's strategy was for the African continent.

Nyerere treated Nkrumah's counter-thesis with contempt. He asserted that to argue that Africa had better remain in small bits than form bigger entities was nothing more than 'an attempt to rationalize absurdity.'

He denounced Nkrumah's attempt to deflate the East African federation movement as petty mischief-making arising from Nkrumah's own sense of frustration in his own Pan-African ventures.

Nyerere was indignant. He went public with his attack on Nkrumah. He referred to people who pretended that they were in favour of African continental union when all they cared about was to ensure that 'some stupid historian in the future' praised them for being in favour of the big continental ambition before anyone else was willing to undertake it." – (Ali A. Mazrui in his lecture "Nkrumahism and The Triple Heritage: Out of the Shadows" at the University of Ghana-Legon in 2002; Ali A. Mazrui in Opoku Agyeman, *Nkrumah's Ghana and East Africa: Pan-Africanism and African Interstate Relations*, Fairleigh Dickinson University Press, 1992, p. 16; Ali Al'Amin Mazrui, *Nkrumah's Legacy and Africa's Triple Heritage between Globalization and Counter-Terrorism*, Ghana Universities Press, 2004, p. 35).

Nkrumah also used President Milton Obote to

undermine Nyerere in his regional venture to form an East African federation. Obote was a friend of both.

Nkrumah argued that such a federation would not be in the best interest of Uganda because Uganda would be no more than a junior member in a union dominated by Kenya and Tanzania. As Philip Ochieng, a veteran Kenyan journalist and political analyst, stated in his article, "Did Nkrumah Kill Off the First EA Community?," in *The East African*, Nairobi, 28 March 2009:

"In the late 1960s, when Yoweri Kaguta Museveni was the leader of the 'revolutionary' wing of the University of Dar es Salaam's student movement, he and his group militantly rebuked the governments of Uganda, Tanzania and Kenya for failing to federate as they had promised.

The Ugandan leader still appears passionate about that union. Last week, he told a news conference that, instead of fighting over an island smaller than a football pitch, Nairobi and Kampala should fight to make Kenya and Uganda one political entity.

Topical again after a lull of many years, one East African republic was a nationalist, pre-Independence theme. Indeed, a treaty of commitment to it was signed by Jomo Kenyatta, Julius Nyerere and Milton Obote just before Kenya's independence.

So what happened? Why hasn't that great idea panned out for us nearly 50 years after the Uhuru fanfare of the early 1960s? I ask this question because, in truth, Museveni may be in a better position than any of the present East African leaders to answer it....In the Ugandan capital's archives – now controlled by his government – there may lie documents that can enlighten us.

Let me jog the president's memory. He and I were in Dar es Salaam in the late 1960s and early 1970s. He will have heard Obote – whom he still deeply admired – being publicly accused as the chief saboteur of the proposal to federate. Official Tanzania was, of course, mum about this accusation. But it came from top-level academics known to enjoy direct links with Mwalimu's State House. The certainty is that it was Nyerere who was feeding them with the lowdown on Kampala.

What did Mwalimu Nyerere and his Cabinet know about Dr Obote that we did not know? The accusing finger I constantly saw whenever I visited the campus at Ubungo was explicit.

Somebody else – far away from East Africa – was extremely unhappy about an East African union and worked tirelessly – mostly through Kampala – to nip it in the bud, so the story went. No, it was not the British (though they would play a central role in frustrating the federation).

So who could it be? The answer: None other than the great Kwame Nkrumah.

This may sound paradoxical because that redoubtable intellectual and nationalist was the father of the pan-Africanist movement. So you would have expected him to be the chief sponsor of all the regional initiatives that might lead to a pan-African government. That again was paradoxical.

According to the story that I kept hearing, it was because Dr Nkrumah wanted to be the father figure of all the regional initiatives, that he sabotaged the East African chapter....

Nkrumah himself sponsored a West African initiative similar to the proposed East African federation...composed of his Ghana, Ahmed Sekou Toure's Guinea and Modibo Keita's Mali....As long as he was the paramount leader of such an initiative, there was no problem.

In East Africa, Nyerere was also taking serious steps to restructure his society. Tanzania (under Nyerere), indeed, is the African country that has gone farthest in dismantling the political, economic and intellectual pillars of colonialism....

Nkrumah...wanted to be the dominant figure in every

147

regional initiative. Like Joseph Stalin for all of the world's non-Maoist communist parties, Nkrumah wanted to be chief policy-maker and policy implementer for every one of the regional groupings. The probable idea was that, if all those regional groupings decided to unite into a single continental government, no individual would be in a position to vie with the Ghanaian leader to be its first president.

That was why Nkrumah could not trust Mwalimu Nyerere as the intellectual spirit behind the East African proposal. For, although they seemed like ideological comrades, the old Tanganyikan schoolteacher was completely independent-minded and would never have been prepared to act as Nkrumah's regional poodle.

With Nyerere thus dismissed and Mzee Kenyatta accused of having surrendered Kenya as a backyard of corporate Britain, the Ubungo intellectuals explained that, in Nkrumah's eyes, Obote now appeared as the only one not too committed one way or the other. That was why – according to the story – it was Obote that Nkrumah latched onto to frustrate all the plans to federate."

Nkrumah's interference in East Africa to neutralise Nyerere's attempt to form an East African federation was a big mistake and portrayed Nkrumah as a trouble maker who was determined to undermine other African leaders who did not agree with him. As Basil Davidson states in his book, *Black Star: A View of the Life and Times of Kwame Nkrumah*:

"Some, like Julius Nyerere of Tanzania, chastised Nkrumah for his interference. East Africa, Nyerere believed, could best contribute to continental unity by moving first towards regional unity. Although knowing little about East Africa, Nkrumah not only disagreed but actively interfered to obstruct the East African federation proposed by Nyerere.... It was one of Nkrumah's worst mistakes." – (Basil Davidson, *Black Star: A View of the Life and Times of Kwame Nkrumah*, Allen Lane, London, 1973, cited by Geoffrey Mmari, "The Legacy of Nyerere," in Colin Legum and Geoffrey Mmari, eds., *Mwalimu: The Influence of Nyerere*, Africa World Press, Trenton, New Jersey, 1995, pp. 179 – 180).

During the OAU summit conference in Accra in 1965, Nkrumah even had listening devices installed in Nyerere's room and in the rooms of the other Tanzanian delegates and those of other African leaders he did not trust or who were a threat to his quest to become the paramount leader of the whole continent. But the director of the Tanzanian intelligence service, Emilio Mzena and his colleagues who accompanied Nyerere to the conference, detected the listening devices. The spying on Nyerere and other delegates from Tanzania by Ghana's intelligence service is one of the subjects addressed by Professor W. Scott Thompson in his book, *Ghana's Foreign Policy 1957 – 1966: Diplomacy, Ideology, and the New State* (Princeton University Press, 1969).

After Nkrumah was overthrown, his espionage activities came to light and were exposed by the new military rulers of Ghana:

"Special attention was devoted to some of these delegates who were thought to be critical of Nkrumah....

Chalet C-4, one of the largest on the grounds of the Star Hotel, also housed Emilio Charles Mzena, a delegate from Tanzania....

At the conference President Nyerere was attended by his personal physician, Dr. A. Nhonoli, who was also an occupant of Chalet C-4." – (*Nkrumah's Subversion in Africa: Documentary Evidence of Nkrumah's Interference in the Affairs of Other African States*, Ghana's Ministry of Information, Accra, Ghana, 1966).

149

Nkrumah had continental ambitions. He wanted to exert his influence on the entire continent. But he also focused on some parts, especially East Africa where he wanted to undermine Nyerere, the most influential leader in the region and one of the most respected across the continent:

"East Africa was high on Nkrumah's list of subversion priorities. At one point, early in 1965, an attempt was made to recruit two sources close to Tanzania's President Julius Nyerere to 'exploit the political contradictions in the East African area.'" – (*Atlas*, a journal, Worley Publishing Company, New York, 1966, p. 22).

One of them was Oscar Kambona, Tanzania's minister of foreign affairs. Perhaps the other one was Kassim Hanga, Kambona's close friend, who briefly served as vice president and prime minister of Zanzibar (January – April 1964) before he became a cabinet member in the union government after Tanganyika united with Zanzibar on 26 April 1964.

They developed their close friendship when they were roommates in London during their student days.

Kambona even sent Nkrumah some money in Conakry, Guinea, where the Ghanaian leader went to live in exile after being overthrown on 24 February 1966. In his book, *Dark Days in Ghana*, Nkrumah thanked Kambona for sending him some money. Only a small amount is mentioned in the book. But sources in the Tanzanian government said the amount Kambona sent Nkrumah was large.

As Tanzania's minister of foreign affairs, and as someone who was so close to Nyerere, Oscar Kambona played a major role in attempting to form an East African federation. Yet he was at the same time secretly working to undermine Nyerere and even wrote Nkrumah telling him any attempts to form an East African federation was an imperialist scheme which would not be in the best interest of Africa. He later became a bitter enemy of Nyerere and was behind an attempt to overthrow and assassinate him.

Kambona told Nkrumah about the plot against Nyerere and Nkrumah supported it, according to sources in Tanzania who saw the letters exchanged between the two leaders when Nkrumah was living in exile in Guinea.

Kambona left Tanzania in July 1967 and went into exile in Britain.

The failure to form an East African federation and other attempts elsewhere on the continent also showed that African countries were more willing to cooperate in the economic and technical fields than they were to form political unions under regional governments, let alone under one government on a continental scale.

Still, the quest for unity remained a perennial ambition. But the mere fact that African countries formed regional groupings or continued to maintain regional institutional structures formed during colonial times showed that they were all aware of the imperative need for unity even if it did not mean forming regional governments.

It is also worth noting that the groups they formed after independence were not strictly regional. The Casablanca Group was formed by North and West African states. The Brazzaville Group – admittedly, more of a neo-colonial than a pan-Africanist institution inspired by France – spanned Francophone Africa, all the way from West Africa to the island nation of Madagascar in the Indian Ocean in East Africa.

The Lagos Charter Group, better known as the Monrovia Group, was also continental in scope and in inspiration. As Dr. Nnamdi Azikiwe, the governor-general of the federation of Nigeria, stated in his speech to the Lagos conference of African heads of state and government on 25 January 1962:

"The main reason for convening this conference is to

151

exchange views among African leaders at the highest possible level for the unity of the political entities comprising the continent of Africa.

There have been conferences of this nature in the past, but this particular conference is very significant because it is the first time in African history that so many heads of state and government have assembled to confer among themselves for the future security and stability of African countries....

The Lagos Conference looks at the continent of Africa as a miniature United Nations....At Monrovia, in May, 1961, the participants of this conference evolved a *modus vivendi* for African states....The principles enunciated in Monrovia include...the right of African states to federate or confederate with any other state or states."[18]

Tanganyika, which won independence on 9 December 1961 – shortly after the Monrovia Group was formed in May the same year – and which was among the first African countries to win independence, attended the conference of the Lagos Charter Group held in the Nigerian capital, Lagos, in January 1962; so did the only other independent East African country, Ethiopia.

Therefore the group was not restricted to West or North African countries which constituted the largest number of the independent African countries during that period.

But Tanganyika, which became increasingly radical taking a militant stand on a number of issues especially on the Congo crisis and the liberation struggle in southern Africa, did not attend subsequent meetings of the Lagos Charter Group. Her increasing militancy led her to identify with the members of the Casablanca Group who together – with the exception of Morocco – even constituted their own group within the Organization of African Unity (OAU) to pursue common goals. As Jorge Castaneda states in his book *Companero*: *The Life and Death of Che*

Guevara:

"Moise Tshombe was despised by the leaders of the OAU, especially its most radical ones - the so-called Group of Six, consisting of Nasser, Ben Bella, Kwame Nkrumah of Ghana, Sekou Toure of Guinea, Julius Nyerere of Tanzania, and Modibo Keita of Mali - who still blamed Tshombe for Lumumba's death....According to Ben Bella, - in an interview with the author in Geneva, on November 4, 1995 - these leaders had a group of their own within the OAU; they regularly consulted and conspired among themselves."[19]

Even before independence, African nationalists from different countries forged links to pursue common goals. For example, in 1958 they attended the Accra Conference convened by Kwame Nkrumah to formulate a common strategy for coordinating the independence struggle across the continent.

The conference was attended by independent African countries – there were only a few then: Egypt, Libya, Tunisia, Morocco, Sudan, Ethiopia, Liberia, Ghana, and Guinea – and by representatives from the countries still under colonial rule. It was held in December and was chaired by Tom Mboya from Kenya, who was then 28 years old. He was one of the most prominent leaders in Africa and was assassinated ten years later in Nairobi, Kenya, in July 1969. He was 39.

One of the organizations which played a critical role in laying the foundation for the establishment of the Organization of African Unity (OAU) was PAFMECSA: the Pan-African Freedom Movement for East, Central and Southern Africa. It was preceded by PAFMECA – the Pan-African Freedom Movement for East and Central Africa – which was the original group founded at its first meeting in September 1958 in the town of Mwanza on the shores of Lake Victoria in what was then Tanganyika under the stewardship of Julius Nyerere.

PAFMECA was an umbrella organization for thirteen African nationalist parties in Kenya, Uganda, Tanganyika, Zanzibar, Ruanda-Urundi, the Belgian Congo, Northern Rhodesia, Southern Rhodesia, and Nyasaland.

It lasted until February 1962 when it was replaced by PAFMECSA after the umbrella organization was extended to the countries of southern Africa still under white minority rule. Nelson Mandela addressed a conference of PAFMECA delegates in Addis Ababa, Ethiopia, in February 1962, where he asked for assistance for the liberation struggle in South Africa after he secretly left the land of apartheid to attend the meeting. The African National Congress (ANC) was invited to the conference and Mandela led the ANC delegation to Addis Ababa. As he stated in his speech:

"The delegation of the African National Congress, and I particularly, feel specially honored by the invitation addressed to our organisation by the PAFMECA to attend this historic conference and to participate in its deliberations and decisions.

The extension of the PAFMECA area to South Africa, the heart and core of imperialist reaction, should mark the beginning of a new phase in the drive for the total liberation of Africa - a phase which derives special significance from the entry into PAFMECA of the independent states of Ethiopia, Somalia, and Sudan.

It was not without reason, we believe, that the Secretariat of PAFMECA chose as the seat of this conference the great country of Ethiopia, which, with hundreds of years of colorful history behind it, can rightly claim to have paid the full price of freedom and independence. His Imperial Majesty, himself a rich and unfailing fountain of wisdom, has been foremost in promoting the cause of unity, independence, and progress in Africa, as was so amply demonstrated in the address he graciously delivered in opening this assembly.

The deliberations of our conference will thus proceed in a setting most conducive to a scrupulous examination of the issues that are before us.

At the outset, our delegation wishes to place on record our sincere appreciation of the relentless efforts made by the independent African states and national movements in Africa and other parts of the world, to help the African people in South Africa in their just struggle for freedom and independence.

The movement for the boycott of South African goods and for the imposition of economic and diplomatic sanctions against South Africa has served to highlight most effectively the despotic structure of the power that rules South Africa, and has given tremendous inspiration to the liberation movement in our country.

It is particularly gratifying to note that the four independent African states which are part of this conference, namely, Ethiopia, Somalia, Sudan and Tanganyika, are enforcing diplomatic and economic sanctions against South Africa.

We also thank all those states that have given asylum and assistance to South African refugees of all shades of political beliefs and opinion. The warm affection with which South African freedom fighters are received by democratic countries all over the world, and the hospitality so frequently showered upon us by governments and political organizations, has made it possible for some of our people to escape persecution by the South African government, to travel freely from country to country and from continent to continent, to canvass our point of view and to rally support for our cause.

We are indeed extremely grateful for this spontaneous demonstration of solidarity and support, and sincerely hope that each and every one of us will prove worthy of the trust and confidence the world has in us.

We believe that one of the main objectives of this conference is to work out concrete plans to speed up the struggle for the liberation of those territories in this region that are still under alien rule. In most of these territories the imperialist forces have been considerably weakened and are unable to resist the demand for freedom and independence - thanks to the powerful blows delivered by the freedom movements.

Although the national movements must remain alert and vigilant against all forms of imperialist intrigue and deception, there can be no doubt that imperialism is in full retreat and the attainment of independence by many of these countries has become an almost accomplished fact.

Elsewhere, notably in South Africa, the liberation movement faces formidable difficulties and the struggle is likely to be long, complicated, hard, and bitter, requiring maximum unity of the national movement inside the country, and calling for level and earnest thinking on the part of its leaders, for skilful planning and intensive organisation.

South Africa is known throughout the world as a country where the most fierce forms of colour discrimination are practiced, and where the peaceful struggles of the African people for freedom are violently suppressed.

It is a country torn from top to bottom by fierce racial strife and conflict and where the blood of African patriots frequently flows.

Almost every African household in South Africa knows about the massacre of our people at Bulhoek, in the Queenstown district, where detachments of the army and police, armed with artillery, machine-guns, and rifles, opened fire on unarmed Africans, killing 163 persons, wounding 129, and during which 95 people were arrested simply because they refused to move from a piece of land on which they lived.

Almost every African family remembers a similar

massacre of our African brothers in South-West Africa when the South African government assembled aeroplanes, heavy machine-guns, artillery, and rifles, killing a hundred people and mutilating scores of others, merely because the Bondelswart people refused to pay dog tax.

On 1 May 1950, 18 Africans were shot dead by the police in Johannesburg whilst striking peacefully for higher wages. The massacre at Sharpeville in March 1960 is a matter of common knowledge and is still fresh in our minds. According to a statement in parliament made by C R Swart, then Minister for Justice, between May 1948 and March 1954, 104 Africans were killed and 248 wounded by the police in the course of political demonstrations.

By the middle of June 1960, these figures had risen to well over three hundred killed and five hundred wounded. Naked force and violence is the weapon openly used by the South African government to beat down the struggles of the African people and to suppress their aspirations.

The repressive policies of the South African government are reflected not only in the number of those African martyrs who perished from guns and bullets, but in the merciless persecution of all political leaders and in the total repression of political opposition. Persecution of political leaders and suppression of political organizations became ever more violent under the Nationalist Party government.

From 1952 the government used its legal powers to launch a full-scale attack on leaders of the African National Congress. Many of its prominent members were ordered by the government to resign permanently from it and never again participate in its activities. Others were prohibited from attending gatherings for specified periods ranging up to five years. Many were confined to certain districts, banished from their homes and families and even deported from the country.

In December 1956, Chief A J Lutuli, President-General

157

of the ANC, was arrested together with 155 other freedom fighters and charged with treason. The trial which then followed is unprecedented in the history of the country, in both its magnitude and duration. It dragged on for over four years and drained our resources to the limit.

In March 1960, after the murderous killing of about seventy Africans in Sharpeville, a state of emergency was declared and close on twenty thousand people were detained without trial.

Even as we meet here today, martial law prevails throughout the territory of the Transkei, an area of 16,000 square miles with an African population of nearly two and a half million. The government stubbornly refuses to publish the names and number of persons detained. But it is estimated that close on two thousand Africans are presently languishing in jail in this area alone. Amongst these are to be found teachers, lawyers, doctors, clerks, workers from the towns, peasants from the country, and other freedom fighters. In this same area and during the last six months, more than thirty Africans have been sentenced to death by white judicial officers, hostile to our aspirations, for offences arising out of political demonstrations.

On 26 August 1961 the South African government even openly defied the British government when its police crossed into the neighboring British protectorate of Basutoland and kidnapped Anderson Ganyile, one of the country's rising freedom stars, who led the Pondo people's memorable struggles against apartheid tribal rule.

Apart from these specific instances, there are numerous other South African patriots, known and unknown, who have been sacrificed in various ways on the altar of African freedom.

This is but a brief and sketchy outline of the momentous struggle of the freedom fighters in our country, of the sacrifice they have made and of the price that is being paid at the present moment by those who keep the freedom flag flying.

For years our political organizations have been subjected to vicious attacks by the government. In 1957 there was considerable mass unrest and disturbances in the country districts of Zeerust, Sekhukhuniland, and Rustenburg. In all these areas there was widespread dissatisfaction with government policy and there were revolts against the pass laws, the poll tax, and government-inspired tribal authorities.

Instead of meeting the legitimate political demands of the masses of the people and redressing their grievances, the government reacted by banning the ANC in all these districts. In April 1960 the government went further and completely outlawed both the African National Congress and the Pan-Africanist Congress.

By resorting to these drastic methods the government had hoped to silence all opposition to its harsh policies and to remove all threats to the privileged position of the Whites in the country. It had hoped for days of perfect peace and comfort for White South Africa, free from revolt and revolution. It believed that through its strong-arm measures it could achieve what White South Africa has failed to accomplish during the last fifty years, namely, to compel Africans to accept the position that in our country freedom and happiness are the preserve of the White man.

But uneasy lies the head that wears the crown of White supremacy in South Africa. The banning and confinement of leaders, banishments and deportations, imprisonment and even death, have never deterred South African patriots. The very same day it was outlawed, the ANC issued a public statement announcing that it would definitely defy the government's ban and carry out operations from underground. The people of South Africa have adopted this declaration as their own and South Africa is today a land of turmoil and conflict.

In May last year a general strike was called. In the history of our country no strike has ever been organized under such formidable difficulties and dangers. The odds against us were tremendous. Our organizations were outlawed. Special legislation had been rushed through parliament empowering the government to round up its political opponents and to detain them without trial.

One week before the strike ten thousand Africans were arrested and kept in jail until after the strike. All meetings were banned throughout the country and our field workers were trailed and hounded by members of the Security Branch. General mobilization was ordered throughout the country and every available White man and woman put under arms. An English periodical described the situation on the eve of the strike in the following terms:

'In the country's biggest call-up since the war, scores of citizens' force and commando units were mobilised in the big towns. Camps were established at strategic points; heavy army vehicles carrying equipment and supplies moved in a steady stream along the Reef; helicopters hovered over African residential areas and trained searchlights on houses, yards, lands, and unlit areas. Hundreds of White civilians were sworn in as special constables, hundreds of white women spent weekends shooting at targets. Gun shops sold out of their stocks of revolvers and ammunition. All police leave was cancelled throughout the country. Armed guards were posted to protect power stations and other sources of essential services. Saracen armored cars and troop carriers patrolled townships. Police vans patrolled areas and broadcast statements that Africans who struck work would he sacked and endorsed out of the town.'

This was the picture in South Africa on the eve of the general strike, but our people stood up to the test most magnificently. The response was less than we expected but we made solid and substantial achievements. Hundreds of thousands of workers stayed away from work and the country's industries and commerce were seriously damaged. Hundreds of thousands of students and schoolchildren did not go to school for the duration of the strike.

The celebrations which had been planned by the

government to mark the inauguration of the republic were not only completely boycotted by the Africans, but were held in an atmosphere of tension and crisis in which the whole country looked like a military camp in a state of unrest and uncertainty. This panic stricken show of force was a measure of the power of the liberation movement and yet it failed to stem the rising tide of popular discontent.

How strong is the freedom struggle in South Africa today? What role should PAFMECA play to strengthen the liberation movement in South Africa and speed up the liberation of our country? These are questions frequently put by those who have our welfare at heart.

The view has been expressed in some quarters outside South Africa that, in the special situation obtaining in our country, our people will never win freedom through their own efforts. Those who hold this view point to the formidable apparatus of force and coercion in the hands of the government, to the size of its armies, the fierce suppression of civil liberties, and the persecution of political opponents of the regime. Consequently, in these quarters, we are urged to look for our salvation beyond our borders.

Nothing could be further from the truth.

It is true that world opinion against the policies of the South African government has hardened considerably in recent years. The All African People's Conference held in Accra in 1958, the Positive Action Conference for Peace and Security in Africa, also held in Accra in April 1960, the Conference of Independent African States held in this famous capital in June of the same year, and the conferences at Casablanca and Monrovia last year, as well as the Lagos Conference this month, passed militant resolutions in which they sharply condemned and rejected the racial policies of the South African government.

It has become clear to us that the whole of Africa is unanimously behind the move to ensure effective

161

economic and diplomatic sanctions against the South African government.

At the international level, concrete action against South Africa found expression in the expulsion of South Africa from the Commonwealth, which was achieved with the active initiative and collaboration of the African members of the Commonwealth. These were Ghana, Nigeria, and Tanganyika (although the latter had not yet achieved its independence). Nigeria also took the initiative in moving for the expulsion of South Africa from the International Labor Organisation.

But most significant was the draft resolution tabled at the fifteenth session of the United Nations which called for sanctions against South Africa. This resolution had the support of all the African members of the United Nations, with only one exception. The significance of the draft was not minimized by the fact that a milder resolution was finally adopted calling for individual or collective sanctions by member states. At the sixteenth session of the United Nations last year, the African states played a marvelous role in successfully carrying through the General Assembly a resolution against the address delivered by the South African Minister of Foreign Affairs, Mr. Eric Louw, and subsequently in the moves calling for the expulsion of South Africa from the United Nations and for sanctions against her.

Although the United Nations itself has neither expelled nor adopted sanctions against South Africa, many independent African states are in varying degrees enforcing economic and other sanctions against her. This increasing world pressure on South Africa has greatly weakened her international position and given a tremendous impetus to the freedom struggle inside the country.

No less a danger to White minority rule and a guarantee of ultimate victory for us is the freedom struggle that is raging furiously beyond the borders of the South

African territory; the rapid progress of Kenya, Uganda, and Zanzibar towards independence; the victories gained by the Nyasaland Malawi Congress; the unabated determination of Kenneth Kaunda's United National Independence Party (UNIP); the courage displayed by the freedom fighters of the Zimbabwe African People's Union (ZAPU), successor to the now banned National Democratic Party (NDP); the gallantry of the African crusaders in the Angolan war of liberation and the storm clouds forming around the excesses of Portuguese repression in Mozambique; the growing power of the independence movements in South-West Africa and the emergence of powerful political organizations in the High Commission territories - all these are forces which cannot compromise with White domination anywhere.

But we believe it would be fatal to create the illusion that external pressures render it unnecessary for us to tackle the enemy from within. The centre and cornerstone of the struggle for freedom and democracy in South Africa lies inside South Africa itself. Apart from those required for essential work outside the country, freedom fighters are in great demand for work inside the country.

We owe it as a duty to ourselves and to the freedom-loving peoples of the world to build and maintain in South Africa itself a powerful, solid movement, capable of surviving any attack by the government and sufficiently militant to fight back with a determination that comes from the knowledge and conviction that it is first and foremost by our own struggle and sacrifice inside South Africa itself that victory over White domination and apartheid can be won.

The struggle in the areas still subject to imperialist rule can be delayed and even defeated if it is uncoordinated. Only by our combined efforts and united action can we repulse the multiple onslaughts of the imperialists and fight our way to victory. Our enemies fight collectively and combine to exploit our people.

163

The clear examples of collective imperialism have made themselves felt more and more in our region by the formation of an unholy alliance between the governments of South Africa, Portugal, and the so-called Central African Federation. Hence these governments openly and shamelessly gave military assistance consisting of personnel and equipment to the traitorous Tshombe regime in Katanga.

At this very moment it has been widely reported that a secret defence agreement has been signed between Portugal, South Africa, and the Federation, following visits of Federation and South African defence ministers to Lisbon, the Federation defence minister to Luanda, and South African Defence Ministry delegations to Mozambique. Dr Salazar was quoted in the Johannesburg Star of 8 July 1961 as saying: 'Our relations - Mozambique's and Angola's on the one hand and the Federation and South Africa on the other - arise from the existence of our common borders and our traditional friendships that unite our Governments and our people. Our mutual interests are manifold and we are conscious of the need to cooperate to fulfill our common needs.'

Last year, Southern Rhodesian troops were training in South Africa and so were Rhodesian Air Force units. A military mission from South Africa and another from the Central African Federation visited Lourenzo Marques in Mozambique, at the invitation of the Mozambique Army Command, and took part in training exercises in which several units totaling 2,600 men participated. These operations included dropping exercises for paratroopers.

A report in a South African aviation magazine, wings (December 1961), states: 'The Portuguese are hastily building nine new aerodromes in Portuguese East Africa (Mozambique) following their troubles in Angola. The new 'dromes are all capable of taking jet fighters and are situated along or near the borders of Tanganyika and Nyasaland'; and gives full details.

Can anyone, therefore, doubt the role that the freedom movements should play in view of this hideous conspiracy?

As we have stated earlier, the freedom movement in South Africa believes that hard and swift blows should be delivered with the full weight of the masses of the people, who alone furnish us with one absolute guarantee that the freedom flames now burning in the country shall never be extinguished.

During the last ten years the African people in South Africa have fought many freedom battles, involving civil disobedience, strikes, protest marches, boycotts and demonstrations of all kinds. In all these campaigns we repeatedly stressed the importance of discipline, peaceful and non-violent struggle. We did so, firstly because we felt that there were still opportunities for peaceful struggle and we sincerely worked for peaceful changes. Secondly, we did not want to expose our people to situations where they might become easy targets for the trigger-happy police of South Africa. But the situation has now radically altered.

South Africa is now a land ruled by the gun. The government is increasing the size of its army, of the navy, of its air force, and the police. Pill-boxes and road blocks are being built up all over the country. Armament factories are being set up in Johannesburg and other cities. Officers of the South African army have visited Algeria and Angola where they were briefed exclusively on methods of suppressing popular struggles.

All opportunities for peaceful agitation and struggle have been closed. Africans no longer have the freedom even to stay peacefully in their houses in protest against the oppressive policies of the government. During the strike in May last year the police went from house to house, beating up Africans and driving them to work.

Hence it is understandable why today many of our people are turning their faces away from the path of peace and non-violence. They feel that peace in our country must

165

be considered already broken when a minority government maintains its authority over the majority by force and violence.

A crisis is developing in earnest in South Africa. However, no high command ever announces beforehand what its strategy and tactics will be to meet a situation. Certainly, the days of civil disobedience, of strikes, and mass demonstrations are not over and we will resort to them over and over again.

But a leadership commits a crime against its own people if it hesitates to sharpen its political weapons which have become less effective.

Regarding the actual situation pertaining today in South Africa I should mention that I have just come out of South Africa, having for the last ten months lived in my own country as an outlaw, away from family and friends. When I was compelled to lead this sort of life, I made a public statement in which I announced that I would not leave the country but would continue working underground. I meant it and I have honored that undertaking. But when my organisation received the invitation to this conference it was decided that I should attempt to come out and attend the conference to furnish the various African leaders, leading sons of our continent, with the most up-to-date information about the situation.

During the past ten months I moved up and down my country and spoke to peasants in the countryside, to workers in the cities, to students and professional people. It dawned on me quite clearly that the situation had become explosive. It was not surprising therefore when one morning in October last year we woke up to read press reports of widespread sabotage involving the cutting of telephone wires and the blowing up of power pylons. The government remained unshaken and White South Africa tried to dismiss it as the work of criminals.

Then on the night of 16 December last year the whole of South Africa vibrated under the heavy blows of

Umkhonto we Sizwe (The Spear of the Nation). Government buildings were blasted with explosives in Johannesburg, the industrial heart of South Africa, in Port Elizabeth, and in Durban. It was now clear that this was a political demonstration of a formidable kind, and the press announced the beginning of planned acts of sabotage in the country.

It was still a small beginning because a government as strong and as aggressive as that of South Africa can never be induced to part with political power by bomb explosions in one night and in three cities only. But in a country where freedom fighters frequently pay with their very lives and at a time when the most elaborate military preparations are being made to crush the people's struggles, planned acts of sabotage against government installations introduce a new phase in the political situation and are a demonstration of the people's unshakeable determination to win freedom whatever the cost may be.

The government is preparing to strike viciously at political leaders and freedom fighters. But the people will not take these blows sitting down.

In such a grave situation it is fit and proper that this conference of PAFMECA should sound a clarion call to the struggling peoples in South Africa and other dependent areas, to close ranks, to stand firm as a rock and not allow themselves to be divided by petty political rivalries whilst their countries burn. At this critical moment in the history of struggle, unity amongst our people in South Africa and in the other territories has become as vital as the air we breathe and it should be preserved at all costs.

Finally, dear friends, I should assure you that the African people of South Africa, notwithstanding fierce persecution and untold suffering, in their ever increasing courage will not for one single moment be diverted from the historic mission of liberating their country and winning freedom, lasting peace, and happiness.

167

We are confident that in the decisive struggles ahead, our liberation movement will receive the fullest support of PAFMECA and of all freedom-loving people throughout the world."[20]

After the Addis Ababa conference, PAFMECA was transformed into a larger organization, PAFMECSA. And it was not long before an even larger organization came into being, replacing PAFMECSA which existed until 1963. It was replaced by the Organization of African Unity (OAU) formed in May the same year in Addis Ababa, embracing the whole continent.

Right from the beginning, PAFMECSA was unique in one respect in the sense that it was composed of nationalist political parties from both colonial and independent countries, while PAFMECA was at first an umbrella organization composed of political parties only from colonial territories, until December 1961 when Tanganyika became independent and the only independent country represented in the organization before its demise in February 1962.

Uganda would have become another independent country as a member of the organization but it did not win independence until October that year when PAFMECA had already been replaced by PAFMECSA.

In the case of some of the independent countries, such as Tanganyika after she won independence in 1961, it was actually the government rather than the local political party or parties which were represented in PAFMECSA. And in independent countries which had a one-party system, the party was in fact the government.

At the PAFMECSA meeting held in December 1962 in Leopoldville, capital of the former Belgian Congo, the following independent countries were represented: Burundi, Congo-Leopoldville, Ethiopia, Rwanda, Tanganyika, and Uganda. Also delegates from the following colonial territories attended the conference: Northern Rhodesia, Southern Rhodesia, Kenya, Zanzibar, Mozambique, and Angola. The meeting was also attended by representatives of the nationalist movements of the African National Congress (ANC) and the Pan-Africanist Congress (PAC) from apartheid South Africa which was an independent country but under white minority rule.

Earlier on 21 March 1960, the Pan-Africanist Congress (PAC) of South Africa under the leadership of Robert Mangaliso Sobukwe, organized a demonstration against the pass laws which led to the massacre of 69 Africans in the township of Sharpeville. More than 180 were injured.

Most of those killed and injured were women and children after a group of black protesters converged on the local police station, offering themselves up for arrest for not carrying their pass books. Police opened fire on the crowd, triggering international outrage and condemnation of the apartheid regime for the massacre. It was a turning point in the history of South Africa and the massacre helped galvanize the struggle against apartheid.

The pivotal role PAFMECSA played in the establishment of the Organization of African Unity (OAU) as we have just seen was also acknowledged by Nelson Mandela in his book *Long Walk to Freedom*:

"In December (1961), the ANC received an invitation from the Pan-African Freedom Movement for East, Central, and Southern Africa (PAFMECSA) to attend its conference in Addis Ababa in February 1962. PAFMECSA, which later became the Organization of African Unity, aimed to draw together the independent states of Africa and promote the liberation movements on the continent....

The underground executive asked me to lead the ANC delegation to the conference....The ANC had to arrange for me to travel to Dar es Salaam in Tanganyika. The flight to Addis Ababa would originate in Dar es Salaam....

Early the next morning we left for Mbeya, a Tanganyikan town near the Rhodesian border....We booked in a local motel (in Mbeya)....We were waiting for Mr. John Mwakangale of the Tanganyika African National Union, a member of parliament....

We arrived in Dar es Salaam the next day and I met with Julius Nyerere, the newly independent country's first president. We talked at his house, which was not at all grand, and I recall that he drove himself in a simple car, a little Austin. This impressed me, for it suggested that he was a man of the people. Class, Nyerere always insisted, was alien to Africa; socialism indigenous.

I reviewed our situation for him, ending with an appeal for help. He was a shrewd, soft-spoken man who was well-disposed to our mission....He suggested I seek the favor of Emperor Haile Selassie and promised to arrange an introduction....

Because I did not have a passport, I carried with me a rudimentary document from Tanganyika that merely said, 'This is Nelson Mandela, a citizen of the Republic of South Africa. He has permission to leave Tanganyika and return here.'"[21]

Although PAFMECSA led to the establishment of the Organization of African Unity (OAU), as did the efforts by the Casablanca and Monrovia Groups, African countries did not – as a step towards African unity – retain the federal structures instituted by the colonial powers to consolidate their rule the way they had agreed to maintain the territorial boundaries they inherited at independence in order to avoid chaos. There were not many federations which had been established by the colonial rulers during their reign. But there were some and were big enough to have made an impact on the international scene had they emerged from colonial rule, intact, as supra-national states each under its own federal government. Only one did, as we will learn shortly.

The French colonial rulers formed two large federations on the continent. There was French Equatorial Africa in West-central Africa comprising Chad, the Central African Republic, French Congo – what is now Congo-Brazzaville – and Gabon. Its capital was Brazzaville. But the federation was dissolved in 1959 when the constituent territories voted to become autonomous republics.

In 1959, the same countries formed a loose federation called the Union of Central African Republics. However, it was a union in name only. In 1960 they became fully "independent" as members of the French Community controlled and dominated by France as her neo-colonial umbrella for her former colonies.

The other federation established by France was French West Africa comprising twice as many colonies: Dahomey, French Guinea, French Soudan (Mali), Ivory Coast, Mauritania, Niger, Senegal, and Upper Volta. Its capital was Dakar, Senegal. Guinea pulled out of the French Community in 1958 when it became independent, the same year the constituent territories became autonomous republics within the French Community. But, like its sister federation of French Equatorial Africa, it, too, was dissolved in 1959.

In the same year, 1959, the colony of French Soudan, renamed the Sudanese Republic, joined Senegal to form the Mali Federation which became independent on 20 June 1960. But political differences shattered the federation. Senegal, led by Senghor, a Francophile, was conservative; Mali, led by Modibo Keita, an ardent Pan-Africanist, was a militant.

On 20 August 1960, Senegal declared itself independent and pulled out of the federation, dissolving it on the same day. The former French Soudan proclaimed itself the Republic of Mali on 22 September 1960 and withdrew from the French Community.

Therefore, none of the federations in Francophone Africa survived to form a basis for union of the member-countries under one government after they won independence. And prospects for unity got dimmer and dimmer through the years as the newly independent states jealously guarded their sovereign status. In fact, the sixties saw no concerted effort among the French-speaking African countries to form any kind of union, except for Guinea and Mali which formed a symbolic union with Ghana that was made impractical by geographical separation and other factors including lack of institutional mechanisms to make the union functional.

But even among Senegalese, who precipitated the dissolution of the Mali Federation when they pulled out, there were those who believed that there was an imperative need for unity transcending territorial boundaries. As Mamadou Dia, who before he became prime minister of Senegal served as vice premier of the short-lived Mali Federation, states in his book *The African Nations and World Solidarity*:

"It would be a fatal error for the nations of the *Tiers-Monde*, especially those just recovering their freedom, to think that the struggle ends with the proclamation of independence....

Narrow nationalisms reflect a lack of historical perspective and surely ill-advised when they hope to guarantee the development of the economies they want to liberate by suddenly reversing their policies, by skillful maneuvering, or by changing partners.

The road to real African independence, constructed on a solid rock of a strong economy, lies not so much in neutralism as in large groupings that permit the concentration of poles, centers, and axes of development. That is why Mali (the Federation) will be an open nation that must expand to fulfill its role."[22]

The Mali Federation was the third and last one to

172

collapse in Francophone Africa. However, the collapse of those federations was lauded even by the imperial Charles de Gaulle when he took a strong stand on the Nigerian civil war and eventually recognized the breakaway region of Eastern Nigeria as the independent Republic of Biafra. As Kaye Whiteman points out:

"De Gaulle based his argument on self-determination, and on hostility to federations in general. All those he mentioned were British creations, including Canada, – where he equally applies the self-determination principle in Quebec – but the real analogy he is making is the two federations the French had created in West and Central Africa, which were systematically dismantled in the late 1950's as independence approached.

France at the time was accused of balkanization – of creating a host of unviable mini-states in order to maintain a neo-colonial influence over them, but of late the French have been emphasizing that their decolonization did at least avoid a Nigerian war. It is significant that wealthy Ivory Coast and Gabon were the 'Biafras' of these failed federations, and it has been claimed that De Gaulle may have been influenced by President Houphouet-Boigny towards Biafra rather than the other way round."[23]

As for the British, they left an enduring legacy in the continued existence of the Federation of Nigeria which is also the only federation on the entire continent formed during colonial times that has survived. But they also formed another one: the Federation of Rhodesia and Nyasaland comprising three territories – Northern Rhodesia, Southern Rhodesia, and Nyasaland. It was formed in 1953 and its capital was Salisbury in Southern Rhodesia.

The British wanted to maintain the federation. But black Africans, fearing perpetuation of white domination as in South Africa without any hope of getting independence soon, were vigorously opposed to it. The federation was already dominated by the white settlers of Southern Rhodesia to whom the British transferred control, ostensibly to facilitate administration but in reality to perpetuate white domination over blacks.

The beginning of the end of the federation started in 1953 – the same year in which it was formed – when Nyasaland, which was almost all-black and hardly had any white settlers unlike Southern Rhodesia and Northern Rhodesia, was forced by the British into the federation. The Nyasaland African Congress founded in 1944 was resolutely opposed to the federation. Opposition continued through the years until the federation was dissolved on 31 December 1963.

However, one African leader with impeccable pan-African credentials was opposed to the dissolution of the Central African Federation as the Federation of Rhodesia and Nyasaland was popularly known. He was Dr. Milton Obote. As Professor Ali Mazrui states:

"Obote's stand on the Federation of Rhodesia and Nyasaland was the more interesting because, while he refused to recognize the present government of the Federation, he was nevertheless against the Federation's dissolution – a stand which put him almost in a class by himself among African nationalists."[24]

Given his pan-African inclinations, it is understandable why he was opposed to the federation's dissolution for the same reason many Nigerians – by no means all – and other Africans were opposed to the dissolution of the Nigerian Federation before and after independence. That is because it was possible to build a strong African macro-nation on the foundations laid by and inherited from the colonialists.

Had the Nigerian Federation been dissolved, there would be no Nigeria today, potentially one of the most powerful and richest black nations in the world. And had the Central African Federation of Rhodesia and Nyasaland survived and emerged from colonial rule as a single political entity under one government, it would have been one of the most powerful and richest black nations in the world together with South Africa and Nigeria; the kind of potential the former Belgian Congo also has.

And had Kenya, Uganda and Tanganyika formed an East African federation – taking advantage of the strong ties which already existed among those countries including a common currency and a common market facilitating the free flow of trade among them as members of the East African Common Services Organisation (EACSO) created by the British colonial rulers – the new supra-nation would have been "a power house," as Nyerere put it, as would have been any other macro-nations formed across the continent.

In fact, Nyerere was such a firm believer in the functional utility of an East African federation that he offered to delay the independence of Tanganyika if that would help facilitate unification of the three East African countries. He said Tanganyika would wait so that all the three countries would win independence on the same day and form a federation under one government.

In one of his last interviews with the *New Internationalist* in December 1998, almost one year before he died in October 1999, Nyerere said that after independence, he and Ugandan President Milton Obote went to see Jomo Kenyatta and told him they should unite and asked him to be the president of the federation. But Kenyatta refused:

"I respected Jomo (Kenyatta) immensely.

It has probably never happened before in history. Two heads of state, Milton Obote and I, went to Jomo and said to him: 'Let's unite our countries and you be our head of state.' He said no.

175

I think he said no because it would have put him out of his element as a Kikuyu Elder." - ("The Heart of Africa: Interview with Julius Nyerere on Anti-Colonialism" in the *New Internationalist*, Issue 309, January-February 1999).

Therefore there has always been a strong sentiment for unity among many Africans especially Pan-Africanist leaders such as Nyerere and Nkrumah. And with regard to the Federation of Rhodesia and Nyasaland, a case could indeed be made that an opportunity which could have been exploited by Africans, if the federation survived and emerged from colonial rule as a single political entity, was lost when it was dissolved. And that is probably what Dr. Milton Obote had in mind when he opposed its dissolution.

He saw a giant African nation emerging out of that if the three British colonies of Northern Rhodesia, Southern Rhodesia and Nyasaland won independence as a collective entity under one government similar to what was envisaged in East Africa had Kenya, Uganda and Tanganyika followed that path. And Africa would have benefited enormously, an achievement which also would have speeded up the collapse of the apartheid regime in South Africa which would have come face-to-face with a powerful and rich black independent nation as a neighbour; as opposed to Nigeria which is so far away, and Congo whose enormous potential – exceeding South Africa's wealth – was wasted during 32 years of Mobutu's kleptocratic rule.

Yet, there was also a perfectly legitimate reason against formation or perpetuation of such large federations by colonial powers: consolidation of white minority rule over vast expanses of territory inhabited by tens of millions of Africans left at the mercy of their imperial rulers. It was a fear the three East African leaders – Nyerere, Obote and Kenyatta – forcefully articulated in their declaration of intent to form an East African Federation which they signed in Nairobi on 5 June 1963:

"In the past century the hand of imperialism grasped the whole continent and in this part of Africa our people found themselves included together in what colonialists styled 'The British sphere of influence.' Now that we are once again free or are on the point of regaining our freedom we believe the time has come to consolidate our unity and provide it with a constitutional basis (for an East African federation).

For some years we have worked together in PAFMECA (Pan-African Freedom Movement for East and Central Africa – later expanded to PAFMECSA to include Southern Africa) where we have accepted common objectives and ideas and created the essential spirit of unity between ourselves and among our people....For forty years the imperialists and local settler minorities tried to impose a political federation upon us. Our people rightly resisted these attempts. Federation at that time would quickly have led to one thing – a vast white-dominated dominion."[26]

Their fears were well-founded. The British imperial government even considered creating, not only an East African federation dominated by white settlers, but also a vast federation stretching from Kenya all the way to South Africa to include all their colonial territories in the region: Kenya, Uganda, Tanganyika, Zanzibar, Nyasaland, Northern Rhodesia, Southern Rhodesia, Bechuanaland, Swaziland, Basutoland, South Africa, and South West Africa which was ruled by apartheid South Africa. As George Bennett stated in "Settlers and Politics in Kenya":

"(There) was an announcement that a commission of the Imperial Government...would visit East Africa to consider federation....

If federation was a 'forced card' as Lord Olivier said, it was forced by two influences of which those in Britain who desired to create a Dominion in East Africa were the prime movers.

In Kenya Lord Delamere had opposed the idea in the 1920 elections, believing that Kenya should stand alone until it was self-governing and that its own problems should be digested first. By 1925, however, he was ready for Grigg's federation plans, and supported the idea of building a Government House at Nairobi to be a worthy centre for the newly established Governors's Conference.

He provided an unofficial background to the Governors' first meeting at Nairobi in 1926 by calling a conference, at Tukuyu in southern Tanganyika...in October 1925, of settler leaders from the whole area from Kenya to Nyasaland and Northern Rhodesia."[27]

Thus, while Africans opposed the imperial federation for good reasons, they failed to form their own – in this case an East African federation – purely for their own selfish reasons.

Not all of them were opposed to federation. In the case of Tanganyika, Nyerere was ready to make a sacrifice. Tanganyika was to be the first East African colony to win independence from Britain. Independence was scheduled for 9 December 1961, but Nyerere offered to postpone it for the sake of federation.

Obote also was in favour of federation but was thwarted in his efforts by separatist threats from Uganda's provinces. The biggest threat which almost plunged the country into civil war during the sixties came from the Buganda kingdom. But other provinces constituted enough threat, as well, to warrant serious attention from the central government. As Colin Legum and John Drysdale state in *Africa Contemporary Record*:

"Although Buganda offered the toughest problem to

the mordenising nationalists, it was by no means the only difficulty they had to face. Each of the other three kingdoms – Toro, Ankole and Bunyoro – and the princedom of Busoga had their own well-structured political systems; each was suspicious of the modern political centre at Entebbe. Also they had traditional rivalries – especially between Buganda and Bunyoro."[28]

Kenya, the most economically advanced of the three countries since it was favoured by the colonialists with its capital Nairobi virtually serving as the capital of East Africa, simply did not want to sacrifice her privileged status and lose many of her benefits – which she enjoyed at the expense of Uganda and Tanganyika – for the sake of federation with her poorer sister-countries.

And nationalism, of course, triumphed over the spirit of Pan-Africanism embodied in the declaration of intent for an East African federation signed by Nyerere, Kenyatta and Obote. Had it not been for the nationalist sentiments and separatist tendencies which prevailed over the leadership in Kenya and Uganda, the federation would have been consummated. Among all the three East African countries, Tanganyika was the only country which strongly advocated federation.

Ten years after Nyerere stepped down as president of Tanzania, ending 24 years of his stewardship of the nation, he stated that failure to form an East African federation was his biggest disappointment. According to James McKinley of *The New York Times* who interviewed Nyerere for an hour in his home village of Butiama in northern Tanzania near the shores of Lake Victoria on 2 September 1996:

"Mr. Nyerere said his greatest failure was that although he managed to form a federation with Zanzibar in 1964 to create Tanzania, he never managed to persuade neighboring countries to form a larger federation, a move he believes would have made the region a powerhouse. 'I felt that these little countries in Africa were really too small, they would not be viable – the Tanganyikas, the Rwandas, the Burundis, the Kenyas,' he said. 'My ambition in East Africa was really never to build a Tanganyika. I wanted an East African federation. So what did I succeed in doing?' he asked. 'My success is building a nation out of this collection of tribes.'"[29]

The failure of the three East African countries to form a federation during the sixties was even more tragic because the three countries had some of the best institutional structures linking them together which could have provided a strong foundation for the establishment of a federation. They had been linked together in a common services organisation for years. And they emerged from colonial rule with the East African Common Services still intact.

The constituent parts of the Common Services includes a transport network known as the East African Railways and Harbours Corporation; communication links collectively identified as the East African Posts and Telecommunications Services; a common airline under the aegis of the East African Airways Corporation; and the East African Scientific Research Institute.

In addition to the Common Services, the three East African countries also had a Common Market with a more or less uniform external tariff, "revenue sharing" rather than "protective" in intent. There was virtually a free flow of trade among the three countries both in goods imported from abroad and in goods produced within East Africa. They also had a common currency issued by the East African Currency Board, and no restrictions at all on the flow of money across territorial boundaries within the region.

After winning independence, they also established a single university system with each of the constituent colleges specializing in some areas to serve the manpower needs of East Africa.

The University College of Dar es Salaam in Tanzania had the largest faculty of law, in addition to other departments in various academic disciplines. Nairobi University College in Kenya was noted for its faculty of engineering and department of commerce, in addition to others. And Makerere University College in Uganda founded in 1922, one of the oldest and best on the continent and regarded as the "Harvard" or "Oxford" of Africa, had the school of medicine and other highly regarded departments including political science and economics among others.

The chancellor of the University of East Africa was Julius Nyerere, the president of Tanzania, himself a leading intellectual. Professor Ali Mazrui described him as the most intellectual leader among the East African presidents and the most original thinker among all the leaders in Anglophone Africa.

The three East African countries also established a common parliament, known as the East African Legislative Assembly, to deal with matters relating to the Common Market and Common Services. The legislators held their sessions on rotational basis in the three capitals of Nairobi, Kampala and Dar es Salaam. Most of the people in East Africa were also, as they still are, united by a common language, Kiswahili, known mostly to outsiders as Swahili.

Yet in spite of all those ties, the three countries failed to form a federation. However, the quest for unity was not a total failure in the region. After the three countries of Kenya, Uganda and Tanganyika failed to form a federation in 1963, Tanganyika and Zanzibar united the following year, on 26 April, and formed one country called Tanzania.

But the union of Tanganyika and Zanzibar was not well-received by everybody, including prominent politicians in East Africa, ostensibly because Zanzibar was said to be under "Communist influence." As Ronald Ngala, Kenya's opposition leader in parliament who led the Kenya African Democratic Union (KADU) which was opposed to a unitary state and favoured a federal structure for Kenya's provinces to protect the interests of smaller ethnic groups, stated upon hearing the news of the impending union:

"I hope...that the overseas influence infiltrated into Zanzibar will not spread to Tanganyika in any malicious way."[30]

But probably Ngala himself and others in East Africa and elsewhere who were not well-disposed towards the union of Tanganyika and Zanzibar would admit that the advantages of unity including regional integration even if not under a single government outweigh its disadvantages. That is why in East Africa itself, the leaders – including those opposed to federation under one government – went on to form the East African Community (EAC) as a vehicle for effective regional cooperation especially in the economic arena despite their political differences.

The EAC was formed in 1967 and superseded the East African Common Services Organisation (EACSO) and restructured the Common Market to accommodate regional differences.

The three countries no longer had a common currency – each went on to establish its own; they also instituted tariffs according to EAC guidelines to protect infant industries in Uganda and Tanganyika and restructure the imbalance in the flow of trade which favoured Kenya at the expense of her partners; and went their own separate ways in other areas but were united in their common desire to maintain economic links and facilitate regional cooperation through their membership in the East African Community (EAC) which they joined voluntarily.

The rationale for such regional cooperation and unification movements elsewhere across Africa is simple. As a developing continent, it is Africa itself which offers the best and safest market for African producers. And it is only regional integration or continental union which can stimulate and facilitate rapid economic growth.

Overseas markets can not absorb all African exports even if they wanted to; other countries have their own products to sell or consume. They are also protectionist, erecting tariff barriers to insulate their own industries and producers from outside competition. And some of them are hostile to African countries including what they produce for different reasons such as political differences and outright prejudice. There could be no stronger reasons for African countries to forge links among themselves in order to establish a common market and trade among themselves.

Formation of the East African Community as an intergovernmental organisation underscored the need for such regional cooperation the three East African leaders – Nyerere, Obote and Kenyatta – had emphasized three years earlier in June 1963 when they signed the "Declaration of Federation by the Governments of East Africa":

"Economic planning, maximum utilization of manpower and our other resources, the establishment of a Central Bank and common defence programme, and foreign and diplomatic representation are areas in which we need to work together.

Such approach would provide greater coordination and savings in both scarce capital, facilities for training and manpower. What is more we would have a total population of some 25 million people – a formidable force and a vast market to influence economic development at home, attract greater investment and enhance our prestige and

183

influence abroad."[31]

The failure of the three East African countries to form a federation demonstrated the great difficulty even countries which have so much in common – for example in terms of economic ties and history as well as a common language as we have shown – are bound to face when they try to submerge their national identities in a supra-national body for the sake of unity under one government.

Even the Arab countries of North Africa which are racially, culturally and linguistically homogeneous and are virtually all-Muslim, failed to unite during the sixties around the same time the East African Federation failed.

Political differences and differences in territorial size contributed to the failure of federation or union government among the North African Arab states which tried to unite: the Maghreb states of Algeria, Tunisia and Morocco.

Algeria was militant, the other two conservative. Algeria was also seen as a threat because it is much bigger and richer than Tunisia and Morocco. And as a nation born in war and bloodshed during its struggle for independence in which one million Algerians died in seven years of guerrilla warfare against the French, Algeria's militancy even before the country won independence was viewed with apprehension by the other two Maghreb states of Tunisia and Morocco.

In spite of all that, the three countries agreed to form a union. But when Algeria won independence in July 1962, Morocco quickly claimed some border regions as hers and threatened annexation of Algerian territory. In October 1963, the two countries fought a brief but intense and bitter war over those claims, dashing any hopes of unity between the two countries in the near future.

Morocco alienated Algerians even further because of her neo-colonial image as a client state of the West, especially the United States and France. By contrast, the Algerian leadership took a very strong stand against neo-colonial penetration of Africa, a position articulated by only a handful of countries on the continent during that pperiod: Egypt, Ghana, Guinea, Mali, Tanzania, Uganda, and Algeria itself. As Algerian President Ahmed Ben Bella said in an interview with Maria Macciochi, a correspondent of *L'Unita*, an Italian daily newspaper, on 13 August 1962, in Algiers:

"I have declared that neocolonialism is our great scourge....Colonialism has been modernized. It has become more progressive, less crude. It understands that people can no longer be dominated by force, by machine guns, and by bloody repression. It seeks new ways of domination – an enlightened colonialism, so to speak – although based on a fictitious equality, a new form of slavery controlling the key positions in our society.

Either there is a revolution under way in the country and we will be able to pursue this course under our own power, or else Algeria will become a revised and improved version of other African governments which have accepted neocolonialism."[32]

Morocco's provocation of Algeria and her attempt to seize Algerian territory may have been interpreted in some quarters as part of a neo-colonialist plot by the West to subvert the Algerian revolution. And it was. King Hussein of Morocco invaded Algeria on his own, but he was also encouraged and "pushed" by the French and American intelligence agencies to attack her neighbour. The Algerian revolution and Ben Bella's ideological orientation were considered anathema to the West. In September 1963, Moroccan troops captured several Algerian border posts, triggering the so-called War of the Desert.

However, the conflict between the two countries was

not atypical on the continent. Although the sixties were euphoric times as Africans celebrated independence every year – until 1968 hardly a year passed without at least one African country winning independence – the decade was also one of crises in different areas, forcing the young African nations to face harsh realities of nationhood. The problems were political and economic as well as military.

At independence, the new African nations lacked many attributes of social cohesion and political stability critical to tackling the arduous task of national development and forging political unity among diverse groups living within the same territorial boundaries. Ethnic diversity presented one of the daunting problems demanding political acumen and statesmanship of the highest calibre. African countries were and still are no more than a collection of different ethnic groups, many of them hostile to each other. Few are well-integrated.

Also, the young African nations lacked trained manpower practically in all areas, resulting in poor performance. In almost all the countries, administrative and technical skills remained at a very low level all the way through the sixties. For example, the former Belgian Congo had only 16 university graduates at independence in 1960; Nyasaland, renamed Malawi, had 34 at independence in 1964; Zambia, formerly Northern Rhodesia, had 109 when it won independence in 1966; and Tanganyika had 120 at independence in 1961.

African countries won independence promising their people not only political freedom but also economic salvation and freedom from disease and ignorance. As Nyerere said in September 1963, although Tanganyikans had won the right to international equality when the country achieved independence, such equality was more apparent than real because a person who was ignorant and could not produce enough food for himself and suffered from disfiguring diseases could not really stand on terms of equality with all the others who were not in his condition.[33]

None of those problems can be solved without economic development. And economic development is impossible without modernization. Unfortunately even today, a modern industrial economy is beyond the reach of most African countries just as it was during the sixties. Yet, there is no alternative to economic development except perpetual misery.

So the fundamental question which was asked then and is still being asked today is, "Which Way Africa?" especially for an underdeveloped and predominantly agricultural continent.

Many economists contend that Africans can develop more rapidly and with less strain if development programmes first emphasize agriculture which is the mainstay of African economies, extractive industry, roads, power plants and light manufactures. Many African countries tried that during the sixties. But they also realized that development of heavy industry seemed to be the *sine qua non* for economic independence. And it is one of the great features which separate developed countries from underdeveloped ones collectively known as the Third World.

Countries such as Ghana and Tanzania also adopted central planning in the quest for rapid economic development and socialist transformation of their societies. And there was a historical precedent for that, China and the Soviet Union.

In the case of the Soviet Union, the country made spectacular achievement and became a super power within 40 years after the Bolshevik Revolution because of its emphasis on heavy industry and education, especially in science, under central planning. It would not have become a super power in so short a time without central planning which enabled the state to channel the nation's resources into specific fields to achieve specific targets within a specified period.

Dr. Nkrumah was one of the African leaders who wanted and tried to take that route towards rapid economic development, placing great emphasis on industrialization including the acquisition of nuclear technology. As he stated at a ceremony launching the construction of Ghana's Atomic Reactor Centre at Kwabenya near Accra on 16 December 1964:

"We must ourselves take part in the pursuit of scientific and technological research as a means of providing the basis of our socialist society. Socialism without science is void....We have therefore been compelled to enter the field of atomic energy because this already promises to yield the greatest economic resource of power since the beginning of man."[34]

Had he been able to achieve his goal, he would have paved the way towards industrialization for other African countries the same way he blazed the trail towards African independence when he led Ghana to become the first black African country to emerge from colonial rule. Unfortunately, shortly after he launched the construction of Ghana's Atomic Reactor Centre, he was overthrown about a year later on 24 February 1966 in a military coup engineered and masterminded by the CIA.

The ouster of Nkrumah was one of the most tragic events in the history of post-colonial Africa.

Nkrumah was the strongest advocate of immediate continental unification, a stand that put him in a class almost by himself. He was also, together with leaders such as Nyerere, Sekou Toure, Obote and Modibo Keita, one of the strongest supporters of African unity in general and of the African liberation movements and an uncompromising opponent of interference in African affairs by world powers and other external forces. And that made him an enemy of the West. He became prime target for the CIA:

"Declassified National Security Council and Central Intelligence Agency documents provide compelling, new evidence of United States government involvement in the 1966 overthrow of Ghanaian President Kwame Nkrumah.

The coup d'etat, organized by dissident army officers, toppled the Nkrumah government on Feb. 24, 1966 and was promptly hailed by Western governments, including the U.S.

The documents appear in a collection of diplomatic and intelligence memos, telegrams, and reports on Africa in Foreign Relations of the United States, the government's ongoing official history of American foreign policy.

Prepared by the State Department's Office of the Historian, the latest volumes reflect the overt diplomacy and covert actions of President Lyndon B. Johnson's administration from 1964-68. Though published in November 1999, what they reveal about U.S. complicity in the Ghana coup was only recently noted.

Allegations of American involvement in the *putsche* arose almost immediately because of the well-known hostility of the U.S. to Nkrumah's socialist orientation and pan-African activism.

Nkrumah, himself, implicated the U.S. in his overthrow, and warned other African nations about what he saw as an emerging pattern.

'An all-out offensive is being waged against the progressive, independent states,' he wrote in *Dark Days* in Ghana, his 1969 account of the Ghana coup. 'All that has been needed was a small force of disciplined men to seize the key points of the capital city and to arrest the existing political leadership.'

'It has been one of the tasks of the C.I.A. and other similar organisations,' he noted, 'to discover these potential quislings and traitors in our midst, and to encourage them, by bribery and the promise of political power, to destroy

189

the constitutional government of their countries.'

A Spook's Story

While charges of U.S. involvement are not new, support for them was lacking until 1978, when anecdotal evidence was provided from an unlikely source - a former CIA case officer, John Stockwell, who reported first-hand testimony in his memoir, *In Search of Enemies: A CIA Story.*

'The inside story came to me,' Stockwell wrote, 'from an egotistical friend, who had been chief of the [CIA] station in Accra [Ghana] at the time.' (Stockwell was stationed one country away in the Ivory Coast.)

Subsequent investigations by *The New York Times* and *Covert Action Information Bulletin* identified the station chief as Howard T. Banes, who operated undercover as a political officer in the U.S. Embassy.

This is how the ouster of Nkrumah was handled as Stockwell related. The Accra station was encouraged by headquarters to maintain contact with dissidents of the Ghanaian army for the purpose of gathering intelligence on their activities. It was given a generous budget, and maintained intimate contact with the plotters as a coup was hatched. So close was the station's involvement that it was able to coordinate the recovery of some classified Soviet military equipment by the United States as the coup took place.

According to Stockwell, Banes' sense of initiative knew no bounds. The station even proposed to headquarters through back channels that a squad be on hand at the moment of the coup to storm the [Communist] Chinese embassy, kill everyone inside, steal their secret records, and blow up the building to cover the facts.

Though the proposal was quashed, inside the CIA headquarters the Accra station was given full, if unofficial credit for the eventual coup, in which eight Soviet advisors were killed. None of this was adequately reflected in the agency's records, Stockwell wrote.

Confirmation and Revelation

While the newly-released documents, written by a National Security Council staffer and unnamed CIA officers, confirm the essential outlines set forth by Nkrumah and Stockwell, they also provide additional, and chilling, details about what the U.S. government knew about the plot, when, and what it was prepared to do and did do to assist it.

On March 11, 1965, almost a year before the coup, William P. Mahoney, the U.S. ambassador to Ghana, participated in a candid discussion in Washington, D.C., with CIA Director John A. McCone and the deputy chief of the CIA's Africa division, whose name has been withheld.

Significantly, the Africa division was part of the CIA's directorate of plans, or dirty tricks component, through which the government pursued its covert policies.

According to the record of their meeting (Document 251), topic one was the "Coup d'etat Plot, Ghana." While Mahoney was satisfied that popular opinion was running strongly against Nkrumah and the economy of the country was in a precarious state, he was not convinced that the coup d'etat, now being planned by Acting Police Commissioner Harlley and Generals Otu and Ankrah, would necessarily take place.

Nevertheless, he confidently - and accurately, as it turned out -predicted that one way or another Nkrumah would be out within a year. Revealing the depth of embassy knowledge of the plot, Mahoney referred to a recent report which mentioned that the top coup conspirators were scheduled to meet on 10 March at which time they would determine the timing of the coup.

However, he warned, because of a tendency to

191

procrastinate, any specific date they set should be accepted with reservations. In a reversal of what some would assume were the traditional roles of an ambassador and the CIA director, McCone asked Mahoney who would most likely succeed Nkrumah in the event of a coup.

Mahoney again correctly forecast the future: Ambassador Mahoney stated that initially, at least, a military junta would take over.

Making it Happen

But Mahoney was not a prophet. Rather, he represented the commitment of the U.S. government, in coordination with other Western governments, to bring about Nkrumah's downfall.

Firstly, Mahoney recommended denying Ghana's forthcoming aid request in the interests of further weakening Nkrumah. He felt that there was little chance that either the Chinese Communists or the Soviets would in adequate measure come to Nkrumah's financial rescue and the British would continue to adopt a hard nose attitude toward providing further assistance to Ghana.

At the same time, it appears that Mahoney encouraged Nkrumah in the mistaken belief that both the U.S. and the U.K. would come to his financial rescue and proposed maintaining current U.S. aid levels and programs because they will endure and be remembered long after Nkrumah goes.

Secondly, Mahoney seems to have assumed the responsibility of increasing the pressure on Nkrumah and exploiting the probable results. This can be seen in his 50-minute meeting with Nkrumah three weeks later.

According to Mahoney's account of their April 2 discussion (Document 252), 'at one point Nkrumah, who had been holding face in hands, looked up and I saw he was crying. With difficulty he said I could not understand the ordeal he had been through during last month.

Recalling that there had been seven attempts on his life.'

Mahoney did not attempt to discourage Nkrumah's fears, nor did he characterize them as unfounded in his report to his superiors.

'While Nkrumah apparently continues to have personal affection for me,' he noted, 'he seems as convinced as ever that the US is out to get him. From what he said about assassination attempts in March, it appears he still suspects US involvement.'

Of course, the U.S. was out to get him. Moreover, Nkrumah was keenly aware of a recent African precedent that made the notion of a U.S.-organized or sanctioned assassination plot plausible – namely, the fate of the Congo and its first prime minister, his friend Patrice Lumumba.

Nkrumah believed that the destabilization of the Congolese government in 1960 and Lumumba's assassination in 1961 were the work of the 'Invisible Government of the U.S.,' as he wrote in *Neocolonialism: The Last Stage of Imperialism*, later in 1965.

When Lumumba's murder was announced, Nkrumah told students at the inauguration of an ideological institute that bore his name that this brutal murder should teach them the diabolical depths of degradation to which these twin-monsters of imperialism and colonialism can descend.

In his conclusion, Mahoney observed: 'Nkrumah gave me the impression of being a badly frightened man. His emotional resources seem be running out. As pressures increase, we may expect more hysterical outbursts, many directed against US.'

It was not necessary to add that he was helping to apply the pressure, nor that any hysterical outbursts by Nkrumah played into the West's projection of him as an unstable dictator, thus justifying his removal.

193

Smoking Gun

On May 27, 1965, Robert W. Komer, a National Security Council staffer, briefed his boss, McGeorge Bundy, President Johnson's special assistant for national security affairs, on the anti-Nkrumah campaign (Document 253).

Komer, who first joined the White House as a member of President Kennedy's NSC staff, had worked as a CIA analyst for 15 years. In 1967, Johnson tapped him to head his hearts-and-minds pacification program in Vietnam.

Komer's report establishes that the effort was not only interagency, sanctioned by the White House and supervised by the State Department and CIA, but also intergovernmental, being supported by America's Western allies.

'FYI,' he advised, 'we may have a pro-Western coup in Ghana soon. Certain key military and police figures have been planning one for some time, and Ghana's deteriorating economic condition may provide the spark.'

'The plotters are keeping us briefed,' he noted, 'and the State Department thinks we're more on the inside than the British. While we're not directly involved (I'm told), we and other Western countries (including France) have been helping to set up the situation by ignoring Nkrumah's pleas for economic aid. All in all, it looks good.'

Komer's reference to not being told if the U.S. was directly involved in the coup plot is revealing and quite likely a wry nod to his CIA past.

Among the most deeply ingrained aspects of intelligence tradecraft and culture is plausible deniability, the habit of mind and practice designed to insulate the U.S., and particularly the president, from responsibility for particularly sensitive covert operations.

Komer would have known that orders such as the overthrow of Nkrumah would have been communicated in a deliberately vague, opaque, allusive, and indirect fashion, as Thomas Powers noted in *The Man Who Kept the Secrets: Richard Helms and the CIA.*

It would be unreasonable to argue that the U.S. was not directly involved when it created or exacerbated the conditions that favored a coup, and did so for the express purpose of bringing one about.

Truth and Consequences

As it turned out, the coup did not occur for another nine months. After it did, Komer, now acting special assistant for national security affairs, wrote a congratulatory assessment to the President on March 12, 1966 (Document 260). His assessment of Nkrumah and his successors was telling.

'The coup in Ghana,' he crowed, 'is another example of a fortuitous windfall. Nkrumah was doing more to undermine our interests than any other black African. In reaction to his strongly pro-Communist leanings, the new military regime is almost pathetically pro-Western.'

In this, Komer and Nkrumah were in agreement. 'Where the more subtle methods of economic pressure and political subversion have failed to achieve the desired result,' Nkrumah wrote from exile in Guinea three years later, 'there has been resort to violence in order to promote a change of regime and prepare the way for the establishment of a puppet government.'"[35]

Although he was overthrown, his influence and continental stature did not diminish. His ideas continued to have a major impact on political discourse on the future of Africa. And his advocacy of industrialization including development of heavy industry won him followers in different parts of Africa, and for good reason.

There is empirical evidence showing that heavy

industry has given countries a quantum leap over others towards economic development and independence. It is true, as the advocates of the heavy-industry approach claim, that emphasis on capital goods production allows a greater rate of reinvestment and therefore fosters a rate of growth that is higher than a more balanced approach between heavy and light industry combined with agriculture.

Moreover, without their own industries, especially heavy industry, African countries can not develop the other sectors of their economies, especially raw materials on which they heavily depend and will continue to be economic plantations for the West and the rest of the industrialized world including China which is destined to become another economic and military super power.

In addition to their underdeveloped status due to lack of manpower and industry, the young African nations were handicapped by their dependence on foreign aid soon after they won independence. And their demand that aid should be channelled through international agencies to avoid strings did not make much sense. All those agencies were and still are dominated by the very same countries, mainly Western, which offered aid. That was one of the harsh realities of nationhood Africans faced when their countries won independence.

Their demand made little sense for another reason. Only about 10 per cent of economic aid was funnelled through multilateral institutions, a negligible amount. The bulk of it came directly from the donor countries themselves. And they called the tune. The only alternative was to reject aid as Tanzania did in 1964 when West Germany tried to dictate policy to her over East German diplomatic representation on Tanzanian soil. Otherwise donor countries have the final say.

But even Tanzania itself was still heavily dependent on foreign aid from other countries besides West Germany, as were all the other newly independent countries on the continent. As Adebayo Adedeji, the Nigerian economist who served as executive secretary of the UN Economic Commission for Africa (ECA) stated:

"We entered the international economy at a time when, in spite of the rhetoric, the rich countries were not as selfless as they pretended to be. Even in the 1960s and early 1970s, when aid was generous, it was usually tied, and because it was tied, it tended to distort the priorities of developing countries and delayed the implementation process.

The donor countries and institutions have the last word, rather than the (African) governments themselves, such as in the recent controversy between the IMF and Tanzania (in 1983). I think, in the final analysis, that the IMF won. This is the grueling reality of poverty. When you are poor, you can never be right. It is the rich country that is right, because it is the only one that can help you out."[36]

As African countries were contending with poverty and tackling the formidable task of economic development without sufficient capital and skills, they also had to deal with political and military conflicts which erupted in different parts of the continent during the sixties. Some of those conflicts were within the countries themselves. A look at some of the important milestones illustrates this point.

The year 1960, probably the most important milestone on the road towards African independence, saw not only the emergence in a single year of the largest number of African countries from colonial rule; it was also a turning point in the history of the Portuguese African colonies, the oldest on the continent.

African nationalists in those colonies, seeing the victory of fellow Africans who had just won their freedom,

197

also felt that their time had come although, as events turned out, they were years off the mark. But they nonetheless drew great inspiration from their brethren who had just won independence in 1960 and thereafter in different parts of the continent.

In 1961, bloody uprisings erupted in Angola, the largest and richest of the Portuguese colonies on the continent. Guerrilla warfare had officially begun.

It was also in the same year, 1961, that Tanganyika became independent, the first country in the region close to southern Africa to win independence.

Soon after independence, Tanganyika became a haven for refugees and training ground for freedom fighters from the white-ruled territories in southern Africa, the bastion of white minority rule on the continent.

When the Organization of African Unity (OAU) was formed in Addis Ababa, Ethiopia, in May 1963, it chose Tanganyika to be the headquarters of all the African liberation movements under the auspices of the OAU Liberation Committee which was also based in the capital Dar es Salaam.

1962 was another important milestone in the history of African liberation when Algeria won independence from France after waging the bloodiest war on the continent which lasted for seven years at a cost of one million Algerian lives.

In 1963, African freedom fighters succeeded in seizing control of parts of Portuguese Guinea, now Guinea Bissau, in West Africa in what came to be one of the most successful wars in the history of African liberation. The war went on for ten years.

The year 1963 also turned out to be an important milestone in another respect in the history of African independence. That was the year in which President Sylvanus Olympio of Togo was assassinated in the first military coup in black Africa.

The assassination of President Olympio started a trend

of assassinations and military coups in Africa, as did Lumumba's in the Congo although in a somewhat different context since the Congo crisis was engineered by Western political and financial interests and turned the country into a theatre of rivalry between the East and the West during the Cold War.

Olympio's assassination showed not only how vulnerable African leaders were but also how precarious the existing order was, and how dangerous a recourse to violence could become to the continued stability of the modern African state.

The early sixties also witnessed some of the most successful campaigns against ethnic centres of power and traditional rulers who were reluctant to submit to central authority.

In Ghana, President Nkrumah subdued the Ewe, members of an ethnic group who live on both sides of the border between Ghana and Togo. He also neutralized the power of the Ashanti kingdom in central Ghana and other traditional centres of power in the northern part of the country to maintain national unity under a unitary state.

In Uganda, Dr. Obote achieved the same goal in the kingdoms of Buganda, Bunyoro and Ankole and in the princedom of Busoga. And in Zambia, Dr. Kaunda was also able to contain separatist tendencies in Barotse Province, also known as Barotseland, in the west, and among the Tonga and Ilunga ethnic groups in the south which supported their native son, opposition leader Harry Nkumbula of the African National Congress (ANC).

In both Rwanda and Burundi, the Hutu and the Tutsi were virtually in a state of war all the way through the sixties. The tension between them even erupted into open warfare now and then through the decade costing thousands of lives.

Other conflicts on the continent had also been going on for years. Besides the Algerian war of independence which started in 1954, there was also the Sudanese civil war which began in 1955, a racial and religious conflict between predominantly Christian blacks in the south and Muslim Arabs in the north. Fighting between the two sides went on throughout the sixties.

And the conflict in the Congo which had been internationalized by the intervention of outside powers went on until 1965. About 100,000 Congolese died in the conflict. It was one of the bloodiest in post-colonial Africa up to that time.

The bloodiest conflict in the sixties besides the Algerian war of independence was the Nigerian civil war.

At least one million people died; some estimates go up to two million. Most of those who died were Igbos in the secessionist Eastern Region of Biafra. A very large number of them were killed by Nigerian federal troops during the war itself. But the majority died from starvation which the federal military government deliberately used as a weapon to starve the secessionists into submission. It amounted to a policy of genocide. Federal Nigerian leaders, especially Obafemi Awolowo and Anthony Enahoro, explicitly stated that starvation was an instrument of war.

There were also, during the sixties, tensions and border conflicts between Kenya and Somalia, Ethiopia and Somalia, Ethiopia and Sudan, Chad and Sudan, and between Chad and Libya; tensions between Malawi and Tanzania over political differences and Malawi's claims to parts of Tanzanian territory; territorial disputes between Malawi and Zambia arising from Malawi's claim to Zambia's entire Eastern Province; disputes between Rwanda and Burundi, Gabon and Congo-Brazzaville, and Congo with her neighbours when Tshombe briefly served as prime minister.

Tensions in varying degrees also strained relations and led to conflict in some cases between Morocco and Algeria, Morocco and Mauritania, and between Egypt and Sudan. But the only conflict of a military nature was between Algeria and Morocco when Morocco invaded

Algeria and tried to annex some territory along the border between the two countries.

Political differences between Ghana and Nigeria also led to strained relations between the two countries because of Nkrumah's Pan-African militancy which led to the denunciation of the Ghanaian leader – and of Nasser – as power-hungry politicians who wanted to dominate Africa. As Ali Mazrui states:

"Nkrumah and Nasser were sometimes regarded as rivals for leadership in Africa. This, at any rate, was the assessment of the *West African Pilot* of Nigeria in one of its attacks against Nkrumah.

On the question of leadership in Africa, the newspaper taunted Nkrumah in the following terms: 'Until recently it was a tournament between Nasser and Nkrumah but Africa today contains many stars and meteorites, all of them seeking positions of eminence.'"[37]

The taunt was published in *The West African Pilot* edition of 18 May 1961. A similar jab at Nkrumah was published in an edition of *West Africa* on 6 May 1961. Yet, in spite of the hostility to Dr. Nkrumah by the Nigerian leadership, many younger Nigerians highly admired him:

"A strong, radically nationalist trend has existed within at least the younger generation of Nigerians.

Following the 1962 Commonwealth Prime Ministers' Conference speculation in Britain started as to why the Nigerian Government, with all its pragmatism, rejected out of hand a proposal for associate membership in the EEC (European Economic Community). Walter Schwartz, speaking on the European Service of the British Broadcasting Corporation (BBC) in October 1962, suggested that 'Nigeria's Government, always open to attack from its own youth for being too lukewarm about its nationalism, simply finds it politically impossible to lag behind Ghana on this issue.'

Visiting newsmen to Nigeria once discovered at a special meeting with young Nigerians at Nsukka that most of the youth were strongly in favour of Nkrumah's brand of militant African nationalism, without by any means necessarily coupling it with hero-worship for Nkrumah. One reference to this meeting appeared in the *The New York Times*, 3 March 1962."[38]

In addition to the tense relations between Dr. Nkrumah and the Nigerian leadership, there were also territorial disputes between Ghana and Togo; political conflicts between Ghana and the West African French-speaking countries all of which, with the exception of Guinea under Sekou Toure and Mali under Modibo Keita who were also Nkrumah's ideological compatriots, accused Nkrumah of trying to overthrow them. Nkrumah denied the charge and even wrote a "letter to President Hamani Diori of Niger denying any link with the attempt to assassinate Diori."[39]

But there is no question that Nkrumah scornfully described all the former French African colonies as "client states" of the former colonial power and of the West in general. The only exceptions were Guinea and Mali which he believed were genuinely independent and pursued uncompromising Pan-Africanist policies.

And some opponents of the Francophile regimes in West Africa, for example in neighbouring Ivory Coast, found sanctuary in Ghana where Nkrumah was sympathetic to their cause. And he helped them try to undermine those regimes which themselves were highly critical of Nkrumah and his policies including his pursuit of socialism; he also interfered in East Africa to thwart attempts to form an East African federation, although that is not why the federation was not formed.

In Francophone Africa, the Ivory Coast under

Houphouet-Boigny was Nkrumah's biggest challenge in the economic arena and also his biggest political adversary.

Senegal and the Ivory Coast also denounced Guinean leader Sekou Toure for his "subversive' activities against their governments. Sekou Toure returned the charge and was vindicated a few years later when the people who invaded Guinea in 1970 in an attempt to overthrow his government included citizens of Senegal and the Ivory Coast. Both countries harboured Guinean dissidents and attempts to topple Sekou Toure dated back to the sixties. Both, Senegal and the Ivory Coast, were deeply implicated in the plot. According to *Africa Contemporary Record*:

"Relations between the two countries (Guinea and Senegal) had deteriorated abruptly after a plot in 1966 to overthrow President Sekou Toure, in which he suspected Senegal of being implicated. The Ivory Coast was also accused of complicity in the plot; but signs of possible *detente* with President Houphouet-Boigny in late 1967 did not lead to any concrete improvement in relations during 1968."[40]

There were also, during the early sixties, tensions between moderates – the Brazzaville and Monrovia Groups – and radicals of the Casablanca Group over the Congo crisis, the Algerian war of independence, and over ideological differences. But after the Organization of African Unity (OAU) was formed in 1963, the Casablanca Group disbanded. The Monrovia Group followed suit.

However, the Brazzaville Group of Francophone countries refused to disband and said it would eventually fuse with the OAU. And tense relations between the moderate states (which included conservative states such as the Ivory Coast and Malawi) and the militant states continued within the OAU. Outside powers skillfully exploited those differences.

But it was the Congo crisis which thrust Africa into the international spotlight and attracted the largest number of outsiders into African affairs.

It was also the Congo crisis which proved to be the most frustrating without the slightest hope of ever being resolved by the Africans themselves; unlike the Rhodesian crisis and the Nigerian civil war both of which drew direct involvement of the independent African countries leading to some positive results strictly from African initiatives.

The Congo crisis was also an exasperating experience for the African countries which showed greater interest in it than others on the continent because their assistance was squandered, and their political input largely ignored, by the very same groups they were trying to help and which claimed to embody the ideals of the country's independence hero Patrice Lumumba.

The Congolese groups also fostered and thrived on one of Africa's worst nightmares: tribalism. And the Congo crisis itself ended up being the worst nightmare for Africa's most progressive states – Algeria, Egypt, Ghana, Guinea, Mali, Tanzania and Uganda – which, after Lumumba's assassination, tried to turn back the tide more than any other African countries which were less involved or did not want to get involved in the crisis.

Probably more than anything else, the Congo crisis demonstrated the weakness and fragility of the modern African state not only against external forces but also against its own internal weaknesses. As Nyerere stated in his speech to the Second Pan-African Seminar in Dar es Salaam, Tanganyika, in August 1961, about four months before he led Tanganyika to independence from Britain:

"There were obvious weaknesses in the Congo situation, but those weaknesses were deliberately used in a scramble for the control of the Congo.

There are obvious weaknesses on the African

continent. We have artificial 'nations' carved out at the Berlin Conference; we are struggling to build these nations into stable units of human society. And these weaknesses, too, are being exploited.

We are being reminded daily of these weaknesses. We are told tribalism will not allow us to build nations. But when we try to take measures to deal with tribalism, we are accused of dictatorship. Whenever we try to talk in terms of larger units on the African continent, we are told that it can't be done; we are told that the units we would so create would be 'artificial.' As if they could be any more artificial than the 'national' units on which we are now building!....Many (people) are deliberately emphasizing the difficulties on our continent for the express purpose of maintaining them and sabotaging any move to unite Africa....

So I believe that the second scramble for Africa has begun in real earnest. And it is going to be a much more dangerous scramble than the first one."[41]

That is what happened in the Congo. One of Africa's biggest and richest countries became a prime target for the big powers right in the heart of the continent. They wreaked havoc at will and the Congo crisis became a test case for Africa. It showed in a very painful and humiliating way how weak Africa was, unable not only to impose peace on herself but to resist foreign intrusion into the continent.

Even collectively, African countries were impotent against external intervention by outside powers from both sides of the iron curtain during the Cold War. And they failed to redeem the honour of Africa in the Congo because of their weakness.

Not long after that, African countries were again humiliated during the Rhodesian crisis when they failed to intervene and oust the white minority regime which had unilaterally declared independence against the wishes of the African majority in Rhodesia and in defiance of the rest of the Africans across the continent who, together with the black majority in that British colony, demanded independence on the basis of majority rule.

The stubborn resistance of the white minority settlers in Rhodesia and their declaration of independence in November 1965 clearly showed that the independent African countries in the sixties were not in a position to help fellow Africans achieve their freedom in that British colonial outpost in spite of the successes they had in uprooting some of the last vestiges of imperial rule on the continent.

Thus, while the sixties was a decade of triumph over colonial rule, it was also a decade of trials and tribulations for Africans in a number of areas including internal conflicts, the worst of which was the Nigerian civil war. It was the bloodiest conflict on the African continent in that decade of independence.

And there are still many lessons to be learned from those years. Many of the problems African countries have faced through the years have their origin in the wrong policies African leaders have pursued since independence in the sixties.

Part II

Uganda

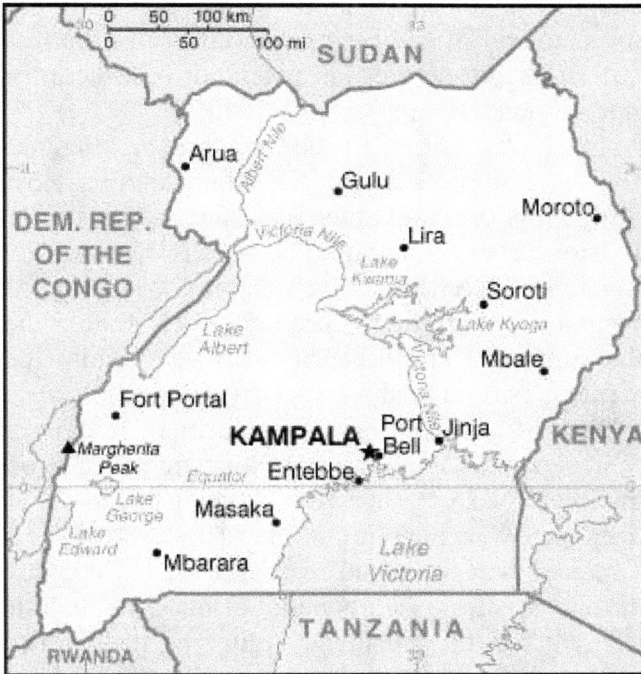

THE following part focuses on Uganda as a case study of an African country during the post-colonial era. Because of the similarities of political developments which have taken place in African countries since independence, it provides some insights into some of the problems other countries have faced and continue to face during the post-colonial period in their quest for political transformation and national development.

As a case study, it looks at the problems the country faced during its first years of independence including the constitutional crisis following the abolition of the kingdoms; the demand by the Buganda kingdom for federal status and its refusal to accept a unitary state; the ouster of Kabaka Mutesa II from the presidency and his subsequent exile to Britain; the paradoxical nature of the demand by Buganda kingdom for federal status under a unitary state and of having a hereditary ruler, Mutesa, the king of Buganda, serving as president of a country that was not under a monarchy.

It also looks at the difficulties in achieving national unity in a country divided by ethno-regional loyalties including kingdoms and other traditional centres of power; the division between Buganda and the rest of the country; the division between the north inhabited by Nilotic ethnic groups and the south that is predominantly Bantu; the role of the military and security forces, dominated by northerners, especially the Langi and the Acholi, in tilting the balance of power in favour of northern leaders during Obote's reign; the 1971 military coup in which President Milton Obote was overthrown and which led to the rise of Idi Amin to power; the reign of terror under Amin and how the centre of power shifted in favour of his people from the northwest; the 1980 general elections which led to Obote's return to the presidency, plunging the country into a civil war that came to be known as The Bush War; and the rise of Yoweri Museveni to power and his status as the longest-serving president in the country's post-colonial history.

The work addresses most of the major events which have taken place and which have affected the lives of most Ugandans since independence. For that reason alone, it

208

can serve a useful purpose as an introduction to the study of Uganda during some of its most turbulent years in the post-colonial era, while at the same time it helps to shed some light on some of the problems other African countries have faced and which they continue to face in the post-colonial era.

Part II

Uganda

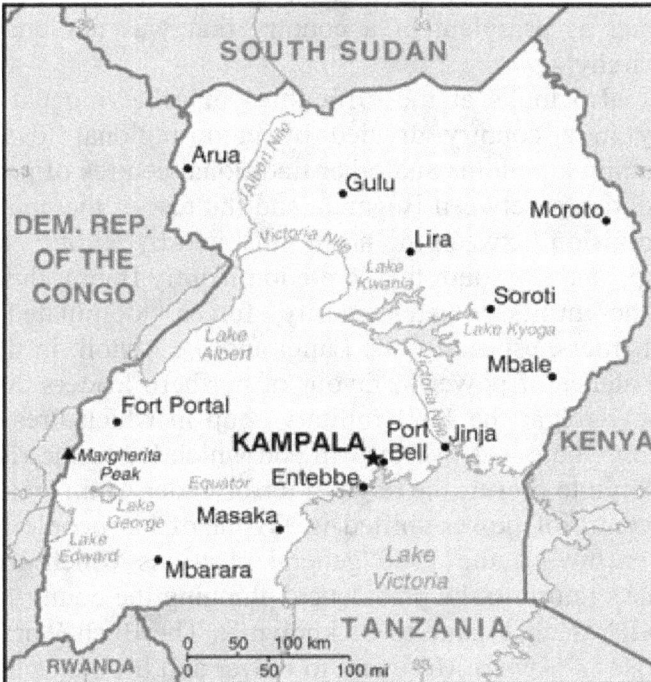

THE following part focuses on Uganda as a case study of an African country during the post-colonial era. Because of the similarities of political developments which have taken place in African countries since independence, it provides some insights into some of the problems other countries have faced and continue to face during the post-colonial period in their quest for political transformation and national development.

As a case study, it looks at the problems the country faced during its first years of independence including the constitutional crisis following the abolition of kingdoms; the demand by the Buganda kingdom for federal status and its refusal to accept a unitary state; the ouster of Kabaka Mutesa II from the presidency and his subsequent exile to Britain; the paradoxical nature of the demand by Buganda kingdom for federal status under a unitary state and of having a hereditary ruler, Mutesa, the king of Buganda, serving as president of a country that was not under a monarchy.

It also looks at the difficulties in achieving national unity in a country divided by ethno-regional loyalties including kingdoms and other traditional centres of power; the division between Buganda and the rest of the country; the division between the north inhabited by Nilotic ethnic groups and the south that is predominantly Bantu; the role of the military and security forces, dominated by northerners, especially the Langi and the Acholi, in tilting the balance of power in favour of northern leaders during Obote's reign; the 1971 military coup in which President Milton Obote was overthrown and which led to the rise of Idi Amin to power; the reign of terror under Amin and how the centre of power shifted in favour of his people from the northwest; the 1980 general elections which led to Obote's return to the presidency, plunging the country into a civil war that came to be known as The Bush War; and the rise of Yoweri Museveni to power and his status as the longest-serving president in the country's post-colonial history.

The work addresses most of the major events which have taken place and which have affected the lives of most Ugandans since independence. For that reason alone, it can serve a useful purpose an an introduction to the study of Uganda during some of its most turbulent years in the post-colonial era, while at the same time it helps to shed some light on some of the problems other African countries have faced and which they continue to face in the post-colonial era.

Chapter Four:

Uganda after Independence:
Obstacles to National Unity

AMONG the three East African countries of Kenya, Uganda, and Tanganyika which united with Zanzibar in 1964 to form Tanzania, Uganda faced the biggest threat to national unity soon after independence.

The threat came from the Buganda kingdom which did not want to be an integral part of Uganda. It wanted to reclaim its status as an independent kingdom which it enjoyed before colonial rule. It was forcibly united with the other kingdoms and traditional centres of power by the British to form Uganda.

Dissatisfaction among the Baganda, under their king known as *kabaka*, led to demands for independence for the kingdom. The demands amounted to secessionist threats. Their complaint was simple. They did not want to be an integral part of Uganda. They wanted to have their own country.

The secessionist threats were swiftly neutralised by

Uganda's first prime minister, Milton Obote, who led the country to independence. He was greatly resented by the Baganda because of his determination to assert control over their kingdom in order to maintain national unity at any cost.

Uganda was also faced with a strange paradox soon after independence. It involved the *kabaka*, king of the Buganda kingdom, a federalist at best and separatist at worst, serving as president of Uganda which was established as a unitary state.

It was Obote himself, leader of the Uganda People's Congress (UPC) and the country' first prime minister after independence, who was responsible for this situation out of political expediency.

He approached Kabaka Mutesa II to form an alliance between the Uganda People's Congress and the kabaka's party, Kabaka Yekka which was solidly Baganda in membership, in order to keep the Democratic Party led by Benedicto Kiwanuka out of power. The *kabaka* became the president of Uganda and Obote remained prime minister.

However, the office of president did not have any executive functions. Real power was in the hands of the prime minister who was the head of government and appointed cabinet members as well as other government officials including ambassadors.

But how could a king serve as the leader of a country that was not a monarchy? Buganda was a monarchy. But Uganda as a country was not. It was a unitary state. And how could someone who sought federal status for his kingdom with the rest of the country be president of a unitary state?

Obote himself resolved this contradiction shortly thereafter when he abolished all the kingdoms and expelled the king of Buganda from the presidency of Uganda to consolidate his position and lay a solid foundation for a highly centralised state.

But it was a solution that soured relations between the people of the Buganda kingdom and the national government for years until Yoweri Museveni became president of Uganda and restored all the kingdoms although only as cultural institutions without any political power.

Some people in Buganda wanted federation for Uganda instead of having a highly centralised state which almost had absolute control over the whole country because power was concentrated at the centre under the national government.

But this concession by some Baganda nationalists – who considered their kingdom to be a nation within a nation but who probably knew they would not succeed in seceding – was also rejected by the national leaders, especially Obote.

The national leaders felt that a federal form of government posed a threat to national unity in a country that was divided along ethnoregional lines with very strong traditional centres of power, especially the kingdoms of Buganda, Bunyoro, Ankole, Toro and the princedom of Busoga whose demands for autonomy could lead to demands for independence.

In fact, the first government formed at independence was no more than a coalition of these regional blocs and various interest groups, including religious ones – Protestant, Catholic and Islamic – which did not even have a common nationalist agenda besides a few leaders who advocated unity at the national level transcending ethnicity and regionalism.

All those divisions and rivalries persisted and became an enduring phenomenon in Ugandan national life years after independence only in varying degrees of intensity.

Compromises to form the first government at independence entailed inclusion – in the cabinet – of some of the leading politicians from the kingdoms and other parts of the country.

Prime Minister Obote came from the north. His stronghold was among his fellow tribesmen, the Langi (also known as Lango) in Lango District. He was also supported by their neighbours, the Acholi.

Mr. Grace Ibingira came from the Ankole kingdom and was also a member of parliament for Ankole West. He also served as justice minister and secretary-general of the ruling Uganda People's Congress (UPC) which drew its greatest strength and support from different parts of the country – especially in the north and in the west – outside Buganda where the dominant party was the Kabaka Yekka whose membership and leadership was almost exclusively Bugandan; while that of the Democratic Party led by Benedicto Kiwanuka, who also came from the Buganda kingdom, was predominantly Catholic.

It was also Grace Ibingira who designed Uganda's national flag.

Other prominent members in the first cabinet (1962 – 1971) who came from different parts of the country included Felix Onama from West Nile District – home of Idi Amin – in northwestern Uganda. He first served as interior minister and later as defence minister. As defence minister, both the military and the police were under his jurisdiction. He also once served as secretary-general of the ruling Uganda People's Congress (UPC).

Others included George Magezi from Bunyoro kingdom, Dr. Emmanuel Lumu, from Buganda kingdom, Cuthbert Obwangor from Iteso, Mathias Ngobi from Busoga, John Babiiha from Toro kingdom, John Lwamafa from Bukiga, Adoko Nekyon from Lango, Alex Ojera from Acholi, N. M. Patel, an Indian; J. T. Simpson, an Englishman; Sam Odaka from Musamia, John Kakonge from Bunyoro, Shaban Nkutu from Busoga, Joshua Wakholi from Bugisu, Lameck Lubowa from Buganda, Max Choudry from Karamoja, and others.

They also represented all the major religious groups in Uganda: Protestant, Catholic, and Muslim.

Yet the cabinet was not a monolithic whole. Its composition was deliberately structured to represent competing and even conflicting interests, local and regional as well as religious, without a single unifying ideology. Its members ranged from the most reactionary to the most revolutionary; from idealists and visionaries to realists and pragmatists; from liberals to conservatives; tribalists to nationalists and pan-Africanists, and so on.

The ruling Uganda People's Congress under Obote faced a formidable task of not only establishing a strong central government; it had to contend with ethnic and regional rivalries – especially among the traditional kingdoms – and instill a true sense of nationalism and patriotism in the people who did not consider themselves to be one. Other countries such as neighbouring Tanzania did not face those problems on the same scale Uganda did. As President Julius Nyerere stated at the annual conference of the Uganda People's Congress in Kampala, Uganda, in June 1968:

"When you consider that one of the really serious tasks facing political parties in Africa is the removal of of outmoded and useless institutions, and their replacement with modern institutions of government capable of producing the fruits of independence for the people of Africa, and bearing in mind the problems the UPC had inherited in this respect, I want to suggest quite seriously that the UPC faced a greater problem of institution transformation than any of her sister parties in Eastern Africa, and that therefore the UPC has been more successful than any of her sister parties of the Mulungushi Club – and certainly more successful than TANU."[1]

While some of the prominent politicians from the kingdoms sought to maintain the territorial integrity of Uganda even if under a highly decentralised federal structure, although they supported Obote in his

219

determination to build a unitary state, the Buganda kingdom sought secession. The kingdom tried to secede even before independence and wanted to attain sovereign status separate from the rest of Uganda.

But that was not the kind of political arrangement Ugandan leaders who led their country to independence wanted to have. They did not want any part of Uganda to secede. And they did not want the country to have a weak government. What was needed, according to Obote and other national leaders, was a strong central government which could keep the country together. As Professor Saadia Touval states in his book *The Boundary Politics of Independent Africa*:

"Uganda's unity has been threatened both before and after independence by separatist sentiments among the important Baganda people who possessed, until 1966, a measure of autonomy in their Buganda kingdom."[2]

Buganda threatened to secede in the fifties. And about two years before independence, it again threatened to secede. That was in 1960. Other kingdoms in Uganda also posed a threat to national unity, only in varying degrees.

Secessionist sentiments among the Banyoro of Bunyoro kingdom were partly fuelled by the Baganda who had territorial disputes with them. What are known as "the lost counties" were transferred from the Bunyoro kingdom to the Buganda kingdom by the British during the advent of colonial rule.

Also, the fact that Buganda was the most powerful kingdom in Uganda played a role in encouraging the Banyoro in their quest for greater autonomy and even for independence to avoid being dominated by the Baganda if they remained an integral part of Uganda. They believed that after independence, Uganda would be dominated by the Baganda who were also the most highly educated people in the country.

Their quest for autonomy was also compounded by nationalism among the Banyoro themselves who did not consider themselves to be a part of Uganda. As James Minahan states in his work, *Encyclopedia of The Stateless Nations: Ethnic and National Groups Around the World*:

"Ganda domination and the Lost Counties controversy initiated the growth of modern Nyoro nationalism.

The movement began as an anti-Ganda popular movement. The Nyoro also saw the British as their enemies, powerful protectors of their ancient rivals in Buganda.

In 1921 Nyoro nationalists formed a political group called Mubende-Bunyoro, which quickly became the kingdom's most popular political party; its demands included the return of the Lost Counties and secession from British Buganda. The British treated the kingdom as conquered territory until 1933, when the king (*omukama*) finally signed a protectorate agreement.

The territorial dispute between Bunyoro and Buganda acquired renewed importance when Britain prepared Uganda for independence. In 1961 the *omukama* refused to attend a constitutional conference until the British authorities resolved the conflict.

The Ganda refused to negotiate, setting off a serious crisis as Bunyoro moved toward secession and prepared for war.

British mediation produced an agreement to hold a plebiscite in the disputed area, finally allowing Uganda to achieve independence in 1962. The Kingdom of Bunyoro reluctantly agreed to accept autonomy and a semifederal status within Uganda.

In 1964 the inhabitants of the Lost Counties voted to return to Bunyoro. The conflict again became a crisis when the Ganda government refused to accept the results of the plebiscite.

Nyoro soldiers gathered in Hoima and prepared for

war, but the dispute quickly lost importance as even more serious threats menaced the kingdoms. The Ugandan government, dominated by non-Bantu northern tribes, instituted laws to curtail the kingdoms' autonomy. In 1966 the government abrogated the autonomy statutes and in 1967 abolished the kingdoms as administrative units."[3]

Minahan goes on to state:

"Nyoro nationalists enthusiastically supported the overthrow of the hated government (of President Milton Obote) in 1971 by a young army colonel, Idi Amin Dada.

Amin's new government, a brutal dictatorship dominated by Amin's small northern Muslim tribe, soon lost all support in Bunyoro. In 1972, Nyoro leaders, sickened by the excesses of the Amin regime, called for Bunyoro secession, but the movement lost momentum as Amin's henchmen systematically eliminated its leaders.

The infamous Amin regime, finally overthrown in 1979, gave way to a series of weak, unstable Ugandan governments. A large resistance movement arose among the southern Bantu peoples of the former kingdoms of the southwest, led by Yoweri Museveni, an ethnic Ankole. After years of bush warfare, Museveni took control of Uganda in 1986 and created the country's first Bantu-dominated government.

Relative peace and democracy permitted the rebirth of Nyoro nationalism, based on demands for the restoration of the kingdom. A more radical minority advocated the secession of Bunyoro from Uganda, arguing that the kingdom's inclusion in the multi-ethnic state had brought it only terror, death, and destruction.

In July 1993 the government allowed the partial restoration of the kingdom and the enthronement of a new Nyoro king, Solomon Iguru, a descendant of Kabarega and the 27th monarch of the Bito dynasty. In September 1993 nationalists demanded the restoration of the kingdom's traditional boundaries, including the Mubende area of Buganda, the Lost Counties.

The first national elections in 16 years were held in Uganda in April 1996. The majority of the Nyoros supported President Museveni, fearing the chaos and violence of the north of the country. The vote generally split along regional lines in Uganda, with the Bantu south supporting Museveni, while the Nilotic north supported opposition leaders.

For decades the Nyoros had been among the poorest of the peoples of Uganda, but in the 1990s they experienced a resurgence due to a new emphasis on cash-crop production by small-scale farmers. New prosperity and the partial restoration of the kingdom fueled demands for greater autonomy and for real political power for the new *omukama*.

Presently, the king is a cultural leader, with no political or administrative power, but under his patronage the Nyoros are striving to salvage and maintain their age-old culture and kingdom....

In May 2001, the kingdom government took control of two palaces, royal burial grounds, and other cultural sites in the region from the Ugandan government. The monarchy has begun to reunite the Nyoros, who have had no unifying symbol since 1967."[4]

Although the kingdom is politically powerless, there are probably many Nyoros who still would like to regain their glorious past when they lived as an independent people under their own leadership.

There is latent nationalism among many people not only in Bunyoro but in other traditional kingdoms as well, although the majority have, even if grudgingly, probably accepted their status as an integral part of the modern nation of Uganda. But a resurgence of nationalism – micro-nationalism, sub-nationalism or proto-nationalism – among them can not be entirely ruled out in the future on a

223

continent where ethnicity remains a potent force in national life.

Toro, an offshoot of Bunyoro, is another kingdom which has experienced nationalist awakening among its people through the years who consider their homeland to be a separate entity although the majority, as in all the other kingdoms, acknowledge that they are an integral part of Uganda. But there has always been an undercurrent of sub-nationalism among the Toro like in other traditional societies and jurisdictions which constituted viable entities once ruled by their own people as nations or micro-nations until the British came and united them to form a bigger country that came to be known as Uganda.

It was also the British colonial rulers who encouraged nationalist aspirations among the Toro although they at the same time wanted to maintain Uganda's territorial integrity for administrative purposes to facilitate colonisation:

"Encouraged by the British, who believed that Ugandan independence was still decades away, the kingdom became the focus of Toro nationalism and identity. In 1953 the Toro royal government demanded federal status and the extension of the Lutoro language to all the kingdom's schools, even in the non-Toro Ruwenzori district.

The issue of Toro nationalism intensified as independence for Uganda neared in the late 1950s. Toro nationalism grew in an effort to keep the revenues from the Kilembe Copper Mine for themselves, and over what they perceived as lesser treatment for their *omukama*. Activists demanded that the *omukama* of Toro be granted the same privileges as the *kabaka*, the king, of Buganda, Uganda's largest and most powerful kingdom."[5]

Inextricably linked with Toro aspirations for autonomy and even for independence if possible is the Rwenzururu secessionist movement in the Ruwenzori – or Rwenzori – mountains in southwestern Uganda on the border with the

Democratic Republic of Congo (DRC).

The Rwenzururu region is home to the Bakonjo and the Bamba, the dominant ethnic groups in the area who strongly resisted integration into the Toro kingdom by the British colonial rulers. As James Minahan states:

"The rapid growth of Toro nationalism parallelled the growing nationalism of the Konjo and Amba, in a reaction to increasing assimilation.

The two mountain peoples demanded separation from Toro and the creation of a separate Ruwenzori district within Uganda. The threat to the kingdom's territorial integrity raised Toro demands for recognition as an independent state before future relations with Uganda were regulated. On the eve of Ugandan independence the kingdom adopted a new constitution that ignored the Ruwenzori people's demands for official recognition of the kingdom's three peoples (Toro, Konjo, and Amba).

In 1962 the Toro accepted semifederal status within the newly independent Ugandan state. Toro nationalists, somewhat mollified by official recognition of the kingdom, blocked Konjo and Amba efforts to separate in a distinct district.

In early 1963 the mountain tribes rebelled, and on 13 February 1963 they declared independence as the Republic of Ruwenzuru, basing their claims to the entire Toro kingdom on historical possession and assertions that the Toro had migrated to the region from Bunyoro and should return to their original homeland.

Uganda's independence government, dominated by northerner Milton Obote, had little sympathy for the traditional Bantu monarchies in the southern districts. In 1967 the Obote government abolished the kingdoms as centers of local nationalism and separatism, and in 1970 the Ruwenzori rebels were finally defeated.

The Ugandan government (was) overthrown in a coup led by Idi Amin in 1971....Initial Toro support of Idi Amin

225

in the belief that he would restore the kingdom quickly disappeared. Princess Elizabeth of Toro formed part of Amin's administration, but she was later framed and dismissed.

Persecution of the Christians fueled a revival of Toro separatism as Amin excesses accelerated (Amin was a Muslim). A strong secessionist movement in Toro ended in 1972 with the murder or disappearance of the majority of Toro's leadership."[6]

Although Toro secessionist attempts were suppressed by Obote and later by Amin, there was no guarantee that they would not be rekindled in the future.

One of the main reasons for secessionist sentiments among many people in the different kingdoms was centralisation of power and dictatorial rule.

There was also, among southerners, opposition to domination of the national government by northerners, especially the Langi and the Acholi. Obote, a Nilotic not a Bantu, was a Langi. The army and security forces were also dominated by northerners. Obote himself had become unpopular in the south especially after he abolished the kingdoms, all of which were in southern Uganda.

After his ouster by Amin in 1971, he returned to power in 1980:

"In 1980 Obote again took control of Uganda but met with stiff resistance in the southern Bantu regions. A Bantu supported resistance movement, led by Yoweri Museveni, rallied the peoples of the former southern kingdoms. Obote's efforts to destroy the rebels led to a great... loss of life....

Museveni finally took control of devastated Uganda in 1986, forming the country's first government controlled by the southern Bantus.

The relative freedom (under Museveni), after two decades of terror and destruction, rekindled Toro

226

nationalism. The land issue, involving claims to territories taken from Toro during the colonial period and turned over to rival tribes, became the focus of the growing national movement.

In July 1993, with the Museveni government approval, the Toro kingdom was partially restored, and Patrick Olimi Kaboyo in 1995 was crowned as the twelfth king of Toro in Fort Portal. The monarchy became a cultural expression, without its former political and administrative powers.

The Konjo and Amba of Bundibugyo District initially refused to relinquish the former royal lands they had occupied, but in March 1994 senior members of the Ruwenzori movement acknowledged the new king, officially ending the conflict that had begun three decades before. The Ruwenzori rebellion resumed in the late 1990s.

The Ugandan government's emphasis on cash crop production in the 1980s and 1990s aided economic recovery. Devastated during the 1960s and 1970s by civil wars and brutal dictatorships, the Toros had slipped back to a premodern existence. The economic resurgence parallelled the cultural and political revival of the kingdom.

Rebel groups in the Ruwenzori Mountains mounted raids on Toro towns in the western districts in early 2000, disrupting the tourism and farming industries. The rebels, mostly based among the Ruwenzoris, sought to separate the mountainous west from the Toro. Reaction to the threat to split their ancient kingdom raised nationalist tension in the kingdom to levels not seen since the early 1960s.

Toro nationalism, led by the Protestant minority, at the turn of the twenty-first century was less separatist than federalist. Many saw the king and the traditional legislature as the logical extension of Ugandan federalism. A completely restored Toro within a Ugandan federation would safeguard the Toro culture and traditions, while federalism and regional autonomy would support the moderate nationalist demands against the more radical aims of the small militant minority.

Many Toros support nationalism on the belief that had the kingdom seceded in 1962 as a member state of the British Commonwealth, they would have escaped the devastation, ruin, and massacres of the Amin and Obote years.

Increasing violence between the Toros and migrants from other areas of western Uganda, particularly the Kigas, became a serious problem in 1997 – 98, and by early 2002 had destabilized many of the rural areas. Many people fled to the relative safety of the towns and cities."[7]

As we have just learned, there were other secessionist attempts in the southwestern part of the country, besides Toro, before and after independence in the sixties and in the following years.

In June 1962, just three months before Uganda won independence in October, the Bakonjo and the Bamba severed ties with the Toro and declared they were not a part of the Toro kingdom. They had their own identity and history, culture and customs. They also suffered oppression and discrimination under the Toro for years and demanded to have their own separate territory, the same demand they made in the fifties.

The British rejected their demand. The Bakonjo and the Bamba responded by launching guerrilla warfare.

It was low-intensity armed resistance and continued even after Uganda won independence. Their nationalist movement was named Rwenzururu. It was secessionist and wanted to establish a kingdom for the Bakonjo and the Bamba.

On 30 June 1963, the Bakonjo and Bamba nationalists declared independence and named their new country the kingdom of Rwenzururu. Isaya Mukirania became king.

But the kingdom did not last long and was brutally

suppressed by the Ugandan army. Toro soldiers in the army played a key role in neutralising the Bakonjo and Bamba secessionists.

However, the secessionists regrouped. They resurfaced years later and posed a great threat to national unity from 1979 to 1982. The government of President Obote reached an agreement with the secessionists. They agreed to abandon secession and accept autonomy for their region.

The odds against them were overwhelming. Unlike the Baganda, the Banyoro and the Ankole, the Bakonjo and the Bamba were not, even when combined, a very large community to be a viable entity had their demand for secession been accepted in order for them to establish an independent state. And there was, of course, the powerful machinery of the state – the central government – to suppress them.

But that did not dissuade them from pursuing their goal, an aspiration that is more common among larger groups. As Professor W. J. Argyle states in *Tradition & Transition in East Africa: Studies of the Tribal Element in the Modern Era*:

"It is, of course, true that size has usually influenced a group's chances of winning and maintaining independence, that ultimate test of nationhood, and it is also true that the most conspicuous attempts to seize independence have been made by large tribes like the Ibo, the Kongo, the Luba, the Lunda, the Ganda. Yet similar bids have been made by much smaller groups.

The Konjo and the Amba of Uganda cannot number more than about 150,000, but in 1962 some of them began a rebellion, followed by the declaration of an independent state and an appeal to U Thant for United Nations' protection against the forces of the Uganda government (Stacey, 1965, p. 81; and *infra*, p. 252ff.).

No doubt many of those who took part in this rebellion saw it merely as a chance to free themselves from the domination of the hated Toro. For its leader, Mukirane, and for his closest followers, it meant something more which would have been recognizable to European nationalists.

Its origin went back to a 'Bakonjo Life History Research Society' – partly inspired by an outsider, Mr Stacey – which Mukirane later turned into a political movement and renamed the 'Rwenzururu Secessionist Movement.'"[8]

He goes on to state:

"After the rebellion had begun, Mukirane set up a rudimentary administration in the mountains with himself self-proclaimed 'President' of the new state of Rwenzururu, which had its own national flag and anthem. A statement justifying the secession included many of the classical nationalist complaints and demands: too few schools and scholarships for Konjo and Amba children; hardly any Konjo or Amba teachers and priests; an unfair allocation of land and of the products derived from it; discrimination against Konjo and Amba in appointments to the bureaucracy.

Such pretensions on behalf of so small a people seem bizarre enough, and it is not surprising that Mr Stacey came, reluctantly, to the conclusion that Mukirane was mad.

Yet was he any madder than, say, the leaders of the Basque nationalists? There are only about three times as many Basques as there are Konjo and Amba,[7] but numbers did not prevent them from demanding and obtaining from the Spanish government in 1932 the same degree of local autonomy as had previously been given to the Catalans, a much larger group.

During the Civil War, Basques took the next step and set up the Republic of Euzkadi with a provisional government headed by a President (Thomas, 1965, pp. 81,

83, 370). The Republic was, of course, suppressed by General Franco's armies, but Basque nationalism and separatism still survive today, and Basques are still being imprisoned for advocating them. Nor are the Basques a unique case in Europe.

The populations of Albania and Esthonia were probably both under a million when they achieved national independence, and that was one argument which their larger neighbours used against their national aspirations. Unless we wish to identify ourselves with Russians, or Serbs, or Greeks or Italians, we surely have no reason to accept the argument. By the same token we cannot, on the grounds of size alone, deny the nationalism of many small groups all over Africa today.

In fact, it has already been implicitly conceded by a few authorities. Not long ago Post (1964, p. 67) pointed out that 'if a nation is conceived as having a common culture, language, and historical experience, as the eighteenth- and nineteenth-century European writers held, then the closest approximation to national sentiment in West Africa must be the 'tribalism' so often denounced by the nationalists.'

What I have done in this paper is to extend the scope of Post's generalization to cover other parts of Africa and to document it by apt illustrations."[9]

The nationalist aspirations of the Bakonjo and the Bamba, two small tribes or ethnic groups in the Ruwenzori mountains in southwestern Uganda, is one such apt illustration of the legitimate aspirations of an oppressed and neglected people using the language of nationalism – taken for granted by larger groups – to articulate their demands.

Their demands may have seemed unrealistic, given the overwhelming power of the state to crush rebellion and because of the small size of their stateless nation that had yet to be realised. But they were no less legitimate.

231

The Bakonjo and Bamba secessionists made another attempt to achieve their goal when they launched a rebellion under the banner of the National Army for the Liberation of Uganda (NALU) in the late eighties and early nineties when Museveni was president of Uganda.

The secessionists had a lot of support among their people. According to a survey conducted by Makerere University in 2008, 87 per cent of the people in Rwenzururu wanted to have their own kingdom. Museveni's government acceded to their demand and declared the Kingdom of Rwenzururu as a cultural institution – but without political power.

Charles Mumbere became the *omusinga* (king) of the Rwenzururu kingdom in October 2009. His authority is strictly social and cultural. Political power is in the hands of the national government. His father, Isaya Mukirane, was the leader of the secessionist movement which was mostly Bakonjo. He was acknowledged as the king of Rwenzururu and was killed when his son Charles Mumbere was only 13 years old.

But Museveni's government also stated that no such kingdom had existed in the past and there was no historical justification to the claim by the secessionists that they were reclaiming lost glory.

Ankole is another kingdom whose sub-nationalism was an obstacle to national unity through the years before and after independence.

One of the four kingdoms in the country, all in the south, Ankole first sought to maintain its status as a sovereign entity during colonial rule just the other kingdoms attempted to do. But it failed to do so and was forced to accept curtailment of its authority by the British colonial rulers.

Suppression of Ankole nationalism did not achieve its goal. Instead, it had unintended consequences. It fuelled nationalist sentiments and aspirations among the people of the kingdom.

Latent nationalism has always existed among the Ankole and the people of the other kingdoms even during the most brutal periods in Ugandan history. It could not be neutralised. And like all the other kingdoms, it has been profoundly affected by the changes which have taken place in Uganda through the years and was one of the first victims of centralisation of power soon after the country won independence from Britain in 1962.

Although the central government exercised control over the country, it also created instability because the kingdoms did not fully accept the new national rulers who had assumed power after independence. As Professor Edward Kannyo, a Ugandan, states in the *International Handbook of Human Rights*:

"The roots of political and social instability in Uganda lie in the fragmentation of the polity at the time of the attainment of political independence in 1962. This fragmentation is traceable to political, administrative, economic, and cultural processes which developed during the colonial regime.

Like virtually all the other African states, Uganda is a creation of the nineteenth-century European colonial expansion. It encloses dozens of cultural and linguistic groups which had previously lived independently of each other. Within the space of sixty years, they were arbitrarily brought under one politico-administrative system.

The colonial regime was a bureaucratic authoritarian system and did not provide for full-fledged political participation by the indigenous peoples at the national level. In Uganda, meaningful African political participation was restricted to local administrative levels which varied in size and form of government.

The kingdoms of Buganda, Bunyoro, Ankole, and Toro enjoyed higher degrees of administrative autonomy than the other parts of the colony. Among the kingdoms, Buganda stood out through its greater size, its greater administrative autonomy and, more particularly, its attachment to the '1900 Agreement' signed with the British government which provided for a higher degree of political autonomy and was regarded as a covenant by the Buganda government, and the resultant special consideration which the colonial regime always showed to the Buganda monarchy.[4]

The restriction of effective African political participation to local levels during the colonial regime was compounded by the uneven socioeconomic development of the country. Buganda took the lead in the development of modern education, commerce, and the cultivation and marketing of export cash crops.

The relative lag of the other parts of the country, compounded by the desire of important segments of the political elites in Buganda to seek independence outside the colonial territorial framework, as decolonization looked imminent, led to resentment on the part of political leaders from other areas which must on balance be considered as having been an obstacle to the evolution of strong national political leadership on the eve of political independence[5]."[10]

There were other factors which contributed to the fragmentation of the Ugandan polity and accentuated ethnic and regional differences and rivalries as well as social cleavages which continued after independence and impeded efforts to achieve genuine national integration. As Professor Kannyo goes on to state:

"Another major colonial legacy has been rivalry based on conflict between Protestant and Roman Catholic political elites.

This rivalry originated in the late nineteenth-century struggles between the French (Catholic) and English (Protestant) Christian missionaries, backed by their respective countries, for control of the kingdom of

Buganda, which became the nucleus and heart of the future Uganda. It was reinforced by the dominant role which the missionaries came to play in the provision of primary and secondary education for their followers.

When national political parties were formed in the 1950s, they came to reflect these religious rivalries. Thus, the Democratic Party (DP) was identified with Roman Catholic elites who sought to redress their discriminatory underrepresentation in national and local administrative bodies, while the Uganda People's Congress (UPC) was, though to a lesser degree than was the case with respect to the DP and Catholicism, identified with the Protestant elites who sought to preserve their overrepresentation.

In the period immediately before and after the attainment of political independence, the major claims articulated by the contending political parties and groups involved the institutional character of the postcolonial state, that is, unitarism vs. federalism and the closely related issue of the terms on which Buganda would be incorporated in an independent Uganda; the redress of socioeconomic inequalities between regions and districts; and the representation of different religious groups in elite political and administrative positions. The resultant pattern of politics was extremely complex.

Broadly speaking, in the period 1961 – 1966, politics revolved around the overlapping and yet conflictual relationships between (1) the two major political parties, the UPC and the DP; (2) the four kingdoms of Buganda, Bunyoro, Toro, and Ankole; (3) the district of Busoga, whose dominant elites wanted to convert it to a kingdom; and (4) the other districts of the country which did not have monarchical institutions and comprised the majority of the population of the country. The dominant elites in these various institutions competed for power and influence at certain times and over certain issues and collaborated at other times and over other issues. The same pattern applied within the institutions themselves.

The four kingdoms were united in their determination to preserve their monarchical institutions and a certain degree of political autonomy. However, in the period leading up to the political independence of the country, the leaders of Bunyoro, Toro, and Ankole would often join with the leaders from other political groups to oppose any attempts on the part of Buganda to secede from the country or to acquire any status which exceeded their own. In addition, Bunyoro had a direct quarrel with Buganda over some border territories which the British had transferred from Bunyoro to Buganda at the beginning of the colonial regime.

The elites in Busoga sought to convert their district into a monarchical unit and to emulate the institutions of the Buganda and Bunyoro kingdoms, with which the region shared important cultural and historical links. As for the rest of the districts in the country, the main goal was to maintain as much parity of status as possible with the kingdom areas.

It was against this complex background that the UPC and the DP competed for control of the postcolonial state. Both parties were united in their desire to preserve the inherited state in its colonial boundaries. In spite of some rhetorical ideological disputes within the UPC between 1964 and 1966, there were no serious class ideological differences between the two parties. The best one can say is that the UPC contained more people who espoused a more radical interpretation of African nationalism and who advocated a more neutralist foreign policy posture than the DP. However, these individuals were far from being dominant within the party.[6] Both parties were compelled to make compromises with the strong prevailing ethno-cultural sentiments.

The two most contentious issues which the political leaders faced at the time of independence were the degree of autonomy which would be enjoyed by the Kingdom of Buganda and the other kingdoms and the question of who would be head of state. The 1962 Independence Constitution provided for a complex political structure granting a high degree of regional autonomy for Buganda, lesser autonomy for the kingdoms of Bunyoro, Toro, and Ankole, and even lesser autonomy for the 'Territory' of Busoga. The rest of the country had a unitary relationship with the central government.

As had happened in other former British colonies, when Uganda became independent, the British monarch became the head of state and was represented in that ceremonial position by a governor-general who, in this as in other cases, was the last British governor. However, it was clear that this was a temporary arrangement and within a year, the question of who would replace the governor-general arose. This was an emotional issue for the various political groups. As George W. Kanyeihamba has recalled:

> While there was agreement on this change the problem was to find the right candidate. The kingdoms would not accept a commoner to occupy the important position of Head of State and thereby become, in importance, greater than their Kings. Buganda went further, no one even if he be King, could be Head of State unless he was the Kabaka [King] of Buganda Himself. The non-kingdoms districts were not silent either. Unused to the regions of Kings they would not accept one of them to be Head of their Independent State.[7]

A compromise solution was found. The head of state would be chosen from among the traditional rulers. However, in order to satisfy the nonkingdom areas, the position of 'constitutional head,' a type of surrogate king, was created for these districts. Any one of these leaders would be eligible for the position of head of state. The head of state was to be known as 'president.' There was also to be a vice president, and both offices were to be held for a term of five years and were to be elected by the National Assembly on a secret ballot.

The *Kabaka* of Buganda became the head of state and

the *Kyabazinga* (king) of Busoga – who was also the UPC vice president – became vice president of Uganda. To quote Kanyeihamba again: 'The Baganda were jubilant, the other Kings happy and the rest of the country satisfied for now there was a possibility that each region was in a position to become produce a President.[8]

It is almost certain that this solution would have failed eventually. The replacement of the *Kabaka* of Buganda as head of state, which would have been demanded to give a chance to another ruler, would have been strongly resisted in Buganda. Moreover, the creation of nontraditional 'king surrogates' outside the kingdom areas was not universally popular and had given rise to conflicts within some districts."[11]

A look at Uganda during its first years of independence in the sixties and in the following decades clearly shows that a number of factors have made it very difficult for the country to achieve unity the way, for example, neighbouring Tanzania has in spite of the fact that it has a very large number of tribes or ethnic groups: about 130.

Tanzania also has substantial numbers of Christians and Muslims – 33% to 35% for each – unlike Uganda which is predominantly Christian. Yet it has managed to avoid ethnic conflicts and rivalries in a way Uganda has not been able to. It has also achieved religious harmony between Christians and Muslims.

The British colonial government in Uganda played a major role in accentuating social cleavages and in fostering ethnic rivalries.

The Buganda kingdom which formed the nucleus of what was to become the country and nation of Uganda – it even gave the country its name, "Uganda" from "Buganda" – was favoured by colonial rulers over the other kingdoms. This kind of favouritism fuelled hostility towards Buganda among many people in the other kingdoms who felt that they were not considered to be as important as the Baganda.

It also laid the foundation for a future secessionist movement among the Baganda who felt they were entitled to rule the whole country after independence; if they could not, they would secede.

There was also a major dividing line between the north and the south. The British focused their attention on the southern part of Uganda in terms of development while virtually neglecting the north. The result was hostility between the two regions fuelled by economic inequalities.

The north remained underdeveloped. Educational opportunities were virtually non-existent in the region while the south had almost all the schools including institutions of higher learning such as Makerere University College founded in 1922.

Religious differences between Protestants – who were mostly Anglican – and Catholics in Uganda aggravated the situation when political competition also assumed a religious dimension, even though this problem was not as serious as ethnoregional rivalries. But it did play a role in impeding progress towards national unity especially when the members of the Democratic Party, which was predominantly Catholic and was led by Benedicto Kiwanuka who came from the Buganda kingdom, made a concerted effort to undermine Prime Minister Obote who was a Protestant and a northerner.

And as in almost all the other African countries, ethnic and regional loyalties have always played a major role in Ugandan politics, clearly demonstrated even during the first years of independence.

The ethnic and regional dimension in Ugandan life and politics was also partly a product of British colonial rule. While the south had the largest number of educated people, in fact one of the largest in East Africa if not the largest during that period, the north provided soldiers.

The largest number of soldiers and members of the security forces during colonial rule and after independence were northerners, mostly Acholi and Lango – or Langi. Obote himself was a Lango.

The imbalance persisted after independence. But it also greatly benefited Obote who, as a northerner, had solid support from the army and other security forces during his term in office until he was overthrown by Idi Amin, a fellow northerner although from the northwest, in January 1971.

But without the support of the army which was then under the leadership of Amin who had been promoted by Obote to that position, Obote may not have been able to survive in office. And he would not have been able to neutralise and oust the *kabaka*, Edward Frederick Mutesa, from the presidency even though the title was more ceremonial than functional; power was in the hands of the prime minister, Obote, during that period.

Although Uganda has survived as a nation, it has had to contend with various forces which could have torn the country apart, especially along ethnoregional lines because of the rivalries among the various ethnic and regional groups which have championed regionalism or micro-nationalism, seeing themselves as nations within a nation. As Professor Joshua Forrest states in his book, *Subnationalism in Africa: Ethnicity, Alliances, and Politics*:

"In Uganda, decades of subnationalist ferment, religious and political strife, and militarized autocracy created a context of intense instability that long preceded Museveni's installment as president.

During the colonial period, powerful ethnoregional leadership structures with direct precolonial roots were strengthened, while the British artificially created several smaller kingships.

The Buganda kingship, with solid links to its precolonial antecedent, was accorded unusual privileges and considerable autonomy.[22]

240

Immediately prior to Uganda's 1962 independence elections, the traditional Ganda leadership, fearful of losing their privileged position, declared that Buganda would secede from Uganda. However, constitutional negotiators enticed the Ganda to acquiesce by promising autonomy and special status for Buganda within a quasi-federal framework.

The western kingdoms of Bunyoro, Toro, and Ankole, along with the very small kingdom of Busoga, were granted nearly as wide a berth of autonomy, despite the fact that the Ankole and Toro kingdoms had been virtually invented by British administrators.[23]

The resultant political stability proved relatively short-lived. In the early 1960s, parliamentary maneuverings by a variety of opponents of Prime Minister Obote considerably weakened his political power. By 1966, the Ganda king Kabaka Mutesa II, who had been granted the largely titular but symbolically significant post of Ugandan president – Prime Minister Obote ran the country – formed a political alliance with parliamentarian backbenchers who opposed Obote's rule.

This proved a strategic error: Obote then preempted Mutesa, removing the king and his political allies from their government positions and subsequently deciding to rescind the formal autonomy that had been granted to the Buganda kingdom as well as to the aforementioned western kingdoms.[24] Buganda reacted by rejecting the authority of the Ugandan national government.

The ending of autonomous status for the kingships exacerbated the level of state-ethnic tension. Subnationalism in Buganda now became strengthened, as Ganda elites, bureaucrats, and ordinary people coalesced both politically and culturally. Territorial and ethnic assertion here converged with popular enmity toward Obote, so much so that Obote felt it unsafe to set foot inside Buganda.[25]

The Bugandan autonomy movement persisted through

241

the Idi Amin and second Obote regimes, serving a potent reminder of the fragility of the political basis on which the integrity of the Ugandan nation-state rested.[26],[12]

But Buganda was only a part of the problem, although the major part of it in terms of posing a real threat to national unity. However, other parts of the country had the potential to cause instability and even promote regional fragmentation. As Professor Forrest goes on to state:

"Meanwhile, long-term economic neglect helped to fuel the generation of separatist movements in the northern and western regions.
During the colonial as well as the postcolonial era, the largely rural northern and western regions remained mostly outside the state-centric development rubric.[27] Frank van Acker uses a district-by-district analysis of road-building and electrification projects to convincingly depict the long-term structural economic neglect of the north and west.[28]
Northern discontent stemming from economic inequity generated uprisings, protests, and demands for autonomy by northern and western region traditional leaders. In combination with Gandan subnationalism, this helped to ensure that Uganda would continue to spiral steadily toward internal fragmentation.
The inability of the Ugandan central government to grapple effectively with rural challenges was made especially clear by the rise of the Rwenzururu separatist movement, which sought autonomous rule based on traditional leadership structures for the Konjo and Amba peoples.
The Konjo and Amba were under the jurisdiction of the Toro kingdom, which was cooperating fully with the Ugandan state. The subnationalists aimed to free themselves of both the kingdom and the nation-state. Tensions led to battles in 1963 – 1964 between the Konjo

242

and the Amba on the one hand, and Toro and Ugandan army units on the other; the latter effectively suppressed the rebels.

However, the Rwenzururu movement reconsolidated over time, and in the wake of the power vacuum left by the collapse of Idi Amin's regime in 1979, it was again able to pose a serious subnationalist threat.[29]

The second Obote administration pursued negotiations with Rwenzururu leaders and reached a settlement in 1982 according to which Konjo and Amba elites agreed to abandon outright secession in return for 'a degree of autonomy'; the appointment of Konjo and Amba to administrative posts; and the provision of economic benefits, such as motorized vehicles, shops, and student scholarships, that would be assigned for distribution by the traditional leaders of these two groups.[30]

The Rwenzururu movement had forced the state to grant power and goods to traditional leaders for the sake of political stability.

In reaction to the monarchical restorations of the 1990s, the Rwenzururu movement was revived yet again, this time with its leaders insisting on separatism. De facto Konjo and Amba control over their claimed districts had already been achieved[31]"[13]

Ethno-regional loyalties and rivalries have always been a part of life in Uganda. That is one of the main reasons why subnationalism has equally been an enduring phenomenon in the country although in varying degrees, at different times.

But it is marginalisation of the groups and regions which have been kept on the periphery or which don't consider themselves to be a part of the mainstream which has really fostered this sentiment.

Had there been equality, meaningful participation in the political process and in the government as well as equitable redistribution of the nation's resources, for all the groups and regions, a lot of this clamour for separation, secession and greater regional autonomy to the detriment of national unity would not have been heard as loudly as it has been through the years.

Even after Yoweri Museveni seized power and tried to build a broad-based national movement to involve people and groups from all the regions of the country, there were still those who felt they were being ignored or deliberately excluded from the political process and other areas of national life because they challenged the president or dared to openly say there is no true democracy in Uganda except for Museveni and his supporters.

Dissatisfaction with the central government, lack of opportunities for members of some groups who feel they have been marginalised, curtailment of freedom, and the government's determination to concentrate power at the centre, have contributed to tensions in a country where many people, probably the majority, have not yet transcended ethnoregional loyalties for the sake of national unity.

Other factors such as lack of economic opportunities, regional disparities in education and income, sociocultural differences, tribalism and other forms of discrimination simply because you are different or you are not one of them, and mistrust of the national government regardless of who is in office, have all contributed to these tensions which have manifested themselves in different ways through the years but with the same tragic consequences: dividing the nation, pitting one group against another, and encouraging regional fragmentation. And as Forrest states:

"Recent tensions reflect the radicalization of monarchists who now insist on complete autonomy and fully independent powers for the Kabaka.

At the same time, a proliferation of new claimants to unrecognized kingships in the restive north and west, especially on the part of the Alur and the Teso, signal further instability, and Lango activists are calling for their own autonomous state.

Adding to this instability is the fact that two of the four officially restored kingships – Ankole and Toro – have now been effectively rendered moribund by the intensity of popular opposition to those kingships within their respective regions.[39]

In these ways, the monarchical reinstallments and the president's attempt to create a stable quasiconsociational political system both reflect and expose the very real limitations to state power and to the integrity of the nation-state.

Uganda's rural regions have repeatedly defied incorporation; they represent elusive redoubts within which the state vainly seeks to fasten its political girders, even when it does so by utilizing relatively loose mechanisms of government control."[14]

It is clear that Uganda faced serious problems in her attempts to achieve national unity soon after independence. One of the major problems was the quest for greater regional autonomy which would have greatly weakened the national government had this goal been achieved by the kingdoms of Buganda, Bunyoro, Toro, Ankole, and the princedom of Busoga which at different times had tried to elevate its status to become a kingdom like the rest.

But the biggest threat to national unity was secession. However, this phenomenon was not peculiar to Uganda. There were other African countries which were also threatened by secession.

In East Africa, Kenya also had to contend with separatist tendencies in the Coast Province whose inhabitants wanted to unite with Zanzibar because of the cultural and historical ties they had. The ties were forged during Arab rule among the people in the coastal regions of Kenya and Tanganyika and on the islands of Zanzibar

245

and Pemba. Like their Arab rulers, the people were also overwhelmingly Muslim, a unifying bond that transcended ethnicity and regional loyalties.

There have been other separatist demands in East Africa. The Somali of the North Eastern Province of Kenya, what was once known as the Northern Frontier District, and of the Ogaden region in Ethiopia have always wanted to unite with their kith-and-kin across the border in Somalia. Their brethren in Somalia have expressed the same desire to unite all Somalis who live in Greater Somalia. Greater Somalia is an area composed of Somalia itself, Djibouti, and the regions in neighbouring countries inhabited mostly by Somalis: the Ogaden in Ethiopia, and northeastern Kenya.

In Zambia also, there were secessionist threats among the Lozi of Barotse kingdom in the western part of the country which is the Western Province. There were also separatist tendencies in the Southern Province among the Tonga and the Ila who straddle Zambia's border with Zimbabwe and Mozambique.

In Congo-Leopoldville, there were strong secessionist tendencies among the Bakongo in the fifties. And after the country won independence, secessionist demands continued not only among the Bakongo but also among the members of other ethnic groups in all of the country's provinces. The strongest demands came from Katanga Province which seceded only 11 days after Congo won independence from Belgium on 30 June 1960.

Another province, South Kasai, seceded on 8 August 1960 and its leader, Albert Kalonji, declared himself king of the new country.

In the Ivory Coast, there was an uprising among the Sanwi in 1959 in their attempt to secede and establish an independent state under a monarchy.

The Tuareg of northern Mali refused to recognise the national government in Bamako and attempted to secede in 1963. Even before independence, they demanded independence for their region. They told the French colonial rulers Mali should be partitioned so that they can have their own country. They were ignored.

In April 2012, following a military coup in Bamako which caused disarray in the nation's capital, leaving a power vacuum, the Tuareg took advantage of the situation to achieve their goal. They seized the entire northern half of Mali and declared independence. They named their new country the Islamic Republic of Azawad. According to a BBC report, "Mali Tuareg Rebels Declare Independence in the North," 6 April 2012:

"A rebel group in northern Mali has declared independence for a region it calls Azawad, after seizing control of the area last week.

The National Movement for the Liberation of Azawad (MNLA) made the statement on its website, adding that it would respect other states' borders.

The MNLA is one of two rebel groups to have gained ground in the area after Mali's government was ousted in a coup.

The African Union has condemned the declaration as 'null and void.'

Former colonial power France and the European Union have also said they will not recognise Azawad's independence....

The army seized power on 22 March, accusing the elected government of not doing enough to halt the two rebel groups - the MNLA and an Islamist group opposed to independence, which wants to impose Islamic law, or Sharia, across the whole country.

'Brink of disaster'

The declaration comes as rights group Amnesty

International warned that Mali was on the brink of a major humanitarian disaster in the wake of the rebellion.

It demanded that aid agencies be given immediate access to the country after days of looting, abduction and chaos in the northern towns of Gao, Kidal and the historic city of Timbuktu, which have all been taken by the rebels.

On Thursday the MNLA rebels declared a 'unilateral' ceasefire after the UN Security Council called for an end to the fighting in Mali.

A statement posted on the rebel website on Friday proclaimed independence, adding it would respect existing borders with neighbouring states and adhere to the UN Charter. The statement also called for recognition from the international community.

'We completely accept the role and responsibility that behooves us to secure this territory. We have ended a very important fight, that of liberation... now the biggest task commences,' rebel spokesman Mossa Ag Attaher is quoted as saying by the AFP news agency.

The Tuareg people inhabit the Sahara Desert in northern Mali, as well as several neighbouring countries and have fought several rebellions over the years, complaining that they have been ignored by the authorities in distant Bamako. But the Tuareg are not the only people who live in the area they claim as Azawad.

Islamists and Tuareg

Journalist Martin Vogl in Bamako says there are two main interpretations for why the MNLA made its declaration now.

Firstly, he says it could be intended to forestall a possible intervention by the West African regional body, Ecowas and secondly to show that it, rather than the rival Ansar Dine group, is in charge of the north.

But he also points to problems with the proclamation, such as the absence of a referendum to prove a popular mandate, as well as reports that the Islamist rebels may control more areas than the MNLA.

Ecowas military chiefs met on Thursday in Ivory Coast. Afterwards, they said they had discussed a proposed force's rules of engagement and would await a response to their suggestions from the region's heads of state. A 2,000-strong force has been put on standby, while France has promised logistical support.

The MNLA was formed last year, partly by well-armed Tuareg fighters returning from Libya, where they had backed former leader Muammar Gaddafi.

But the UN has voiced alarm at the presence of Ansar Dine, which has links to an al-Qaeda franchise which operates in the region.

Correspondents say that Western powers are more concerned by a growing Islamist threat throughout the region than a Tuareg issue which is considered a political internal problem.

The MNLA could possibly expect greater autonomy rather than independence if it came back to negotiations and helped fight the Islamists, they say.

Mali has been in disarray ever since the 22 March coup enabled the rebels to secure territory in the north.

People are continuing to flee the area and buses to the capital have been packed with people desperate to get out. Reports say the situation in the northern town of Gao, in rebel hands, is particularly tense.

The Algerian government also says seven of its staff were kidnapped by unknown gunmen in Gao. The consul and six colleagues were forced to leave their diplomatic mission at gunpoint.

The Algerian government says it is doing all it can to find them.

Ecowas has closed Mali's borders to trade, frozen its access to funds at the central bank for the region's common currency and slapped travel bans on the coup leaders and their supporters.

The coup and Tuareg rebellion have exacerbated a humanitarian crisis in Mali and some neighbouring countries, with aid agencies warning that 13 million people need food aid following a drought in the region."[15]

Although Tuareg separatists came nowhere close to achieving their goal in the sixties and in the following decades, they remained a source of instability in Mali, especially in the north where they continued to campaign for autonomy and independence sometimes by violent means.

Ghana under Kwame Nkrumah also had to contend with separatist threats among the Ashanti in the central region. They posed the biggest threat to national unity.

The Ewe in the east also posed a threat. There was an irredentist movement among the Ewe in the Volta region seeking to unite the Ewe of Ghana and Togo who had been separated by the boundary between the two countries during colonial rule.

There were also separatist demands among the Dagomba and members of other ethnic groups in northern Ghana, a region that was once known as the Northern Territories.

Nkrumah effectively neutralised all those threats by establishing a highly efficient centralised state with power concentrated at the centre just as Obote did in Uganda, Jomo Kenyatta in Kenya and Kenneth Kaunda in Zambia although in varying degrees.

It was fear of the domino effect: once one region or province goes, the rest will go and become independent states. That is why many African leaders were very suspicious of those who demanded regional autonomy. They feared such devolution of power to the regions or provinces could eventually fuel demands for secession and even lead to secession in some cases. And as Touval states:

"The ethnic composition of the African states has been an important influence in shaping governmental attitudes and policies on boundaries. Boundaries may be likened to the external shell of the state. Since the majority of African states have not yet attained internal cohesion, it is in their interest to preserve this shell intact.

In many cases, the maintenance of the status quo has come to be associated with the self-preservation of the state. It was feared that, were the right to secede granted to any group or region, such a grant could stimulate secessionist demands from additional regions or groups, and thus threaten the disintegration of the state. The danger of such disintegration has been vividly exemplified by the secessionist movements that have sprung in several states....

The interest of states in preserving the status quo is reflected also in the qualms many states have shown about annexing regions or tribes from neighboring states."[16]

The only leader in Ugandan post-colonial history who attempted to claim some land from neighbouring countries was Idi Amin who, in October 1978, annexed about 700 square miles of Tanzanian territory in Kagera Region in the northwest bordering Uganda. Tanzania fought back and drove out Amin's occupying forces. Amin also claimed parts of western Kenya and southern Sudan without success.

Most African leaders, including Ugandan, want to maintain the borders inherited at independence.

The problems most African countries face are internal, not external. One of them is ethnic and regional rivalries. Uganda is one of the countries on the continent which have had to contend with this problem since independence. And it has not been fully resolved as different groups continue to demand autonomy for their regions from national leaders who are determined to maintain a highly centralised state as the best guarantee for national unity.

251

Most African leaders articulate the same position on a continent where they fear their countries can easily disintegrate along ethnoregional lines if extensive devolution of power to the regions is allowed in order to defuse tensions and resolve ethnic and regional rivalries.

That is why decades after independence in the sixties, most African countries have not adopted a federal form of government which would have enabled regions or provinces to have autonomy, reducing the power at the centre over the rest of the country. They have remained highly centralised states with no prospect for devolution of power to the regions.

Chapter Five:

Post-colonial Uganda:
National consolidation

UGANDA has gone through major changes since independence in the sixties. They have mostly been violent.

The first one involved the removal of Kabaka Mutesa II in February 1966 when his palace on Mengo Hill in Kampala was attacked by soldiers led by Idi Amin. It was alleged that Kabaka Mutesa had ordered some weapons and that the weapons were being kept in the palace.

The Kabaka himself conceded in his book, *Desecration of My Kingdom*, that he did indeed seek weapons from Britain as president of Uganda but the British government turned down his request.

What were the weapons for? Even the prime minister, Milton Obote, asked him that question. And he had no authority to order the weapons because his title, as president, was only ceremonial. Real power was in the hands of the prime minister who was the head of the government. Kabaka Mutesa was not an executive president.

Obote denied ordering the attack on Mengo Hill and implied Amin exceeded his authority when he used violence during the siege of the palace. As he stated in an interview with Ugandan journalist, Andrew Mwenda, which was published as part of a series in the *Daily Monitor*, Kampala, Uganda, in April 2005 a few months before before he died in October the same year:

"I did not order an attack on Lubiri in 1966.

On February 9th, Muteesa called the British High Commissioner and asked for massive military assistance. When I asked Muteesa why, he said it was a precaution against trouble. I asked him, 'Trouble from whom and against whom?' He just waved me to silence.

Although he was president, head of state and commander in chief of the armed forces, Muteesa did not have powers to order for arms.

Later, I sought the advice of my Attorney General, Godfrey Binaisa QC. He told me that given what Muteesa had done, I had to suspend him from being president of Uganda; the only way I could was to suspend the constitution itself....

Regarding the attack on the Lubiri, I regret it only in as far as I was the head of government. I had nothing to do with it.

I was having a luncheon at Kampala Lodge with Bulasio Kavuma, Badru Kakungulu and Elidad Muwonge of Bugerere when we heard at about two o'clock, a bomb at Lubiri.

We later found out that it was Idi Amin's soldiers who were bombing Lubiri. I called for Amin, he came and we discussed it.

Amin tried to justify his action saying that the men who were in the Lubiri wanted to overthrow the government, wanted to overpower the army. I did not accept that one. I ordered him to return the troops to the barracks, which he did.

By this time, the battle of Mengo was over, although many authors have said the battle went on into the night. Unfortunately Mutesa was my friend."[1]

If Obote did not order the attack on the palace (Lubiri), who did? Since it was supposed to be a matter of national security, was it his first cousin, Akena Adoko, head of the intelligence service – General Service Unit (GSU) – who was also the second most powerful man in Uganda after Obote himself, who ordered the attack? Or was it Amin, on his own, who decided to use violence? He was the commander of the army.

The General Service Unit was founded by Obote's government. Obote also had a paramilitary force, the Special Force Units. Most of the members of this private army came from his tribe and home region. They were mostly Langi (Lango). The Special Forces Units worked closely with the army and the police.

In his book, *Desecration of My Kingdom*, Kabaka Mutesa II contends that it was Obote who ordered the attack on the palace:

"It was not yet dawn – about 5:30 in the morning – when I was awakened suddenly by the sound of gunfire: quite near, I reckoned, certainly inside the wall that surrounds my palace and grounds....

Troops from the Uganda Army were attacking my palace on the orders of the Prime Minister, Dr. Obote. So much was clear. Nor should it have been in the least surprising. We had been suspecting such a move for weeks, and I myself had been surprised when nothing happened the previous evening. Yet I was filled with a sense of outrage now that it was happening....

Many people from the city, Kampala, and the villages had come up and waited round the palace the previous day,

255

not from knowledge of imminent disaster, but instinctively, uncertain whether they were giving or receiving protection....

There seemed to be an endless follow-up supply of enemy soldiers, many of whom were occupied with destroying my rooms. I think they believed their own stories about hidden supplies of arms, and even indulged in fanciful ideas that a king must have hoards of treasure buried beneath his palace....

Once I was overwhelmed with emotion, and foolishly returned to the palace garden alone. There I selected a looter and shot him out of honest rage. I felt calmer and somewhat uplifted as I made my way back."[2]

The attack on Mengo was one of the most tragic incidents in Uganda's post-colonial history. It had far-reaching consequences which reverberated through the years.

There were some casualties. But there is a dispute on the number of people who were killed. Some reports say about 1,000 people were killed. They were mostly civilians. Kabaka Mutesa escaped and fled to Britain where he died in London three years later when he was 45 years old.

The most violent phase the country went through involved Amin during his eight-year reign of terror after he seized power from Obote in a military coup in January 1971. His rise to power was the most dramatic development in the country's history up to that time. It had tragic consequences for Uganda and beyond and the country has not yet fully recovered from his brutal reign.

There have been other changes, including constitutional, such as the abolition of kingdoms in 1967 and their restoration in 1993 by President Yoweri Museveni although only as cultural institutions without any political power as in the past. But the biggest changes have involved transfer of power from one government or regime to another.

Also, when Obote returned to power in 1982, his resumption of office had serious implications and tragic consequences for the country.

Another major change came in 1986 when Museveni took over the country after waging guerrilla warfare against the government. He won the war and the country entered another phase.

Uganda has witnesses some of the worst excesses of African leadership in its 50 years of independence. It has yet to see the best its leaders have to offer.

Like other African countries, its history during the post-colonial era is one of broken promises and unfulfilled hopes. It is also one of horrendous tragedies, mostly a product of state-sponsored terror.

When the country won independence from Britain in October 1962, it had all the attributes of a potentially successful nation including a significant number of highly educated people, although they were mostly Baganda from the Buganda kingdom. But they were still Ugandans destined to play a major role in the development of their country.

The British also left an infrastructure which facilitated economic growth after independence, although the infrastructure was skewed in favour of the southern part of the country.

But it was Obote's government which laid the foundation of modern Uganda during the first few years of independence until his ouster in 1971. His government built roads, schools and hospitals across the country; increased economic growth and income for the average Ugandan; and expanded manufacturing and boosted export trade.

Uganda also had an abundance of natural resources many African countries did not have; it still does. In fact, Uganda and a number of other African countries had a higher per capita income than some southeast Asian countries did. Yet those countries, the Asian tigers, are now some of the most developed in the world; a point underscored below:

"In 1965, Nigeria was richer than Indonesia, and Ghana richer than Thailand. Today Indonesia is three times richer than Nigeria, and Thailand five times richer than Ghana.

In 1965, Uganda was richer than South Korea. And in 1967, Zambia also was richer than South Korea. Zambia had a per capita income of $200, and South Korea, $120. After 30 years, South Korea's gross domestic product per person was more than $10,000 in 1998, and Zambia's $400.[4] Yet, by African standards, Zambia is considered to be one of the richest countries on the continent in spite of all the misery, hunger and starvation ravaging this country endowed with abundant minerals and arable land more than enough to feed its entire population....

African countries have become international beggars. And they have been begging since independence in the sixties. Yet, some of these very same countries had the potential to develop and outstrip their southeastern Asian counterparts which are now known as the Asian tigers because of their brilliant economic performance. And the contrast is glaring.

In the sixties, the southeast Asian countries were as poor as or poorer than some African countries which are now on international welfare, dependent on donors for their very survival. They include 'prosperous' ones today such as Uganda. As Ugandan President Yoweri Museveni said in a speech to the United National General Assembly in February 1997, in 1965 Uganda was 'more prosperous than South Korea and Nigeria more prosperous than Indonesia.'[8]

So what happened?

It is also worth remembering that the year 1965 when Nigeria was richer than Indonesia, Ghana richer than

Thailand, and Uganda and Zambia richer than South Korea, was around the same time when all those African countries had just won independence from Britain; which means it was *not* the African governments which made those countries prosperous when compared to their southeast Asian counterparts. It was the British colonial governments which did that.

Ghana won independence in March 1957, Nigeria in October 1960, Uganda in October 1962, and Zambia, formerly Northern Rhodesia, in October 1964; hardly enough time - by 1965 - for the new African governments to have made any appreciable impact on their countries' economies to achieve significant progress within so few years and outstrip the southeast Asian nations."[3]

The Ugandan economy performed reasonably well during the sixties. But all those gains were reversed during the seventies when Idi Amin was in power. He destroyed the economy. It was not until the mid-1980s that the economy started to improve after major economic reforms were introduced and implemented, with the biggest gains made under Museveni.

The economic ruin of the seventies under Amin was preceded by a crisis of legitimacy for the state under Obote in the sixties.

Obote consolidated his position, with the army dominated by fellow northerners tipping scales in his favour, after he expelled Kabaka Mutesa. But he was far from being accepted as the legitimate leader of Uganda especially in the south where he had abolished the kingdoms. He was greatly resented by the people in the former kingdoms, especially Buganda, for stripping their traditional rulers of power and taking their position as the leader of the former kingdoms which were an integral part of Uganda of which he was the leader.

But his ruling party, the Uganda People's Congress (UPC), also enjoyed significant support in the former kingdoms – except Buganda – because it was broad-based and inclusive, embracing people from all parts of the country unlike political parties in the Buganda kingdom – the Democratic Party (DP) and Kabaka Yekka (KY) – whose membership was solidly Baganda. And he enjoyed strong support in the north, his stronghold and homeland.

Yet his government had to resort to coercive tactics to achieve its goals because of the strong opposition it faced especially in the south. Ethnicity continued to play a major role in national life and in the government. It was also used as a bargaining tool and as a weapon to extract concessions from the government. Obote also used it to consolidate his position, for example, by offering leading Baganda politicians cabinet posts and other high-ranking jobs in the government.

By including some of his opponents in the government, he demonstrated the imperative need for compromise as a cardinal principle in politics and in the conduct of national affairs. And ethnic and regional considerations were a central component in the successful administration of the country.

There was a need for regional balance in the government although it was not fully implemented in all areas. Obote felt that it was necessary to build national consciousness in place ethnic loyalties if Uganda were to survive and develop as a country and as a cohesive whole. But the crisis of legitimacy for his leadership especially in the south continued to be a major problem for his government. As Dr. Juma Anthony Okuku, a lecturer in political economy at Makerere University, Kampala, Uganda, states in his paper, "Ethnicity, State Power and The Democratisation Process in Uganda":

"The post-colonial practices of the mainstream nationalists, who inherited the national state, saw the reproduction rather than the deconstruction of ethnicity in Uganda's body-politic....

The post-colonial practices enhanced rather than deconstructed ethnic consciousness....

The post-independence government led by Milton Obote, 1962 – 71, had a number of assumptions. First, the task of nation-building called for uniting all the forces of society. To him, diversity of ethnic identities was inherently negative and obstructive to successful nation-building and development. As Obote stated in 1963:

> The tribe has served our people as a basic political unit very well in the past. But now the problem of people putting the tribe above national consciousness is a problem that we must face, and an issue we must destroy. (Hansen, 1974: 63).

This set the stage for the clash between the UPC, a republican party, and KY, an ethnic chauvinist and monarchist party devoted to the preservation of the special status of Buganda Kingdom in the post-colonial setup."[4]

Even before independence, Obote warned against the preservation of the monarchy in the Buganda kingdom, contending that it would militate against national unity, as would the preservation of the other traditional centres of power in other parts of the country. According to *Africa Contemporary Record: Annual Survey and Documents*:

"President Milton Obote's first decade in parliament was celebrated in August/September 1968.[1]

In almost his first speech in the Uganda Legislature on 6 May, 1958, the almost unknown young radical nationalist from Lango (he was 32) in a criticism of colonial policies had said:

> If the Government is going to develop this country on a unitary basis, how on earth can the Government develop another state within a state?
> Does the Government really think that, when self-government comes to this country, the state of Buganda will willingly give up the

powers it has already got now, in order to join with other outlying Districts or provinces? I do not think so.

Now, ten years later, Dr. Obote had not only seen the accuracy of his prophecy; he had also become the instrument for breaking the power of the State of Buganda, as well as sweeping away much of the country's Old Order.

For him, 1968 was a decisive turning point: his leadership was under challenge, and with it his plans for unifying Uganda within a modernising political system.

Uganda's basic political problems at independence in 1962 were dominated by the rigid and strongly-based determination of the Kingdom of Buganda to maintain its distinctive identity – either by achieving a political ascendancy over the rest of the country as was largely the case in the heyday of Buganda's overlordship, or through secession.

Thus Buganda's politics had two parallel drives: the thrust to leadership for control of the modern political system, and the thrust towards separatism.

Because Buganda lies at the heart of modern Uganda's economy and metropolitan development, and since its people – the Baganda – were the best-educated and most sophisticated among the Ugandans, its threat to those who opposed it was formidable: more especially since the modern young Kabaka – a tough, shrewd and entirely inflexible leader – was strongly backed by the Buganda parliament, the Lukiiko, and supported by a closely-controlled system of rural government through a hierarchical chieftaincy system dependent on the Kabaka; these were buttressed by a close-knit system of Palace politics.

All these threads of Buganda's power and authority were brought together in the Kabaka's hands on Mengo Hill – the seat of his palace and local parliament above Kampala."[5]

Obote inherited the ethnic configuration of Ugandan politics left by the British and whose biggest beneficiaries were the Baganda. His attempts to control the dynamics of ethnicity and change the social order and political landscape were fiercely resisted by the Baganda and, to a lesser degree, by the members of the other kingdoms.

Even attempts to resolve disputes by constitutional means were opposed by Buganda when the monarchy felt resolution of the disputes would not be in the best interest of the kingdom. One of the best examples was the case of the "lost counties" which once belonged to Bunyoro but which were given to Buganda by the British for the role the Baganda played in helping the colonial rulers to take over Bunyoro. As Okuku states:

"One explosive political problem the government handled constitutionally was the long-standing dispute between the Buganda and Bunyoro Kingdoms over the so-called 'lost counties.' These were counties that belonged to the Bunyoro Kingdom before the onset of colonialism but were given to the Buganda Kingdom as appreciation for its assistance in the conquest of the Bunyoro Kingdom by the British.

The colonial government left it to the government of the newly independent state to settle this issue through a referendum. The referendum was held in 1964 as was required by the independence constitution. The population in the two counties voted overwhelmingly for their return to the Bunyoro Kingdom.

This democratic solution to the problem of ethnic conflict provoked instead ethnic antagonism between Buganda and Bunyoro on the one hand, and the central government and the Buganda Kingdom, on the other. The Buganda Kingdom was not content with the way the dispute was handled by the government of Milton Obote. This resulted in a strain between the Buganda Kingdom and the central government culminating in the breakup of the UPC/KY alliance formed at independence (Karugire, 1988: 184).

The ethnic conflict, militarism and authoritarianism that followed between 1964 and 1971 during the Obote I regime had this tension as one of its sources. The leadership on both spectrums of the 1964 wrangle was rather antagonistic and confrontational, a recipe that democratic practice is not made of.

The 1966 crisis, which resulted in the violent overthrow of the independence constitution, was a culmination of *three* political developments. First, the breakup of the UPC/KY alliance, second, the leadership wrangle in UPC, using the Congo gold scandal[2] as an excuse to overthrow Obote. This resulted in Obote's detention of his own cabinet ministers for the plot and third, the unilateral suspension of the Independence Constitution in 1966.

Using authoritarian methods in what was essentially a civil conflict that could have been handled politically compounded the problem. The long-term effect of this was to exacerbate ethnic mobilisation and destroy any chance of democratic solutions to such cleavages. Because the opposition to Obote came from mainly Bantu politicians, the crisis came to take on a North-South dimension.

While it is true that Obote was trying to break up the heaviest concentration of power in the land in order to safeguard his position and perhaps concentrate on the nation-building objective, instead of using democratic means, he did so through the use of ethnicity. The treatment of Buganda between 1966 and 1971 lent little credibility to his declared intentions of reducing the significance of the ethnic factor in Uganda's politics.

The Baganda were still regarded as so hostile and unreliable that the region was kept in a state of emergency throughout this period (Hansen, 1974: 66 – 71). Suppressing the Kingdom of Buganda and the imprisonment of Southern politicians without trial simply politicised ethnicity in the country's body politic. Obote's partisan authoritarianism played a key part in keeping ethnic consciousness alive in the country waiting for an opportunity to re-assert itself....

The Congo gold scandal refers to allegations by an opposition parliamentarian in 1965, that the prime minister, Milton Obote, his defence minister, Felix Onama, and army commander, Idi Amin, were involved in smuggling gold and ivory from eastern Congo. The Uganda army had been sent to aid the Lumumbist rebellion led by Mulele Congo in its military operations."[6]

Ethnicity continues to play a role in Uganda politics and in life in general fifty years after independence despite professions to the contrary by some people, especially national leaders who, in their rhetoric, emphasise the imperative for national unity and talk as if ethnic considerations don't play a major role across the spectrum – social, political, and economic.

What may sometimes be overlooked when examining the ethnic factor in Ugandan national life is the fact that even if the kingdom of Buganda did not exist, Ugandan nationalist leaders – Obote and his colleagues – would still have faced a formidable task in their attempt to unite the country.

There were other kingdoms, as well as other traditional centres of power, which even by themselves – individually or collectively – did make the task of nation building difficult because they did not subscribe to the national ethos of one Uganda espoused by Obote and his compatriots.

The advantage the national government had was coercive power, including military power, the kingdoms did not have. Even Buganda, the most advanced and most powerful among the kingdoms, did not have the military might to resist let alone defeat the national army and security forces, as was tragically demonstrated when Kabaka's palace was attacked and destroyed, as the king fled in a humiliating way.

But in spite of their military weakness, the kingdoms were a formidable force in the political arena with or without the combined strength of other traditional societies which were also opposed to the central government in Kampala. As Colin Legm and John Drysdale state in their co-edited work, *African Contemporary Record*:

"Although Buganda offered the toughest problem to the modernising nationalists, it was by no means the only difficulty they had to face.

Each of the other three kingdoms – Toro, Ankole and Bunyoro – and the Princedom of Busoga had their own well-structured political systems; each was suspicious of the modern political centre at Entebbe. Also they had traditional rivalries – especially between Buganda and Bunyoro – this, however, had advantages for the nationalists since it helped prevent southern Kingdoms – mainly Bantu-speaking – developing an alliance of traditional interests.

Also, in the centre of the country, are two large areas, Teso and Lango, which – having entered into the modernising economic and education system at a fairly early stage – constitute important political units; but they lack the strong tradition of centralised leadership.

To the North – among the Nilotic peoples stretching to the frontiers of the Sudan and the Congo – are scores of scattered ethnic groups who fared least well under colonialism, and who got into the modernising process several decades behind the Southerners. Bringing them forward rapidly was an obvious priority for their own leaders; but those who undertook this task were in danger of being accused of wishing to favour 'the North' – with its Islamic contacts – against 'the South' – with its Christian traditions and Bantu cultures. Both these elements were conveniently exploited by politicians in the North and the South."[7]

All those different traditional societies in different parts of the country made integration very difficult. They knew they were all an integral part of the modern nation of Uganda. But they wanted to remain separate to manage their own affairs and even pursue goals – ethnic and regional – which were in conflict with national interests.

Although the national leaders tried to bring the different parts of the country together in order to build one cohesive nation, ethnic and regional loyalties continued to play an important role across the spectrum; a phenomenon that has haunted Uganda since colonial times.

Even when some leaders seemed to be determined to transcend ethnicity and regionalism, the problem continued to resurface. In fact, no government of Uganda – civilian or military – during the post-colonial era has been able to insulate itself from this problem.

Obote himself was not entirely immune from that. Some of the most highly prominent or sensitive posts in his government were given to fellow northerners including his relatives. For example, he chose his first cousin, Dr. Akena Adoko, to be the head of the intelligence service which was known as the General Service Unit (GSU). Adoko was the second most powerful man in Uganda after the president. Another cousin of Obote, A.A. Nekyon, was a cabinet member and one of his closest advisers.

However, most of the senior posts in the government were held by southerners, not by northerners as some critics of Obote have alleged, a dominance attributed to the high level of education among southerners contrasted with northerners. Yet, it is equally true that ethnicity was an influential factor even in the government of Obote who espoused principles of meritocracy and truly nationalist policies embracing everybody. And as Okuku states:

"In spite of the various regimes' apparent aversion to ethnicity in Uganda, they have rested on distinctly ethnic political foundations and reproduced themselves on the basis of definable, and in most cases, narrow ethnic alliances. The ultimate result of authoritarianism, militarism and the stifling of civil society organisations was that it did not get rid of ethnicity and regionalism and construct a nation-state....

The other part of the state where the political leadership failed to transform its ethnic base was the military. The introduction of militarism and the mobilisation of ethnicity in the military, impacted negatively on political development in Uganda.

During both Milton Obote's regimes in the 1960s and the early 1980s, Idi Amin's regime in the 1970s, and including Yoweri Museveni's since 1986, militarism was and has been employed as a means of capturing and maintaining power. As a result, the resolution of the problem of ethnicity through democratic means in the foreseeable future has been postponed.

The scourge of military power that looms throughout Uganda's post-independence period was introduced in Uganda's politics between 1964 and 66. Between 1964 and 66, democratic solutions were abandoned and Obote resorted to militarisation of the country's politics as a strategy for crisis management (Okoth, 1995: 123). The loss of the 1964 – 65 power struggle between the Prime Minister, Obote, and the President, *Kabaka* Mutesa, within the UPC/KY ruling coalition, resulted in the retreat of Mutesa into enclave, chauvinistic Ganda ethnicity and aggressive, militarist ethnicity on the part of Obote, with a reliance on the army which was dominated by the northerners.

By 1967, th army had been dragged into Uganda's politics, thereby eroding the relative degree of democracy and pluralism that had prevailed in the country between 1962 and 1966.

Militarisation only exacerbated the ethnic question. This is because the army had been used in a showdown with an ethnic group in the 1966 invasion of Kabaka's Lubiri (King's Palace). The army could no longer be regarded as an organ that was neutral in an ethnic sense (Hansen, 1974: 66).

The deliberate recruitment of the Specialised Paramilitary Corps into the Obote regime along ethnic lines lent little credence to his fight against ethnicity. Obote initiated a massive expansion of a Special Paramilitary Corps, Special Force, and created a lavishly equipped intelligence service, the General Service Unit, GSU, under the command of Akena Adoko, his cousin, and recruited almost solely from his own ethnic group, the Langi (Hansen, 1974: 88).

The result was the rise of an ethnically organised state. Obote failed to resolve the contradictions inherited from the colonial political economy.

Every regime in Uganda since then, Yoweri Museveni's National Resistance Movement (NRM) included, has used ethnicity in the military and other state organs to retain power."[8]

Idi Amin also used his ethnic base to seize power in 1971. When he overthrew the government with the help of the British and the Israelis, he used soldiers in the army who came from the West Nile District, his region in the northwestern part of Uganda. Soldiers – the Langi and the Acholi – from the north-central part of northern Uganda, Obote's home region, remained loyal to the president and even contemplated a counter-coup to reinstate him. But it was too late.

There is no question that all Ugandan leaders have used and have benefited from ethnicity or ethnic and regional loyalties at one time or another only in varying degrees. But, although Obote was one of those leaders, it is also true that his government was not filled with northerners even if it seemed to be controlled by them mainly because the army and security forces, dominated by fellow northerners, tipped scales in his favour.

Even as late as 1968, six years after independence and not long before he was overthrown about two years later, most government jobs, especially in the civil service, were filled by southerners. And the cabinet reflected regional balance, north versus south. According to *Africa Contemporary Record 1968 - 1969*:

"A recurrent feature of political controversy in Uganda is the allegation that under President Obote there had been a persistent attempt to impose Northern domination on the rest of the country; this allegation is used to buttress the cause for a 'Bantu alliance' among the Southerners.

Sometimes it is also argued that there is a secret understanding between Uganda's Northerners to ally themselves with the Luo political forces of Kenya led by Mr. Oginga Odinga: this is frequently referred to as 'Rule by the O's' since so many Nilotic names – Obote, Odinga, Onama – begin with O.

What these allegations fail to explain is that the overwhelming majority of senior posts in Uganda are filled not by Northerners, but by Southerners; and that the composition of Obote's Cabinet reflects more or less the same ratio of Southerners to Northerners as existed before the crisis of 1966.

It is possible that pressures of the Northerners – latecomers to modernisation – for a fair share of the posts in the central government might help to explain the suspicions about 'a Northern push.'"[9]

However, what happened two years earlier in 1966, with strong ethnic overtones, did set the stage for what was to take place in the following years and decades in terms of political changes in Uganda.

The 1966 crisis which led to the ouster of Kabaka

Mutesa was a turning point in the history of Uganda. As the king of the Buganda kingdom, his ouster, especially by a government led by a northerner and by soldiers who were also predominantly northerners, had serious ethnic implications and repercussions across the country and throughout the post-colonial period.

Almost every major change or political event that has taken place in Uganda in the following decades can be traced to that critical moment. Here is how the events unfolded:

"Unlike most African countries, religion has played a role in Uganda's modern political development – mainly between Protestants and Catholics. Latterly, too, the Muslim factor has been introduced.

In the politics of pre-independence the nationalist forces were divided and thus weakened; the traditionalists were strong but divided, and so less effective than they might otherwise have been. This enabled the running to be made by the Democratic Party (DP), led by Mr. Benedicto Kiwanuka, which appealed nationally to the Catholic vote.

His temporary majority in the Legislature was a challenge to both the nationalists and Buganda. To defeat him Obote's Uganda People's Congress (UPC) entered into a political alliance of convenience with its arch political enemy, the Kabaka of Buganda.

To both sides this uneasy alliance offered temporary advantages; first, to rid themselves of Kiwanuka's DP; second, to manoeuvre against each other from a base of shared power at the centre – with the Kabaka as President (the Royal Republican), and Dr. Obote as Prime Minister.

Neither side had any illusions about each other's intentions.

At first it seemed that Obote's nationalist forces had the better end of the deal; but in 1966 the pendulum swung unexpectedly against Obote when he discovered that an influential group within his own Cabinet were not only

271

working secretly against his leadership but had entered into a convenient alliance of their own with the Kabaka.

This produced the familiar post-independence crisis shattering the brief period of relative stability. Obote struck back fast and had to retain his initiative: what happened in the succeeding months is directly relevant to understanding the situation which Obote faced in 1968.

22 February, 1966. Prime Minister Obote ousts Kabaka as President; suspends the Constitution; arrests five of his leading Ministers – Grace Ibingira, Dr. Emmanuel Lumu, George Magezi, Balaki Kirya and Mathias Ngobi. He announces: ' We are introducing a new era and new issues in Uganda's politics. It would be unfortunate to go back now to a government at Mengo controlled by the Kabaka.'

15 April, 1966. A temporary Constitution is introduced with an Executive President, abolishing the Prime Minister. Obote assumes the Presidency.

20 May, 1966. Lukiiko demands Uganda's expulsion from Buganda Kingdom by 30 May.

20 – 23 May, 1966. Considerable violence in Buganda.

24 May, 1966. Obote again takes the initiative, sending a small group of his forces to investigate reports that the Kabaka has imported arms into Mengo. After a sharp skirmish, Kabaka escapes and Mengo Hill is occupied. State of emergency declared in Buganda.

1 May, 1967. President loses two of his closest Ministerial colleagues – his cousin, Mr. A.A. Nekyon, who is the President of the National Association for the Advancement of Muslims; and Mr. Godfrey Binaisa, the senior Buganda politician in the Cabinet, who gives ill-health as the reason for resigning as Attorney-General.

9 June, 1967. President announces policy to abolish all four Kingdoms and to turn Uganda into a Republic.

22 June, 1967. National Assembly is converted into Constituent Assembly to discuss a new Constitution.

10 July, 1967. President dismisses Mr. Cuthbert Obwangor, his Minister of Planning and Economic

Development, a prominent nationalist politician from Teso, following a public disagreement over the new Constitution.

8 September, 1967. Constituent Assembly passes the new Constitution and Public Order Act against the protests of the Opposition. It provides for an Executive President, a Republic, abolition of the status of the four Kingdoms, the division of Buganda into four Administrative Districts in line with the rest of the country, central control over Local Administration, and a Preventive Detention Act.

President Obote, having survived the crises within his own ruling UPC and in the Kingdoms, was faced in 1968 with the huge task of making the Constitution work and of carrying out the revolutionary changes initiated by the creation of new institutions.

His main challenge still came from Buganda; but despite many alarms about a Buganda uprising – stoked up by the Kabaka and his Court in exile in London – they remained passive, though by no means won over to the new order. Nevertheless, the Baganda in the Cabinet and in senior positions in the civil service remained loyal to the President; and a number of Buganda politicians came over to join the UPC."[10]

The constitutional challenges Obote faced in the late sixties, and the acrimonious debate that ensued over the constitutional overhaul, led to other developments. Obote was accused of being intolerant of criticism and of instituting a dictatorship. There were also charges of censorship.

Critics said the government was too sensitive to criticism and was unwilling to tolerate dissent, although Obote himself was open to criticism and even debated leading academics such as Professor Ali Mazrui.

Mazrui taught political science at Makerere University during that time. Obote once asked him if he knew the difference between being a politician and being a political

273

scientist.

It was also during that period that some of the most highly influential people in Uganda were arrested on charges of sedition. One was Abu Mayanja, a veteran of the independence struggle. He was one of the founders of the leading political party in the country in the fifties, the Uganda National Congress (UNC) together with Obote, Ignatius Musaazi and others, and served as its first secretary-general.

In the April 1968 issue of *Transition*, he criticised the 1967 Uganda constitution, thus incurring the wrath of the government which brought sedition charges against him. He was acquitted of the charges but was re-arrested under the Emergency Powers Act which became effective on 1 November the same year.

Another prominent figure who was arrested was Rajat Neogy, editor of *Transition*, a highly influential scholarly journal published in Kampala and considered to be the most intellectual magazine ever published in Africa:

"A new Emergency Powers Act, effective on 1 November (1968), empowered the appropriate Ministers to make regulations for securing the defence of Uganda, public safety, effective government, maintenance of public order, enforcement of the law, and the maintenance of necessary supplies and services.

The regulations cover the detention or restriction of people and deportation of non-citizens, the performance of labour or services, and the possession of property. They also provide for amending or suspending any law, including the prohibition of strike action.

A member of Parliament, Mr. Abu Mayanja, and Mr. Rajat Neogy, editor of the magazine *Transition*, were arrested in November and charged with publishing and printing a seditious publication. The charges referred to a letter which appeared under Mr. Mayanja's name which repeated what the writer called 'a rumour' at the appointment of Africans to the Uganda Judiciary had been held up mostly for tribal reasons. The prosecution alleged that this brought into hatred or contempt the President, Dr. Obote.

These two arrests provoked considerable criticism abroad, as well as in Uganda. In a personal statement on 19 October, Professor Ali Mazrui of Makerere College, said:

'I personally know of no two people who have contributed more to the intellectual liveliness of Uganda than Rajat Neogy and Abu Mayanja.

I did not always see eye to eye with either of them. In fact, Abu Mayanja and myself have been on opposite sides in almost every debate in which he and I have taken part in the Main Hall of Makerere, and the differences between us were real. But Uganda's reputation as an open society was secure for so long as there was one Abu Mayanja free to speak out his mind, and one *Transition* leading the rest of Africa in sheer intellectual verve.

There is a sense in which intellectual freedom is indivisible. On a day like this I feel lonely and shaken.'

The government responded to these criticisms by promising to put both men on trial in open court.

However, there appear to have been other suspicions in the mind of the Government so far as Abu Mayanja is concerned.

Although he started his political life as a radical nationalist, he had in recent years moved increasingly towards leadership within the Muslim community. He became prominent in the affairs of the East African Muslim Association, which is in rivalry to the National Association for the Advancement of Muslims with which Mr. A.A. Nekyon is involved.

There had been a clash between the rival Muslim groups in the remote Karamajong area which had led to violence and killing. Mayanja, it is alleged, had been on a trip to the Middle East in August (1968) to seek support for his Association's activities. The authorities also seem to

275

suspect that there is a secret agreement between the East African Muslim Association – whose patron is H.H. The Aga Khan – and the *Kabaka Yekka* which is working for the restoration of the ex-Kabaka."[11]

The late sixties were some of the most turbulent years in Ugandan history. Not long after that, Amin seized power. It was the beginning of a new era and a downward spiral for Uganda.

Chapter Six:

Amin's regime

WHEN Idi Amin overthrew Obote, Uganda entered a new era and the most violent period in its history. It was also years of lawlessness. Laws meant absolutely nothing. It was a reign of terror that lasted for eight years. Uganda has never been the same since.

Amin may have had his own reasons for overthrowing Obote. His move may have been a pre-emptive strike against Langi army officers who were going to arrest him and his supporters in the army. It was said Obote gave the order to arrest Amin because he posed a threat to his government. Amin was also accused of embezzlement involving millions of dollars.

Somehow word about his imminent arrest leaked out and he made the first move. Before he left for the Commonwealth conference in Singapore, President Obote reportedly gave the order to have Amin arrested, prompting him to overthrow the government.

But the real players on the Ugandan political scene

during that period, who are the ones who were really behind Obote's ouster, were the British and the Israelis. They are the ones who engineered and masterminded Obote's ouster. The horrendous tragedy that befell Uganda under Amin's brutal dictatorship which included massacres of hundreds of thousands of people was in a way a direct result of their involvement in Obote's downfall.

At the very least, the suffering the people of Uganda endured under Amin can partly be attributed to the British and the Israelis because they are the ones who put him in power. Had they not do so, the world would not even have heard of Idi Amin. And the history of Uganda would have taken an entirely different turn.

The British, the Israelis, and the Americans who also helped Amin, did not care about the suffering of Ugandans and continued to support him. It was only after he turned against them that they withdrew their support from him.

The rise of Amin to power was a tragedy not only for Uganda but for Africa as a whole, especially for East Africa where his reign of terror had repercussions throughout the region:

"The rise of Idi Amin to power in Uganda introduced a destabilizing factor on the East African political scene as never before. And his ouster by Tanzania eight years later also set a precedent as the first case of direct intervention by one African country in another in the post-colonial era; besides incursions by apartheid South Africa into neighbouring countries which were supporting South African freedom fighters, and the apartheid regime's almost successful takeover of Angola in the seventies, until Fidel Castro sent Cuban troops to halt the advance.

South African troops penetrated deep into Angola and were headed towards the capital, Luanda, before they were pushed back by the Cubans. Tanzania's intervention in Uganda was also the first time that an African country captured the capital, and overthrew the government, of another country on the continent.

Amin came to power in a military coup on January 25, 1971, which would probably not have been launched, let alone succeeded, without external help. In announcing his seizure of power on Radio Uganda, Amin made a short speech and tried to assure his fellow countrymen in the following terms:

'Fellow countrymen and well wishers of Uganda. I address you today at a very important hour in the history of our nation.

A short while ago, men of the armed forces placed this country in my hands. I am not a politician, but a professional soldier. I am therefore a man of few words and I shall, as a result, be brief.

Throughout my professional life, I have emphasized that the military must support a civilian government that has the support of the

1

people, and I have not changed from that position.'

The contradiction is obvious. And the people who placed Uganda in Amin's hands, to paraphrase what he said, were not just the Ugandan soldiers but Israeli agents as well, with the support of the British government. The British supported the coup against President Milton Obote because of his uncompromising stand on apartheid South Africa and Rhodesia. His policies towards the apartheid regime in South Africa were diametrically opposed to those of Britain which was friendly towards the racist government and did not want to impose severe economic sanctions on the white-dominated country because of her large investments there.

African countries demanded such sanctions in order to force the apartheid regime to abandon its racist policies. In the case of Rhodesia, the British government was hostile towards President Obote because of his uncompromising stand on the white minority regime in Salisbury, demanding that Britain actively intervene in her colony with military force to end the rebellion by Prime Minister Ian Smith who had unilaterally declared independence,

279

excluding the African majority from power.

Britain also supported the coup against Dr. Obote because he nationalized British companies in Uganda after he adopted socialist policies in pursuit of economic independence. And Western countries in general, including the United States, supported the coup against Obote as a containment strategy to neutralize 'communist penetration' of East Africa through Tanzania which was friendly towards the People's Republic of China and other Eastern-bloc nations more than any other country in the region; a false accusation, since Tanzania was not communist or communist-oriented but fiercely independent, a stance that antagonized the West as much as Uganda's under Obote who was also a close friend of President Julius Nyerere of Tanzania. Obote's Pan-African militancy and socialist policies as well as his friendship with Eastern-bloc countries, like Nyerere's, were anathema to the West and could be neutralized only by ousting him from power.

It was a grand conspiracy, further confirmed when Western countries were the first to recognize Amin's regime, and before any African country did. Britain was the first Western country to do so; an implicit admission of her involvement in Obote's ouster, or, at the very least, of her strong desire to see him ousted. But Britain's complicity and involvement in the coup was obvious; a point underscored by Western analysts as well, including the *Executive Intelligence Review*:

'General Amin came to power in Uganda, in a military coup against President Milton Obote. British sponsorship of the semi-illiterate Amin, son of a sorceress, was quickly evident; Britain was one of the first countries in the world to recognize the Amin government, long before any African country. And when relations with Britain had soured after Amin expelled the Asian business community from Uganda, British intelligence operative Robert Astles remained as Amin's mentor in Uganda until the very end. Amin's tyranny, lasting until 1979, trampled Uganda's political and economic institutions, leaving the country a wreckage from which it has never recovered.'

Israel's involvement in the Ugandan military coup was even more direct. The coup was masterminded by Israeli agents working in Kampala, Uganda. It could not have succeeded without them. As Dr. Milton Obote stated:

'It is doubtful that Amin, without the urging of the Israelis, would have staged a successful coup in 1971... Israel wanted a client regime in Uganda, which they could manipulate in order to prevent Sudan from sending troops to Egypt.... The coup succeeded beyond their wildest expectations.... The Israelis set up in Uganda a regime, which pivoted in every respect to Amin, who in turn was under the strictest control of the Israelis in Kampala.... The Israelis and Anya-Anya were

3

hilarious; the regime was under their control.'

The Israelis wanted to prevent Sudan from sending troops to Egypt - a frontline state in the Arab League against Israel and the most powerful in the Arab world - by tying down her troops in a war against the rebels, known as Anya-Anya, fighting for self-determination in southern Sudan against the Arab-dominated government in Khartoum in northern Sudan. Israel's support of the black rebels was motivated by self-interest more than anything else including humanitarian concern. So was the coup against President Obote.

The ouster of Dr. Milton Obote had striking similarities to the coup against President Kwame Nkrumah of Ghana five years earlier on February 24, 1966. Both leaders were ardent Pan-Africanists and strong supporters of liberation movements in Africa. Both antagonized the West because of their Pan-African militancy and the socialist policies they pursued. And both were overthrown - with Western help including the CIA - when they were outside their countries: Nkrumah, while on his way on a peace mission to Hanoi at the invitation of Vietnamese

President Ho Chin Mihn to help end the Vietnam war (and in pursuit of Nkrumah's ambition to make Africa an important player on the global scene and in major international affairs); and Obote, when he was at the Commonwealth conference in Singapore where he had gone, at the urging of President Julius Nyerere, to make a strong case against Britain because of her insistence on selling arms to apartheid South Africa and her unwillingness to take stern measures against the apartheid regime and the white minority government in Rhodesia.

Obote did not want to go to Singapore because of the internal political situation in Uganda which he felt, and rightly so, that his enemies would try to exploit in his absence. And there has been some speculation that had he not left Uganda, as urged by Nyerere, he probably would not have been overthrown. Nyerere was undoubtedly outraged by the coup against Obote who was also his friend and ideological compatriot.

But to say that he took military action against Idi Amin in order to reinstate Obote - hence make amends for his "mistakes" - because he had contributed to his downfall by urging him to go to Singapore to attend the commonwealth conference, is to distort history.

Idi Amin invaded Tanzania on October 30, 1978, and announced on November 1 that he had annexed 710 square miles of her territory in the northwest region of Kagera, triggering a counterattack by Tanzania, which eventually drove him out of Uganda. The atrocities perpetrated by Amin through the years in which hundreds of thousands of people were massacred were ignored by most African leaders and by the international community; a situation Nyerere found to be unacceptable, thus prompting him to intervene in Uganda to stop the atrocities by getting rid of Amin.

Therefore, even if President Obote had died in office and Amin or someone like him had usurped power and went on to perpetrate unspeakable horrors, as Amin did,

Nyerere would still have intervened in Uganda out of humanitarian concern to stop the madness. He did not need Obote to be overthrown to do this. Obote could even have resigned, which is highly speculative, and Nyerere would still have intervened if Obote's successor - Amin or somebody else - went on to unleash terror on a scale Idi Amin did. It is in this larger context that Nyerere's outrage against the military coup by Amin should be viewed; a perspective that eludes a number of analysts or is deliberately distorted to conform to their interpretation of events at that critical juncture in Ugandan history. As Professor Ali Mazrui states in 'Nyerere and I':

'In 1971, did Julius Nyerere convince Milton Obote to leave Uganda and go to Singapore to attend the Commonwealth conference of Heads of State and government? Milton Obote had hesitated about going to Singapore because of the uncertain situation in Uganda. Did Nyerere tilt the balance and convince Obote that he was needed in Singapore to fight Prime Minister Edward Heath's policy towards apartheid South Africa? Obote's decision to go to Singapore was disastrous for himself and for Uganda. In Obote's absence, Idi Amin staged a military coup and overthrew Obote. Eight years of tyranny and terror in Uganda had begun.

I never succeeded in getting either Nyerere or Obote to confirm that it was Nyerere who convinced Obote to leave for Singapore. But we do know that Nyerere was so upset by the coup that he gave Obote unconditional and comfortable asylum in Tanzania. Nyerere also refused to talk to Amin even if the policy practically destroyed the East African Authority which was supposed to oversee the East African community. Was Nyerere feeling guilty for having made it easy for Amin to stage a coup by diverting Obote to Singapore?

I shall always remember Nyerere's speech in Tanzania upon his return from Singapore. I was in Kampala listening to him on the radio. Nyerere turned a simple question in Kiswahili into a passionate denunciation of Idi Amin. Nyerere's repeated question was 'Serikali ni kitu gani?' ('What is government?'). This simple question of political science became a powerful speech to his own people and against the new 'pretenders' in Kampala.

I visited Milton Obote at his home in Dar es Salaam during his first exile. Obote and I discussed Idi Amin much more often than we discussed Julius Nyerere....

In 1979, Nyerere paid his debt to Milton Obote. His army marched all the way to Kampala and overthrew the regime of Idi Amin. My former Makerere boss, Prof Yusufu Lule, succeeded Idi Amin as President of Uganda. But Nyerere was so keen on seeing Obote back in power that Nyerere helped to oust Lule. Was Nyerere trying to negate the guilt of having encouraged Obote to go to Singapore for the Commonwealth conference way back in 1971? Was that why Nyerere was so keen to see Obote back in the presidential saddle of Uganda in the 1980s?

Unfortunately, Obote's second administration was catastrophic for Uganda. He lost control of his own army, and thousands of people

4

perished under tyranny and war. Was Julius Nyerere partly to blame?'

If Nyerere was partly to blame for Obote's ouster, then he was equally guilty of the atrocities perpetrated by Idi Amin, since he "helped" pave the way for Amin's rise to power by encouraging Obote to go to Singapore to attend the Commonwealth conference; a far cry from reality, and a stretch of the imagination even Idi Amin - let alone his sponsors - would have found to be laughable. The Israelis and Western powers would still have tried and might even have succeeded, sooner or later, in overthrowing Obote with Amin's help even if he had not gone to Singapore, and even if Nyerere did not exist on the political scene to "influence" Obote one way or another.

Whatever the case, the coup which catapulted Amin into power was one of the biggest tragedies in Africa's post-colonial history and one of the most tragic cases of foreign intrigue on African soil by outside powers. And an illiterate who never went beyond standard two - what Americans call second grade - took over the leadership of one of the most prosperous countries in Africa, and ruined it.

Yet, in spite of his wicked nature and bestial character, Amin was also capable of presenting himself in an amiable way as someone who could be trusted, although he could not hide his ignorance. As Henry Kyemba, who once served as Amin's private secretary and as health minister before fleeing to Britain, said about him: 'Amin never knew anything about how a government is run. He could not write and he had problems reading. So it was very hard to work with him.'[5]

Kyemba also described Idi Amin, whom some people called the Black Hitler, as one of the friendliest people he ever met, yet had the rage of a wounded buffalo. And his government and army were dominated by illiterates who were no better than he was. As another former Amin's cabinet member, Birgadier Moses Ali who later served as Third Deputy Prime Minister under President Yoweri Museveni, also bluntly stated: 'Illiterates and sycophants were some of the people who spoilt Amin's government. They could not even read maps, they excelled in praising him, they were no better than Amin himself.'[6]

Amin's willingness to be used by external powers to overthrow Dr. Obote - one of Africa's most prominent and influential leaders - was one of the most treasonous acts in the history of post-colonial Africa. As an expression of gratitude to those who had sponsored the coup, Amin took a strong pro-Western stance immediately after he seized power and declared that Israel and Britain were his close allies.

The United States, like Britain, also supplied him with weapons. And the CIA as well as Britain's MI6 intelligence service, together with Israel's intelligence agency Mossad, trained Amin's security forces; including the dreaded and notoriously brutal Public Safety Unit and the State Research Bureau, euphemisms for secret police. They also provided them with weapons and other supplies. And Israeli troops also trained the Ugandan army and air force even when Obote was president, giving them a strategic advantage when they helped Amin execute a military coup a few years later. And Amin himself once received paratrooper training in Israel.

A former CIA official publicly confirmed in March

1978 that the coup against Obote was planned by the British MI6 and the Israeli Mossad intelligence services. And it had been confirmed earlier that a British agent operating under diplomatic cover at the British High Commission in Kampala, Uganda, planned the failed assassination attempt on President Obote on December 18, 1969.

Israel's role in the execution of the coup proved to be critical when, on the advice of an Israeli colonel in Israel's army and with the help of Israeli agents in Uganda, Amin was able to secure control and command of a mechanized battalion - of paratroopers, tanks, jeeps and armored vehicles - which was able to overwhelm the majority of the soldiers and officers in the Ugandan army still loyal to President Obote. Firepower compensated for numerical disadvantage to Amin's benefit. And the ease with which the coup was carried out also confirmed Obote's suspicion that the Israelis had played a direct and critical role in his ouster.

Obote may still or may not have been overthrown had he stayed in Uganda to mobilize support among his followers against any uprising. And although he knew that the security situation in Uganda was not very stable when he left for Singapore, he agreed with Nyerere that he would be needed at the Commonwealth conference to help present strong opposition to the sale of weapons to the apartheid regime of South Africa by Britain. The strongest opponents were Nyerere and Kaunda, and Obote provided much needed support to them at the conference where other African leaders were also opposed to the sale.

At a meeting in Singapore during the conference, Nyerere, Kaunda and Obote told British Prime Minister Edward Heath that their countries would withdraw from the Commonwealth if Britain proceeded with the sale of arms to the apartheid regime. In the ensuing debate, Heath is reported to have told the three leaders: 'I wonder how many of you will be allowed to return to your own countries from this conference?'[7]

It was an ominous warning, confirmed shortly thereafter, when Obote learned in Nairobi, Kenya, on his way back to Uganda from the conference that he had been overthrown. And it directly implicated Britain in the coup. Britain's involvement in the coup was further confirmed only a few days later when the British government became the first to recognize Amin's military regime exactly one week after he seized power.

The British also rejoiced at Obote's ouster and gave Amin extensive coverage in the media, portraying him in a very positive way as Uganda's savior. According to *The Daily Express*: 'Military men are trained to act. Not for them the posturing of the Obotes and Kaundas who prefer the glory of the international platform rather than the dull but necessary tasks of running a smooth administration.'[8] And *The Daily Telegraph* bluntly stated: 'Good luck to General Amin.'[9]

The thrill in government circles was equally evident, as reported by *The Times*: 'The replacement of Dr. Obote by General Idi Amin was received with ill-concealed relief in Whitehall.'[10]

And Amin wasted no time in reciprocating these feelings.

He earned British confidence when he reversed Obote's policies in a number of areas. Unlike Obote, he supported the sale of weapons to apartheid South Africa by Britain. He also returned to private ownership British companies and other businesses nationalized by Obote. In return, Britain increased economic aid to Uganda, supplied weapons and provided further training to the Ugandan army. But the honeymoon was short-lived, and Britain as well as the United States and Israel soon learned that Amin was not the kind of leader they thought they could manipulate at will.

Amin had expansionist ambitions to conquer Tanzania and ostensibly gain access to the sea. He also toyed with the idea of annexing parts of western Kenya bordering Uganda, and even parts of Sudan, prompting Sudanese President Gaafar Nimeiri to remind Amin that he was Sudanese himself - Amin's small Kakwa tribe straddles the Ugandan-Sudanese-Congolese border, with part of Amin's lineage being on the Congolese and Sudanese side. He also threatened to destroy neighbouring Rwanda. He antagonized almost all his neighbours including Kenya whose western province, the burly dictator claimed, belonged to Uganda. But his immediate goal in this expansionist scheme was to conquer Tanzania mainly because Nyerere had offered sanctuary to Amin's nemesis, Obote. And he became incensed when Britain refused to supply him with combat jets and other sophisticated weapons to fulfill his mission.

Amin's desire to 'flatten Tanzania,' as he put it, became an obsession which made him turn to Israel to seek weapons he needed to accomplish his mission. He asked for Phantom jets and other advanced weapons. But because these weapons were manufactured in the United States and sold to Israel with permission from the American government, the Israelis could not transfer or resell them to Uganda without Washington's approval. But Israel did not even go that far.

The Israeli government refused to sell the weapons to Amin, saying that his request 'went beyond the requirements of legitimate self-defence.' The rejection of Amin's request was a prime factor in the expulsion of the Israelis from Uganda in April 1972, and in his unconditional support of the Palestinian cause and solidarity with Arab countries - and fellow Muslims - in their conflict with the Jewish state. And the failure to acquire the weapons he felt he needed, did not in any way discourage him from pursuing his expansionist ambitions to conquer Tanzania and secure a corridor to the sea.

Although he did not get the weapons he needed to inflict heavy damage on Tanzania, in his misguided belief that he would be able to conquer and occupy such a large country several times Uganda's size in terms of both area and population and which was believed to be militarily the strongest country in East Africa, Amin was provided with strategic advice and information in pursuit of this goal from an indispensable source. The advice came from a British major, working with the British intelligence service, who lived on the Tanzanian-Ugandan border on the Kagera River. He was in touch with Amin who frequently flew in a helicopter to the border for consultations with him on the planned invasion of Tanzania.

The British major had been an officer in the Seaforth Highlanders and a member of the International Commission of Observers sent to Nigeria during the 1967 - 70 civil war to investigate complaints by the Igbos and other Easterners in the secessionist territory of Biafra that they were victims of a systematic campaign of genocide by the federal military government. But he was expelled from the international observer mission because he compromised his neutral observer status when he offered his services to the Nigerian military regime as a mercenary in the war against Biafra.

However, at a hearing on his dismissal before the National Insurance Tribunal in England where he protested his expulsion from the observer mission, the major made a "startling" revelation that his real mission in Nigeria was to collect intelligence for the British government and provide strategic military advice to the Nigerian federal forces in their campaign against the Biafran secessionists and their supporters. The British government vehemently denied this, but the tribunal accepted his testimony and described him as a 'frank and honest witness.'[11]

He also proved to be an indispensable tool for Amin,

as a spy, collecting vital intelligence for Amin's planned invasion of Tanzania. 'The Major took Amin's invasion plan of Tanzania seriously, undertaking spying mission to Tanzania to reconnoiter the defences and terrain in secret. He supplied Amin with a strategic and logistical plan to the best of his abilities, and although lack of hardware was an obstacle, evidence that Amin never gave up the idea came in the fact that the invasion of Uganda by Tanzanian and exiled Ugandan anti-Amin forces in late 1978 which eventually brought his rule to an end on 10 April 1979, was immediately preceded by an abortive invasion of Tanzania by Amin's army.'[12]

Full-scale war between Tanzania and Uganda began after Idi Amin announced on November 1, 1978, that his troops had captured and annexed 710 square miles of Tanzanian territory in the northwestern part of the country, Kagera Region.

Amin would not have been able to invade Tanzania and cause a lot of destruction in Kagera Region had he not been armed and kept in power by outside powers. British and Israeli involvement has received more attention than America's, but the United States' role in sustaining Amin's brutal regime cannot be underestimated.

In July 1978, Jack Anderson, a hard-hitting American columnist, revealed in one of his columns that 10 of Amin's henchmen from the notorious Public Safety Unit were trained at the International Police Academy in Georgetown, a suburb of Washington, D.C. The academy was run by the CIA, one of the three foreign intelligence agencies - together with Britain's MI6 and Israel's Mossad - which helped sustain Amin in power, especially during the early years of his brutal eight-year reign. And as *The Economist* remarked, concerning the relationship between Britain and Amin's regime, 'The last government to want to be rid of Amin is the British one.[13]"1

Amin's reign of terror was first directed against the supporters of Obote, especially the Langi and Acholi soldiers in the army. Being northerners like Obote, they supported him as a fellow northerner and had in fact tipped scales in his favour when he was in office because they were the dominant groups in the army. Now that he was out of power, they became the prime target of Obote's opponents, especially Idi Amin and his henchmen most of whom came from his home region, the West Nile District in northwestern Uganda.

Some of the biggest opponents of Obote were the Baganda. Many of them hated Obote because of what he did to them. He forcibly removed their king, Kabaka Mutesa II, from power. And he abolished all kingdoms, including Buganda.

Most Bugandans and other people in the other kingdoms were jubilant when Obote was overthrown and embraced Amin as their liberator. Some of them may even have hoped that the new military ruler would restore the kingdoms which had been abolished by Obote.

Yet it was Amin who, only a few years earlier as head of the army, invaded Kabaka Mutesa's palace and almost killed the king who was forced to flee into exile in Britain. The people of the Buganda kingdom seemed to overlook that. They were in jovial mood, celebrating Obote's downfall.

Although the new ruler was embraced by many Ugandans after he seized power, he remained a soldier and had no intention of returning the country to civilian rule. He instituted an oppressive machinery and went on to rule Uganda as if the whole country was a military garrison. Army officers and ordinary soldiers were given high positions in the government and in state-owned agencies. Even civilian government officials including cabinet members were subordinate to a military council composed of army officers who were the real government. But real power was in the hands of Amin himself.

He did not care about merit. Many soldiers who were given high government positions could not even read and write. Amin himself was virtually illiterate. He only had standard two education. He could barely sign papers. Because he couldn't read and write, he gave all orders by word of mouth. He sometimes used the radio to do that.

Military barracks became government headquarters, ministries and departments, with battalion commanders having absolute power in their areas and collectively constituting an oppressive apparatus for the whole country. They were exceeded only by Amin himself in terms of power. No one challenged them.

Amin created his own intelligence agencies, the State Research Bureau (SRB) and the Public Safety Unit (PSU), which became notorious for torturing people to death. Countless were also summarily executed through the years. Among the victims were prominent Ugandans.

Besides Benedicto Kiwanuka, who was Uganda's first prime minister not long before independence, other prominent figures who were killed by Amin included the Anglican Archbishop Janan Luwum. An Acholi, he was reportedly killed for criticising Amin's brutal dictatorship. It was said he sent Amin a note protesting against numerous killings which had taken place and which continued unabated. Amin accused him of being an agent of Obote, a fellow northerner. He was arrested on 16 February 1977, together with two cabinet members, Erinayo Wilson Oryema and Charles Oboth Ofumbi. They were all killed the following day. The government claimed they died in a "car accident." Their bodies were riddled with bullets.

However, there is another version that sheds some linght on the events which led to Archbishop Luwum's assassination. According to Professor Phares Mukasa Mutibwa in his book *Uganda Since Independence: A Story of Unfulfilled Hopes*:

"One occurrence which sent a wave of horror throughout and beyond the Christian world was the wanton murder of the Anglican Archbishop, Janani Luwum, in the company of ministers Erunayo Oryema and Charles Oboth-Ofumbi.

Why Amin killed the Archbishop has never been explained. However, it appears that at that time an attempt to stage a coup was being organised by some Acholis and Langis based in Nairobi. Archbishop Luwum was never involved, but he was informed of it by some Acholis in Uganda. When the archbishop was asked to join the group, he declined, saying that as a churchman his concern was with preaching not fighting; the plotters left him.

What led to Luwum's death was the fact that he did not tell Amin of this plot. Other people who knew of it warned Amin, and among these were a senior consultant at Mulago hospital and a senior police officer. Amin then personally accused Luwum of failing to warn him of the danger from outside the country, which meant that the Archbishop too wanted to see him overthrown.

Perhaps the killing of Oryema and Oboth-Ofumbi, who like Luwum were Luo-speakers, was for the same reason."[2]

Another victim was Frank Kalimuzo, vice chancellor of Makerere University, who was killed in October 1972. He was taken from his house. He came from Kisoro District which borders Rwanda. Amin accused him of being a spy for the Rwandan government. He also accused him of being a strong supporter of Dr. Obote:

"Frank Kalimuzo was accused by President Amin of Uganda of being a disloyal Rwandese masquerading as a Ugandan....In reality he was a Ugandan by birth and ancestry, but he came from an ethnic group in Uganda that was related to the Rwandese.

In broad daylight Kalimuzo was arrested in 1972 by

Amin's soldiers from his home on campus, never to be seen again. He must have been murdered soon after his arrest. Did he die partly because his ethnic group of Ankole district was linked to Rwanda? His murder shook many intellectuals so deeply that some left Uganda for refuge in the Western world.

It was not until 1986 that the tide turned when Museveni, ethnically linked to Kalimuzo and to the people of Rwanda, captured power in Uganda. The Tutsi and the Hima of Uganda were ethnic cousins."[3]

The terror unleashed by Amin is well-documented. It was intended to eliminate his opponents, real and imagined, but also to instill fear in the entire population so that he would continue to rule without being challenged by anyone.

Some of the reasons he gave to explain the elimination or disappearance of some prominent figures were far-fetched even though he did not have to give any since he was the absolute ruler of the country. As Mutibwa states:

"Benedicto Kiwanuka, the Chief Justice, was arrested in his chambers and later murdered. Kiwanuka had earlier released a detained British businessman named Stewart and commented that the soldiers had no right to detain individuals arbitrarily.

It is also said that Amin killed Kiwanuka after finding out that he had agreed to work with Obote for his overthrow. This has been disputed by Grance Ibingira who says that, from what he knew of Kiwanuka, this would have been impossible.[27] However, the point is that, whether or not Kiwanuka agreed to work with Obote against him, Amin found out that the two men were in contact with each other, and this was reason enough to eliminate the Chief Justice.

The murder of Kiwanuka has also been attributed to Amin's fear of him as an alternative choice for the leadership of Uganda, due to his popularity and standing within Uganda society.[28]

Another victim of Amin at this time was Frank Kalimuzo, Vice-Chancellor of Makerere University, who was picked up from his official residence and killed later at Makindye.

Amin had on several occasions accused Kalimuzo, who was from Bufumbiro/Risoro, of being a spy for the government of Rwanda – and for Amin this suspicion was conclusive.

Basil Bataringaya, who had chaired the meetings that were planning to stop Amin's coup in January 1971, was dismembered alive outside the town of Mbarara and his severed head displayed on the end of a pole. His wife too was killed soon after, allegedly by Juma Bashir, the Governor of Western Province....

The reign of terror unleashed on the population did not spare the youth, particularly members of NUSU – the National Union of Students – at Makerere and other institutions of higher learning, of whom many fled into exile.

Others killed...included Francis Walugembe, the Mayor of Masaka, and John Kakonge, James Ochola and Shaban Nkuutu, former ministers in Obote's government. Mr (Joshua) Wakholi (former minister of public service) and Alex Ojera (former minister of information)...were captured and later murdered. Of the twenty cabinet ministers in Obote's government, eight had been killed and four were in exile within two years of the coup.

The killings were extended to the armed forces, where of the twenty-three officers of the rank of lieutenant-colonel or above at the time of the coup, only four were still in the service three years later, including Amin, the Paymaster and the Chief Medical Officer. Thirteen of these officers had been murdered.

By the beginning of 1973, Amin's true nature was emerging – what Grace Ibingira has described as 'a combination of guile, buffonery and utter ruthlessness in killing anyone even remotely suspected by him or his subordinates of being unfriendly.'"[4]

Yet in spite of the absolute power Amin had, including killing people at will, he failed to contain led alone end rivalries and divisions in the army and in other parts of the country. Ethnic and regional rivalries intensified during his reign. Even the people from his home region, the Kakwa and the Lugbara, turned against each other. When Obote was overthrown, they seemed to be united against a common enemy: the Langi and the Acholi who were Obote's biggest supporters. After killing the Langi and the Acholi, they started killing each other. The Kakwa and Lugbara became enemies.

Even some of Amin's fellow tribesmen in the army, the Kakwa, turned against him not long after he seized power. Kakwa army officers tried to overthrow him in April 1973 and again in March 1974. They were the last people he expected to turn against him.

Although Amin was identified as a Kakwa, only one of his parents, his father, was a Kakwa. His mother was a Lugbara. He took his father's identity because it is customary among many African ethnic groups – including mine, the Nyakyusa of southwestern Tanzania – for children to take the identity of their father.

The army mutiny against Amin in March 1974 was led by the chief of staff, Brigadier Charles Arube, a Kakwa. He was a Catholic and the first person to be appointed the army chief staff under Amin.

He was the most prominent army officer to attempt a coup against Amin. Amin accused Arube of collaborating with Lugabra army officers in a conspiracy to overthrow him.

Earlier, in 1972, Lugbara army officers also attempted to overthrow Amin. That was not long after Amin himself overthrew Obote. It was a clear signal that he had enemies even among his own people from the West Nile District on whom he depended so much to stay in power.

He also had enemies from other parts of the country within and outside the army. Ironically, the biggest threat to his regime came from the army itself, the most powerful institution in the country and of which he was in charge. As Professor Phares Mukasa Mutibwa, a Ugandan who once taught at Makerere University in Kampala, states in his book, *Uganda Since Independence: A Story of Unfulfilled Hopes*:

"In an endeavour to tighten security the Military Police were given greater powers even than the regular army, police and prisons. A new decree (no. 19) empowered them to arrest people without a court order or an arrest warrant. They could arrest a wide range of 'criminals,' on the basis of suspicion only.

As for the armed forces, some promotions were made in May 1973 to keep them contented, but these did not stop some officers from thinking of ways of changing the leadership of the country, and the first major coup attempted by some of the most senior officers took place in March 1974. It was an event that had a lasting effect on Amin and influenced subsequent events.

However, this coup attempt was not the first against Amin since the September 1972 invasion (launched by Ugandan exiles from neighbouring Tanzania); there had been one led by Colonel Wilson Toko, commander of the Air Force, in April 1973. It was Toko who had read the citation for the decoration of Amin after the expulsion of the Asians!

Up to that time, the threats to Amin had come from outside Uganda, particularly from Tanzania; this was the first major coup attempt mounted from within. The 1974 coup was organised and led by Brigadier Charles Arube who, with Elly (Colonel Elly Aseni) and a few others (including Justice Mathew Opu), had just returned from attending a course in Moscow. It was spearheaded by the Malire Reconnaisance Regiment whose commander, Major Juma, did not particpate.

Arube's coup almost succeeded; all the important installations – Malire, Makindye and Kampala – were captured, and all that remained was to announce the overthrow of the government on Radio Uganda. In fact, the coup started so well that in the early hours of Sunday, 25 March 1974, Arube started celebrating its success with a dancing party at his house, but he was then arrested by soldiers loyal to Amin and shot and killed there and then.

It would seem that one of the major causes for Arube's coup attempt was dissatisfaction at Amin's appointment of non-Ugandans to key posts in the army and government agencies. For instance, he had elevated Malera, a Sudanese, to the high post of Army Chief of Staff, and he later relied heavily on Brigadier Taban, Lt.-Col. Gole, Lt.-Col. Sule (all Sudanese) and Brigadier Issac Maliyamungu (a Zairean). Other influential Sudanese nationals in Amin's regime at that time were Farouk Minaawa, Chief of the State Research Bureau, and Ali Towelli of the Public Safety Unit.

According to some sources, the aim of the coup organisers was to arrest Amin, Brigadier Malera and the other notorious killers from southern Sudan and place them on public trial at the Clock Tower in Kampala, where the guerrillas were executed in February 1973.

Amin was shaken by the attempted coup, which had been organised and led by Kakwa officers, his fellow-tribesmen. He felt betrayed and abandoned, but because there were very few officers whom he could appoint, he decided not to eliminate his betrayers. Instead, officers such as Lt.-Col. Elly were sent abroad as ambassadors.

Throughout 1974 Amin continued to feel threatened from all sides. On top of the abortive coup of March 1974, reports of guerrilla invasions from Tanzania in August and Sudan in November alarmed him further, and caused him to live in constant fear of being toppled by Obote.

He also believed there was an international conspiracy to unseat him, engineered by international media such as BBC and British and Kenyan newspapers. That was partly why, early in June 1974, his government banned all 'imperialist' newspapers in Uganda 'for, among other points, their perpetual stand against the Ugandan government.'

It was in these circumstances that so many innocent Ugandans died or disappeared, all suspected of working against him.

It is impossible to fathom the extent to which Amin really believed in these stories of invasions, but those who were in Uganda at that time cannot forget the tension that existed between Tanzania and Uganda, which put the country on a war footing.

Because of the increasingly serious security problems from the time the Economic War was declared, particularly in view of Toko's attempted coup in June 1973 and Arube's in March 1974, Amin took measures to strengthen his position in the army. After Arube's attempt, Amin was never the same again, a point to which those who served in his cabinet at the time have testified.

However, the reorganisation of the army to bring it directly under his control began well before March 1974, although it was speeded up thereafter. Thus in November 1974 Uganda was divided into five military commands. At the same time, civilians and non-West Nilers were removed from cabinet posts and (other) key positions."[5]

It was also clear that without ethnic and regional loyalty from his people in the West Nile District in the northwest, Amin would not have been able to exterminate the Langi and the Acholi in the army most of whom remained loyal to Obote, even though there were also divisions among them, with the Langi, his fellow tribesmen, being the most loyal to him.

After the other northwesterners abandoned or turned against Amin, the only people Amin could depend on were the Nubians and former rebels from southern Sudan, the Anya Anya, who had settled in Uganda especially in the West Nile District, his home region.

Ethnoregional loyalties in the military and the police played a prominent role in determining the balance of power between the northerners and the rest of Ugandans after independence, tipping scales in favour of the north especially when coercive power of the state had to be employed. As Donald L. Horowitz, professor of law and political science at Duke University in the United States, states in his book, *Ethnic Groups in Conflict*:

"Obote placed a loyal Northerner in the position of Inspector General of Police. The overwhelming majority of the police had long consisted of Northerners. A Lango himself, Obote packed the army with Langi and Acholi officers and men, and expanded its budget rapidly in the early years of independence.[28] Conservative estimates gave the Acholi, less than 5 percent of the population, at least one-third of the army.[29] Northern N.C.O.s were frequently commissioned, particularly after the East African army pay strikes of 1964 and the repatriation of British officers that followed. The paramilitary General Service Unit, composed heavily of Langi, was strengthened.

Like the army, the GSU was distinctly hostile to the Baganda and clashed with them from time to time.[30] Both the army and the GSU got their chance when Obote's forces attacked the palace of the Kabaka of Buganda in 1966, driving him into exile. At that point, many of the remaining Baganda officers fled the army.

When Obote further suppressed the Baganda and banned all opposition parties after an unsuccessful attempt on his life in 1969,[31] there were no further southern threats, electoral or military, to his control. The equilibrium had been destroyed.

Instead, the locus of conflict moved to the North."[6]

Professor Horowitz goes on to state:

"The Northerners who supported Obote were far from homogenous, and there is evidence that in the end he trusted only Langi, preferably relatives. He placed his cousin at the head of the GSU (General Service Unit) and the secret service[32]....

A Northerner, Amin was neither an Acholi nor a Lango, but a Kakwa.[34] In the army, he seemed to command the special loyalty of members of the Kakwa, Lugbara, and Alur ethnic groups from his own West Nile district and of the Madi next door.

Amin was also in contact with Southern Sudanese rebel groups, and it is said that he supplied them with arms to be used against the Khartoum government.[35] The Kakwa straddle the Uganda-Sudan-Zaire border.

Himself a former N.C.O., Amin maintained contact with N.C.O.s after losing favor with Obote.[36] In the months preceding the coup, Amin also manipulated the ethnic composition of certain army units. He relied particularly on West Nilers and 'Nubians,' the latter an elastic category that includes descendants of Muslim Sudanese brought to Uganda as soldiers in the nineteenth century, certain groups of West Nile Muslims, and apparently even some recent converts to Islam.[37] Amin packed one unit with Nubians, only to have Obote break it up in late 1970.[38] By then, however, Amin had transferred some twenty-two Nubian and West Nile officers to another unit, the Malire Mechanized Battalion.

By the time of the coup in 1971, thirty-two of the Malire unit's forty-three officers were Nubian, Kakwa, or Lugbara; only five were Acholi, and three were Langi.[39] When the coup came, the loyalty of this unit to Amin was a key factor. When Obote threatened to move against

301

Amin in January 1971, troops from Malire surprised Obote's forces and seized power.[40,7]

The ethnicization of the military by both Obote and Amin deeply divided the armed forces as well as other security organs including the police and entrenched ethno-regional loyalties across the spectrum. Amin exploited those sentiments when he launched a military coup against Obote. He divided the country even more when he targeted the Langi and the Acholi for elimination because they were supporters of Obote. He also fuelled regional hostilities when he favoured his fellow tribesmen and their allies from the West Nile District by recruiting them into the army in large numbers to replace the Langi and the Acholi:

"Amin's coup depended on ethnic loyalties. Its perpetrators were principally West Nilers and Nubians, as well as some Southern Sudanese recently recruited into the Uganda army.[41] The results were visible soon after the coup.

The General Service Unit was abolished, and Acholi and Langi soldiers were massacred to the point where virtually no officers from either group were left in the army.[42] (Most of Obote's guerrillas who later invaded Uganda from Tanzania were Acholi and Langi who had fled the army in 1971). Much of the killing was done by the Malire unit. Punitive expeditions were launched into the Lango district, where AWOL soldiers were hunted down, there to be killed with their families.[43]

West Nile men were promoted to take the places of the Acholi and Langi officers and soldiers. The army was expanded. Many of the new recruits were also West Nilers. Of the twenty-four top military posts in 1973, only three were not held by West Nilers; some of the new commanders had formerly been N.C.O.s.[44] Among West Nile groups, the Lugbara in particular assumed a new prominence in the army.

If 'Northerner' is not a homogeneous category, neither is 'West Niler.' With the Acholi and Langi decimated, fissures developed among their military successors. Madi and Alur officers were rather quickly purged; they were gone by 1973. The Lugbara proved more persistent.

Beginning in May 1972, and extending over the next two years, Lugbara officers planned a series of at least seven coup plots, assassination attempts, and confrontations with Amin, all of which miscarried.[45]

Amin had begun to rely increasingly on Muslim officers, particularly Kakwa. In 1972, for example, the armories were placed securely in Muslim hands. Whether these steps provoked disquiet among Lugbara in the army or resulted from it, the reliance on Muslims and the Lugbara unrest were certainly related. No longer certain of their loyalty, Amin transferred a number of prominent Lugbara officers. Finally, in March 1974, Lugbara troops, from a unit whose Lugbara commander had been replaced by a Kakwa, staged an unsuccessful revolt.[46] No senior Lugbara officer remained in the army thereafter."[8]

The ethnic cleansing by Amin did not stop there. Other groups were targeted as well.

The intention was to achieve hegemonic control of the entire country by his people, the Kakwa, and the few allies they had from his home region, the West Nile District.

In the southern part of the country, the biggest victims of Amin's purges were the Baganda. It was also time for the Asians to go, about whom we will learn more later:

"While this sorting out was taking place among West Nile groups, the very few remaining Southern sources of power were also being eliminated. Prominent civil servants, among them many Baganda, were dismissed or murdered in 1972 – 73. West Nilers, and especially Muslims, succeeded to many of these positions, as they also did to many of the businesses left by the Asians Amin expelled from Uganda at about the same time.[47]

Then, in 1974 and again in 1977, there were attempts by air force officers to kill Amin. There were still some Baganda officers in the air force – as might be expected, given the difficulty of replacing highly trained personnel in a short time. These plots 'had a definite 'Buganda flavor,' '[48] and they led to more bloody purges of Baganda in the armed forces and civil service.

In the four years following the anti-Obote coup in 1971, all of the most sensitive positions – including defense minister, armed forces chief of staff, and air force squadron commander – came to be occupied by Muslim Kakwa, Nubians, and certain increasingly prominent groups of foreigners.

The various secret police and terror units were commanded and staffed by Nubians. There was an increase of Southern Sudanese, some of them ex-Anyanya rebels, in the army, as well as some ex-Simba rebels from Zaire. The military police was commanded by a Southern Sudanese. Most of the young cadets and officers sent abroad for military training were Kakwa, Nubians, Sudanese, or Zaireans. The presidential bodyguard was composed of some 400 Palestinians.[49]

At each stage of this narrowing process, ethnic rivals were eliminated, and then the previous successful alliance disintegrated. First the North-South conflict was resolved on terms unequivocally favorable to the Northerners, who were left in control of the government and the army; then the Northern groups supporting Obote, the Langi and Acholi, were eliminated by the West Nile groups; and then the Alur, Madi, and Lugbara were eliminated by the Kakwa and Nubians....

Ultimately, Amin ended up ruling with the active support of ethnic groups comprising well under 10 percent of Uganda's population[50]."[9]

In fact, Amin's regime was more divided than Obote's ruling Uganda People's Congress Party was.

Amin divided the country even further when he decided to expand the army. He recruited soldiers mainly from the north, especially from his home region in the northwest, unlike Obote who recruited soldiers from all parts of the country although even during his presidency, the army was dominated by northerners, especially the Acholi and the Langi, an imbalance inherited from colonial rule when the British depended on the north to recruit soldiers.

To remain in power, Amin also spent lavishly on the army. Such lavish expenditure proved to be a big financial burden on the country and almost drained the treasury. He also promoted many soldiers to make them happy even though they were illiterate.

He also severed relations with Israel and expelled all Israelis from Uganda in order to forge and strengthen ties with Arab countries, especially Libya. He accused the Israelis of plotting against his government.

Establishment of strong ties with Arab countries was an expression of solidarity with the Arabs in their struggle against Israel for the rights of Palestinians although it also had financial benefits. Amin also identified with the Arabs as fellow Muslims since the majority of them are Muslim.

After expelling the Israelis, he seized all property owned by Israelis in Uganda:

"Before the Asian expulsion, President Amin turned his attention to another group of people, the Israelis. Early in 1972, he left to visit West Germany, and on his way back visited Libya, Chad and Ethiopia. In Libya, President Amin and Col. Gaddafi signed a communique affirming their support for the Arab people in their struggle against Zionism and imperialism, and for the right of the Palestinian people to return to their land and homes.

Until this time, relations between Uganda and Israel

305

had been close and cordial. Some Israeli companies were carrying out large building contracts in Uganda for the Government, and Israel had a close link with the Uganda Army which dated from 1964, when Israel supplied material and assistance to form a Uganda Air Force.

Now, however, President Amin alleged that Israel was planning subversion against Uganda, and ordered first the Israeli military training personnel, and then all Israelis, out of Uganda. Uganda broke diplomatic relations with Israel on March 30, 1972, and something like 700 Israelis were expelled. President Amin has since stated that he took this action because Israel was insisting on being paid for work done in Uganda, and for material supplied to that country, and he has said that this is the reason he expelled them."[10]

After Amin expelled the Israelis and established strong relations with Libya, Libyan military ruler Muammar Gaddafi responded by providing Amin with financial and military assistance.

Amin also strengthened ties with Saudi Arabia in order to secure financial aid.

A substantial amount of all that money was spent on the army. Soldiers were happy. In return, Amin secured protection from them although some of them did not like him and even tried to kill him. Even a lot of the property he seized from the Asians whom he expelled from the country was given to soldiers.

But it was his decision to expel the Asians, including those who were Ugandan citizens, which had far-reaching consequences politically and economically. The decision thrilled black Ugandans. It made him extremely popular across the country. He told them it was the ordinary people including the poor who would be the biggest beneficiaries of the economic war against the Asians.

However, the biggest beneficiaries turned out to be those who were closest to him, mostly soldiers. They seized property owned by the expelled Asians, including shops, houses and cars. Many other black Ugandans, especially those with ties to the government, also shared the loot.

Amin said he expelled the Asians after God told him in a dream that he should kick them out. The decision amounted to a declaration of war on the Asians. It was an economic war waged in the name of black African nationalism to Africanise the economy and everything else in Uganda, a country which belonged only to black Ugandans, according to this rationale.

He gave the Asians 90 days to leave the country.

An event which set the stage for their expulsion was a speech Amin delivered to the leaders of the Asian community on 6 December 1971. He called the meeting to express a number of grievances against the Asians which he said caused disharmony in the country between the indigenous people and the Asians. The speech was an ominous warning to the members of the Asian community. But no one thought it would lead to their expulsion from Uganda.

It was a prepared speech. Amin did not write it himself. It was written for him. But it reflected his thoughts and was perhaps dictated by him. Everything in the speech was what he had in mind. It was probably all his ideas, although he did not have the intellectual sophistication to express and elaborate them the way they were in the speech.

And he did get some help from his subordinates to polish the language in order to present it in good English. He did not have any formal education – only up to standard two – and did not want to deliver his speech in broken English which he normally spoke. This is what he said:

"This particular Conference has been convened as a follow-up of the many public statements and letters in the press complaining against the Asian community in this country.

At this Conference you as representatives of Asian groups throughout Uganda can brief the Government about the different aspects which have made Africans in this country complain against the Asians.

My aim is to ensure that like a father in a family, understanding and unity between the different communities in this country is established on a permanent basis.

I am sure that, having received your views as expressed through this Conference, and the memoranda which you produced to the Chairman, Hon. A.C.K. Oboth-Ofumbi, the Minister of Defence, whom I directed to chair your Conference, and having listened to what I am going to tell you this afternoon, I hope the wide gap between the Asians and the Africans in the different economic and social fields will narrow down, if not disappear altogether, so that all of us, whether citizens or non-citizens, African or non-African, can live a happier life in the Republic of Uganda.

No one doubts the various positive contributions which you Asians have made since the arrival of your forefathers in East Africa as railway builders. Some of the Ugandan Asians even received Government assistance to undertake different types of courses, including post-graduate training in medicine, engineering, law and other professional fields. Whereas some of these people after completing their training joined the Government, and have done a good job, I regret to point out to you that many of them have shown total disloyalty to the same Government which financed their training and enabled them to use other training facilities.

For instance, between 1962 and 1968, the Government of Uganda sponsored as many as 417 Asians for training as engineers. Today, however, only 20 of the 417 Asians work for the Government. Within the same period, the Government sponsored 217 Asians to train as doctors, but to date not more than 15 doctors of these are working for the Government.

Finally within the same period, the Government sponsored 96 Asians to undertake law courses, but of these only 18 are now serving in the Government.

You can ask yourselves the question as to where the majority of the Asians trained by the Uganda Government have disappeared. My information is that many of them either took up private practice immediately after their training or joined the Government but resigned to go into private practice. In view of the fact that it is extremely expensive to sponsor a student to undertake a professional course at graduate level, I consider that these Asians who deliberately refused to return to serve the Government, or who did so briefly and then left, have cheated this nation.

I am further informed that some of these Asians who were sponsored to take courses abroad refused to return to Uganda after they qualified, which means that they have contributed absolutely nothing in return for the training benefits which they received from this Government. Moreover, I am told that some of them who resigned from Government service did so on very selfish grounds, such as working in the Government on the condition that they would not be transferred away from either Entebbe, Kampala, Mbale or Jinja to up-country stations.

Although some of them gave the excuse that they would not agree to be transferred up-country because of lack of schools, housing, appropriate medical facilities etc., yet we know fully well that in most cases their refusal was due to the fact that a good number of them have side businesses outside the Civil Service, such as shops, garages, transport businesses etc., from which they get extra huge sums of money, and which therefore they dislike to leave behind while they go on up-country transfer.

My government deplores this attitude and I wish to direct all the Ministries in which Asians are employed at any level to report to me from now on any Asian who refuses to go on up-country transfer for any reason at all.

I am particularly disturbed in this matter because according to reports which the Minister of Health has given me, some of the Asians who refused to be transferred to hospitals such as Gulu, Apach, Aturtur, Iganga, Soroti and even Butabika Mental Hospital, and who in some cases resigned in protest against those transfers include some consultants on whom the Government obviously heavily relies for the improvement of the medical services to residents of Uganda at large. This is but one of the many disturbing aspects of your community.

Having made the above point on the general disloyalty of some members of your community to the Government, I now wish to turn to probably the most painful matter around which public statements and correspondence in the press have centred. That is the question of your refusal to integrate with the Africans in this country.

It is particularly painful in that about 70 years have elapsed since the first Asians came to Uganda, but despite that length of time the Asian community has continued to live in a world of its own; for example, African males have hardly been able to marry Asian girls. For example, a casual count of African males who are married to Asian females reveals that there are only six. And even then, all the six married these women when they were abroad, and not here in Uganda.

In the cases where there have been moves by Asian girls to love Africans, it has been done in absolute secrecy. I as well as you yourselves certainly know that these girls are under their parents' strict instructions never to fall in love with Africans.

On the other hand, it is interesting to note that many Asian men in this country are loving and living with African girls without favourable pressure from the parents of those girls. This is the sort of attitude which I would welcome because it points the way to integration between Africans and Asians. Asian parents should leave their sons and daughters free to integrate with Africans, instead of imposing against them social restrictions that are completely out of date.

Although I am aware that this lack of integration between the Africans and the Asians is due to the extension of the Asian caste system and ways of life generally, the Government of the Republic of Uganda is of the firm view that if there is goodwill on the part of the Asian communities it is possible for you to reach an understanding whereby integration among all the people in this country would be easy. I am therefore appealing to you here as the representatives of all the Asian communities in Uganda to consider this point seriously in the interest of integration between you and the Africans at all levels. I am saying this because I know that if we do not integrate in this country the situation which would be build up could easily lead to serious racial disharmony.

I am aware that one of the causes of the continuing distant social relations between the Asians and the Africans in this country was the policy of the colonial Government which ensured that the Africans, Asians and Europeans had entirely separate schools, hospitals, residential quarters, social and sports clubs and even public toilets – with the facilities to serve the Africans being of the poorest quality and hopelessly inadequate. We have, of course, now changed all this, but there are Asians who still live in the past and consider, like the former colonialist Government, that the Africans are below them. This living in the past cannot help Asians in any way, nor can it foster the desired harmony and unity.

One sector which greatly disturbs my Government are the numerous malpractices which many of your community members are engaged in. We are, for instance, aware of the fact that some Asians are the most notorious people in the abuse of our exchange control regulations.

Some of you are known to export goods and not to bring the foreign exchange back into Uganda. On the other hand some of you are known to undervalue exports and overvalue imports in order to keep the difference in values in your overseas accounts. Another malpractice for which many of you are notorious is that of smuggling commodities like sugar, maize, hoes etc. from Uganda to the neighbouring territories.

This has on many occasions created an artificial shortage of those commodities within Uganda, with the result that whatever was left here at home was finally sold at unduly high prices.

You are all aware of the recent importation of sugar from India. In this particular case, the Government was told that the shortage of sugar within the country was due to the drought which had hit sugar production at Kakira and Lugazi. What we know, however, is that the sugar shortage which we suffered was mainly due to the fact that a number of Asian businessmen and smuggled sugar into the neighbouring countries.

Another bad practice which many Asian businessmen practise in the hoarding of goods in order to create an artificial shortage, again resulting in higher prices for these goods. A typical example is the recent court case in which Hussein Shariff Velji Mawji was convicted for hoarding oil and selling it at black market above the Government-controlled price.

These malpractices show clearly that some members of your community have no interest in this country beyond the aim of making as much profit as possible and at all costs. As I have already said on other occasions, my Government will not tolerate those malpractices and will take all necessary measures to stamp them out. If any businessman is found smuggling or hoarding goods in this country, such businessman should not expect any mercy and he will permanently lose his trading licence whether he is a citizen of this country or not.

My government also feels strongly about the practice of some of your traders in deliberately sabotaging government policy by, for instance, renting to African traders only the front room in the shops in controlled areas, while retaining the back rooms, toilet and the cooking facilities.

Your community made use of the policy of establishing their own commercial and trading organisations which played a big part in the economic life of this nation. Here I am thinking of thousands of shops which the Asians built all over Uganda to deal in a wide variety of goods. I am further thinking of big industrial concerns and farming activities which, for example, have all along been spreaheaded by such outstanding families as the Madhavanis, Mehtas, etc. All these activities have assisted employment opportunities without which some people might have been forced to take up criminal activities.

Besides your contribution to the commercial and industrial life, I must also mention the part some of you have played in the expansion of educational and medical facilities in Uganda.

I should also like here to pay tribute to some of your members who have served and are serving in the different fields in the Government. There is no doubt, therefore, that the work of some of your people as judges of the High Court, magistrates, doctors, engineers, teachers, accountants, etc., has been vital in the development of the country.

But, and this is a big but, there are several disturbing matters which I now want to point out to you frankly as, indeed, this is the purpose of this Conference. Firstly, I want to say that it is a well-known fact that the Uganda Government has made available facilities for the training of Ugandans as well as non-Ugandan Asians in the local and overseas educational institutions.

Some Asians have deliberately locked up their premises in areas which have been declared restricted areas, and have refused to rent them to African businessmen. It is also common knowledge that some of you who decided to rent their premises to the African traders did so at inflated rates.

I must remind you that any Government worth its name cannot sit back and allow a minority group of any kind deliberately to work against the policies of that Government, which are aimed at the overall national development of that country. I therefore intend to instruct the Ministry of Commerce, Industry and Tourism to double its efforts in tracking down such offending Asian traders in order to completely wipe out these malpractices that are aimed at defeating government policy.

Another malpractice I may mention is that of under-cutting African traders, and unfair competition. It is well-known that you are generally importers, wholesalers, and retailers at the same time. Many of you have taken advantage of this position to frustrate aspiring African businessmen in every possible way. Again, many of practise price discrimination against African traders, in that you supply your fellow Asians with goods at lower prices than those at which you supply your African traders. In this respect, it is up to you Asian businessmen to do everything possible to see that the competition between you and the African businessmen is conducted fairly, with the aim of balanced commercial and economic development of this country, otherwise here again Government will be forced to take action.

While still on the subject of malpractices in trade, I should like to mention the tendency of Asians to keep all their business within their family circles.

When Government insisted that you should absorb as many Africans as possible into your businesses, some of you started to employ some outstanding Africans in the posts, for instance, managing directors, personnel managers, sales managers etc. What we know, however, is that all these appointments were mere window-dressing, and that those Africans whom you have employed, although they earn fat salaries, know next to nothing as far as the secrets of your enterprises are concerned.

Apart from this, I also regret to note that you have been most reluctant to trust Africans in your different trades. Thus you find that even the Africans you employ at your counters in your shops have to consult you practically every time a customer approaches them, to ask the price of whatever you will sell. This shows that, apart from your giving them the jobs in your shops, you have not given them the necessary authority and trust to finalize even simple deals with customers.

It is also disturbing to note that some of your members have carried out practices which are meant to evade the payment of income tax. They do this, for example, by keeping two sets of books. One set is specially for inspection by the Income Tax Department, whilst another, which shows the true and correct accounts of the business, is kept for your own use.

Of course, one of the advantages which you derived from the Colonial Government in this case is that you were also permitted to keep your accounts books in your Gujarati writing which cannot be read by your African directors and the officials of the Income Tax Department. It is not my intention to direct the Minister of Education to introduce Gujarati in our schools yet, but I urge you to refrain from such practices which made the reading of accounts by the authorized officers impossible.

It is also very well-known that many Asians in this country believe that they cannot get any services rendered to them by any Government department or para-State organisation without their extending favours to the officers who are dealing with their problems. There appears to be a belief that unless one corrupts somebody one might not get such things as licences, passports, tenders, applications for citizenship, medical treatment, a plot in the town, or eating-house licence approved at all, or approved quickly enough.

This malpractice has unfortunately been generally accepted by some of the public officers in this country, because of the constant pressure they receive from the members of your community who practise corruption. This practice of corruption by some Asians has, therefore, interfered with some of the officers' decisions which should otherwise be based on truth, equality, nationality and justice.

As I appealed to the taxi-drivers to report any cases of policemen who asked them for bribes, I appeal to report any case where any public officer asks you for a bribe. Equally, I expect all of you to stop tempting public officers with bribes.

I turn to the question of citizenship. As already stated on many occasions in the past, my Government is committed to upholding all the legal obligations inherited from the previous Government. This means, in short, that in the matter of citizenship my Government will respect all citizenship certificates which were properly issued before the 25th January 1971. However, with respect to such certificates as were illegally obtained, these will not be respected and will be cancelled in accordance with the provisions of the law.

Concerning old applications for citizenship which were outstanding as on the 25th January 1971, my Government does not consider itself in any way bound to process such applications and regards them as having been automatically cancelled by lapse of time. Some of them had been outstanding for as many as seven or eight years.

For the future, all those who are interested in obtaining Ugandan citizenship will have to make fresh applications, and these will be processed in accordance with new qualifications which my Government is in the process of formulating and which will be announced in due course. In this respect, information and particulars which Government will obtain from the recent census of Asians, when finally worked out, will be relevant and of much use.

However, my Government is disturbed because it is clear that many of you have not shown sufficient faith in Ugandan citizenship. This is indicated by the fact that the vast majority of you refused to apply for citizenship which was offered after independence.

Another point is the practice whereby one family is composed of individuals all of whom are citizens of different nationalities. For example, whereas a head of the family may be a British passport holder, his wife may turn out to be a an Indian or Pakistani citizen, whilst their children might be citizens of either Kenya, Uganda or Tanzania. Sometimes two brothers are registered as different citizens. This shows clearly that many of you have no confidence at all in Uganda or any of the other countries, for that matter. I will not hesitate to say that you are gambling with one of the matters which my Government takes most seriously, and that is citizenship.

Therefore I will remind you that, if there is any blame which you might later on wish to bring against my Government about your citizenship, the persons responsible for any confusion were yourselves.

Having drawn your attention to the above points, I now strongly wish to appeal to you to come together as a single community and discuss these points and present to Government a memorandum showing clearly what you are going to do in order to eliminate the complaints I have made against your community. My Government is going to take steps to see where the malpractices stated above are a breach of the laws of this country or exploitation of loopholes.

Those laws will then either be amended so that they work more tightly, or their enforcement will be strengthened. What I do not want to convey to the group whom you represent here this afternoon is the impression that Government considers your community an abandoned child. It is yo yourselves, through your refusal to integrate with the Africans in this country, who have created this feeling towards you by the Africans. But as far as my Government I concerned, and until the issue of the Asians who hold British passports is cleared, I consider you as one of a family of this nation.

Therefore, when you discuss what to do in order to eliminate the misunderstanding which has been created between you and the Africans in this country, you should remember that the solutions you are looking for are for the improvement of the relations within this family – Uganda. Furthermore, I wish to reassure those of you who might be panicking because I called this Conference, that this Conference, like the Uganda Development Master Plan Conference, the Baganda Elders' Conference, the Muslim Leaders' Conference, the Church of Uganda Leaders' Conference, and the Agricultural Officers' Conference, is meant to fulfill the aspirations of this Government, which is to improve the unity, understanding, love and racial integration among all the people of this country.

In other words, this is not an isolated Conference which is aimed at attacking your community because of the malpractices which I have outlined above. What I want of you is self-examination and the correction of any weaknesses which affect your community and which have made the Africans speak and write against you. I am doing this because I believe in God in Being Frank. That is why I did not discuss the public allegations against you secretly with my Cabinet or the Defence Council, but I decided to put it to you as prominent leaders of the Asian community in this country.

I, therefore, hope that you will take my address to you this afternoon and probably the whole night counting nthe various malpractices which are common among the Asian community, particularly in commerce and industry, but as it is not my intention to accuse, but rather to remedy an unsatisfactory situation, I consider that the examples I have given are sufficient to illustrate the concern of the public and of my Government over the activities of your community in this country."[11]

The speech was published in the *Uganda Gazette 1972*, Government Printer, Entebbe, Uganda.

Amin used mild yet very strong language in his speech to the leaders of the Asian community. And it was clear he intended to warn them strongly of what was to come, although he was not specific. But there was no question Asians were no longer welcome in Uganda as long as he was president.

Still, many of them did not think he would take the extreme or drastic measure he did by confiscating their property, including money in the bank, and by kicking them out of the country.

There were those who left even before he gave that speech. They believed he was hostile towards them. But the majority stayed. They never thought he would expel them or simply hoped for the best.

I remember their expulsion well. It was during the same period that I left my home country, Tanzania, for the United States for the first time aboard East African Airways (EAA).

I left Dar es Salaam on 4 November 1972. After a stop in Nairobi, Kenya, the plane flew to Entebbe, Uganda. Almost all the people who boarded the plane at Entebbe were Asians, expelled by Amin, on their way to Britain and elsewhere.

I did not get off the plane. Relations between Uganda my country were very bad during that period and I did not want to take chances with my life by getting off the plane even for just a few minutes.

When the expelled Asians boarded the plane, an elderly man, who was one of those expelled, came to sit next to me. I knew he was one of the victims. He asked me where I was going. I told him I was going to school in the United States. He wished me the best and remained quiet during most of the flight, probably pondering his future after being expelled from Uganda. As I state in one of my books:

"I remember the expulsion well. I was on the same flight, East African Airways (EAA), with some of the expelled Asians in November 1972 on my way to Britain, and got the chance to talk with an elderly Indian sitting next to me. He was one of those kicked out of Uganda by the burly dictator and talked about this forced exodus, about which I had known when I was a reporter at the *Daily News* in Dar es Salaam, Tanzania.

The flight originated from Dar es Salaam, Tanzania's capital, where I caught the plane on my way to the United States for the first time as a student. Our first stop was Nairobi, Kenya; next, Entebbe, Uganda, where the expelled Asians boarded the plane on their way to Britain and whatever other countries would take them in.

Stripped of their possessions including financial assets, they landed in Britain, and in other countries such as Canada and the United States, destitute. Most of them ended up in Britain, Uganda's former colonial ruler. Almost all the passengers on the flight I was on from Uganda were Asians expelled by Idi Amin, as were those on subsequent flights, booked full.

President Julius Nyerere of Tanzania publicly condemned Idi Amin for expelling the Asians and called him a racist. Two other African leaders, President Kenneth Kaunda of Zambia and President Samora Machel of Mozambique, also criticized Amin for his brutalities and eccentric behaviour in general.

But it was Nyerere who was most explicit in his condemnation of Amin, and strongly criticized other African leaders for their silence and tolerance - and even admiration - of the Ugandan despot and for practising tyranny in their own countries.

He reminded them that had Idi Amin been white, and

had the apartheid regime of South Africa gone on a genocidal rampage, slaughtering blacks across the country, these same leaders would have been furious. There would have been an outcry across the continent, calling for severe sanctions and even military action against the white murderers. But because Amin was black, other African leaders simply looked the other way, as they did when other atrocities were being committed across the continent by fellow Africans. Black leadership had become a license to kill fellow blacks."[12]

Amin claimed he wanted to put the economy in the hands of Africans, a term synonymous with blacks. But the expulsion of Asians proved to be disastrous. The economy, once robust but then in tatters because of mismanagement under his leadership, virtually collapsed.

He had accused the Asians, mostly of Indian and Pakistani origin but mostly Indian, of economic sabotage. Yet it was he who ended up destroying the economy by expelling them and by appointing people who were not qualified to help him govern the country.

Many stereotypes against the Indians – a collective term of ethnic identity since the vast majority of the Asians who were expelled were of Indian origin – were used to justify the expulsion. The term "Indians" also denotes a broad or an elastic category comprising all the people of the Indian subcontinent and their descendants – originally from India, Pakistan and Bangladesh.

They were labelled as exploiters whose only objective was self-enrichment at the expense of the indigenous people.

They were accused of hoarding wealth. They were accused of milking the economy. They were accused of overcharging Africans and discriminating against them.

Everything that went wrong with the economy was blamed on them. Africans were poor because Indians were exploiting them. The economy was not growing because of the Indians. They were guilty of economic strangulation. They were also guilty of impeding progress across the spectrum because they controlled the economy. It was time to declare war on them. But in the long run, the war proved to be too costly for Uganda in more than one way:

"Some of the Asians had been born in Uganda and were Ugandan citizens, whereas many others held foreign passports. For Amin, this did not matter – they were foreigners and spies in his country and needed to be expelled.

The Asians held many civil service jobs and essentially formed the middle class. With their expulsion, Amin established the foundation for the destruction of the Ugandan economy. He seized the pillaged Asian assets and properties for himself and his cronies. Some estimates suggest that this amounted to more than five thousand firms, factories, ranches, and agricultural estates and about $400 million in personal possessions.

In January 1973 Amin decided to nationalize all British-owned businesses in Uganda – without compensation. This naturally strained ties between Great Britain and Uganda, and the situation came to a head when Amin embraced Libya and the former Soviet Union over Britain and Israel, Uganda's traditional allies.

The United States closed its embassy in Uganda in 1973, and Britain followed suit, shuttering the doors of its high commission in 1976....

Amin's economic war was initially met with jubilation from many Ugandans, who believed that Asians were foreigners who had profited off the backs of Ugandans. Little did they know at the time that Amin's pillaging would not stop with the Asians' property and assets.

The impact of Amin's economic war on the Ugandan economy was not felt immediately, because the nation's main export, coffee, continued to do well on the international market. But by 1977 the Ugandan economy was in shambles, with inflation averaging 1,000 percent. The Ugandan infrastructure was also in bad shape, with an inept civil service. Soon the economy collapsed. Peasants refused to grow coffee, as often they were not paid for months, if at all."[13]

Forty years after the Asians were expelled from Uganda, one Asian, Nina Lakhani, recalled that tragic event in her article, "After the Exodus: 40 years on From Amin's Terror Offensive Against Asians in Uganda," in *The Independent*, London, 24 June 2012:

"A dozen or so children are gathered outside 2 Nile Gardens in Jinja, Uganda, playing and preparing mogo (cassava), as we pull up outside the detached, corner bungalow around lunchtime. They all stop, momentarily shy of strangers, but relax as my mum explains in Swahili that this was her home 40 years ago – and she has just come back to remember the old days.

The children are excited to hear her stories, following her around the house as she points out the old bedrooms, a coal-room, the store-room for sacks of rice and flour, and the tiniest room, which once served as a mini-temple in which my grandmother would pray.

The wide-eyed kids can hardly believe her tales, as 40 years later, this once-comfortable bungalow is now in a dilapidated state: many windows are broken and there is no running water or electricity. Once home to my prosperous, extended family, these days it houses 10 extremely poor Ugandan families, one to each cramped room.

The best-preserved part of the house is the shady veranda out front, where every afternoon the women would once have gossiped while chopping vegetables and the toddlers played. Back then, the older children could usually be found outside on the oblong grassy gardens,

323

around which 20 Asian families lived for decades.

It was from this very veranda that my mum got her one and only glimpse of General Idi Amin Dada, not long after he overthrew the elected government in a military coup in January 1971. 'He was standing on the corner of the neighbour's house talking politics, and we secretly watched him from here. He was so big, tall and fat, with big, red eyes. We were all scared of him because he was a military man and they used to say he drank human blood.'

Then, Ansuya Lakhani was a 27-year-old mother of one, and little did she know that this scary man, fanciful rumours aside, would go on to become one of the world's most brutal dictators. In eight short years, Idi Amin, the self-professed 'Last King of Scotland,' slayed hundreds of thousands of his countrymen suspected of harbouring loyalties to the previous government, and oversaw devastating economic and social ruin.

In 1972, Amin expelled more than 70,000 Asians, including my family, as part of his incoherent, sadistic plans that he claimed would make Uganda thrive. This decisive intervention led 29,000 Asians to come to Britain over a three-month period – one of the largest diasporas since the Second World War – uprooting my family from the only country they had ever called home and, in doing so, determining the course of my life before I was born.

In 2012, the year that marks the 40th anniversary of the Asian exodus, I have come to Uganda for the first time, to the place that would have been home.

I grew up with romantic stories about the old life, in the country known as the Pearl of Africa, so fertile that a few chilli seeds carelessly thrown out of the kitchen window would bestow a new plant.

My dad and his seven siblings were born in Jinja, where the majestic River Nile begins its journey across Africa. Ironically, Uganda's second city has, since 1963, been twinned with Finchley, a north London suburb where more than a handful of Ugandan-Asians ended up.

My mum, now 67, laments the pitiful state of her former marital home, which is the most ramshackle on the square. 'It makes me want to cry to see what it has become. We lived a good life here. We worked hard, but it was a relaxed life, it was our home.'

Nile Gardens was, back then, part of Asian Town, exclusively home to the city's 10,000 or so Asians, with every shop on Main Street owned by and largely catering for their needs. British-imposed segregation, broadly accepted by the 1.2 million Asians then living in Africa, had meant that before Ugandan independence in 1962, it was rare for the three racial groups to mix in school, work or play.

The sprawling Rock View School in Tororo, my mum's home-town near the Kenyan border, is now attended by almost 3,000 primary-aged schoolchildren, many travelling far from surrounding villages for a chance to learn. But it opened in 1942 as the fee-paying Indian public school, with only Asian teachers teaching only Asian girls, no more than 20 per class.

'It wasn't until we went to Britain that we really understood that what we had been doing was so bad. We never hated the Africans, and we never once treated them badly, but we never played together, or lived together. We wouldn't even use the same plates,' admits my mum.

'They lived in their areas, we lived in ours and the British lived in Europe Town, that's just the way it was and I didn't question it. When I saw how some of the British people treated us [when we arrived], I understood, and felt so bad about how we had lived our lives in Africa.'

It was in Tororo that Amin announced on 4 August 1972 his decision to rid the country of the 'bloodsucking' Asians who he declared were sabotaging the country's economy and taking African jobs. His intention to rid the country of what he called the 'British Asians' sent shockwaves around the world, nowhere more than here.

Three-quarters of East African Asians had opted for a

British passport at independence, though most were still subject to strict immigration controls. But worsening race relations and dwindling job opportunities meant more and more Asians wanted to emigrate, from Kenya in particular. MPs such as Enoch Powell warned of an impending race-relations crisis, so in 1968 the Labour government stemmed the flow of immigrants (legally British citizens) by introducing an annual quota system.

Yet, in August 1972, Edward Heath's Tory government was suddenly faced with having to honour promises made to colonial subjects a decade earlier.

At first nobody believed Amin, but within days it became clear that this was no joke – and my family was among tens of thousands of Asians forced to flee. Further absurd decrees from Amin, together with violence and looting by his undisciplined army, spread fear across the country. The mood was exacerbated by the British government's initial refusal to accept responsibility for its citizens.

Officials first tried to negotiate with the General, whom they believed to be a man Britain could work with, and then tried to offload as many evacuees as possible to other Commonwealth countries. Government documents reveal attempts to find an island on which to house (some might say dump) the Asians, amid fears that the public wouldn't tolerate such a huge influx of coloured migrants.

My mum remembers those dark days well: 'Everyone was frightened for their lives. We would hear stories of dead bodies floating in the Nile, dumped from trucks by Amin's men; we were too scared to go outside.'

The expulsion came at a time when my family had been prospering. Several aunts and uncles were working or studying in the UK, my dad was progressing at Standard Bank and the family's transport business was expanding fast; they were on track to becoming millionaires when the carpet was pulled from under their feet. But, at the same time, many families were almost destitute – banned from jobs under Africanisation policies – and so cheered when Amin forced the British to accept them as citizens.

My mother and grandmother, who arrived in Uganda in 1934 from India aged 13 after marrying my grandfather, always described Tororo as an idyllic place where everybody knew everybody else, and children played with bottle tops, filling their bellies from fruit-laden mango and papaya trees.

This magical place turns out to be a twee two-street affair with a roundabout and an impressive, imposing rock overlooking the town as its most notable landmarks. My grandfather's shop, which had sat on the main street selling bicycles, hardware and textiles, is now a lawyer's office and mobile-phone shop.

Next door, the tailor, Owino William, who owns the shop where he once worked, immediately recognises my mum: 'Matoto ya matoto,' he exclaims, jumping up to embrace her. 'The little girl of the little boy' – the latter being how my grandfather was known from the time he arrived from Gujarat at the age of 13 to the day he reluctantly left his beloved Africa 48 years later. Like the vast majority of Asians in East Africa, he had come voluntarily in hope of a better life, encouraged by the colonial masters to help develop the economy and provide goods and services for the coolies brought over to build the railways.

The long, narrow, very simple one-storey house behind the shop is almost unchanged. Local land disputes are now resolved from the old lounge which once doubled as a bedroom for my mum and her sisters. Behind that, the rest of the house is office and home to the lawyer Opino Walter Simali, who couldn't be more welcoming.

His father had moved in not long after my grandparents left, but Mr Simali only bought the place from my family after – in the late 1980s – Uganda's current president, Yoweri Museveni, allowed Asians to claim back properties in the hope they might return to help rebuild the economy.

By happy coincidence, my mum bumps into an old neighbour, Ramesh Pathani, who she hasn't seen for more than 40 years. He lives in London, too, but has been in Tororo for 10 months, embroiled in legal shenanigans to reclaim the house and soap factory his family left behind.

Their factory, like all Asian businesses, had been handed over to favoured Ugandans by Amin as part of his great economic war. The move was a populist one – but had catastrophic consequences, as most new owners had no business experience, which, together with trade embargos and blocked credit, quickly led to desperate shortages.

In Jinja, we meet shop owner and landlord Hitesh Dahia, whose family was permanently split by the troubles. His grandmother went back to India; he, his mother and sister were allowed into Britain; but his father and grandfather, Ugandan citizens, were not, so they, along with several hundred others, stayed put and tried to carry on. The pair were personally guaranteed protection by Amin, but in 1976, the grandfather was shot dead in his shop by military looters. It was a sign that Amin was losing his grip.

Dahia, like most Asians who have returned to Uganda, divides his time between this country and Britain, with economic and emotional ties to both.

As does Alibhai Kara, 69, who in 1972 left his textiles shop in the safe hands of an African childhood friend. In 1987 he left his family in Bolton, to return to a city that he found was in dire straits. 'The roads were ruined; so many people had been killed, it was a mess. But I was born here, it is my home, and anyway, who would give someone my age a job in the UK?'

These shopkeepers stand out in Jinja's high street amid the new generation of immigrants from India, thousands of whom have come on work permits from one rural region of Gujarat over the past 10 to 15 years. They own many of the country's mini-supermarkets and predominantly employ only Indians because, they tell us, local people cannot be trusted to work hard or to be left with money.

The blatant and insidious racism dished out by some of this new and expanding population is fuelling tensions, which are never far from the surface. In 2007, two Indian men were killed after protests triggered by a controversial government plan to sell part of a protected forest to an Asian sugar-cane mogul turned into full-blown race riots.

'These new Indians treat the local people as if they are doing them a favour by selling them something,' says Dahia, 'so I don't blame them for being so upset. We had a meeting in the town hall recently, and the local government told the Indians to behave better or get out.'

In Iganga, a small town between Jinja and Tororo, we get into an argument with some shop owners. 'Haven't you people learnt anything from what happened to us?' asks my mum. 'You are in someone else's country and you can't even treat people properly with a little respect; you are all asking for the same trouble.'

A few minutes later we get chatting to three Ugandan market stallholders while buying some sugar. 'Thank you, mama, for teaching your children good manners,' says one woman to my mum. 'The Indians here don't even reply when we say 'Jambo' [Hello] – we want you people to come back.'

My mum looks heartbroken. She never wanted to leave, but nor can she imagine going back after so long.

My parents holidayed in Britain in 1971, when my dad's younger brother, Himat Lakhani (who ran away from Uganda in 1962 for a better education) tried to convince them to buy a house in Golders Green, going cheap for £5,000. 'I told him not to be stupid,' says my dad. 'Uganda was our home and when we got old, we had ideas of retiring in India, never Britain.'

So when Amin's explusion took effect a year later, my mum and dad, aged 28 and 33, seriously considered a life in India. Not that they had ever been, but for them, it somehow seemed less alien, less of a risk than coming to the UK, because neither had an education to fall back on (my mum left school at 12, my dad at 18). 'But we knew it would be better for our children if we came to the UK, as they would get a good education,' explains my mum.

My family was temporarily split during those mad three months. One aunt left quickly with three of her four children because they had a coveted unrestricted passport, foiling the looters by "smuggling" out the family's gold jewellery among the children's bags.

Most people queued for hours in the heat to get the correct paperwork from the somewhat unsympathetic British High Commission, and then outside the Bank of Uganda to buy plane tickets and exchange 1,000 shillings for £50 – the total foreign currency each person was allowed to leave with.

Daily reports of brutality in Uganda, allied with Amin's declaration of allegiance with Hitler and government assurances that the Asians were middle-class, educated people who would easily assimilate into British life, meant that by the time the first chartered plane landed at a wet and dreary Stansted Airport on 18 September, the British public was largely persuaded that these were worthy victims.

My parents, brother Deven, two, and cousin Avni, three, were among the last to leave, at the end of October 1972. The family left behind five trucks, two cars, a lifetime of belongings and most of their money – split between their staff. For some reason they shipped blankets, pots and pans, and huge cooking utensils with hollow handles stuffed with pound notes, which miraculously arrived in London, box by box, over the coming months. Those saucepans are still used: 'They came this far, how can I throw them away,' we're always told.

My family was lucky: they were quickly reunited,

while many, including thousands of Ugandan passport-holders declared stateless, spent months apart in different countries, waiting for refuge. Most of my family started out in a rented house in Sudbury, north-west London, where the kids got their first glimpse of a TV. But my dad went to Stradishall, a former RAF station in Suffolk, one of 17 refugee camps set up by the government's Ugandan Resettlement Board. More than 20,000 people spent time on these disused barracks in far-flung places such as Yeovil, Greenham Common and Tywyn in north-west Wales, which were criticised for being cold, cramped, unfit for purpose, isolated.

Despite protests from the National Front and strikes by Smithfield meat porters (presumably worried about their jobs), hundreds of volunteers rallied with a war-like spirit to help out, with church groups, the WRVS and Citizens Advice on hand with warm clothes and welfare counsel.

My dad stayed in Stradishall for almost two months, filling out job applications, trying to acclimatise himself to his new country. He was offered a junior post by both the Midland and Standard banks, with a clerk's starting salary of £1,400 per year.

But then along came Peter Black, a Jewish man who had escaped the Nazis by hiding in a truck, and now wanted to help someone in a similar plight. 'He offered me a job in the accounts department of his factory in Yorkshire for £1,500 a year, but also free accommodation for a year,' explains my dad. 'We had never heard of Yorkshire, and of course I personally would have preferred a bank job, but I needed a house for your mum and brother, so we said yes and took the train to Keighley.'

They spent nine years in West Yorkshire, where they had two more children – my brother Mehul and me – improved their English and bought their first house. 'It was so cold, it snowed and snowed, but I felt so embarrassed to wear trousers because I thought everyone was laughing at me,' says my mum. 'But we didn't have too many problems

– sometimes people would call us 'Paki' or say, 'Go back home,' but we just ignored them. We made friends, but we were lonely as we had never lived without the rest of the family.'

Mum got her first ever job in Peter Black's factory, but became depressed and lonely– so when my dad got the chance to start his own business with a friend in London, a toy shop near West Ham's stadium, they headed south.

My dad, now 72, was perhaps too trusting to be truly successful in business, and after trying his hand at a succession of small ventures, settled at a friend's post office, where he still works. My mum "retired" in 1997 to care for my grandmother – for it was the elderly who found the exodus most difficult, arriving in the UK too old to learn the language or find a job; too cold to venture outside much; and never again really feeling free. This trip made me realise just how much families like mine gave up – not just their homes and jobs, but their identities, relationships, often hopes and dreams. Though we hear about how successful these immigrants became, this truth is anecdotal rather than being based on any real evidence about what became of their lives.

Being witness to some hateful racism dished out by those Indians who have more recently made the move to Uganda has made me think not that Amin was justified or right, but why he might have thought it would be a popular decision. The long-standing mutually beneficial relationship between the Asian businessmen and President Museveni cannot last forever. What happens to the Asians then... well, anything is possible.

Naturally, I've often wondered what my life might have been like had Amin not been a deranged despot. It's odd but I felt something I can't quite explain when I was in Uganda – though not the powerful connection I had visiting India for the first time. And I now can't stop thinking about how different I might have been. My mum's take on these musings: 'Don't think too much, everything happens for a reason.' Spoken like a true survivor."[14]

The expulsion of the Asians from Uganda by Amin was only one aspect of his brutal dictatorship. His reign of terror covered every aspect of Ugandan life. It was synonymous with destruction. He left his imprint everywhere, in every part of Uganda, and on the life of every Ugandan. Even after he was long gone, evidence of his destruction was clearly visible. No part of Uganda was left untouched.

Farmers, on whom the country depended so much, resorted to smuggling since they were not being paid enough for their products. Many simply stopped growing cash crops, such as coffee and cotton, or produced very little. It was a major blow to the country. Agriculture was the backbone of its economy. Without it, it was doomed.

Most of the smuggled goods went to Kenya. Amin gave orders to shoot smugglers on sight. His adviser, Bob Astel, a British, was given the responsibility to take whatever measures he considered appropriate to address the problem. But that did not save the economy from collapsing.

He did not even have the people to help rejuvenate or revive the economy. The infrastructure and institutions such as the civil service had also collapsed. Technocrats and other skilled people were either dead or had fled the country.

Uganda suffered a tremendous loss of its highly trained manpower during the seventies. That was when about a third of its highly skilled people and professionals were killed or fled into exile. Newly trained ones overseas refused to return home.

All sectors of the economy became paralysed. Even the vibrant manufacturing sector, which functioned well under Obote, came to a grinding halt. The treasury was almost empty and the people who were put in charge of the economy did not not know what they were doing.

Amin made a complete mockery of merit.

Even the army, on which he depended so much, was not spared. He appointed many civilians as army officers and promoted them rapidly. Most of them were illiterate or barely literate. They were mostly members of his tribe, the Kakwa, or of other tribes from his home region, the West Nile District, in northwestern Uganda. One of his most bizarre appointments was when he chose a former telephone operator to be the head of the air force.

The West Nile District was one of the most neglected. Under Amin, it was the most favoured. When he doubled the size of the army by 1977, most of the soldiers who were recruited during that period came from the West Nile District.

He also recruited into the army many people from neighbouring countries – Sudan, Zaire and Rwanda – whom he believed would be loyal to him by doing them such as a favour. But such a policy had unintended consequences. A very large number of soldiers in the army were not only foreigners; they could not communicate well because they spoke different languages. Not all of them understood or spoke Kiswahili, or Swahili, a language that is commonly used in the armed forces.

There were also disciplinary problems. Some army officers and their units were out of control and virtually established independent fiefdoms, terrorising local civilians, without the slightest fear of punishment from the central government because it had no control over them and didn't even care to discipline them. Thus, while Amin was the overall military ruler of Uganda, a number of army officers were also absolute rulers in their own areas. And they ruled with impunity.

The security forces Amin established, especially the State Research Bureau (SRB) and the the Public Safety Unit (PSU), grew rapidly and had about 15,000 people by 1979. They were some of the most brutal and most efficient agents of state-sponsored terror, probably the worst in post-colonial Africa up to that time, rivalled only by President Masie Nguema's regime in Equatorial Guinea where an entire third of the country's population was either wiped out or was forced to flee into exile.

Amin's terror squads which collectively constituted his security forces started to undermine themselves. They competed and fought against each other along tribal lines. The Kakwa, Amin's fellow tribesmen, were the most influential. They had the highest and most powerful posts in the State Research Bureau, the Public Safety Unit, the army, the air force and the police. Members of other tribes and ethnic groups including foreigners such as Sudanese in the army resented that.

The Lugabara fought the Kakwa, although they were allies and fellow northwesterners. The Sudanese also tried to undermine the Kakwa. Other groups in the army were also involved in violent conflicts, further weakening the army.

The economy also continued to deteriorate. And during the same time, Amin was faced with another major problem: attempts by Obote and his supporters to overthrow him.

The first attempt took place in September 1972 when a small and ill-equipped invasion force entered Uganda from northwestern Tanzania in order to capture a military post at Masaka and spark an uprising against Amin. They failed to capture the military post. And no uprising against Amin took place. The invaders were routed and fled back to Tanzania. Some of them were killed. But Obote did not give up. He was determined to return to Uganda and lead the country again.

The invasion by Ugandan exiles living in Tanzania scared Amin and his supporters. His security forces became even more brutal. They spread fear throughout the country, arresting, torturing and killing suspected opponents of Amin. Countless were killed. Most of them

335

were innocent civilians who were not involved in any plot to overthrow Amin.

To instill even more fear in the population, Amin used a very effective scare tactic by having his subordinates announce on the radio the names of some of the people who were about to "disappear." Lives of his fellow countrymen, even some who were very close to him, meant absolutely nothing to him.

As terror intensified, even some of the people who were closest to him fled. Some were killed. Amin himself was under siege.

The beginning of the end came when troops of the Malire Mechanised Regiment mutinied. Ironically, it was the same regiment which played the most decisive role in the January 1971 military coup and helped Amin to seize power. In October 1978, Amin sent loyal troops to quell the rebellion. The mutineers fled to Tanzania. Even some of the troops loyal to Amin crossed the border and joined his opponents in Tanzania.

Amin blamed Nyerere for all that. He accused him of trying to overthrow him. In order to divert attention from domestic discontent with his brutal dictatorship, he tried to mobilise his fellow countrymen against an external enemy, Nyerere, and invaded Tanzania.

On 1 November 1978, Amin ordered the Suicide Battalion in Masaka and the Simba Battalion in Mbarara to invade Tanzania and annex part of its territory. His soldiers occupied about 700 square miles of Tanzanian territory in Kagera Region in the northwest and claimed it as Ugandan territory.

Tanzania fought back and drove Amin's troops back into Uganda. The Tanzanian army, known as the Tanzania People's defence Forces (TPDF), was joined by an army of Ugandan exiles, the Uganda National Liberation Army (UNLA), who were trained in Tanzania and began the long march to Kampala to oust Amin. His friend Gaddafi sent 3,000 troops to help save him. But they were no match for

Tanzanian soldiers and were easily routed. Many of them were captured or simply surrendered.

Kampala fell on 10 April 1979 and Amin fled to Libya. He lived in Libya until 1989 when he fell out with Gaddafi and sought exile in Saudi Arabia where he spent the rest of his life. He died on 16 August 2003.

He was at least in his seventies when he died. Most biographers claim he was born in 1925. Other sources say he was born in 1923; yet others claim in 1928. He probably was born in the mid-1920s.

338

Chapter Seven:

Obote returns to power

AFTER Amin was ousted, Obote started to make plans to regain power. But before he could do that, there were other Ugandans who led the country.

It was a period of uncertainty. And the person who was really in charge of Uganda during that period was President Julius Nyerere of Tanzania. His admirers and detractors alike concede that Nyerere was the real president of Uganda during that time. Nothing was done in Kampala without his permission. He was effectively president of two countries at the same time: Tanzania and Uganda.

The first person to lead Uganda after Amin was overthrown was Yusuf Lule. He became president on 13 April 1979. It was Nyerere who put him in power. Lule was replaced by Godfrey Binaisa on 20 June 1979, also with Nyerere's support and approval. As John Kato stated in an article, "Julius Nyerere, the Godfather of Uganda's Political Set-up," in *New Vision*, Kampala, Uganda, 4

April 2012:

"In June 2011, prayers were held at Namugongo Martyr's Shrine for Nyerere, in which President Museveni made one of the brightest eulogies about him: 'I am happy when I speak of Nyerere because I am his supporter. He was the greatest black man that ever lived. There are other black men such as Nelson Mandela and Kwame Nkrumah, but Nyerere was the greatest...,' Museveni said.

Between 1979 and 1980, Tanzanian leader Julius Nyerere was the 'defacto' president of Uganda. Nothing was done without consulting him and anything attempted without consulting him was quashed.

'Even if you wanted to sneeze or move your leg, you had to first inform Julius Nyerere about it,' mused late President Godfrey Binaisa, in his testimonials, *Binaisa ne Yuganda*. That was the depth of Nyerere's influence in Uganda. It is easy to understand why Nyerere is attracting all these praises. At the peak of the anti-Amin struggle, many Ugandan exiles – politicians, academicians and otherwise, sought refuge in Tanzania, and were directly aided by Nyerere.

Among them were Milton Obote, Yoweri Museveni, Oyite Ojok, Tito Okello and Bazilio Olara Okello. When time came to organising and hosting the Moshi Conference in 1979 to determine Uganda's future, Nyerere was at the forefront. Most anti-Amin fighters were in Dar-es-Salaam with their families, all funded by Nyerere.

'The good people in Mwalimu's office assisted us to get an apartment in another neighbourhood called Upanga,' Janet Museveni, who too was in Tanzania with her husband, Museveni, recalls. 'Milton Obote was living in the presidential guest house in Musasani, supported by Mwalimu's government,' Janet wrote in her book *My Life's Story*. It was also clear that on Obote's behalf, Nyerere was willing to fight Amin.

'On return to Dar-es-Salaam, Nyerere told me the

Tanzanian army had suggested that if I could find a pilot, some of my men could be flown to Entebbe on the night of the invasion. The plan was for the government of Tanzania to commandeer an East African Airways aircraft from a Tanzanian airport,' Obote wrote.

He adds:

'From 1973 to 1978, I requested President Nyerere to allow me to arrange for the infiltration of the men to Uganda, but the president who was always very kind to me, who used to come to my residence, sometimes twice a week, for conversation and would invite me to functions at his house, rejected every request.'

Obote also wrote that when Idi Amin's forces invaded Tanzania via Mutukula on the Ugandan southern border President Nyerere briefed him and concluded: 'This is the opportunity we have been waiting for.' This culminated into the struggle led by the Tanzanian army and the Ugandan exiles that ended the bloody rule of Idi Amin in 1979.

Apparently, Nyerere had learnt that sections of Ugandans did not want Obote to return as president. This is why he accommodated other fighters like Yusuf Lule, who later became president after the toppling of Amin, and Godfrey Binaisa. Earlier, while Obote had advised Nyerere against bringing a young man called Yoweri Museveni closer, Nyerere embraced Museveni. You can as well argue that other than Idi Amin and Sir Edward Mutesa, all the other Ugandan presidents, seven out of the nine, had Nyerere's blessing."

Binaisa was ousted on 12 May 1980, again with Nyerere's approval, and was replaced by Paulo Muwanga, Obote's close associate who paved the way for Obote's return to power. Muwanga served as president of Uganda from 12 – 22 May 1980 when was chairman of the ruling

341

Military Commission. He was replaced by the Presidential Commission whose members were Saulo Musoke, Polycarp Nyamuchoncho, and Joel Hunter Wacha-Olwol. Muwanga also served as prime minister of Uganda from 1 August – 25 August 1980.

The Presidential Commission led Uganda from 22 May – 15 December 1980.

General elections were held on 10 December 1980 and Obote was declared the winner. Muwanga was the chairman of the Electoral Commission. But there was a bitter dispute over the elections.

Obote's opponents, including Yoweri Museveni, claimed the elections were rigged. Muwanga was blamed for rigging the elections in favour of Obote. Museveni launched a rebellion to overthrow Obote. But it took years before he finally succeeded in doing so.

Yet it was those elections which set the stage for Museveni's rise to power years later. They galvanised the opposition and helped plunge the country into a civil which came to be known as the Bush War.

The Commonwealth election observers conceded there some irregularities but concluded that the elections were fair; a conclusion that was not accepted by Obote's opponents.

Obote's ally, Paulo Muwanga who was chairman of the Electoral Commission, had full control of the electoral process and even disqualified Obote's opponents, especially members of the Democratic Party (DP) led by Paul Ssemogerere, from the ballot although there was evidence showing that some of them had defeated the candidates of Obote's Uganda People's Congress (UPC).

It was also alleged that many ballot boxes of the Democratic Party (DP) were simply seized on orders from Muwanga and given to the Uganda People's Congress to give Obote's party more votes. Empty ballot boxes were also allegedly stuffed for the same purpose, enabling the Uganda People's Congress to get even more votes.

It was easy to seize the ballot boxes of the Democratic Party, UPC's main challenger, because there was no secret ballot. Muwanga had decreed that each candidate should have his own ballot box, making the electoral process even less democratic but securing an easy victory for Obote. And as Professor Frederick K. Byaruhanga, a Ugandan, states in his book, *Student Power in Africa's Higher Education: A Case of Makerere University*:

"President Binaisa was removed from power after serving just a few months and was placed under house arrest, to be replaced by Paulo Muwanga, who was appointed not as president, but as Chairman of the Military Commission.

The appointment of Paulo Muwanga, a UPC enthusiast, was seen by many as a clear pathway for the return of former President Obote. Muwanga quickly lifted the ban on political parties and began preparations for multiparty general elections, which took place December 10, 1980.

Former president Obote and his UPC party won the elections, which were widely considered rigged and fraudulent. As a result, many of Obote's opponents, including the current president Yoweri Museveni, took up arms to wage guerrilla warfare against the government."[2]

Even if Obote could still have won the election because his party was better organised across the country and was better financed, although he probably would have won with a smaller electoral mandate if he were to win at all, the fact that his party employed coercive tactics because it controlled the electoral process means the legitimacy of his victory was seriously in doubt even among some of his supporters although it was at the same time validated by international observers who concluded that he did, indeed, win, although there were some violations during the electoral contest.

On the other hand, the Democratic Party claimed victory at the polls. And some analysts believed the party did indeed win the election. Others said the Democratic Party did not win but would have won if the election was free and fair.

The opposition capitalised on all that and did everything it could to discredit Obote and the Uganda People's Congress because of what Muwanga and his subordinates had done to help the UPC secure many votes it was not entitled to.

Therefore the UPC discredited its own victory, thus legitimising claims by Museveni other opponents of Obote that Obote did not win the election.

Had the election not been manipulated by Muwanga and other UPC supporters who controlled the Electoral Commission, Obote's opponents would have had a hard time building a case against him. And they would not have been able to mobilise forces against him across the country on the scale they did – except in northern Uganda, Obote's traditional stronghold with the exception of the West Nile District in the northwest which was Amin's home region.

The 1980 elections were also held during a period when Tanzania exerted a lot of influence on Uganda because of the role she played in ousting Amin. And it was taken for granted that whoever was to be elected the next president of Uganda had to have the approval and blessings of Tanzania's president, Julius Nyerere, who on 14 November 1978 ordered the Tanzania People's Defence Forces – popularly known as TPDF – to launch a counteroffensive against Amin's forces which had annexed the Kagera Salient in northwestern Tanzania:

"The forces which overthrew Amin contained a variety of groups with different ideologies and aspirations, whose only common goal had been to remove Amin.

The Tanzanians remained powerful behind the scenes, retaining a sizeable military force in the country....

Throughout, the Tanzanians appeared determined to re-establish Obote in power....

Acholi and Langi soldiers in the Uganda National liberation Army (UNLA) proceeded to revenge the massacres of Amin. Indiscriminate killings in West Nile, Idi Amin's home area, destroyed most of the town of Arua. According to the UN High Commission for Refugees, over a quarter of a million refugees from West Nile fled to neighbouring countries like Sudan and Zaire (Karugire, 1980).

The general election which followed Binaisa's overthrow was contested by the traditional political parties – the Protestant anti-Baganda Uganda People's Congress (UPC) led by Obote, and the Catholic and Buganda Democratic Party (DP) – as well as the new Uganda Patriotic Movement (UPM), led by Yoweri Museveni.

The election was rigged, however. Although it appears clear that the DP won the majority of votes, the Military Commission declared Obote the winner."[3]

The reaction by opponents of Obote to what was widely perceived to have been a rigged election varied. The biggest challenger, the Democratic Party, decided to operate within the system by assuming the role of official opposition in parliament. Museveni, who had been vice-chairman of the Military Commission under Paul Muwanga which ruled the country before the election, stayed out and chose to go to war against Obote's government.

And although the Democratic Party did not win the election according to official results, it still managed to win a significant number of seats even under those circumstances. As George Lugalambi, a lecturer and head of the mass communication department at Makerere university, states in his work, *An Assessment of Democratic Deliberation in Uganda*:

"Four parties contested the elections: UPC fielded Obote as its candidate; DP fielded Paul Ssemogerere; Uganda Patriotic Movement (UPM) fielded Museveni; and the Conservative Party (CP) fielded Jehoash Mayanja-Nkangi.

UPC won 73 of the 126 parliamentary seats and returned Obote to power. DP won 52 seats, UPM one, and CP none.

Obote's controversial return to power marked what became known in public parlance as the Obote II regime.

There is wide agreement that the 1980 general elections were marred by extensive irregularities and fixed in favor of UPC. Whereas all losing parties disputed the results, DP opted to join parliament as the opposition party. Museveni, on the other hand, opted to mount an armed rebellion against Obote's UPC regime."[4]

The general consensus that the 1980 general elections were rigged has been validated by different analysts. They articulate the same position. As Professor Kefa Otiso, a Ugandan, states in his book, *Culture and Customs of Uganda*:

"In December 1980, a general election monitored by a Commonwealth team saw Obote regain the presidency, even though his Uganda People's Congress (UPC) was accused of electoral fraud."[5]

According to Edward Khiddu-Makubuya, a renowned Ugandan lawyer, in his work, "Violence and Conflict Resolution in Uganda," in *The Culture of Violence*:

"In December 1980, Uganda held its first general elections since independence. The campaigns leading up to the elections were partially characterized by violence and intimidation; some candidates were violently prevented from even processing or presenting their nomination papers.

A few shooting incidents were reported and, and one candidate was abducted and murdered shortly before the elections (Bwengye, 1985; commonwealth Secretariat, 1980).

In the end, the Uganda People's Congress (UPC) was declared the winner; it formed a new government headed by President Obote. The election was immediately denounced as a fraud by several influential groups within and outside Uganda."[6]

The election also intensified rivalries between the people of northern Uganda, especially the Langi and the Acholi who strongly supported Obote, and those of the southern regions; a division which historically has also been viewed as a competition between the Nilotic people of the north and the Bantus of the south.

Many Ugandans were also not satisfied with the results because they believed that the electoral process was manipulated by Tanzanians, even if by remote control, because they wanted Obote to return to power. And as Professor Devra C. Moehler of the University of Pennsylvania states in her book, *Distrusting Democrats: Outcomes of Participatory Constitution Making*:

"In 1980, Uganda held its postindependence general election. Four parties contested the election: the UPC, led by Obote, the DP, headed by Paul Ssemogerere; the Uganda Patriotic Movement, recently formed by Museveni; and the Conservative Party of Baganda tradionalists.

The UPC was declared the winner, but international observers and opposition candidates argued that gross malpractise had occurred (Kasozi 1999, 136 – 43).

The period that followed the contentious 1980 election is dubbed Obote II, and many observers consider it the most brutal time since independence (Human Rights

Watch 1999, 34 – 35; Kasozi 1999, 145). Rebel groups became active throughout the country, and government troops responded with massive abuse and killing.

Museveni's Popular Resistance Army, which later became the National Resistance Army, was among the guerrilla movements that formed in opposition to the Obote government (Kasozi, 1999, 165). The movement was militarily most active in the central Buganda region known as the Luwero triangle.

Many of the Baganda who aided the NRM (National Resistance Movement) in their struggle did so in the hope that removing Obote would allow for the restoration of their former kingdom and federal status (Mulondo 2001)."[7]

When Obote became president for the second time on 17 December 1980, Uganda was in shambles. But there was also a lot optimism, considering what the country had gone through during eight years of terror and destruction under Amin. Obote also did achieve early success during the first years after he returned to power:

"Just like his predecessor, Idi Amin, President Obote's initial moments were accompanied by much hope and enthusiasm on the part of the population. Amin fatigue, as well as the obvious substandard performance exhibited by the successive interim governments, provided a positive political environment for the new government.

President Obote's immediate approach was to jump-start the economy and to re-establish relations with his neighbours. He made an immediate move to attract foreign investment, especially by encouraging and facilitating the return of Asians, his long time allies, whom Idi Amin had expelled in 1972. In addition, the president was able to obtain financial support from bilateral and multilateral funding organizations, such as the World Bank, IMF and (the) European Economic Community, which identified prospects for economic growth.

Evidently, the country's economy began to show positive signs – up to 5% growth by 1982 and 1983, leading to the first recorded balance of payments surplus in 1984 (Furley, 1987).

But the economic gains were eclipsed by reports of gross human rights violations. The army, which was President Obote's most formidable power base, used its military power and privilege to suppress any kind of opposition – often with massive brutality, resulting in killings and disappearances, as well as a colossal outflow of asylum seekers, reminiscent of Idi Amin's dictatorship."[8]

Obote did not even have the chance to do much because of the instability in the country. Therefore his successes and failures during his second presidency have to be measured against that background.

But his government was also at war with its own people. Suppression of dissent led not only to large-scale abuse of human rights; it also led to more instability across the country, providing fertile ground for rebellion against his rule.

Obote did not have the electoral mandate to rule. This democratic deficiency compromised his ability to lead the country and win acceptance from his fellow countrymen besides his supporters. As Professor Joshua B. Rubongoya, a Ugandan teaching in the United States, states in his book, *Regime Hegemony in Museveni's Uganda: Pax Musevenica*:

"Following the fall of Idi Amin in 1979, a series of leaders from Lule to Binaisa and, then, finally to Milton Obote tried their luck at rebuilding the state without much success. The main proposition is that at the root of the failure in state reconstruction was the continuing deficiency in democratic legitimacy....

349

Obote rose to power in 1980 by way of a botched election. This very fact, which was itself a consequence of failure to muster broad popular support, seems to have forecast the character of Obote's government between 1980 and 1984. The illegitimacy of the 1980 election and, therefore, of Obote's power was soon thereafter exposed by the emergence of a strong guerrilla opposition mounted by what would become the NRA/M (National Resistance Amry/Movement).

Thus, not unlike his first term, Obote's second term presented unique challenges to democratic governance. In his analysis of the illegitimate government of Obote, Khadiagala argues that

> Obote had again to resort to segments within the military to subdue a growing opposition. As before, despotic power used without infrastructural power confirmed the vulnerability of state managers and, at most, emboldened opposition factions. (1995: 38).

Right from the start, Obote had to wrestle with an economy that had one leg in the grave and the other in intensive care. The state was hobbling along under the weight of the *magendo* economy and its accompanying moral and ethical malaise. Social cleavages between town and country, between Christians and Muslims, and between haves and have-nots left very limited room for national unity.

The chasm between northerners and southerners represented another political fault line.

All told, the political culture was too distorted to support a democratic civil society, but equally important was the fact that the policies of Obote II restricted the emergence of an effective civil society.

To add to this mix, the political parties of old were reintroduced to contest the 1980 elections, thus, creating new political and social fault lines.

There were several credible reports confirming claims

of election fraud and rigging carried out with the express intention of ensuring victory for Obote's UPC party. Indeed, it was in response to the contested nature of the 1980 elections that Obote's Minister of Defense Yoweri Museveni abandoned the government to launch a rebel opposition that would lead to the ouster of Obote in 1986.

What, then, could any post-Amin government do, to restore the rule of law, democratic legitimacy, accountability, and economic productivity? Success in these three (sic) areas would at least restore the instrumentalist prerequisite of legitimacy, namely, state effectiveness."[9]

It was therefore a combination of problems Obote faced during his second presidency. He inherited the post-Amin state that was in shambles. It was not his fault. It was Amin who destroyed the country during his eight-year reign of terror. But Obote also created his own problems for the country and exacerbated the situation when he went into office without full mandate from the electorate. He also alienated many people who could have joined him to rebuild the country when he resorted to draconian measures to achieve his goals by suppressing dissent. And as Professor Rubongoya goes on to state:

"First, with respect to the economy, Obote's 1981 budget speech announced the following policies in order to correct state-imposed economic distortions and to end the black market:

The shilling was allowed to float in order to wipe out arbitrary profits.

Administered profits were removed from all consumer goods except petrol, to permit prices of state-owned commodities to rise to their market value.

Prices paid to growers for export commodities were raised and border patrols were reinforced to reduce coffee

351

smuggling and to encourage production of other export crops, and in 1982, a 'second window' for purchasing – by auction – foreign exchange for business purposes was opened, this was an effort to break the black market in currency that had survived the float.

These policies helped stem the intensity of coffee smuggling and the foreign exchange black market known locally as *kibanda*. However, state prices for cash crops remained fairly low relative to what farmers were paid by the *mafuta mingi*. Furthermore, the state apparatus was still unable to protect the peasant from the violence of the *mafuta mingi* that, as Kasfir argued, could still seize agricultural produce with impunity, thus, creating an opportunity for primitive accumulation outside and independent of the state (1983: 97). It is quite possible, also, that *mafuta mingi* funds ended up supporting UPC campaigns, thus, compromising the ability of the government to act as honest broker between state and society."[10]

Whatever achievements Obote's government made in the economic realm were also compromised by corruption which was a major problem during his second presidency.

In an interview with Ugandan journalist Andrew Mwenda of the *The Monitor* in April 2005 in Lusaka, Zambia, where he lived after being offered asylum by President Kenneth Kaunda soon after he was overthrown for the second time, Dr. Obote maintained that he was not corrupt. He also said his ministers were not corrupt and that subsequent investigations even by Museveni, his nemesis, produced no reports which showed investigators had found or uncovered evidence of corruption.

But even if Obote himself and his cabinet members were not corrupt, which is questionable, it is hard to believe that his entire government was not corrupt.

There was corruption in his government during his second presidency, probably even more so than in the first.

But many corrupt officials and state agents as well as UPC functionaries were not exposed or arrested because of the culture of secrecy to protect each other and during a time when opponents of the government were muzzled, suppression of dissent was institutionalised, and when the primary focus of the government was on fighting the rebels who were trying to overthrow Obote. As Rubongoya states:

"As Obote's second tenure wore on, the above-mentioned policy achievements were weakened by rampant corruption, mostly among agents of the state entrusted to realize financial commitments to the war against rebel insurgencies. By 1985, inflation was out of control, unemployment high, and foreign investment was declining. As the economy worsened and the Museveni-led rebel attacks intensified, Obote's attempts to restore the institutional logic of the state began to wane and so did the chances of reconstituting viable sources of legitimacy.....

Obote had the difficult task of winning popular support ...because of perceptions of electoral fraud....The bungled elections further weakened his claims to legitimacy and forced him to concentrate power in a few trusted supporters. Secondly, it became increasingly difficult to separate the UPC regime from the state. Yet, the post-Amin UPC party was a weakened party, in fact, a shadow of its old self. It was not only split along several political and ethnic factions, but it was also facing a stronger and resurgent Democratic Party (DP) and a highly politicized military with representatives in the Parliament.

UPC MPs were beholden to the members of the executive branch, specifically to President Obote personally. The president had control over the party, the executive branch, and a very politicized military. The UPC was too weak internally to perform the functions of mass mobilization, interest aggregation, and provider of viable policy alternatives. Under these circumstances state-society relations were so constrained as to block the emergence of a governance realm.

Values of trust, reciprocity, accountability, and authority were all linked to party loyalty or to personal relations with the president and other high-ranking party/government political elites. Limitations on political space precluded the expected activities of opposition parties, civil society, and particularly the media.

The peasantry once again exited the formal economy, resorting instead to smuggling, trading in local foodstuff, or simply subsistence agriculture. As the prospects for establishing a governance realm dwindled, the ensuing legitimacy deficit was only reinforced by the emergence of a fortified statist regime type and a neopatrimonial state.

Obote could not extricate himself from the forces that had been central to his political resurrection, namely, the Uganda National Liberation Front and its military wing, the Uganda National Liberation Army (UNLA). He used them in his futile attempts to restore law and order. Not only did influential elements in these bodies pave the way for Obote's political fortunes, bu they also threw their support behind the political parties, particularly the UPC. In this process, two crucial developments emerged: the militarization of politics on the one hand and the politicization of the military, on the other. The result of this syndrome was that interests peculiar to the military would be taken care of by military representatives, and military representation would also enable the army to participate in the decision-making processes in top civilian organs.

The military, therefore, became increasingly central not only in maintaining law and order, as had been the case in Obote's first government, but also in administration. The reinstitutionalization of the General Service Unit and other intelligence organs perfected the structure of coercion without which Obote could not maintain control. The military, together with the political elites, formed a strong alliance that used the state as a conduit for the delivery of patronage to select groups of clients. This form of patrimonial legitimacy sealed any hopes of a transition to democracy in Uganda.

Ironically, Obote allowed the ethnic factor – a policy responsible for his downfall in his first term – to undermine the coherence of the military and its capacity to keep the peace and defend the nation. This is because he once again sought to purge the army of the Acholi elements while elevating his fellow Langis – a sign that even in the military, support for him was narrow and, in fact, tenuous. In the spirit of this policy, Obote's commanders disproportionately deployed the Acholis to the frontline to face a strengthened guerrilla force in the name of the National Resistance Army (NRA).

So, while Obote relied on the army to maintain order by rounding up, torturing, detaining, and terrorizing suspected citizens in several urban centers, his policy of ethnic cleansing within the military seemed to undermine the very institution he needed to gain legitimacy, if not control. It was, indeed, the victims of this ethnic cleansing, the Acholi army officers, who led a coup that toppled Obote for the second time."[11]

Obote made a fatal mistake not only by alienating the Acholi in the army who eventually overthrew him; he failed or was unwilling to reach out to other groups who did not support him or vote for him in the 1980 general elections, especially when he knew that he did not have the mandate of a substantial segment of the population to rule. There was widespread belief in Uganda and among other observers and analysts that he did not have majority support to lead the country.

He could have formed an inclusive government which reflected a broad consensus across the spectrum not only to sustain himself in power but also as a concession to his opponents and as a compromise to appease the people whose fundamental democratic rights were violated when the 1980 elections were rigged by his supporters led by Paulo Muwanga.

And just for the sake of peace and stability, he should have agreed to hold another election, to avoid civil conflict, especially for a country that was in such political turmoil after eight years of terror under Amin. It had barely emerged from its dark past.

If Obote knew or really believed that he won the first election, he also should have believed he was going to win the second one. He should have had nothing to fear to legitimise his victory for the second time by holding another election, as demanded by his opponents, just to save his country, instead of allowing the situation to degenerate into chaos and civil war.

The legitimacy of the state under Obote was further eroded and compromised as time went on and by the continued use of coercive tactics including violence to achieve his goals.

The erosion of this legitimacy was compounded by the effects of the war against the rebels whose ability to destabilise the country demonstrated that Obote's government was not in full control of the situation.

But in spite of all those problems, there were some achievements during Obote's second presidency especially in the economic arena although they were not longterm. They were also compromised by corruption.

Obote implemented austerity measures demanded by the IMF to rejuvenate the economy under structural adjustment programmes (SAPs) as a condition for aid. He had undergone an ideological conversion and renounced his past policies which he implemented during his first presidency to achieve socialist transformation of his country. Those polices were enunciated in *The Common Man's Charter* in 1969. In an interview with Andrew Mwenda of the Ugandan newspaper, *The Monitor*, in April 2005, Obote conceded that his first government made a mistake when it pursued socialism and nationalisation. As he put it:

"I also regret the move to the left. With hindsight, I think we should not have attempted socialist or nationalisation policies."[12]

After Uganda adopted free-market policies under Obote, the economy improved although the people also suffered because benefits did not trickle down to the grassroots as as the neoliberal advocates of economic liberalisation claimed they would.

Still, there were some economic gains in a number of areas during Obote's second tenure, even for some people on the lowest rung of the economic ladder, just as there were some during his first in the sixties when he achieved even more economic success. But they were negated by the cost of the war against the insurgents during his second term and could not be sustained in a chronic state of uncertainty and instability as the conflict with the insurgents went on.

Adoption of IMF-mandated policies also won Obote some credibility from donor nations as a responsible leader who also had the experience to rebuild his country. Also, Obote's assumption of power during his second presidency coincided with the recommendation of structural adjustment programmes by the IMF to Third World countries as a solution to their economic plight. As Dr. Frederick Golooba-Mutebi, a senior research fellow at the Institute of Social Research, Makerere University, Kampala, Uganda, states in his work, "Economic Liberalization and Politics in Uganda," in *Economic Liberalization and Political Violence: Utopia or Dystopia?*:

"The second Obote administration – Obote II – inherited a virtually collapsed economy, a political

357

environment that was already poisoned by accusations of electoral rigging, and a realistic threat of renewed civil war by losers unwilling to accept the election results. Rather than devote its energies and resources to repairing the country's torn political fabric and rebuilding the economy, the new regime found itself caught up in an insurgency that further poisoned the political environment and polarized the country's political elites.

The new administration made an effort to implement, with the support of the World Bank and the IMF, economic reforms and even scored some successes. However, their sustainability was undermined by the civil war and the damage it inflicted on the productive sectors and, consequently, the country's revenue-earning capacity.

The accession to power by the Obote II government coincided with the beginning of pressure by Bretton Woods institutions on African governments for economic reform. In Uganda it was therefore the Obote II government which was the first to implement the IMF's earliest economic restructuring programs in Africa....

(But) the 1980 elections which were held after nearly a decade of dictatorship, were not the outcome of the pressure donors were exerting on African governments to adopt multi-party politics alongside economic liberalization. Instead, they were the outcome of acrimonious debate among local political elites about the form of government best suited to the country's circumstances following years of despotism and political turmoil.

Rather than usher in a period of peace and stability as would have been expected by war-wary Ugandans and foreign observers, the elections sparked a five-year civil war responsible for the limited success of the IMF-backed economic reform program and which eventually led to the collapse of Obote's second administration."[13]

Had the 1980 elections been free and fair, the

358

economic recovery programme would probably have been implemented on long-term basis regardless of who was in power, even if it was Obote himself who was reviled so much by his opponents for rigging the electoral contest, had he won fairly. And there probably would have been no civil war to wreak havoc across the country, at least not on the scale it did during Obote's second tenure.

Golooba-Mutebi goes on to state:

"By 1980, the economic devastation wrought by the Amin regime rendered efforts at economic reconstruction an absolute necessity. As with other countries undergoing economic reform, in Uganda the central objective was to reduce the need for external financial support.

In 1981, under the guidance of the IMF, the government embarked on programs of economic stabilization. In what has been characterized as 'the first experiments in structural adjustment programs for Third World countries,' the donor community insisted on 'liberalizing (or floating) the Uganda shilling and a considerable reduction in state expenditure as the price of financial assistance' (Hansen and Twaddle, 1998, p. 2). They sought to 'halt the deterioration of the economy, revive production, restore confidence in the Uganda shilling, eliminate price distortions, improve fiscal and monetary discipline, and lay a firm foundation for sustained recovery' (Ochieng, 1991, p. 44).

The economy responded positively, leading to the transformation of GDP growth rates from negatives to positives during 1981 – 83. In 1982 and 1983, all the sectors experienced positive growth. Only electricity (1982) and agricultural primary processing (1983) did not.

However, the economy had negative growth rates during 1983 and 1984. Although in agriculture the area planted and production of all food crops increased between 1980 and 1983, both declined between 1983 and 1985. While for cash crops there was no change in the area

359

planted, production increased between 1980 and 1983, only to decline and register negative growth rates from 1984.

The industrial sector also showed signs of revival in capacity utilization, but only temporarily. Only soft drink and cigarette production maintained the revival momentum and were operating at 40 percent and 75 percent capacity respectively by 1985, while other industries operated at less than 20 percent capacity utilization (Ochieng, 1991, p. 46)."[14]

Therefore, in spite of the problems the country faced, there is evidence to show that it was able to achieve economic growth in some sectors even if for only a short period. But economic recovery was also a daunting task because of the war and corruption; a point underscored by Golooba-Mutebi:

"Under Obote, the adjustment program had therefore managed to attain only short-term success in reviving the economy.

The major cause of the government's failure to sustain its reform success was the damage inflicted by the civil war on the productive sectors and its drain on the government's meager resources.

There were, however, other factors not related to the war. According to Hansen and Twaddle (1998, p. 2), the reforms begot a great deal of corruption among ministers and officials seeking to benefit from the black market sale of foreign currency, which discredited Obote's government and increased support for the insurgents.

In July 1985, the embattled Obote government fell to a military coup led by the army commander, General Tito Olara Okello. Behind the coup were ethnic divisions that had severely factionalized the military, and its inability to contain the insurgents.

The putsch ushered in a short-lived government which,

following failure to negotiate peace with the insurgents, was toppled in 1986 by the Museveni-led National Resistance Movement (NRM), the largest and best-organized of the several armed group that had declared war on the Obote II regime following the 1980 elections.

The failure by the Obote government to sustain the initial successes of its economic reform efforts and to carry out a successful economic reconstruction program was the outcome of the civil war into which it was plunged after the elections.

The civil war itself was the consequence of two related phenomena. First was the failure by the country's political elites to reach a consensus about how to move the country forward following the collapse of the Amin regime. Second was the systematic and arrogant manipulation of the pre-election political process and the elections themselves by Obote's allies in the transitional Military Commission government. Also, after the war broke out, the government steadfastly refused to engage the insurgents in talks to try and resolve their differences peacefully, and instead sought to defeat them militarily.

Further, as the civil war grew in intensity, the Obote government and its allies took to harassing and eliminating members and supporters of opposition parties – activities that served only to isolate it from major sections of the general public."[15]

Another major problem during Obote's second tenure was widespread lack of discipline which led to chaos and even amounted to anarchy in some areas, facilitated by the security forces themselves which had no respect for the law. Security agents constituted terror squads. Soldiers fighting insurgents brutalized civilians with impunity and even in areas where there was no fighting.

There was no-one to discipline them. They were above the law. The government had lost control over its own forces of law and order.

All that had unintended consequences. The security forces and the military, hence the government itself, became one of the best recruiting agents for the insurgents. State-sponsored terror became a blessing for the rebels. It fuelled the rebellion:

"Furthermore, the government failed to impose discipline on and create cohesion within the military and the security agencies. Widespread indiscipline culminated in the military and security agencies committing atrocities against civilian populations, especially in areas where the insurgents were active, thereby forcing many civilians to join the armed rebellion.

Conflicts within the military, especially between the dominant Acholi and Langi factions, undermined its effectiveness as a fighting force, leading to a failure to defeat the insurgents and eventually to the Acholi-led coup d'état of 1985.

Such were the demands on the government's energies, resources, and organizational capacities that made failure in the twin arenas of economic reform and post-war reconstruction inevitable. Indeed, it was in the midst of trying to respond to the exigencies of the civil war and its effects, against the advice of the IMF, that the latter withdrew its support.

It is clear, therefore, that the main factor behind the failure of reform under the Obote II regime was political instability and its underlying sources: elite polarization and the consequent zero-sum politics underlain by the desire on the part of competing political factions, once they acquired power, to monopolize it and hold on to it for as long as possible."[16]

The failure of Obote's second presidency was a direct result of the rigged 1980 general elections. His economic recovery programme was not fully implemented because of the devastating impact of the civil war, itself a product of the rigged elections.

Obote's opponents went to war against him because of the rigged elections.

And he could not govern effectively because he did not have the electoral mandate to lead the country except from his supporters – who were outnumbered by his opponents who did not have the opportunity to express their wish because the 1980 elections were rigged in his favour. Had the elections not been rigged, the country would not have been plunged into civil war. And the economic recovery would probably have been successful.

In less than three months after Obote assumed power for the second time, he faced rebellion. Museveni, one of the leading political figures in the country, announced in February 1981 that he and his supporters had formed the National Resistance Army to fight Obote. There was a lot of resentment against the government which suppressed the opposition and because of the unfair elections which had taken place in December, rigged by Paulo Muwanga who was now serving as vice president and minister of defence under Obote.

Museveni said Obote's opponents were going to overthrow the government by launching a popular rebellion, drawing support from ordinary people, especially peasants who constituted the bulk of the population. That was the beginning of what came to be known as the Bush War. It was, up to that time, the most successful grassroots insurgency against an established government in post-colonial Africa.

Museveni's group was the best-organised. There were others which tried to undermine Obote's government. But they were disrupted and defeated by the security forces including the army.

Museveni mobilised forces in the former kingdoms of Buganda, Bunyoro, Toro and Ankole where Obote was not very popular because he had abolished the kingdoms; his government waged a bitter campaign against his opponents in those areas; and he was a northerner and a Nilotic who was accused of favouring his fellow northerners against southern Bantus.

Most of Museveni's support during the campaign against Obote came from the rural areas. But his operational stronghold was in the central part of the former Buganda kingdom not far from the capital Kampala.

And there were enough complaints against the government to justify a sustained campaign of popular opposition. Although Museveni came from Ankole in the southwestern part of the country, he also had enough support in the other western kingdoms – Bunyoro and Toro – and in Buganda in the central part of the country – to be able to wage a prolonged military campaign which eventually toppled Obote. And as Moehler states:

"Museveni claims that he 'went to the bush' to wage guerrilla war in response to the rigged election, government corruption, political manipulation of sectarian interests, and gross human rights abuses (Human Rights Watch 1994, 34; Mukholi 1995, 24; Museveni 1997, 123).

The NRM's political philosophy was enshrined in the 'Ten-Point Programme,' the first point of which was the restoration of democracy. This democratic rhetoric was accompanied by generally democratic behavior during the insurgency (Kasfir, 2005).

Museveni maintained strict control over the use of violence by his soldiers against civilians. In areas 'liberated' by the NRM, the Resistance Council (RC) system of elected local officials was established (Kasfir 2005; Okoth 1996, 58)."[17]

Obote spent four years to try to crush his opponents. The toughest was Museveni's National Resistance Movement. In an attempt to do so, the army wreaked havoc in many parts of the country, especially in central Buganda which came to be known as the Luweero

Triangle during the war and which is where Museveni launched his guerrilla campaign.

Launched in 1983 and known as Operation Bonanza, the government military offensive against the rebels earned Obote even more enemies.

It also drove many civilians into the rebel camp. They joined the insurgency or supported the rebels by various means.

The military campaign also divided the country even further, between north and south, because most of the government soldiers waging the war against the insurgents and brutalising civilians were northerners, Langis and Acholis, Obote's traditional supporters and fellow northerners. The perception among the victims, most of whom were southerners especially the Baganda in the former Buganda kingdom, was that this was a war between the north and the south; it was also a war between the Nilotic tribes of northern Uganda and the Bantu tribes in the south.

At least 100,000 people died in the conflict. Some sources give higher figures, as high as 500,000, equal to or more than the number of victims who perished under Amin. Others say more people were killed under Obote. Estimates of those who were killed under Amin range from 300,000 to 800,000.

Even Obote himself conceded that he lost control over his army which caused a lot of misery and destruction including many deaths during the war against the rebels, especially in the Luweero Triangle in the central part of the former Buganda kingdom. But he blamed Museveni and his rebels for most of the deaths, implying those caused by his army was mere collateral damage, a byproduct of the justified military campaign against the insurgents.

It is difficult to imagine how Museveni and his insurgents would have deliberately killed so many people in the Luweero Triangle, only to alienate their supporters in an area where he launched the rebellion and among the people on whom he still depended so much to carry on his campaign against Obote.

It is much easier to see how the national army, composed mostly of northerners, the Acholi and the Langi, would have gone on the rampage killing the Baganda in the Luweero Triangle since they had no love for southerners and saw them as their enemies simply because they were not fellow northerners.

It is also hard to believe that Obote had many supporters among the Baganda in the kingdom he abolished in the sixties, let alone in the Luweero Triangle which was the operational base of the military campaign against him only a few miles north of the national capital Kampala.

In an interview with Ugandan journalist Andrew Mwenda in Lusaka, Zambia, where he and his wife lived in exile, Obote admitted that failure to control his army was his biggest mistake during his second presidency. As he put it:

"I regret that my second administration was unable to stop the killings and massacres of innocent civilians in Luweero by Museveni and his insurgent army."[18]

The conflict also assumed ethnic and regional dimensions. Many Langis and Acholis – Obote's traditional supporters – who had joined the Uganda National Liberation Army to overthrow Amin went on to attack the people of the southern tribes, just as Amin did, who were opposed to Obote. Many of them were not even in the army. But they still had weapons and military uniforms they wore during the war against Amin. And there were those who remained in the army which toppled Amin and which became the national army known as the Uganda National Liberation Army (UNLA).

The destruction they unleashed was not limited to the

southern part of the country. They also fanned out into the northwest, Amin's home region, exacting retribution for the atrocities committed against them by Kakwas, Lugbaras and other northwesterners during Amin's eight years of terror.

They did not identify with southerners who were Bantu. They also did not identify with the people of the northwest in the West Nile District, although they were fellow northerners and fellow Nilotics, because of what the kinsman of those northwesterners, Idi Amin, did to them. They also came from a different part of northern Uganda. The Langi and the Acholi homeland is in the central north.

After Amin seized power, he exterminated the Acholi and the Langi in the army and even sent killer squads to the north to hunt down Acholi and Langi soldiers who had left the army and fled there for security. Those who were found hiding among their tribal kinsmen were killed by Amin's soldiers – who were mostly Kakwa, Lugbra and Nubian – together with their families and others. The Acholi and the Langi never forgot that. It was now time for vengeance. And the northwest became another killing field.

As Museveni's rebellion intensified, the government decided in 1983 to remove hundreds of thousands of people in the Luweero Triangle in order to deprive the rebels of an operational base and civilian support. It was a massive relocation involving about 750,000 people and resulted in massive violations of human rights and countless deaths.

The people were forcibly relocated in internment camps, similar to what happened to the Hutu in Rwanda and Burundi during the civil wars in those countries under Tutsi-dominated armies, and led to many abuses without any intervention by the government to stop the violations including rape and looting. Any civilians who lived outside the camps were automatically considered to be

367

rebels or rebel sympathisers, targeted for elimination.

Amidst all this, Obote still tried to rebuild the economy and even got foreign aid to do so. His government also worked with the International Monetary Fund and followed austerity measures recommended by the IMF. He was also concerned about his country's international image and tried to curb excesses unlike Amin who had no use for diplomacy or any respect for international law.

Obote was one of the leading African statesmen and had won international respect as one of the founding fathers of modern Africa and as a staunch supporter of the liberation movements in southern Africa together with leaders such as Kwame Nkrumah, Julius Nyerere and Kenneth Kaunda all of whom were also his friends. He was also a strong advocate of African unity and greatly admired fellow Pan-Africanists such as Nkrumah, Nyerere, Kaunda and Ahmed Sekou Toure. He stood tall and as an equal among them as an embodiment of Pan-Africanism.

He also had experience running a country which he acquired during his first presidency. Many donors felt, because of all that, he would be able to restore stability and rebuild the economy. But he failed on both counts.

The rebellion led by Museveni continued to gain momentum. The Ugandan national army could not neutralise the insurgents and it became notorious for human rights abuses. Torture and murder became common. It is estimated that between 1981 and 1985 when Obote was ousted, about 300,000 Ugandans lost their lives, according to Amnesty International.

The CIA said the death toll was more than 100,000, implying it did not reach let alone exceed 300,000.

The highest death toll was in the Luweero Triangle, the site of the bloodiest conflicts between the army and the rebels.

The Red Cross estimated that in the Luweero Triangle alone, hundreds of thousands were killed. According to

Human Rights/Watch Africa in its work, *The Scars of Death: Children Abducted by the Lord's Resistance Army in Uganda*:

"According to Kasozi and Omara-Otunno, Obote's return to power also restored the Acholi and Langi dominance within Uganda's military, and heralded the beginning of another period of widespread violence. Yoweri Museveni's guerrilla National Resistance Army – dominated by southerners and westerners – sought to topple Obote by force, and the International Committee of the Red Cross ultimately estimated that fighting in Uganda's Luwero triangle region left several hundred thousand dead. The bulk of the dead were civilians."[19]

Obote's government sought assistance from North Korea which sent military advisers to help the army fight the insurgents in what was supposed to be the final offensive against the rebels. The war was already draining the nation's resources, making economic recovery impossible. It was time to take decisive military action to end the conflict and start rebuilding the country. Obote's government was determined to win the war at any cost. Victory became its priority to the exclusion of everything else.

But such victory against the National Resistance Army (NRA) proved to be impossible because of its stamina, organisational skills and ability to wage a sustained guerrilla campaign. As Robert Barlas states in his book, *Uganda: Cultures of the World*:

"In the government that succeeded Idi Amin, Museveni served briefly as Minister of Defence. After Obote rigged the general election in 1980, Museveni opposed the tyranny of the Obote regime.

During the struggle, Museveni's troops achieved a very high level of leadership and managerial skills, as well as

369

clear political and military policies. They also established excellent working relations with the civilian population in areas where they operated.

After a five-year guerrilla war against the regimes of Obote and his successor Tito Okello, Museveni became president of Uganda on January 26, 1986. He formed a broad-based government in which formerly hostile factions were brought under the unifying influence of the National Resistance Movement (NRM).

His reading of liberal Western thinkers such as American economist John Kenneth Galbraith shaped his intellectual and political outlook."[20]

The guerrilla fighters frustrated the army which was soon beset by combat fatigue. It also suffered another major blow when the army chief of staff, Major-General Oyite Ojok, died in a helicopter crash on 2 December 1983. He was 43.

Ojok was a highly respected soldier with great combat skills and even won admiration from his enemies as a great soldier.

When he was army chief of staff, he planned and carried out effective military campaigns against the National Resistance Movement (NRM), and the Uganda Freedom Movement (UFM), led by Dr. Andrew Kayiira, which also had guerrilla fighters trying to overthrow the government. The UFM was based in the capital Kampala, unlike the NRM which operated from the rural areas of the Luweero Triangle.

Major-General Ojok distinguished himself as a great strategist and successfully neutralised the guerrillas in a number of battles. But the campaigns by the army were so brutal that civilian populations suffered immensely. In addition to those who were killed in the Luweero Triangle, many people in Kampala also became victims of violence at the hands of soldiers. They were rounded up and taken to army barracks where they were tortured and killed.

The fighting in Kampala intensified when the Uganda Freedom Movement (UFM), waging urban guerrilla warfare, attacked government buildings and other institutions which had to do with the government. The army fought back and easily neutralised the rebels by cordoning off areas where they launched search-and-destroy missions to hunt down the rebels. Civilians in those areas were tortured until they were forced to tell the soldiers where the rebels were hiding. Within two years, the UFM was defeated, earning Ojok credit for leading a successful military campaign against the guerrillas.

It was an entirely different story fighting the NRM rebels. They used typical guerrilla tactics, operating from the bush, and ambushing army patrols and convoys, then melting into the general population. They used hit-and-run tactics effectively.

After defeating the UFM rebels, Ojok turned his attention to the NRM rebels who proved to be much tougher.

He did achieve some success and would have consolidated his gains as time went on had he not suddenly died in a helicopter accident. His death was such a blow to the army, which was already demoralised, that it began to fall apart from sustained attacks by the NRM rebels since it no longer had a leader of his calibre to carry on a successful military campaign against the insurgents.

There was much speculation about Ojok's death. Some sources, including Obote's government, said it was just an accident. Others said it was shot down by NRA fighters; it probably was. As Professor A.B. K. Kasozi, states in his book, *The Social Origins of Violence in Uganda 1964 - 1985*:

"His (Ojok's) success in storming the UMF camps gave him the hope that the NRA would be as easy to crack. In June 1982 Oyite Ojok commanded the five-battalion offensive termed 'Operation Bonanza' against the NRA,

371

but the Resistance Army was victorious.

UNLA soldiers vented their wrath on civilians, whose skulls still litter the Luwero Triangle. Further offensives against the NRA between 1983 and 1984 proved equally futile as the Resistance Army grew from strength to strength.

Having built a fighting force that could engage Obote's army effectively, the NRA turned from guerrilla to conventional warfare and successfully attacked Masindi, Hoima, Gombe, and other areas formerly not considered part of the fighting zone.

Obote's decline in the period 1983 – 84 was partly brought about by a change in international attitude towards his regime. As evidence of his brutality leaked to the outside world, he began to lose credibility. His stay in power was financed, in large measure, by foreign sources. When these backers began to shuffle their feet, his problems increased. The Canadian and Australian members of the Commonwealth Military Team were withdrawn in this period.

There was an erroneous assumption that Obote's problem was the lack of a well-trained army, so trainers were sent in to help him. Their trainees were, however, no match for the NRA.

Outsiders did not want to recognize that Uganda's problem was mainly political; that unless the political problem was resolved nothing could be accomplished.

The NRA sent videos overseas exposing the atrocities of the UNLA and the Obote regime against civilians. The IMF and World Bank began to reassess their involvement in Obote's Uganda. Although he had done almost everything they had asked him to do, Obote's misrule frustrated their hopes that Uganda would become a 'model' of economic structural adjustment.

Decreasing financial resources and intensification of armed struggle led to thousands of casualties in Obote's camp, among whom was Oyite Ojok, the chief of staff, whose helicopter was shot down by the NRA – though the government claimed it was an accident. Soldiers began to resist having to face the NRA 'gorillas,' as they called them; in 1983 many soldiers mutinied rather than fight.

As usual in Uganda, sectarian cleavages began to emerge. The Acholi complained that their deaths were disproportionately high and that only Langis were being promoted. They were confirmed in their belief when Obote, bypassing senior officers, chose a Langi, Smith Opon Acak, as his new chief of staff. The cabinet was divided."[21]

As the fighting went on, the army began to fracture along ethnic and regional lines. The national army under Obote was still dominated by the Acholi and the Langi as much as it was during his first presidency and even during the colonial era when the British recruited northerners into the army in disproportionately high numbers. But it now began to fall apart.

After Ojok died, Tito Okello became the head of the army. Like Obote, Ojok was a Langi; Okello, an Acholi. The conflict in the army pitted the Langi against the Acholi. Most of the foot soldiers were Acholi. They suffered the highest casualties during the war against the rebels and wanted to end the fighting by negotiating with the insurgents. In remarkable contrast, elite troops and most of the army officers who were very close to President Obote were his fellow tribesmen, the Langi. They did not want to negotiate with the rebels. The split between the two northern groups in the army became final when Ojok died and Okello took over as the army chief of staff.

But the rivalry between the Langi and Acholi was not a surprise. Although the two groups were allies and worked together as fellow northerners since colonial times, they did not constitute a monolithic whole. They had their own differences and interests as distinct and separate ethnic groups even though they had a common identity as

Nilotics and as northerners who were different from southern Bantus.

The conflict between the two northern tribes and former allies was another major blow to Obote and his government. It provided impetus to the insurgents who now sensed victory.

Obote himself further alienated the Acholi when another Langi, Smith Apon-Achak (Opon-Acak), a junior army officer, was chosen to be the new chief of staff after Ojok died, instead of an Acholi.

Obote said he did not appoint Apon-Achak to be the army chief of staff; he said he did not even know him. He said it was the military commission which chose Apon-Acak to be the new chief of staff after Ojok was killed in a helicopter crash which Obote blamed on Museveni. He said he believed it was Museveni's fighters who shot down the helicopter in Luweero.

Yet there was a perception that it was Obote himself who, as president, was responsible for Apon-Achak's promotion to be the new army chief of staff. Or, at the very least, he should have vetoed the decision in order to refute claims that Apon-Achak got the position because he was a fellow tribesman, especially after the death of Ojok who also was a Langi and whom Apon-Achak replaced. As Obote stated in an interview with Andrew Mwenda:

"Sometime in 1983, I was in India on a state visit and Paulo Muwanga rang me to say he was giving me sad news.

He said, 'We have lost Oyite Ojok in Luweero, it is a helicopter crash.' Then he explained the details. I stopped him.

I said, 'Paul, stop there, go back to the beginning.' So he started again from the beginning. He explained, I understood.

Then he said, 'I am sending you a cable,' which he did. That same day I informed Indira Ghandi, the prime minister of India and a close personal friend and political ally that we could not continue with the state visit and she graciously accepted the state visit to stop and we returned to Uganda the same day.

I still think it was Museveni's guns that shot the aircraft, but other people think it was an accident. Even in government there were two views; there were people who thought it was Museveni's guns, there were people who thought it was an accident. Peter Otai knows the details better than me.

Then the Ministry of Defence did not immediately produce a replacement. I was not running the Ministry of Defence; the suggestions should have come from the Ministry of Defence for a replacement.

I used to write to them asking them to propose a name. Paulo Muwanga used to reply only informally, 'You know I have only two names and I can not propose one.'

There was only Smith Opon and Bazillio Okello both of whom were brigadiers. Muwanga used to say that he could not propose Bazillio Okello because he had been promoted above his level of education and training and Smith Opon was good on paper qualifications but weak in administration and command.

Later, after one and a half years, the two names were brought to the Defence Council, which I chaired, and included Otai, Samwiri Mugwisa, Tito Okello and Muwanga. In the middle of the vetting of the candidates, Muwanga and Okello asked to be excused to go out and consult.

They returned to the meeting and proposed that we drop Bazillio Okello and consider only Smith Opon Acak which we all accepted.

Some people then began to claim that I appointed Acak because he was a fellow Langi.

My only contribution to his appointment was ceremonial i.e. that I chaired the Defence Council, and that it is the commander in chief who was the appointing authority.

I personally did not know Acak. At least I knew Oyite Ojok and he was a personal friend. I did not appoint Oyite Ojok as army chief of staff. I found him in that job just like I found Tito Okello army commander.

Tito Okello was an ignorant person, he should not have remained army commander. I accept that to have been a mistake, actually a fatal one, we made."[22]

Many Acholi army officers expected Bazilio Olara-Okello to be the new chief of staff. He was a senior army officer who was also one of the commanders of the Uganda National Liberation Army (NLA) which together with the Tanzania People's Defence Forces (TPDF) ousted Amin. Instead, it was alleged that Obote chose a fellow tribesman to lead the army.

Whoever made the decision to appoint Acak (Achak) as the new chief of staff, it was a choice which helped pave the way for Obote's ouster by Acholi army officers and soldiers about two years later on 27 July 1985.

Obote was already beset by accusations that he rigged the 1980 elections and had even lost some cabinet members who decided to join the opposition demanding new elections. As Jacob J. Akol states in his book, *Burden of Nationality: Memoirs of an African Aid Worker/Journalist 1970s – 1990s*:

"Accusations that Obote had rigged the 1980 elections persisted. Some of his own ministers deserted and joined the opposition to demand fresh and fair elections. Obote took offence and declared war on any opposition; he began to rely more and more on the military personnel who had toppled Amin in 1979 and paved the way for his return to power.

But the military itself was now more divided than ever and was riddled with corruption and tribal rivalry between the Langi, his tribe, and the Acholi. Obote's own reversion to tribalism became apparent when, in August 1984, he tactlessly insisted on appointing his fellow tribesman Lt. Col. – later Brig. – Smith Opon Acak as his chief of Staff while more senior officers from the Acholi tribe were overlooked."[23]

The military coup against Obote was led by General Tito Okello and Brigadier Olara-Okello. The two Okellos were not related but shared a common Acholi name.

Olara-Okello commanded a brigade composed mostly of Acholi soldiers which executed the coup. It was also said that, not long before the coup, Obote gave orders to have Olara-Okello arrested by the Special Force Units which were dominated by Langis.

After overthrowing the government, Olara-Okello served for only a few days as chairman of the powerful military council, hence as Uganda's head of state. He was replaced by General Tito Okello, a fellow Acholi, who became president. Olara-Okello was promoted and became a lieutenant-general and head of the army.

The split between the Langi and the Acholi in the army could have been avoided if Obote did not favour his fellow tribesmen at the expense of the Acholi. The Acholi also complained that they did not even get the rewards they were entitled to for serving in the army and for fighting the rebels. The split also made it impossible for the army to wage an effective military campaign against the rebels of the National Resistance Army (NRA).

It was a rivalry which not only facilitated Obote's downfall but also Museveni's victory and rise to power. As Professor Byaruhanga states:

"One of President Obote's major challenges was the multiple rebel forces, most portentous of which was the National Resistance Movement led by Yoweri Museveni. This aura of uncertainty was further exacerbated by the growing rift between Obote's trusted factions in the army –

the Langi, his own tribe, and the Acholis, their neighbour.

The Acholis accused the president of sectarianism – favouring his own tribe (the Langi) by awarding them with frequent promotions, and intentionally putting Acholis and other tribes in harm's way during the incessant combat engagements with the rebels.

It was against this background of power struggle within the army, that President Obote was overthrown, July 27 1985 by Acholi army officers led by Tito Okello, who became President.

But the Okello military government lasted only a few months, a period that was characterized by violence and political uncertainty. Meanwhile, as the Nairobi-based peace negotiations with Yoweri Museveni's National Resistance Movement failed to reach fruition, Museveni and his National Resistance Army (NRA) overran the capital of Kampala and took over power January 25, 1986. Yoweri Museveni then became president and has been at the helm of power to date."[24]

There has also been an undercurrent of suspicion between the Acholi and the Langi for tribal reasons since colonial times, although they have been allies through the years and have always been collectively identified as "northerners" in contrast with southerners. The suspicion and even tensions between them have also been exacerbated by the disparity in the number of soldiers from the two groups. The Acholi have always outnumbered the Langi and other groups in the army. There was a time when an entire half of the army was Acholi.

It was during Obote's leadership when the Langi made quantum leaps in terms of promotion and recruitment into the army, although they were already there in substantial numbers since colonial times, surpassing members of other tribes but not the Acholi. It was also during his presidency that tensions and rivalries between the two northern tribes degenerated into violence and destroyed the bonds which existed between them as close allies against southerners because the Langi were favoured by Obote. Without unity between the two in the army, it was impossible for Obote to survive in office. As Professor Moehler states:

"Obote's reliance on the military to maintain power eventually led to his downfall. As rebel activity against the government intensified, ethnic cleavages deepened between the Langi and the Acholi, two ethnic groups from the north that dominated the military.

In July 1985, Obote, a Langi, was once again removed from power in a military coup, this time led by Brigadier Bazilio Okello and General Tito Okello, two Acholi officers (Kasozi 1999, 171 – 74). Museveni's NRM made great progress in its guerrilla war and continued to fight the Okello government until the NRM captured Kampala and the Ugandan government on January 26, 1986 (Human Rights Watch 1999, 35 – 36; Mukholi 1995, 24)."[25]

Obote's second presidency was dominated by tensions, instability, and by civil war almost from the beginning. The first priority was to win the war and bring peace without which nothing else could be done, especially to rebuild the country after years of destruction by Idi Amin.

But Obote himself ruled that out when he excluded his opponents from meaningful participation in the political process when he had the election rigged in his favour. The result was war which eventually drove him out of office.

He may also have underestimated Museveni who eventually emerged as the winner. Besides all the resentment and plots against him by Acholi soldiers, Museveni was the person to watch.

Since his student days at the University of Dar es Salaam in Tanzania, he had shown great interest in revolutionary changes and even worked with FRELIMO guerrillas in Mozambique when they were fighting against the Portuguese colonial rulers.

He also fought against Idi Amin and was one of the prominent leaders in the anti-Amin coalition which was formed in Tanzania. As Akol states:

"Museveni was still studying (at the University of Dar es Salaam in Tanzania) when Obote was overthrown by Amin in 1971. He remained in exile in Tanzania till 1979, when he returned to Uganda as a leading member of the Uganda National Liberation Front (UNLF), which had kicked out Amin.

He later formed the Uganda Patriotic Movement (UPM) to fight the 1980 elections. His party won only one seat in the elections, which, supposedly democratic, brought Obote back to power. He was so upset by his defeat and so disgusted by the way the elections had been rigged that he took to the bush and formed the National Resistance Army/Movement (NRA/M).

When Obote heard that Yoweri Museveni had formed the NRA in order to remove him by force, he derisively referred to him: 'A *Mnyarwanda!* What can he do?' meaning a foreigner from Rwanda could not succeed in removing him.

But Obote should have known better. As a student in the University of Dar es Salaam, Museveni's idea of a worthwhile holiday was reportedly to join the Mozambique nationalist fighters, FRELIMO, to fight against Portuguese colonialism there.

As time went by and the NRA/M gained more ground militarily and politically, the hallmark of the movement became 'discipline.' This fact, more than anything else, won the movement more and more supporters and respect all over the country.

Even Obote's own Vice President, Paulo Muwanga and Prime Minister Otema Alimadi, were said to be secretly in league with the NRA/M long before Obote lost power for the second time through a military coup. The two Acholi generals who later spearheaded the coup in 1985 were said to be in contact with the NRA, though the NRA has consistently denied this."[26]

The rivalry and violence that erupted between the Langi and the Acholi in the army also signalled the beginning of the end of Obote's second presidency. He could not depend only on his fellow tribesmen, the Langi, to keep him in power in an army that had more Acholis than Langis.

It also meant that the ethnic and regional solidarity Obote had depended on so much to stay in power since the sixties had come to an end. It was the alliance between the two northern groups in the army, the Langi and the Acholi, which tipped scales in his favour against his rivals, including Kabaka Mutesa II who was ousted by military means – mostly by Langi and Acholi soldiers and security forces – in May 1966 under the leadership of another northerner, Idi Amin, although a member of the Kakwa tribe from the northwest. As Akol goes on to state:

"Following NRA's gains in the west of the country, a dispute between the two main Nilotic tribes, who dominated the army, began to surface.

The Acholi troops had long complained that the new Langi Chief of Staff, Opon Acak, expected them to do the brunt of the fighting with the NRA. The Acholi soldiers rebelled against the Langi 'Special Force' soldiers who were sent by Acak to take them from Jinja to the front in early June (1985). They would rather fight the Langi forces than face the guerrillas of Museveni.

The Jinja rebellion was followed by a more serious confrontation between the two tribes early in July at Mbuya barracks near Kampala. The dispute over the ownership of a large cache of weapons left 30 dead. The

Langi overwhelmed the Acholi troops, took them to Makindye barracks and murdered them.

Army Commander Tito Okello, together with many Acholi soldiers and their weapons, hurried north to the Acholi capital of Gulu, where they joined Basilio Okello, who was already there as Commander of the Northern Brigade.

The Acholi troops, led by the two Okellos, attacked Acak's forces at Karuma Falls on the River Nile. Soon afterwards, the Lango capital, Lira, was taken without resistance.

In the end, it took less than a day for the Acholi-led troops to sweep down to Kampala through Soroti and Jinja in the east and Bombo in the west. Obote and Acak fled to neighbouring Kenya in a helicopter with only minutes to spare.

The mid-day coup was successful and the victorious tribal-led army announced on Radio Uganda:

The tribalist government of Milton Apolo Obote has been overthrown. We appeal to our brothers in the bush and honourable Yoweri Museveni to join us.

There was no immediate response from Museveni.

The two Okellos then set up 'an interim government' in Kampala and promised a general election within a year.

However, reports of atrocities being committed by the soldiers were coming in daily and it seemed that, apart from Obote's absence, nothing much had changed. In contrast, the areas controlled by the NRA in the west were reportedly peaceful.

It was now clear to the NRA that the new military government in Kampala was nothing but old wine in, well, old bottles really, since the generals had been part and parcel of the Obote regime.

Peace talks, and even an agreement, between General Okello's government and Museveni's NRA/M took place in Nairobi under the Chairmanship of the Kenyan President Daniel arap Moi. But all that came to nothing, as Museveni soon adopted a winner-take-all attitude.

On January 25, 1986, Museveni's NRA took the capital, Kampala, from the generals.

But Lt. Gen. Basilio Okello and former Defence Minister, Col. Wilson Toko, had retreated to their home town, Gulu, and tried to convince the people that the NRA was coming to loot, rape and savage them.

For the first two weeks, thousands of Acholis and their Nilotic cousins, who had been warring among themselves, now buried the hatchet and congregated daily at Gulu army barracks to be given weapons. The seeds of the present opposition to the government of Museveni were thus sown."[27]

Although northern leaders – Obote and later the two Okellos – were swept out of power, northern opposition to southern leadership of the country, whose most prominent symbol was Museveni, did not stop. Museveni was the first leader from the south to lead Uganda since independence. And northerners were determined not to make it easy for him if they could not overthrow him.

He also faced strong opposition from fellow southerners, including his former allies during the struggle against Obote and the Okello regimes. Others were his own people who had left the National Resistance Movement to oppose him:

"Museveni's honeymoon in Kampala was over only six months into power. By the end of 1986, a full-blown war between the NRA and the northern rebels was already underway.

In a Christmas Eve attack on the NRA near the town of Kitgum, the rebels claimed having killed more than 100 NRA soldiers and taking 50 prisoners. The NRA claimed they killed 115 rebels while they lost 'only 23 men, due to some mistake' on their part.

The significance of that attack was that a new chapter in the unending cycle of killings in Uganda had been ushered in. The players had merely switched places, with the former rebels now the government while the former rulers were now the rebels.

As if the opposition in the north were not enough, opposition within the government had become apparent. By January 1987, some former allies of Museveni, the leader of the Uganda Freedom Movement (UFM), Dr Andrew Kayiira, and the leader of the Federal Democratic Movement (FEDEMO), David Livingstone Lwanga, were already in jail, charged with treason. Also, 18 top-ranking army officers were arrested and charged with plotting a coup against the government.

Dr Kayiira was murdered in a BBC correspondent's home shortly after his release from five months' detention. The correspondent, himself a Ugandan, went underground and later turned up in Kenya, claiming that Dr Kayiira's killers were NRA soldiers. His movement, Uganda Freedom Army (UFA), announced their return to the bush in the south to fight Museveni.

But UFA would be just one of the multitude of armed anti-NRA/M movements which have since been formed.

In spite of the wide publicity given to the so-called 'Holy Spirit Movement,' which was led by Alice Lakwena, that organisation was never a real threat to the government of Museveni. The 'Holy Spirit' followers were massacred each time they mounted their suicidal attacks against the NRA. The real problem came from the 'Uganda People's Democratic Army' (UPDA")."[28]

Dr. Andrew Kayiira, who once was a cabinet minister under President Yoweri Museveni, was killed on 9 March 1987 only about a year after Museveni seized power. He was was born on 30 January 1945 and was 42 when he was killed.

His death was an assassination.

Kayiira's assassination raises some questions about Museveni's leadership and the National Resistance Movement (NRM) among many Ugandans including some NRM supporters because of the alleged involvement by the National Resistance Army (NRA) in that brutal murder. As Ugandan journalist David Kibirige stated in his article, "Who Killed Kayiira?" in *The Monitor*, Kampala, Uganda, 6 March 2004:

"For 17 years now, mystery still surrounds the gruesome murder of former minister and guerrilla leader Dr Andrew Lutakome Kayiira.

Kayiira was the Uganda Freedom Movement (UFM) military leader with lawyer Francis Bwengye as head of its political wing.

On March 7, 1987 Kayiira was shot dead at the home of a friend, then BBC correspondent Henry Gombya, at Konge, Makindye on the outskirts of Kampala.

Mr Gombya, who was around the house at the time of the murder, later fled to exile in Britain.

Because of its high profile, President Yoweri Museveni ordered that the famous Scotland Yard investigate the murder.

Scotland Yard did come and investigate but several years later, nothing is known about the report, or who killed Kayira.

Not surprisingly, Kayiira's death has dogged the country and at every presidential election, his ghost returns to haunt President Yoweri Museveni.

In 1996 when Paul Kawanga Ssemogerere stood against Museveni, Kayiira's death became a hot issue.

Fingers were pointed at Museveni saying it was he who did not want the Kayiira report made public.

Ironically Mr Ssemogerere was the minister of Internal Affairs at the time of Kayiira's death.

The police, which carried out initial investigations, fall

under the Internal Affairs ministry.

Ssemogerere resigned his ministerial post in 1995 to contest for the presidency.

So the question is why has Ssemogerere kept quite all this long?

Contacted by *Sunday Monitor* on Wednesday Ssemogerere said he could not discuss the Kayiira issue on the phone. He said he was going to attend a funeral. Again *Sunday Monitor* tried to speak to him on Thursday in vain.

Kayiira was a Democratic Party (DP) firebrand politician who as early as 1986 had started calling on Ssemogerere to relinquish party leadership.

Again in the March 2001 presidential elections, Kayiira's death cropped up.

Museveni's closest challenger, Dr Kizza Besigye, challenged the president to tell Ugandans who had killed Kayiira.

Again ironically, Besigye was time minister (sic) of State for Internal Affairs, at Kayiira's death.

In his book *The Price of Freedom* which he wrote after Kayiira's death, Mr Bwengye blamed government for the murder. Informed sources told *Sunday Monitor* that government bought off all copies. Even Bwengye does not have one.

Highly placed sources told *Sunday Monitor* that after writing the book, government sent then national political commissar, Col. Kizza Besigye and Lt. Gen Salim Saleh off all copies in addition to 'oiling Bwengye's hand' which persuaded him to come back home.

Bwengye conceded that it was Saleh and Besigye who negotiated his return but denies ever receiving money.

'The book was published abroad and I had no contact with government, so how could I have negotiated for a buy off,' Bwengye told *Sunday Monitor* on March 4.

Asked if *Sunday Monitor* could borrow his copy since as the author he might have one, Bwengye said; 'My copies were borrowed and never returned.'

Again asked why there is no reprint, Bwengye said; 'I am not a publisher. So I do not know.'

He however said that at one time he requested *The Monitor's* then managing editor, Charles Onyango Obbo, to publish the book but that he received no reply.

Last month during Monitor FM's popular Andrew Mwenda live programme, Bwengye gave his reasons why he suspects elements in government eliminated Kayiira.

'I and Kayiira were acquitted of treason charges because there was no evidence. Peter Kabatsi [then solicitor general] said we were free. Two days later, President Museveni while addressing the Law Society said although people like Kayiira were released, they were guilty. Two days later Kayiira was killed,' Bwengye said.

Pressed if he thought it was Museveni who killed Kayiira, Bwengye said: 'soldiers did it.'

When asked if he thinks Museveni can assassinate someone, he said: 'I do not think Museveni is an assassinator (sic) but a man who has been fighting wars can not shoot into trees.'

Advised to drag the government to court for killing Kayiira, Bwengye said; 'When Lule was removed, some people went to court and court ruled that he had been removed illegally but nothing happened. There have been many court rulings but this does not change the system.'

Museveni-Kayira background

Immediately after the December 10, 1980 general elections, Kayiira was of the view that a guerrilla war was inevitable.

On the other hand Ssemogerere as party leader said they should form the opposition in parliament.

So Kayiira formed the Uganda Freedom Movement (UFM). In fact it was Kayiira who went to the bush first; to be followed by other guerrilla groups including that of Yoweri Museveni.

387

Kayiira felt that by telling the youths not to join the bush fighters, Ssemogerere denied him a block of Baganda fighting force.

In fact when Museveni appointed Kayiira minister after the fall of the Gen. Tito Okello Lutwa's junta, he (Kayiira) felt that it was not because of his DP leanings but because he had a fighting force.

As early as 1986 Kayiira had shown 'signs of being problematic.'

For instance even before the whole of Uganda had been 'liberated' by the NRA, he was telling Museveni to come clean on issues like multiparty politics and federalism.

Some of his commanders were arrested and killed by the NRA. This was on suspicion that elements within UFM were planning to overthrow Museveni's government.

At the end of 1986, Capt. Abbey Kalega Sserwada, one of the UFM commanders was arrested and detained at Lubiri. Up to now no one knows his fate but *Sunday Monitor* has learnt he was probably tortured by senior NRA officers and had his ears cut off before he was killed.

On October 7, 1986 Kayiira, then minister of Energy, was arrested for allegedly planning to overthrow Museveni's government. He was arrested with two cabinet colleagues; Evaristo Nyanzi and Dr David Lwanga.

Baganda army officers had apparently spied on them.

During court proceedings senior Baganda officers came out and testified that the politicians had approached them. They had recorded proceedings which the court dismissed on technicalities.

The Baganda officers who featured prominently in the treason case included Col. Fred Bogere and Col Drago Nyanzi (RIP).

Later some people tried to kill Bogere by showering his car with bullets.

Court acquitted Kayiira for lack of evidence.

A few days after his acquittal in the wee hours of

March 7, 1987, armed people stormed Gombya's place and showered Kayiira with bullets.

Uganda police makes arrests

After the death, police arrested five men who it alleged had killed Kayira. Government said two had escaped from Luzira. They were Robert Magezi and Sylvester Wada. Those paraded in court were John Katabazi, Peter Kiwanuka alias Backfire and Musisi Kizito.

In the trial that followed, Justice C.M Kato of the High Court acquitted them but they were re-arrested by security operatives outside court and to date, their whereabouts remain unknown.

Scotland Yard comes in

When there was a general outcry that government was covering up investigations, Museveni suggested that the famous Scotland Yard should carry out independent investigations.

British officers came, carried out investigations and compiled a report, which is a top government secret up to now.

Sniffer dogs that were used had moved from Kayiira's house and had reportedly led investigators to the Lubiri barracks. That is when the matter became tricky.

Though government might not have been involved, some elements within the army may have had a hand in the high profile murder.

Because of these developments, the matter took a very dramatic turn.

Top security sources told *Sunday Monitor* that police did not have access to the report but it was with State House.

Criminal Investigations Department (CID) boss Elizabeth Kuteesa was cagey when contacted March 4.

Asked whether as the boss of CID she had the report, she said; 'That is not a priority matter now, as there are many files. I will check and see if that report is here.'

Asked how soon she could avail the report to *Sunday Monitor* she said, 'I do not know; I do not work according to your deadlines.'

She could not delve more into the matter.

The president's legal assistant and acting principal private secretary, Fox Odoi, said the report was not given to State House.

'The report was given to the Attorney General for legal advice since he is the chief legal advisor of government and, then Directorate of Public Prosecution was directly under him,' said Odoi.

Justice Joseph Mulenga who was the attorney general then says he does not remember receiving the Scotland Yard report.

'I do not recall receiving the Scotland Yard report. That is not something one can easily forget. I recall the trial but I do not recall ever getting that report,' Mulenga told Sunday Monitor on March 5.

More and more mystery

Days after the murder of Kayiira, Capt. Sajjad Sooria alias Sajjabi, a Pakistani fled the country. He was a UFM mercenary and Kayiira had employed him in 1981.

Just days after the murder, Gombya also fled to exile where he has lived up to now.

Gombya had apparently managed to divide Shs 40 million into two – under the hail of bullets – after they had been attacked and reportedly threw at the attackers to buy his escape.

This was the official version Gombya gave to the press then and even in the 1990s he maintained his explanation in articles he used to write for *The Monitor*. And with his weight, Gombya apparently managed to jump from a fifteen feet high wall and fled.

In April 1987, Bwengye during a press conference in London attended by Sajaad announced that the UFM was returning to the bush to fight Museveni's government. Bwengye insisted government had killed Kayiira.

Who was Kayiira?

He was born in Mawokota, Mpigi district. He went to St. Peter's Nsambya Primary School in Kampala before proceeding to Namilyango College.

After secondary school he joined the Prison Service as a cadet officer. He left for Britain for further studies.

On his return he was promoted to the rank of assistant superintendent of prisons.

In 1968 he went to the USA to study at the University of New Haven where he did a degree course in criminology and mathematics. He did a master's degree in criminology, themed on criminal justice.

In 1975 he returned to complete his research paper on kondoism – armed robbery – for his PhD. He spent much of his time at Makerere Institute of Social Research when he was writing the paper.

He married Betty Mutema after which he returned to the USA. He joined groups which were fighting Amin. He formed the Uganda Freedom Union with other people like former president Godfrey Lukongwa Binaisa and Olara Otunu, a former Foreign minister and now based at the United Nations.

After Binaisa, the firebrand Kayiira became UFU leader.

He represented UFU at the Moshi Conference, which charted the way forward after Idi Amin's government. He was elected a member the National Consultative Council (NCC).

He was a deputy minister of commerce in the short-lived Yusuf Kironde Lule's government, which replaced that of Amin.

He later became minister of Internal Affairs.

After the removal of Lule he formed the Uganda Freedom Movement with the mission of fighting to restore the professor.

Kayiira's deadly missions

On June 10, 1976 Kayiira participated in an assassination attempt on President Idi Amin Dada during a passout parade at Nsambya Police barracks. Three grenades were hurled at the presidential jeep.

Idi Amin's driver was killed prompting Amin to drive the jeep up to Mulago.

Panic-stricken soldiers opened fire into the crowd killing more than 50 people.

On February 23, 1981 Kayiira's Uganda Freedom Movement (UFM) attacked Lubiri army barracks and the battle lasted eight-hours.

UFM was one of the groups, which was fighting Apollo Milton Obote's government after the December 10, 1980 elections, which were allegedly rigged in favour of UPC.

UFM lost 67 fighters while government claimed it lost 5 soldiers.

UFM claimed that Museveni had assured them that his National Resistance Army (NRA) would reinforce the attacking but betrayed them at the last moment.

Lt. Col. Sonko of UFM delivered a truckload of guns, which Kayiira had captured, to Museveni.

He later defected to NRA.

This caused bad blood between Museveni and Kayiira.

After the unsuccessful attack on Lubiri, Kayiira left for the USA to secure funds for his group.

While he was away there were differences within his group leading to the formation of the Federal Democratic Movement of Uganda (Fedemu).

Before he could reorganise his group, Tito Okello Lutwa and Bazillio Okello overthrew Obote's government.

He joined the Military Council with Lutwa as head of state.

He constantly warned the military council not to underrate the NRA.

By the time the NRA captured power, Kayiira was in charge of parts of Kampala. He was in charge of areas like Ggaba, Konge, Muyenga and parts of Makindye.

Kayiira's six children and wife live in the USA."[29]

Kayiira's assassination sheds some light on the National Resistance Movement – and its army, the RNA) – as an organisation whose leaders will not hesitate to use any means including extra-judicial killings to silence its opponents and as a warning to others in spite of its reputation as a "disciplined" movement which respects the rights of all Ugandans.

Ugandan journalist, Rodney Muhumuza, talked to one of the NRA soldiers sent to kill Kayiira. As he stated in his article, quoting the killer, entitled, "I Took Part in Kayiira Murder," published in *The Monitor*, Kampala, Uganda, 13 January 2007:

"In a voluntary confession that is likely to send shock waves across the nation, a former National Resistance Army (NRA, now UPDF) child soldier (kadogo), Corporal Eddie Sande, has come forward to say he was part of a platoon of 33 government soldiers that murdered former Energy Minister Dr Andrew Lutaakome Kayiira in March 1987.

Dr Kayiira, the leader of the former rebel group, the Uganda Freedom Movement, was murdered shortly after being acquitted of treason. Less than a week before his murder, President Yoweri Museveni told the BBC World Service Radio that even though the High Court had acquitted Kayiira, Museveni was sure he was guilty of

393

treason, based on the intelligence reports available to him.

Cpl. Sande says he was a member of the NRA's Lubiri-based Central Brigade, which the Democratic Party (DP) has said is implicated in the murder by a still secret investigative report into the murder by Britain's Metropolitan Police of New Scotland Yard.

On the late evening of Saturday, October 14, 2006, Cpl. Sande took this reporter by surprise when he walked into the *Daily Monitor* offices in Kampala and volunteered to tell the story of Dr Kayiira's assassination at the home of his friend, BBC journalist Henry Gombya.

The short and slender Sande, who claims he participated in other 'liquidations,' wanted to see a journalist who would help him write the story of his life. He initially asked for *Daily Monitor's* Political Editor, Mr Andrew Mwenda, who is away in the United States.

He then asked for our former Editor in Chief, Wafula Oguttu, who was unavailable, following which he told this reporter a shocking story.

Cpl. Sande gave his army number as RA 34452, which records from the Chieftaincy of Military Intelligence have since showed to be valid.

The records, confirmed on Thursday by army spokesman Maj. Felix Kulayigye, show that Cpl. Sande is currently attached to State House, and has been involved in a number of 'special intelligence assignments' on behalf of the state. Although there are some inconsistencies in the dates Sande gives in his story, the army records tally with most of his claims. Maj. Kulayigye said it was possible the corporal had deserted the army and gone underground.

In a series of interviews, initially clouded by some doubts from this reporter, Cpl. Sande recalled the events of an evening in 1987 when soldiers from the 19th battalion of the Central Brigade were allegedly briefed about a mission to eliminate an 'adui' [Swahili word for an enemy] that turned out to be Dr Kayiira.

'Before going to Libya [for training], in 1987, I was in

the 19th battalion [Central Brigade] under [now Brigadier] Peter Kerim. When we were called in the evening, I was at the headquarters in Lubiri. We were called for assembly at night [and told] that we were going for an operation,' he said. 'That was after people who were supposed to go for patrol had already left. We were all from the Brigade headquarters, not from companies.

'By then, the OC (Officer-in-Charge) of Headquarters was one Otto, sometimes called John Byuma Otto. I understand he is now in Lira.' (*Sunday Monitor* has confirmed the existence of this officer but has been unable to locate him and has not been able to obtain his confirmation or denial, and we urgently want to hear his side of the story – Editor).

Although the call to get ready for the operation was made by Kerim, Sande recalled, it was the brigade's Intelligence Officer, (now Lt. Col.) David Kaboyo, who briefed the platoon of some 33 soldiers before heading to Makindye, the Kampala suburb in which Kayiira was sharing a house with Mr Gombya, who mysteriously survived the attack and fled into exile.

'Peter Kerim, the 19th battalion commander, told us that we were going for an operation. For that operation, he told us, there was someone who would brief us. And then we left the barracks and went to the brigade headquarters. When we reached there, we met the brigade intelligence officer. He was called Kaboyo.'

Sunday Monitor has since independently confirmed that 19th Battalion was under the 163rd Central Brigade and that Lt. Col. Kaboyo was indeed Intelligence Officer at the time. We have also confirmed Brig. Kerim was at the time Commander of the 19th Battalion.

Brig. Kerim is now the army's Director of Training, operating under the office of the Deputy Chief of Defence Forces. Lt. Col. Kaboyo is still in the army as a zonal commander of land forces in the Lake Albert (Bunyoro) region.

'Kaboyo talked to us and there was another officer present called Peter Nkola. Kaboyo told us we were going for a crucial mission 'right now'. We asked him what the mission was. He said: 'No, jeshi apana wuliza maswali [soldiers do not ask why].''

Contacted for comment, Lt. Col. Kaboyo turned down several requests from *Sunday Monitor* to say anything about Cpl. Sande's claims or the murder of Dr Kayiira. He would neither confirm nor deny anything on record, saying 'the government which I serve does not allow me to comment on that issue.'

Sunday Monitor has since been told by intelligence sources that the Chieftaincy of Military Intelligence became aware of this newspaper's intention to publish this story a few days ago and that all soldiers named by Sande had been ordered to make no comment.

Other security sources have since told *Sunday Monitor* that Kaboyo's role was to 'secure the scene of crime' of Kayiira's murder but they declined to clarify whether this took place before or after the crime and this newspaper is still keen to obtain Col. Kaboyo's comment.

Cpl. Sande claims on that fateful March 6 1987 night, his platoon of soldiers took a truck ride to the house in which 'the enemy' [Dr Kayiira] was said to be residing, and although they were there by 8.30 p.m., it would be a long wait before the mission was executed. He said that although they travelled under the command of Otto, the NRA's deputy army commander, the late Maj Gen Fred Rwigyema (a Rwandan Tutsi and founder and leader of the Rwandan Patriotic Front – RPF – together with the current Rwandan President Paul Kagame), later joined them. Sande says the Isuzu truck on which they travelled was driven by one 'Godie,' whom he has since lost contact with. He insists the truck belonged to the 163rd Central Brigade.

'When we reached there, we were asked to get out of the vehicle. Then Rwigyema came and found us. He was in a jeep. But for us, we had gone with Otto, who is now retired. We got out of the vehicle, and we were told to line up and take positions. There were some selected people who advanced. We were told that if we heard gunshots we should advance up to the scene, and be ready.'

Cpl. Sande says he and other soldiers present were told to shoot any suspicious person moving in their direction and to preserve their concealment, although some of his senior colleagues were frequently radioed.

But it would be hours before they heard the gunshots, he recalled. 'It was late in the night when soldiers entered the house. So when we heard a gunshot we advanced as we were told,' he said, explaining that they soon stumbled upon a man lying in a pool of blood – the victim of gun-wielding assassins who were still hovering over the corpse when Sande arrived.

Sande's account, however, does not tell who actually pulled the trigger. He told *Sunday Monitor* he did not know the identity of the actual killers because he arrived after the murder. 'When we reached the scene we saw a tall, big man lying in a pool of blood. Then (the late) Major Dr Peter Baingana (a former NRA Director of Medical Services) told Rwigyema (the two later led the Rwandan liberation war but were killed in its first month) that 'mission imeisha' [mission is complete] after checking [the body].'

Cpl. Sande claims that after Dr Kayiira's killing, Maj. Gen. Rwigyema – travelling in a jeep, and followed by some soldiers among whom was Cpl. Sande – travelled to the Kololo home of the then Central Brigade Commander, Gen David Tinyefuza, to convey the good news.

'We followed Rwigyema up to Kololo, where we found the afande. He was up (awake). 'Tumerudi [we are back],' Rwigyema allegedly told Tinyefuza, to which Tinyefuza allegedly replied, 'pole kurudi [welcome back].'

This part of the account attracted much sceptical questioning from this reporter because Tinyefuza was a subordinate to Rwigyema and whether he would therefore report back to him after a mission appeared highly unlikely. It also appeared unlikely that the Deputy Army Commander would take part in such an operation. Cpl. Sande said he also found it strange.

But he suggested that, judging by the brevity and nature of their discussion, Rwigyema's reporting to Tinyefuza could have been more in the spirit of comradeship than hierarchy. Tinyefuza has vigorously denied any involvement in the murder of Dr Kayiira, whom he says was killed by his former comrades in UFM and its breakaway faction Fedemu.

Contacted for detailed comment, Gen. Tinyefuza said there was no truth in the claims. 'It is not possible...I don't recall any of that. In any case, it is strange. All that is not true. Kayiira was killed by his true friend,' Gen. Tinyefuza said but did not name the purported killer.

Cpl. Sande said he does not know for sure if Brig Kerim was physically present during the operation. 'I don't know, because when we were called for fall-in at around 7 p.m., he [Kerim] came and told us that we were going for [an] operation and that someone would come and take us. Then he entered his short chassis Cross Country and drove to his residence in Kololo.'

In response to Sande's claims on Monday, Brig. Kerim showed no surprise at the Corporal's account, and went on to say that he had waited 20 years for a journalist to ask him questions over him questions over Dr Kayiira's death. Describing it as 'a terrible trend,' Brig. Kerim denied any involvement in the murder of Kayiira but said Cpl. Sande's account seemed to 'have good information.' But he said he was 'not supposed to talk much' since he was still a serving UPDF soldier.

Brig. Kerim, however, corroborated the historical aspects of Cpl. Sande's account and confirmed that he knew the names mentioned by the former kadogo. Recalling that Peter Nkola was a signaller and that David

Kaboyo was an intelligence officer, Brig. Kerim argued that while he did not know about the Kayiira mission, it was possible that the execution could have been the work of intelligence operatives who did not have a duty to report to him.

Brig. Kerim said 19th Battalion was the biggest battalion under the Central Brigade, and that it was composed of many companies. He said the Brigade headquarters had 180 soldiers and that each company and platoon had its own commander. 'I don't know who commanded that platoon but what happens depends on individual commanders. If Kaboyo took Sande [for that operation], he took him illegally.'

'I do not remember anything about that mission. I don't do secret missions...that is intelligence work...,' Brig. Kerim said. The Brigadier also denied any link with Maj. Gen. Rwigyema.

Asked whether he would feel hurt by this newspaper publishing this story, which names him, the apparently unperturbed Brig. Kerim said 'you seem to have good information.' Asked whether this reporter should proceed with the story, he answered, 'That is already a story, if a man has come out openly...'

After Kayiira's murder, the NRM government contracted Scotland Yard, the British Metropolitan Police, to investigate the case at a cost of $250,000. Uganda's tax revenue at the time was only $40 million. Scotland Yard was called in because of widespread suspicion in the country that Kayiira had been killed by Museveni's government. The government has never released the report to the public, resulting in a full-blown storm, 20 years later.

Last week the Democratic Party threatened to release the report at a rally at Constitution Square on January 6, but they did not succeed as police dispersed them with teargas and rubber bullets in running street battles that paralysed business in the city. They later said they would release the report on Saturday at another rally in Masaka. *Sunday Monitor* has however learnt that a decision was taken on Friday not to release the report at the rally.

Later in the day, DP, quoting from the said report, issued a press statement saying Kayiira's killers were drawn from the then Central Brigade under a top General.

In the statement, DP President Ssebaana Kizito said the report identified one of the killers as Suicide Brewery, a reference to the late Maj. Marius Katungi, who he said is named by Scotland Yard as having participated in the killing of Kayiira. The late 'Suicide' was known in the army for his spontaneous cruelty and was one of the NRA (now UPDF) bush war commanders.

In an interview published in *Daily Monitor* on Thursday, Mr Gombya, in whose house Kayiira died, said the soldier who shot Kayiira was a Muganda officer who is now a Brigadier in the army. Brig. Kasirye Ggwanga, a Muganda officer, has denied any role in the murder but said Kayiira 'deserved death.'

Last week, at the height of DP's claims that there was evidence for the army's complicity in Kayiira's death, Security Minister Amama Mbabazi denied such a role by the army. The army spokesman, Maj. Felix Kulayigye, said he could not comment. 'Well, what can I say? No information, no comment,' he said.

Asked whether he wanted his story published, Cpl. Sande said, 'It is better if it is there on record (he accepted to be photographed and tape recorded) because even if you hear tomorrow that Sande Eddie is dead, you can then bring the tape. That's why I came here instead of going to *The New Vision* (a government-owned daily newspaper).'

He said he joined the NRA in 1985 at Mulima in Mount Rwenzori. 'I was under the protection of [Moses] Kigongo. We were there with men like [John] Nagenda and Jacob Asiimwe.' He said he was recruited into Brig Kerim's 19th Battalion (which he says was then still under the late Col Patrick Lumumba) by one Corporal Kalibbala.

Cpl. Sande claims he later attended the Mbarara Kadogo School and was trained in Libya. He does not remember his parents but says Cpl. Kalibbala, who recruited him at a tender age, told him his father used to deal in secondhand clothes and was a supplier to Kalibbala, who sold the clothes in Luwero, where he was also an NRA informer. Sande says during the war, he spent some time at Mulima (Mount Rwenzori) with other child soldiers.

Brig. Kerim told *Sunday Monitor* that most of his 19th Battalion recruits were child soldiers from the Rwenzori and Fort Portal region."[30]

The assassination of Dr. Kayiira by NRA soldiers still haunts Museveni's government and the ruling National Resistance Movement (NRM). It is also now and then used as a weapon by the opposition to discredit Museveni and his Movement.

Although Museveni continued to face opposition in the southern part of the country after he came into power, his biggest challenge was in the north, the ethnic and military stronghold of the Uganda People's Democratic Army (UPDA) which was fighting the National Resistance Army (NRA).

The Uganda People's Democratic Army (UPDA) was formed by Acholi soldiers under the leadership of Brigadier Odong Latek. The soldiers had left the national army – the Uganda National Liberation Army (UNLA) – after the government of Tito Okello was overthrown by Museveni. They fled north and sought sanctuary in southern Sudan. They returned to northern Uganda when the National Resistance Army (NRA) of Museveni occupied Acholiland in January 1986. They formed the Uganda People's Democratic Army in March the same year to push the NRA out of Acholiland which was also the homeland of the ousted Ugandan military head of state, Tito Okello.

The UPDA attacked NRA forces – who then, as now, constituted the Ugandan national army – in the north in August 1986 and got a lot of support across Acholiland. It was Acholi subnationalism at its best. The NRA forces, composed mostly of southerners, were seen by Acholis as an army of occupation by foreigners in Acholiland who had to be driven out.

It was nothing new but a resurgence of the same phenomenon, only in another form (armed resistance), that has been an integral part of Ugandan national life in a country where ethno-regional loyalties play an important role across the spectrum. Even the composition of the cabinet – as well as allocation of other posts – has to reflect regional balance for the sake of national unity and stability; that is also the case in many other African countries.

Northerners felt they were left out under Museveni, partly because of their support for Obote, their opposition to Museveni's leadership, and for simply being northerners who had little in common with southerners who were now in control of the government.

The National Resistance Army occupying Acholiland alienated the Acholi even further when they brutalised the people in retaliation for the attacks by the Acholi rebels of the UPDA. Many of them were killed, further encouraging them to support the UPDA fighters.

But the National Resistance Army proved to be too strong for the rebels. Although the rebels controlled most of the rural areas and knew the region well since it was their homeland, they failed to dislodge the NRA from the towns and started losing the war.

But they refused to concede defeat and many of them turned to the Holy Spirit Movement led by Alice Auma – better known as Alice Lakwena – who led her followers south in an attempt to take over the capital Kampala and end Museveni's rule. As they moved south, she and her followers got a lot of support on the way from other ethnic groups who, like the Acholi, were opposed to the national government under Museveni. But they were defeated by the national army in a forest near Kampala.

Other Acholi soldiers from the UPDA began to support other rebel groups including one led by Joseph Kony. Kony's group, also opposed to Museveni's rule, became the Lord's Resistance Army (LRA) which gained international notoriety through the years for attacking villages and killing civilians in northern Uganda – mostly in Acholiland itself – and for abducting children and turning them into child soldiers and sex slaves.

On 3 August 1988, the UPDA signed an agreement with the government to end the war. The agreement also called for an inclusive democratic government. But the UPDA founder Odok Latek refused to sign the agreement and joined the Lord's Resistance Army. However, most of his officers gave up fighting. It was a final blow to the UPDA. The rebel group died out by early 1989, the same year Odok was reportedly killed by NRA soldiers in Nyono Hills in northern Uganda.

It is one of the tragedies of Ugandan history that ethnicity has always played a prominent role in national life – in the political and economic arenas, educational and sociocultural spheres and so on – to the detriment of national unity as has been the case in most African countries. The conflict in northern Uganda, and even the crisis in the Buganda kingdom in the sixties which led to the ouster of Kabaka Mutes II and his subsequent exile in Britain, would not have occurred if the people were allowed full participation in the political process on equal basis and if all the regions were equally represented in the government.

Unfortunately, the leaders themselves have exploited and continue to foster and exploit ethno-regional sentiments and loyalties in the post-colonial era the same way the colonial rulers did in the past to serve their own interests, not those of the nation. Their primary interest is domination from which everything else flows. Uganda is one of the countries which have suffered the most in this context. As Aaron Griffiths and James Katalikawe state in "The Reformulation of Ugandan Democracy" in *Can Democracy Be Designed? The Politics of Institutional Choice in Conflict-torn Societies*:

"Both the colonial and the nationalist governments failed to find structures to accommodate politicised ethnic group difference and the ambitions of 'tribal leaders' in a democratic polity. It is a problem that colonialism – both in the longer term and in the reforms it attempted in its dying hours – bequeathed to much of Africa, but in most places the experience led to less bloodshed and volatility than in Uganda.

Since independence, tensions have persisted between different parts of the country, especially the developed central part and and the undeveloped North.

Northern dominance in the military and inter-ethnic conflicts between different factions in the army only added to the strife.

Depending on who is in power, some consider themselves central to the country's mainstream political activity, while others feel marginalised and out of the reckoning.

The ethnic and tribal variation underlying Uganda's cleavages – 56 ethnic groups, four different linguistic categories and over 30 different dialects – does not mean that it is therefore impossible to forge a harmonious society within a stable nation state. Political institutions often failed in Uganda because they mediated these cleavages in a polarising rather than a cross-cutting way. The potential for Acholi Catholics to ally with Baganda Catholics, for example, thus reducing North-South polarisation, has rarely been realised, except in the early years of independence when the religious division of parties did give some cross-ethnic unity.

The roots of the problem must be traced to Uganda's colonial experience, which left damaging military, economic, religious and political legacies.

The British favoured recruitment from the 'martial races' of the northern Acholi and Langi, a tradition and military model which continued after independence. Northern soldiers, whenever trouble has erupted, 'were usually over-zealous in restoring order among the southerners' (Furely 1987: 2). On the other hand, the British preferred to grow their cash crops in the more fertile South, which developed the best infrastructure. The North and West did not share in colonial economic development.

Finally, the rivalry between the competing branches of Christianity persistently materialised as violence. During the early crystallisation of political parties, the Democratic Party (DP) emerged as mainly Catholic, while the Uganda People's Congress (UPC) became mainly Protestant – both parties marked more by these characteristics than by any concerted ideology.

The political legacy of the colonial state was a narrow relationship with society, one of domination rather than representation, that left it unsuited to being a legitimate institution at the moment of independence. Further, the British formed differing relationships with the different tribal-political groups they encountered, and the governments they variously called kingdoms, territories and districts 'had no socio-political or economic network linking them to one another' (Odongo 2000: 33).

The British relationship with Buganda was to be particularly significant. The *Uganda Agreement 1900* had appeared to set Buganda apart from the rest of Uganda and conferred on the Kabaka – the King of the Baganda – and his chiefs 'special privileges' in return for their cooperation. It set the scene for the disunity of Uganda when in the 1950s the Baganda resisted reforms of the Legislative Council: instead of agitating for more African

405

representation they sought assurances that the council would not affect the Agreement. This led to the abrogation of the latter, the declaration of a state of emergency in Buganda and the deportation of the Kabaka – who returned two years later.

The idea of a unitary form of government for Uganda, which the British authorities supported, was in shambles, and no mass nationalist movement emerged, as it did in Tanzania or Kenya, to counterbalance the sectarian nature of political groupings."[31]

The result is what you see today: a fragmented Uganda, divided along ethno-regional lines, although it has not fallen apart.

The two leaders who have had the most significant impact in trying to unite the country are Obote and Museveni. Especially during his first presidency, Obote formed a cabinet and made other appointments reflecting regional balance, north and south, and from all the kingdoms. But all that was counterbalanced, hence neutralised, by the army and security forces which were dominated by his fellow northerners – a colonial legacy – and who tipped scales in his favour.

Obote also divided the country during his second presidency when he rigged or allowed the general elections – which propelled him into office – to be rigged by his supporters.

He had the opportunity to make amends for the wrongs done by him and his supporters in the 1980 general elections by forming an inclusive government of national unity – embracing all political and ethno-regional groups – which should have included all of his opponents to avoid plunging the country into civil war.

He should have listened to them. He should have shared power with them on meaningful basis. He should have discussed with them on how to move the country forward after the disputed elections. And he should have conceded to their demands instead of listening only to his supporters in the Uganda People's Congress.

By locking out his opponents, he also locked out the majority of Ugandans because the majority did not vote for him.

It was a recipe for catastrophe. As Professor Phares Mukasa Mutibwa states in his book, *Uganda Since Independence: A Story of Unfulfilled Hopes*:

"Obote had promised to form a national or broad-based administration after a UPC victory, but once in power his group forgot this commitment and instead formed an administration composed entirely of UPC members, with the military as its ultimate source of support. Had Obote fulfilled his promise, it is possible that he would have mitigated some of the harm done in stealing the election. Indeed, had Obote formed such a broad-based government, it would have brought a measure of consensus to the confrontational style of politics that has existed in Uganda since independence. But power to Obote is like oxygen to a man, and there could be no compromise with those with whom he disagreed.

Thus, the UPC government did not have the support of those who mattered, particularly in central Uganda which was the heart of the nation containing capital. It soon became clear that, much as in the late 1960s, Obote's regime operated from within an enemy's camp, surrounded by hostile Baganda with whom he had now established a relationship of intense mutual suspicion and hatred. Thus it is important to understand the thinking of the Baganda and other southerners on the one side and of Obote and his military men, headed by Tito Okello and Oyite-Ojok, on the other at the start of Obote's second presidency.

The mere return of Obote from exile in Tanzania in May 1980 had cast a chill over a large section of the Bantu nationalities of southern Uganda who were not in the UPC camp; it was regarded as an ominous event.

When, on 11 December 1980, they saw on Uganda TV Obote taking the oath as President, the bad dream had come closer to reality. The people in Kampala and Buganda generally felt that they were in an occupied territory – mere local inhabitants who would be looked upon as hewers of wood and drawers of water for the ruling group. Lacking guns, they resigned themselves to what Obote and his military establishment would mete out to them....

Luckily for Obote, he still had many of his former lieutenants around, some of a younger generation than himself – men with whom he had lived in the sweltering tropical forest of Owiny Ki-Bul in southern Sudan in 1971 and then in the heated politics of Tanzania and who finally planned his return to the presidency during the UNLF (Uganda National Liberation Front) administrations.

Obote knew that he was disliked by the DP (Democratic Party), CP (Conservative Party) and UPM (Uganda Patriotic Movement) and the people they represented. It did not matter; what mattered was the power and influence he would use in the service of himself, his close lieutenants and the native regions of most of his supporters, both civilian and military. He did not ignore the political wrangles going on outside his encamped headquarters: time and guns, he mused, would take care of those problems and of those responsible for such misguided doings.

In this, perhaps, lies part of the real cause of Obote's failure in his second administration: his inability to accept that the Uganda to which he had returned in 1980 was very different from what it had been in 1971. Obote came back as a wounded buffalo, determined to crush all those whom he believed had supported Amin in the early days of his rule, and he was not prepared to offer any real reconciliation or compromise. If Obote ever knew what the English philosopher Thomas Hobbes taught three centuries earlier – that 'there is no valid reason for sovereigns to desire to oppress their subjects, for the strength of sovereigns is directly dependent upon the strength and wellbeing of their subjects' – he ignored it now.

To Obote there was no common ground, no common strength and well-being, between himself as a 'sovereign' and the people, his hapless and helpless subjects. It is for this reason that Obote is felt to have lacked a clear vision of his country's future when he assumed power for the second time in 1980; he was a fighter at a time that demanded conciliation, a short-sighted politician at a time that demanded statesmanship."[32]

It is difficult to reconcile such short-sightedness with the astuteness of a politician like Obote. But it did happen. And the main reason was the quest for power: his determination to regain the presidency that was taken away from him by force in 1971 even if it meant using the same weapon, force, that was used against him although there was a better way, by democratic means, if the people really wanted him back in power. Professor Mutibwa goes on to state:

"Obote was able to defy his opponents because of the assurance he had received that the army – the UNLA (Uganda National Liberation Army), headed by the veteran soldier Tito Okello, with David Oyite-Ojok as Deputy Commander and the driving force behind its strategies – would support him. It was clear that Obote regarded the UNLA not as belonging to the nation but as his own and the UPC's army that would keep him in power at all costs. This was partly demonstrated during the 1980 election campaign, when Obote would challenge the DP leader to show him *his* army.

Obote knew that although he did not, like the DP, have a civil constituency, his own military constituency was solidly Nilotic. He knew that the Acholi-Langi hegemony which provided the underpinning for his administration was sure and strong, and supported by other soldiers from the peripheral areas in the east – such as Teso – and some Bantu-speakers from the south and west.

As we know, confronted with the decision whether or not to join Obote and the UPC in parliament after the disastrous December 1980 election, the DP leaders grudgingly swallowed their pride – some say they also swallowed their principles – and decided to join parliament. It is said that after the UPC coup, the UPM leaders approached the DP and asked what course it intended to take. According to some sources, the DP leaders replied that they were joining the parliament because they had been rightfully elected. 'Not all votes were stolen,' they appeared to be telling Museveni's party; otherwise the DP would not have won fifty-one seats.

A staunch DP member has stated that there was a long debate on the issue of whether or not the elected DP members should take up their parliamentary seats. But they eventually did agree to take up those seats, perhaps in response to Obote's promise to give them the post of Deputy Speaker and the nomination of four of ten Specially Elected Members who would be chosen.

Obote, with 'magnanimity,' agreed to Paul Ssemogerere becoming the 'Leader of the Opposition' and Alex Waibale 'Opposition Whip.'

The DP parliamentarians would continue condemning the UPC government for its rigging of the elections, but Obote and his supporters saw the DP's presence on the Opposition benches in parliament as the party's acknowledgement of the validity of the 1980 election.

However, some Ugandans – prominent among them being Yoweri Museveni – refused to give support to a government that had obtained power through fraud.

Museveni has been blamed for rejecting the results of the 1980 election since he had been Vice-Chairman of the Military Commission that organised it. Indeed, one critic has even said that not only was Museveni 'a key person in ensuring that the election was not rigged...[but] if anything, he could have been in a position to rig the election in his favour.'

Such criticism is not only unfair, but also shows how some commentators on these events had little idea of what was actually going on in Uganda at that time. Those with eyes to see knew that Museveni was no more than a figurehead within the Military Commission, as indeed was reflected by the nature and size of the room he occupied on the third floor in the parliamentary building. The real rulers in the Military Commission at the time we are talking of were Paulo Muwanga and David Oyite-Ojok.

Be that as it may, the UPM refused to accept the election results and some of its members, soon joined by other peace-loving Ugandans in other parties but especially in the DP, decided to oppose Obote through the use of the gun, since that was the only language Obote understood. They started a guerrilla war against his regime. The outbreak of this guerrilla movement from the moment when he stepped into State House once again compounded Obote's problems right from the start of his administration."[33]

Thus, right from the beginning, Obote denied himself the opportunity to govern and implement his policies effectively by refusing to reach out to his opponents and offer them meaningful concessions. He refused to work with them and relied solely on his fellow UPC members and supporters at a time when the country was deeply divided after the 1980 general elections. He was, in a very tragic way, partly responsible for his own failure and destruction and tarnished his image as one of the leading African statesmen.

Unlike Obote during his second presidency, Museveni tried to establish a broad-based political movement and succeeded, to a limited degree, in bringing different groups together in pursuit of national unity. But he failed to mobilise support in the north and bring in northerners to the degree that he should have.

And he fell short of instituting democracy which he promised he would after seizing power, although his government was not a full dictatorship; it had redeeming qualities even if they did not amount to full democracy. But it could not claim democratic legitimacy when the opposition was not allowed full participation in national politics and in the electoral process.

Chapter Eight:

Uganda under Museveni

YOWERI MUSEVENI became one of the most well-known political figures in Uganda after Idi Amin was ousted in April 1979.

In 1980, he formed a political party, the Uganda Patriotic Movement (UPM), to run for president.

Museveni's main opponents in the general elections in December 1980 were former president, Dr. Milton Obote, leader of the Uganda People's Congress (UPC) which led the country to independence, and Paul Ssemogerere, leader of the Democratic Party (DP).

The Conservative Party (CP), led by Jehoash Mayanja Nkangi, also took part in the elections. Nkangi once served as prime minister of the Buganda kingdom under Kabaka Mutesa II and was in office when the *kabaka* was ousted in 1966.

But the Conservative Party did not pose a major challenge to the other contenders because of its limited

413

regional appeal. It was mostly a party of Baganda traditionalists and drew its support almost exclusively from the former Buganda kingdom.

The most formidable challenge to Obote's Uganda People's Congress came from the Democratic Party which was moderately conservative. Although it had roots in the Buganda kingdom and was predominantly Catholic and appealed to Catholic voters in the sixties, it broadened its appeal and became a major contender in the 1980 general elections. It was strongest in the south while Obote's UPC's stronghold was the north, his home region.

Although the Democratic Party performed better than Museveni's Uganda Patriotic Movement (UPM) in spite of electoral rigging by Obote's UPC supporters, it lost some credibility among many Ugandans when it became the official opposition in parliament, thus inadvertently legitimising Obote's "victory" at the polls. Other groups, including the Uganda Patriotic Movement exerted a lot of pressure on the Democratic Party to dissuade its leaders from joining parliament but were unsuccessful.

However, such intransigence cost the Democratic Party some valuable members including Andrew Kayiira who decided to launch guerrilla warfare against the government. They formed an urban guerrilla group, the Uganda Freedom Movement (UFM), which had spectacular success in some parts of Kampala before it was finally defeated by government forces.

The group which became Obote's fiercest and most dangerous opponent was the National Resistance Movement (NRM) led by Museveni whose name is synonymous with what came to be known as the Uganda Bush War, also known as the Resistance War or Luweero War, because he was the driving force behind it.

The war was fought from 1981 to 1986, first against President Obote, and then against Tito Okello, the military head of state who replaced Obote after a military coup.

The military wing of the National Resistance

Movement (NRM) which waged the war was the National Resistance Army (NRA).

After Museveni announced that he and his supporters were going to launch a popular rebellion to overthrow Obote, he and his followers sought a safe haven in the southwest, his home region, where they formed the Popular Resistance Army (PRA).

The PRA later united with the Uganda Freedom Fighters (UFF) led by former president, Yusuf Lule, to form the National Resistance Army (NRA). They also formed the National Resistance Movement (NRM) as the political arm of the NRA to articulate and propagate the ideals of the struggle against Obote's rule and against any other kind of unrepresentative form of government, with the underlying principle that the people, not the leaders, are sovereign.

There were two other rebel groups during that time opposed to Obote: the Uganda National Rescue Front (UNRF) and the Former Uganda National Army (FUNA). Both were formed in West Nile District, Idi Amin's home region. They were supporters of Amin and waged war against the Uganda National Liberation Army (UNLA) – which was the national army under Obote – in West Nile District.

The war by the National Resistance Army was formally launched on 6 February 1981 when NRA fighters attacked an army installation in Mubende District in the former Buganda kingdom in central Uganda. It was a war that would change the political landscape of Uganda and other parts of the Great Lakes region for years to come because of Museveni's role in other conflicts as well.

He supported the Tutsi-dominated Rwandan Patriotic Front (RPF) which launched its attack on the Hutu-dominated government of Rwanda from Ugandan soil with his approval and finally overthrew that government in 1994, ending the Rwandan genocide. He also, together with Rwandan RPF ruler Paul Kagame who was trained in

415

Tanzania as an intelligence officer and who served as the intelligence chief of the Ugandan army after Amin was overthrown, helped overthrow President Mobutu Sese Seko of neighbouring Zaire. And the armies of both countries, Uganda and Rwanda, went on to dominate eastern Congo, former Zaire, for years on orders from Museveni and Kagame.

When the RNA started its guerrilla war against Obote's government, no-one knew how far-reaching its impact would be if Museveni won and became president of Uganda, although he already had ambitions beyond Uganda and knew that he would try to overthrow Mobutu, his enemy, one day and help Rwandan refugees – mostly Tutsi – living in Uganda return to their homeland by force.

He already had military experience fighting against Idi Amin. He was the leader of the Front for National Salvation (FRONASA) which he formed in Tanzania and which was one of the military groups that joined the Tanzanian army, the Tanzania People's Defence Forces (TPDF), to overthrow Amin. He also had some knowledge about guerrilla warfare after spending sometime with the freedom fighters of FRELIMO – Front for the Liberation of Mozambique – in Mozambique when he was a student at the University of Dar es Salaam in Tanzania. And he used that knowledge to mobilise forces in Uganda against Obote's government.

To mobilise forces and civilian support, he focused on the areas where Obote was not popular; Obote was in fact hated by many people in those areas.

His primary focus was on the rural areas of Buganda, especially the central and western parts of the former kingdom which became his operational base in an area near the capital Kampala; his home region of Ankole and other parts in the southwest; and in Bunyoro also in the western part of the country.

He started his campaign in Ankole and continued to

mobilise grassroots support in other parts of the southwest. The campaign included political education, not just military training. As Professor Joshua Rubongoya states in his book, *Regime Hegemony in Museveni's Uganda: Pax Musevenica*:

"His decision to attend the University of Dar es Salaam, a hotbed of socialist and Marxist political paradigms, further strengthened Museveni's *Weltanschauung* or worldview and convinced him of a need for a fundamental transformation of both the socioeconomic structure of the peasantry and the peasants' consciousness of it.

Drawing from his social roots,Museveni makes the observation that African societies are precapitalist – and in a sense patrimonial – based on identity rather than rationality and are, therefore, vulnerable to local or international elite manipulation.

Because of these characteristics he argues that peasant ideology is still guided by an insidious form of superstition that limits entrepreneurial capacities, thus, perpetuating backwardness.

Out of this thinking emerges Museveni's opposition to political parties in general and multiparty democracy in particular. He reasoned that Uganda's political history was replete with examples of political parties that served as conduits through which parochial, ethnic, and religious interests have subsumed national priorities. They have perverted the development of national unity and consciousness, thus, undermining the roots of a modern economic system.

Indeed, his reasoning is that superstition, sectarianism, and the absence of a capitalist class have slowed the development of modern productive forces and left the peasantry open to the machinations of uncouth, irresponsible political party elites. In order to deal with these pathologies, Museveni advocated and implemented what has come to be known as 'movement' or 'no-party' democracy (Nelson Kasfir 2000). This explains his Johnny-come-lately advocacy for multiparty politics.

Nonetheless, when Museveni announced his desire to bring about 'fundamental change' on (his inauguration day) January 29, 1986, he meant not only restructuring society but also changing the political culture of Uganda's political elite. He campaigned for a shift from, in his words, the cheap, backward, and myopic forms of leadership to principled, disciplined, and scientific management of the state (Museveni 1997, 2000).

In practical terms, Museveni exhorted NRM leaders to mobilize and educate the masses, which explains why he personally went around the country teaching, lecturing, and debating issues pertinent to his political vision and philosophy (Museveni 1997, 2000). This form of communication earned President Museveni the label of democratic populist because it blends well with the local cultures in which consultation and talks between leader and the citizens is widely accepted and is, therefore, legitimizing. Indeed, much of Museveni's early popularity hinged on his virtuosity in combining paternalistic and populist elements in his leadership style.

The charismatic authority flowing from these elements has allowed Museven to inspire, *inter alia*, local community development projects and volunteerism, especially by LC committees and Local Defense Units (LDUs) that complemented national law enforcement and security units.

Museveni's leadership style appeared to reflect an intimate acquaintance with the everyday life and experiences of the masses. To ignore this background is to miss an important trajectory in the growth of his thinking and leadership, both as a guerrilla fighter from a peasant background and as president of Uganda since 1986. Indeed, much of what sets Museveni apart from his predecessors is rooted in the particularities of his social background.

Some have argued that Museveni was never an ally of the peasant/working classes, but a good political tactician. Be that as it may, Museveni's social roots cannot be divorced from the character, nature and outcome of the bush war or from the political vision he projected after assuming state power – these form the normative foundation for the early period of *Pax Musevenica*. Indeed once in government, these same political values became the springboard from which he would launch sweeping changes to the political, social, and economic landscape of Uganda.

What were the challenges that redirected Museveni's vision for Uganda? What political choices did his leadership make, and why? Which ones were imposed on him? What were the missed opportunities during this very pivotal moment in Uganda's history? And central to this study, how much democratic legitimacy did the NRM gain and to what extent was it used to further state institutionalization."[1]

There was also the question of how Museveni was going to become Uganda's president in order to implement the values and policies he had in mind probably since his student days at the University of Dar es Salaam in Tanzania.

He could have tried to seize power through a military coup. He already had military training and experience and took part in the ouster of Idi Amin. He also had contacts in the military since he had once served as defence minister under Obote after Amin was overthrown. But there were several factors which militated against a military takeover had he and his colleagues decided to attempt that to oust Milton Obote soon after Obote regained the presidency.

Museveni also ruled out other options which did not include right from the beginning participation of the masses, especially the peasants in the rural areas, in the struggle against Obote's government which he described as undemocratic since it came into power after the 1980 elections were rigged by Obote's supporters. As Rubongoya states:

"When Museveni left for the bush in 1981, as he had promised he would if the previous year's elections were rigged, Uganda was in the grip of Obote's second dictatorship.

The decision not to organize a possible coup against the now newly formed government of Obote was critical in shaping the future of the Museveni revolution. The success of a possible coup against Obote was in doubt, considering that over 1000 Tanzanian soldiers were still in Uganda following the overthrow of Idi Amin.

The other alternative was to appeal to the international community to annul the election results, but foreign election observers had already declared the elections 'free and fair,' thus, lending the all-important external legitimacy to the outcome of the polls.

The third alternative would have been to wage an urban campaign using assassinations of ruling elites and the destruction of state institutions as the main methods of opposition.

Museveni rejected all of these options, favoring instead the more protracted and arduous process of launching a grassroot, peasant-based guerrilla war. Not only would this option mobilize the support of peasant/working classes, but it would also ultimately lead to the Movement uprooting the elites and institutions of neopatrimonial governance. This decision was initially important in shaping the dynamic and ideological orientation of the Movement because the latter was freed of external obligations. Peasant- and working-class participation would provide the strongest foundation both for the revolution and for the post-Obote system of government, especially at the local level.

The first and critical component of Museveni's revolution was the institutionalization of a force that would impose military resistance to the Obote regime. Museveni started with a military 'force' of twenty-six men and hardly any ammunition. The February 8, 1981, attack on Kabamba Military Training Wing would be the first of many such raids on military installations inside Uganda. Since the expected consignment of arms from foreign sources did not materialize, these raids were absolutely vital – as weapons supply sources – for an internal, incipient guerrilla force. But more, more importantly, during this initial phase, Museveni was faced with two challenges, namely, to be self-reliant in weapons acquisition and to find and train recruits for his embryonic army.

Furthermore, Museveni was determined not to repeat the mistakes of both the colonial and the previous postcolonial states in their policies of recruiting, training, and disciplining their militaries. Thus, the recruitment, partly out of necessity and partly out of a conscious decision, targeted both men and women – it sought to close the traditional gender gap in the military. The training of recruits included not only military discipline and know-how, but most importantly political education as well. While peasants involved in actual combat received more advanced training, the noncombatants underwent military training involving drills and gunhandling. Also included in the training courses were military songs, physical exercises, and group dynamics and cohesion.

But the popularity of these courses rested on the NRM rationale, namely, that such preparations would enable Ugandans to defend themselves in the event of a return to state-directed tyranny. And, in Buganda, in particular, this claim was poignant considering Obote's systematic slaughter of innocent citizens in the Luwero triangle from 1981 to 1984, for which his wife, Miria Obote, would later apologize."[2]

421

He goes on to state:

"Turning now to political education, the 'curriculum' consisted of 'daily lectures on topics such as African and Ugandan history, colonialism, law and justice, democracy, the practicalities of the LC (Local Council) system, civic rights and responsibilities, women's rights and economic development.' These courses – known locally as *mchaka mchaka* – were very popular because there was consensus among the peasantry that the acquired knowledge would cure the 'political immaturity' prevalent among the rural majority. The fact that this way of thinking among the rural masses fit perfectly with Museveni's paternalism contributed to his legitimacy early on, this was because the training – and the concomitant LC system – was seen as a democratization program that ran *with* the grain of local political culture rather than against it.

It was out of these mutations that that NRM/A was able to construct a social foundation upon which the basic political thrust of the anti-Obote movement would manifest, flourish, and lead to regime change. Even though *mchaka mchaka* programs later became propagandistic tools by which the NRM sought to exert state hegemony, in the beginning they were effective instruments for establishing badly needed regime legitimacy. Because such programs were unprecedented, NRM elites were able to distinguish themselves from previous regimes by strengthening their claims to fundamental change. But more importantly, by enabling ordinary Ugandan peasants to defend themselves against state tyranny, the NRM gained credibility and trust while improving value-based reciprocity between state and society. It is from these early strategies that a governance realm would begin to emerge during this early period of power consolidation.

Museveni inculcated a new culture and ideology built around respect for civic virtue and the rights that flow from it. With these principles in place, the initial force of twenty-six individuals gradually expanded to include the mostly disenfranchised and alienated peasants and workers in the Buganda region that was later to be known as the Luwero Triangle. The latter became the geographic nucleus of Museveni's guerrilla movement.

The NRA itself was an amalgamation of Museveni's initial organization, the Popular Resistance Army (PRA), which was mostly made up of the Banyankore and the Baganda-dominated Uganda Freedom Fighters (UFF) led by Professor Yusuf Lule. This measure was undertaken to begin the construction of a non-sectarian military force in contrast to previous postcolonial armies that were dominated by northern ethnic groups. The institutionalization of a gender neutral and ethnically balanced military was a key decision not only in legitimizing the army, but also in turning it into an instrument for improving civil-military relations. The latter objective would become a key factor in the success of the guerrilla struggle itself."[3]

Whether or not Museveni truly identifies with masses – the peasants and workers – the way his political mentor Julius Nyerere did, is highly debatable. He undoubtedly projected the image of a populist when he mingled with the peasants during his preparation for guerrilla war that would later end Obote's rule. However, years later, after being in office as president, he does not seem to be the same Museveni the people knew earlier when he was mobilising forces in the rural areas to fight Obote.

Unlike Nyerere who remained humble and simple until his last days, Museveni is no different from other African leaders who are known for their extravagance and lavish lifestyles and for dispensing favours to their friends and family members including sending them overseas for medical treatment and giving them high government positions as Museveni himself has done in spite of his claim that he identifies with the masses and lives modestly. He has even appointed his wife as a cabinet member.

His fellow countrymen have been outraged by his lavish spending, including the purchase of an expensive presidential jet and sending his daughter to Germany to give birth, which cannot be reconciled with his image as a man of the people. According to a report, "Outrage at Ugandan President's Plan to Buy Himself £25 million Private Jet," subtitled, "Under Fire: Yoweri Museveni Wants to Blow Millions of Pounds on a Jet," in the *Daily Mail*, London, 19 December 2007:

"Uganda's president was today slammed over plans to spend £25 million on a private jet despite the average voter earning just £3 a week.

Members of poverty-stricken country's parliament claimed Yoweri Museveni's lavish gift would be a national asset.

But critics say Uganda, which has been devastated by AIDS with 2 million orphans from the disease, cannot afford the luxury Gulfstream jet.

'Why should a leader of a poor country fly a jet when leaders of some of the industrialised countries he begs from travel on commercial flights?' the *Weekly Observer* wrote in an editorial.

But a committee of lawmakers have endorsed the proposal to buy the plane which can comfortably fit up to 19 passengers.

'We believe this is not a luxury for the president. It is a national asset,' parliamentary committee chairwoman Mary Karooro said.

She also said the new plane would require less fuel than Museveni's existing presidential jet, need fewer inspections and stopovers on long-haul flights and be cheaper to maintain.

The government will either take out a loan from HSBC

to buy the jet or borrow $28 million from the central bank, the rest of the cost being covered by proceeds from the sale of his existing plane.

Money-burning Museveni's frequent use of his presidential jet has sparked controversy in the past.

In 2003, he enraged critics by using it to fly his daughter to a hospital in Germany so she could give birth, at a cost of $15,000 to the taxpayer."[4]

The money spent to send Museveni's daughter to Germany to give birth also caused an outrage in Uganda and beyond. As Regina Jere-Malanda stated in her article, "Special delivery--the VIP baby: President Museveni has been trying hard to rebuff critics who have denounced his grandchild's costly birth at a German private clinic. But why did it happen?," in the *New African*, November 2003:

"President Yoweri Museveni has been under fire for flying his heavily pregnant daughter on his presidential jet to deliver her second baby in Germany at a reported cost of $90,000. But he has defiantly defended his action which his critics has condemned as needlessly uneconomical.

Museveni, who claims to live a 'modest lifestyle' and regularly condemns lavishness and wastefulness among Africans, says he had to send his daughter, Natasha, and an unnamed daughter in-law (due to give birth at the same time), abroad for the costly delivery--because he cannot trust local doctors and medical services.

'When it comes to medical care for myself and my family, there is no compromise,' he said in a defiant statement released to the local media who had widely condemned the action as an unnecessary wastage of limited public hinds, a view echoed by opposition politicians who only recently moved a motion in Parliament asking the First Family to trim down their 'luxurious lifestyle.'

In the statement, Museveni points out that he detests a

wasteful lifestyle, but that as a leader, he is a constant target for plots to kill him and he believes some would-be assassins would not hesitate to use local doctors.

'I regard myself and my immediate family as a principal target for criminal forces,' he said in the strongly-worded statement which one of his senior advisors said the president wrote himself. 'He even described some doctors in Uganda as hostile, who cannot be trusted,' wrote the BBC's Will Ross.

President Museveni tried to dismiss the criticism even further by claiming that the whole affair cost 'only' US $27,000. But as one news paper reported, a Ugandan on the national average wage would take 85 years to turn that much.

The *Sunday Monitor* newspaper in Kampala, quoting a member of parliament with some knowledge of the aviation industry, broke down the cost as follows: it costs US$5,000 for every hour the presidential jet is airborne, and it takes--on average--Eight hours to any destination in Europe from Uganda's Entebbe airport. And it took the presidential jet on this special mission at least 18 hours to and from Germany—a whooping $90,000!

The two women were accompanied by an entourage of 10 other carers, including the First Lady herself, Mrs Janet Museveni. The expenses for their 10 days' upkeep – hotel, loud and probably shopping – while waiting for the babies to be born are not included in the above figure.

Apparently, however, nothing the president did here, is outside the law. In fact, according to Museveni's press secretary, Maria Karooro, the First Family in Uganda is perfectly entitled to such luxuries. 'The constitution says so.'

'The law provides for such a flight,' Karooro said. 'The Presidential Emoluments and Benefits Act provides that each biological or adopted child of the president shall be entitled to one trip abroad per year,' she told The *Sunday Monitor.* 'The law says such trips shall be at the expense of the State,' she added.

What prompted the president to send his daughter to deliver the baby at the unnamed private clinic has not been explained.

There has been speculation, however, that the president was concerned that rebel fighters or sympathisers of the Lord's Resistance Army (LRA) had got wind of where Natasha was to give birth locally and planned an attack.

Normally, most airlines advise heavily-pregnant mothers against air travel--Natasha was only a few days away from her delivery date when she was flown out. She has another older daughter whom she gave birth to at a local private hospital and everything went perfectly fine then.

President Museveni's supporters have defended him as a humble and modest man who only gets an annual presidential salary of about 30,000 [pounds sterling]. 'Nobody who knows hint would describe him as a lavish man. His idea of a perfect meg would be a bowl of millet-meal washed down with a glass of milk,' says his senior advisor, John Nagenda. He adds: 'But as head of state, he has the right to do anything to protect his family if he has any reason to suspect they might be in harm's way.' However, critics say, the cost of having his grandchild delivered abroad could have paid for 1,200 Ugandan mothers to have a once in a lifetime chance of giving birth at a local private hospital in Kampala.

Most importantly, perhaps, $20,000 would have gone a long way in a malaria prevention programme – the country's biggest killer – of children or better still purchased basic medical supplies such as gloves and wound dressings which are routinely in shore supply in most local hospitals, but which come at a fraction of the cost of delivering the presidential grandchild."[5]

That is in sharp contrast with Nyerere.

Museveni says he considers himself to be a disciple of

427

Nyerere. But he obviously means not in terms of lifestyle.

Nyerere lived a very simple lifestyle and did not even carry any money in his pocket, according to those who knew him well and who were very close to him. Throughout the years when he was president, he did not live in his official residence, The State House. He used it only for visitors and for meetings. Instead, he chose to live in a very simple house, also of medium size, which he built after getting a loan from a bank in Dar es Salaam, Tanzania.

He was the lowest-paid head of state in the world, earning no more than $5,000 per year.

After he stepped down from the presidency, he returned to his home village of Butiama near the eastern shores of Lake Victoria in Mara Region in northern Tanzania to work on the farm as a peasant using simple tools – hoes, sickles and pangas (machetes) – and live in a simple house that was not even in good shape.

All that is unheard among leaders, let alone presidents. As James Mpinga stated – not long after Nyerere died on October 14th – in an article "With Mwalimu Gone, Free Bread for Butiama Children Goes Too," in *The East African*, Nairobi, Kenya, November 3, 1999:

"There is little to show that Butiama, the birthplace of Julius Nyerere, raised one of Africa's greatest sons.

Mud huts surround the Catholic Church where Nyerere used to pray, and both the church and the mud huts tell a story. From the mud huts came the children who knew exactly when Mwalimu would have his breakfast, and dutifully came to share it with him every morning, and in the church their parents shared a common faith and prayer.

'At first, it was bread and butter for both Mwalimu and the kids. Soon I couldn't cope with the increasing numbers of children joining him for breakfast, so I downgraded it to porridge and *kande* – (a boiled mixture of maize off the cob and pulses),' recalls Mwalimu's former housekeeper,

Dorothy Musoga, 74, now living in retirement in Mwanza at a house built for her by Mwalimu.

I met Dorothy by sheer coincidence during Mwalimu's funeral at a pub put up by the Tanzania Peoples Defence Force (TPDF) building brigade at Butiama. Like all Mwalimu insiders, she was full of praise for the departed former president but, above all, worried about the future of his family and what she called Mwalimu's 'other children' who loved to share his breakfast.

'With Mwalimu dead, free breakfast for poor villagers will become a thing of the past,' Dorothy reflected, almost to herself, between sips of warm beer. The poverty of their parents remains, as does the lack of infrastructure at Butiama, which Mwalimu didn't want to transform into an edifice to be envied by Tanzania's 8,000 registered villages.

During the last week of October, vehicles thronged the dusty road to Butiama, which runs 11 kilometres from Makutano Juu along the Mwanza-Sirali highway. In fact, the road to Butiama was only made passable by last-minute grading. The net result, however, was a far from comfortable drive. The workmen had, in effect, only succeeded in increasing the circulation of dust.

The drive was a journey through abject deprivation and grinding poverty. On the way we saw small plots of cassava, much of it wilting under the searing heat. The land was mostly bare.

On Saturday, October 23, when Mwalimu was buried, Butiama may well have started to slip back into oblivion, to become what it once was, an unknown village in the middle of nowhere. With Tanzania's propensity for neglecting matters until they become a crisis, Butiama's transition from a collective shrine to an ordinary village is likely to be swift.

The process may, indeed, have started earlier, with Mwalimu's own house, which stands obscured from view by the relatively more affluent boma where the reigning patriarch of the Wazanaki, Chief Japhet Wanzagi, lives. By village standards, the chief's boma stands out as an island of prosperity in a sea of deprivation.

Many people take their first house as a proud possession, but the sewage system at the late Nyerere's first house bears marks of his self-denial. Children fetch water from a public standpipe and their mothers wash clothes in the open. The house itself could do with a fresh coat of paint. Nearby, and just as hidden, is the house where Nyerere's mother, the late Mugaya, lived.

However, judging from the relatively wealthier homestead of the chief, Mwalimu was no more than a peasant - which the Tanzanian government would want the world to believe. The truth is that the former president was in fact a prince who simply chose to shun the trappings of privilege out of his own conviction.

The day after the burial, October 24, I arrived at the village just as villagers in their Sunday best were leaving church. They behaved as if nothing had happened, a stark contrast to the day before when some of them had broken down, unable to reconcile themselves to a future without Nyerere. I was now seeing a different scenario; a people resigned to their common fate.

Only one person, Dr Ebenezer Mwasha, still remained in the past, eleven days after it had all happened. Dr Mwasha is among the scores of professionals who worked closely with Mwalimu both as individuals and as public servants. 'I always looked forward to Mwalimu's homecoming. I never thought I would have the misfortune to receive his body one day,' Dr Mwasha said ruefully a day before Tanzanians and their well-wishers buried Mwalimu.

I met Dr Mwasha again the Sunday after the burial, and he was still unable to believe the obvious. He and his wife were waiting to see Mama Maria, Mwalimu's widow, before he could drive back to Machame in Kilimanjaro region, where he now runs a non-governmental organisation dealing with primary health care. He told me he had been helping Mwalimu to put up an appropriate sanitation and water supply system at his new house, the one the Tanzania Peoples Defence Forces (TPDF) had built for him.

'It is sad that the old man didn't have much time to stay in it,' Dr Mwasha said. Others at Butiama echoed his words. 'It was God's will, we cannot do anything' a primary school teacher, Gambiwa Masubo, said.

Gambiwa accosted me with poems for which he wanted me to find a publisher. 'Can *The East African* publish them, please?' he pleaded. Unfortunately, all them were in Kiswahili. In one of the poems, Gambiwa says Mwalimu has 'cleared the bush' so that the rest of Tanzania can move forward.

When I later visited the compound of Mwitongo, where Mwalimu was buried not far from the graves of his parents, only a few insiders and the late Nyerere's close family members had remained, among them his former press secretary Sammy Mdee and former aide-de-camp Philemon Mgaya. At the grave itself, TPDF soldiers from the army's building brigade were erecting a permanent structure.

The mood was still sombre, but noticeable was lighter than before. Some of the mourners took turns to have their pictures taken at the graveside. Was this some transition from mourning to a heritage industry? Now people had accepted the inevitable, Mwalimu's grave was already taking on the air of a world heritage site.

When Chairman Mao was asked what he thought about the French Revolution, a century and a half after it had taken place, he retorted: 'It's too early to say.'

Few in Tanzania can give a better answer about the impact of Nyerere's death. For the poor children of Butiama, however, the days of free breakfast with their beloved grandpa are gone. It is hard to imagine what will follow."[6]

That is the leader Museveni says is his mentor and proudly adds: I am a disciple of Nyerere.

The contrast between the two is glaring.

Museveni greatly admired Nyerere not only as a great pan-Africanist committed to the unification and liberation of Africa including the liberation of Uganda from Amin's tyranny; he also greatly admired Nyerere for his humility and simplicity and uncompromising commitment to the well-being of the masses, the poorest of the poor.

He also greatly admired Nyerere as a great thinker, an assessment shared by other people including Nyerere's critics such as Professor Ali Mazrui who also at the same time always admired Nyerere and who stated in his work, *General History of Africa VIII: Africa Since 1935* :

"Julius Nyerere is the most enterprising of African political philosophers. He has philosophized extensively in both English and Kiswahili.

He has tried to tear down the language barriers between ancestral cultural philosophy and the new ideological tendency of the post-colonial era. Nyerere is superbly eloquent in both English and Kiswahili.

He has allowed the two languages to enrich each other as their ideas have passed through his intellect.

His concept of *ujamaa* as a basis of African socialism was itself a brilliant cross-cultural transition. *Ujamaa* traditionally implied *ethnic* solidarity. But Nyerere transformed it from a dangerous principle of ethnic nepotism into more than a mere equivalent of the European word 'socialism.'

In practice his socialist policies did not work – as much for global reasons as for domestic. But in intellectual terms Nyerere is a more original thinker than Kwame Nkrumah – and linguistically much more innovative.

Nkrumah tried to update Lenin – from Lenin's *Imperialism: The Highest State of Capitalism* to

432

Nkrumah's *Neo-Colonialism: The Last Stage of Imperialism.* Nyerere translated Shakespeare into Kiswahili instead – both *Julius Caesar* and *The Merchant of Venice.*

Nkrumah's exercise in Leninism was a less impressive cross-cultural achievement than Nyerere's translation of Shakespeare into an African language.

Yet both these African thinkers will remain among the towering figures of the twentieth century in politics and thought."[7]

Professor Mazrui also had this to say in *Governance and Leadership: Debating the African Condition*:

"Nyerere's) great experiments and inspirational ideas an indication that the mystique of Nyerere is not simply in his being an intellectual. It is also in his being a gifted and imaginative one.

Of all the top political figures in English-speaking Africa as a whole, Nyerere is perhaps the most original thinker....The originality of Nyerere consisted not in the policies advocated but in the arguments advanced in their defense."[8]

Mazrui was also interviewed by Professor Seifudein Adem on a wide range of issues about Africa including leaders such as Nyerere, Nkrumah and Mandela, and stated the following in that interview which was published in *The Gambia Echo*, 25 July 2008:

"The fact that Nkrumah had a greater positive impact on me than has any other leader does not necessarily mean that I admire Nkrumah the most.

Intellectually, I admired Julius K. Nyerere of Tanzania higher than most politicians anywhere in the world. Nyerere and I also met more often over the years from 1967 to 1997 approximately.

433

I am also a great fan of Nelson Mandela. By ethical standards Mandela is greater than Nyerere; but by intellectual standards Nyerere is greater than Mandela."[9]

And in his lecture on intellectualism in East Africa entitled "Towards Re-Africanizing African Universities: Who Killed Intellectualism in the Post Colonial Era?" in Nairobi, Kenya, on 14 September 2003, Mazrui had this to say about Nyerere:

"The most intellectual of East Africa's Heads of State at the time was Julius K. Nyerere of Tanzania – a true philosopher, president and original thinker....

In Tanzania intellectualism was slow to die. It was partially protected by the fact that the Head of State – Julius Nyerere – was himself a superb intellectual ruler. He was not only fascinated by ideas, but also stimulated by debates....

In my own personal life I was respected more as an intellectual by Milton Obote in Uganda and Julius Nyerere in Tanzania than I was by either Mzee Kenyatta or Daniel arap Moi in Kenya.

Even Idi Amin, when he was in power in Uganda, wanted to send me to apartheid South Africa as living proof that Africans could think. Idi Amin wanted me to become Exhibit A of the Black Intellectual to convince racists in South Africa that Black people were human beings capable of rational thought."[10]

Nyerere was admired even by some of his most ardent critics. As Jonathan Power, who was highly critical of Nyerere's policies and one party-rule, stated in his article, "Lament for Independent Africa's Greatest Leader":

"Tanzania in East Africa has long been one of the 25 poorest countries in the world. But there was a time when it was described, in terms of its political influence, as one of the top 25. It punched far above its weight. That formidable achievement was the work of one man, now lying close to death in a London Hospital....

His extraordinary intelligence, verbal and literary originality... and apparent commitment to non-violence made him not just an icon in his own country but of a large part of the activist sixties' generation in the white world who, not all persuaded of the heroic virtues of Fidel Castro and Che Guevara, desperately looked for a more sympathetic role model.

Measured against most of his peers, Jomo Kenyatta of Kenya, Kwame Nkrumah of Ghana, Ahmed Sekou Toure of Guinea, he towered above them. On the intellectual plane only the rather remote president of Senegal, the great poet and author of Negritude, Leopold Senghor, came close to him.

Not only was Nyerere financially open, modest and honest, he was uncorrupted by fame or position. He remained throughout his life, self-effacing and unpretentious....

Many of us will mourn Julius Nyerere when he is gone. He was, without any doubt...the most inspiring African leader of his generation."[11]

Kenyan journalist and political analyst, Philip Ochieng' who worked at the *Daily News* in Dar es Salaam, Tanzania, in the early seventies also had a lot to say about Nyerere. As he stated in his article, "Africa's Greatest Leader Was A Heroic Failure, " *The East African*, Nairobi, Kenya, 19 October 2009:

"It takes extraordinary personal strength for a leader to admit in public that he is a failure.

Julius Nyerere is the only one I know who has ever done it.

Some time towards the end, he stood on a podium to announce that he had failed to achieve the social goal that had driven him into leadership.

But if you have genuinely tried, failure is to be respected.

Julius Nyerere is among the extremely few world leaders who have selflessly attempted great things for their national peoples.

Other African leaders -- notably Leopold Senghor and Tom Mboya -- have spoken of 'African socialism' as a means of restoring human dignity to the African person after a protracted era of colonial brutalisation and dehumanisation. But none has ever offered a plausible definition of 'African socialism.'

Mwalimu Nyerere was the first -- probably the only -- African nationalist leader to cast a serious moral and intellectual eye upon Africa's 'extended family' tradition and weave a practical national development philosophy around it.

Ujamaa had two basic components.

The Ujamaa Village was an attempt to revive traditional rural communalism -- bringing groups of villages together, investing collectively in them and running them through modern democratic precepts.

Since the turn of the 21st century, Kenya's own leaders have divided and sub-divided what used to be called districts into veritable village units, claiming a purpose similar to 'Nyerereism' -- to bring utilities and social services 'closer to the people.'

The second component was much more theoretically shaky -- a series of nationalisations intended to bring urban commerce and industry under state control, the state purporting to be the public's trustee.

But the 1967 *Arusha Declaration* in which this doctrine of 'socialism and self-reliance' was enunciated opened a Pandora's box of ideology. Ideas ran from the extreme right to others that were so leftist that, in the circular prism of ideas, they actually bordered on the right!

In a single-party system, all these ideas were forced to

contend with one another within that party.

It was no wonder, then, that Marxist-Leninists, Bepari (capitalists) and even Kabaila (feudalists) held central positions both in the party and in government.

This, indeed, was where Nyerere began to reveal his greatness.

In other 'socialist' situations -- such as Sekou Toure's Conakry -- every thought and activity deemed dangerous would simply have been banned, often on pain of death.

Nyerere encouraged even his bitterest opponents to express themselves freely and without fear.

And he often took them on -- not by means of such state machinery as our Nyayo House basement, but intellectually, replying to each critic point by point.

The Nationalist (the party's own organ) and *The Standard* Tanzania (the government publication on which Ben Mkapa and I worked – later renamed *Daily News*) routinely published news, features, columns and letters expressing the most diverse views.

Nyerere demanded only that his detractors produce the facts and figures and weave these into cogent thought.

'Argue, don't shout!' he once admonished his equivalents of the loudmouthed but empty-headed coalition that rules Kenya.

No, Mwalimu was not a revolutionary in any Marxist sense.

Like all of Africa's petty bourgeois radicals in power at that time -- Ben Bella, Kaunda, Keita, Nasser, Nkrumah, Obote, Toure -- he rejected outright all of Marx and Lenin's theories on class, revolution and party organisation.

His, said he, was a national mass movement in which every Tanzanian must participate.

Such a policy might sound noble, but it was what finally proved Dr Nyerere's Achilles heel.

You cannot implement any 'socialist' programme except through a committed vanguard.

For his Ujamaa Village projects, he relied on the peasantry, a property-owning class whose members, as a rule, are interested only in their small individual property.

For his nationalisation programme, he relied on another property-owning class, what the Kiswahili Academy called vibwanyenye.

This propertied urban class was led by the educated elite who monopolised the civil service, the police, the provincial administration, the army, the classroom, the shrine -- a social stratum deeply drilled right from the classroom in liberal Western individualism and self-pursuit.

In 1972, goaded by Idi Amin's overthrow of Milton Obote -- the ally across the Great Lake -- Mwalimu issued a set of ruling-party 'Guidelines' called *Mwongozo*, which, among other things, introduced an elaborate leadership code.

But to no avail. Soon the Ujamaa Village administrative network, as well as the two custodians of nationalised property -- the National Development Corporation and the State Trading Corporation -- were drowning in a well of corruption deeper than Lake Tanganyika.

Mwalimu reacted by decentralising the leaderships of both those bodies and the central governance system -- succeeding only in spreading bureaucratic ineptitude thinner on the ground, thus making corruption much more difficult to detect.

By replacing the colonial educational structure with what he called Elimu yenye Manufaa ('functional education'), he enabled Tanzania to kill up to five birds with one stone.

Tanzanian is the only African country that has totally banished illiteracy, and the Three Rs are solidly linked to vocational interests.

In the process, Tanzania became the African country with the highest degree of national self-consciousness and

-- through it and through Kiswahili -- has almost annihilated the bane of Kenya that we call tribalism.

But, as a rule, internal policy is what guides a country's foreign policy.

Any nation that tries to cultivate self-sufficiency, self-efficiency, self-respect and self-pride will find it morally compelling to share these ideals with other nations the world over.

Ujamaa inspired Tanzania into spending much of its meagre resources on liberating the rest of Africa and the world from the colonial yoke.

At a time when Nairobi was drowning in crude elite grabbing, Dar es Salaam was a Mecca of the world's national liberation movements, and a hotbed of global intellectual thought.

From this perspective, it is justifiable to say that Mwalimu Julius Kambarage, son of Chief Nyerere, is the greatest and most successful leader that Africa has ever produced since the European colonial regime collapsed 50 years ago."[12]

Another Kenyan journalist Barrack Muluka also stated the following about Nyerere in the *Standard*, Nairobi, 15 October 2011: "It shall take Africa ages to produce another philosopher like Nyerere."

Unlike most leaders, Nyerere not only mingled and identified with the masses who paid him the highest tribute after he died by saying "he was one of us"; he was also comfortable exchanging ideas with intellectuals, including some of the best like Professor Ali Mazrui, unlike many African leaders who are intimidated by them.

And probably more than any other East African president, it is Museveni who has tried to fill Nyerere's shoes and assume the mantle of leadership as the eminent leader in the region.

He may not be of Nyerere's calibre as a leader and as

an intellectual. But he has harboured ambitions to be the the next Nyerere in the region and on the continent as a whole. And he wants to achieve what Nyerere failed to achieve by establishing a political federation of the East African countries Nyerere attempted to do in the sixties.

Although President Museveni has not reached that level in East Africa as a leader of Nyerere's stature and calibre, he has distinguished himself in Uganda where he did an excellent job in the early years when he was preparing for guerrilla warfare against Obote.

He was able to convince the peasants in the critical areas where he mobilised forces and established operational bases that he was on their side.

He also had a clear vision for Uganda and policies which would bring about fundamental change if they were implemented properly.

He also had a guerrilla force which was inclusive and even had non-Ugandans, mostly Rwandans, who were ready to take part in the revolution to bring about fundamental change in Uganda but also with the expectation that Uganda would in turn help them bring about such change in their own country. And that is exactly what happened.

Tutsi refugees who had lived in Uganda for many years, many of them since childhood, were some of the soldiers who constituted the National Resistance Army. One of them was Fred Rwigema (sometimes misspelled as Rwigyema). He was the commander of RNA guerrilla fighters. Museveni's half-brother, Salim Saleh, was the deputy commander.

Rwigema was also a friend of Paul Kagame and both planned the invasion of Rwanda from Uganda as the main leaders of the Rwandan Patriotic Front (RPF).

The RNA fighters used typical guerrilla tactics, moving around in small units, ambushing government military vehicles and convoys, and using hit-and-run tactics, and then melting into the civilian population.

The national army composed mostly of Acholi and Langi soldiers from northern Uganda randomly attacked civilians, ostensibly to flush out the guerrillas as the Americans did in Vietnam, but mainly to terrorise and brutalise them simply because they belonged to southern tribes which were against Obote, a northerner.

Massive relocation of civilians by government soldiers in the area that was the main battleground in that conflict, the Luweero Triangle, led to further abuses and countless deaths.

RNA guerrilla fighters were also responsible for many atrocities although not equal to those committed by government soldiers. NRA fighters planted mines which killed many civilians in the rural areas. They also used child soldiers.

The national army (UNLA) – which really became Obote's army with fellow northerners, the Langi and the Acholi, constituting the vast majority of the soldiers and officers – fought well against the NRA guerrillas when it was led by Oyite Ojok. But internal wrangling split the army along ethnic lines, Acholi versus Langi, as the Acholi complained of discrimination by the Langi who were members of Obote's tribe and who constituted the majority of the army officers.

The National Resistance Army took advantage of the internal dissension within the army and capitalised on the split between the Acholi and the Langi. When the Acholi soldiers overthrew Obote, Museveni and his fighters sensed victory. They knew it was only a matter of time before they could seize power from the military rulers who overthrew Obote and whose army was now weak because of internal divisions.

After Museveni signed a peace agreement with Uganda's military head of state, Tito Okello, in Nairobi, Kenya, in December 1985, he began counting days when he would seize power. He had no intention of honouring the agreement. He knew the NRA would have an easy victory over the national army which was now mostly Acholi without the support of their fellow northerners, the Langi, many of whom had left after their kinsman, Obote, was overthrown by the Acholi.

The following month, on 25 January 1986, the NRA fighters entered Kampala, led by Museveni's brother Salim Saleh. They met virtually no resistance as Tito Okello and his fellow Acholi soldiers fled north, to their homeland. The National Resistance Army became the national army. It was renamed the Uganda People's Defence Force (UPDF) probably in honour of the Tanzania People's Defence Forces (TPDF) who had played such a major role in ending Amin's tyranny and thus helping pave the way for Museveni's rise to power years later. It was probably Museveni himself who chose the name. The RNA was renamed UPDF in 1995 after the country adopted a new constitution.

After seizing power, Museveni began to consolidate his base of support in the south. He portrayed himself as a civilian and not as a soldier in power. He tried to mobilise the masses and university students by identifying himself as a man of the people, using socialist rhetoric and focusing on the well-being of the vast majority of the people most of whom were poor. He also emphasised law and order after years of lawlessness and tyranny under Amin and Obote.

He also embraced the people of the northwest, Amin's homeland, and gave high government positions to a significant number of them.

One of them was Amin's sons. Another prominent figure from the northwest was Brigadier Moses Ali, former minister of finance under Amin, who was the leader of a rebel group, the Uganda National Rescue Front (UNRF), which first fought against Obote and then Museveni. Many UNRF fighters joined Museveni's National Resistance Army after Obote was overthrown in July 1985 and after signing a peace agreement with the government. They also, together with other UNRF members, joined the National Resistance Movement which was the country's ruling party under Museveni.

But Moses Ali had a somewhat tempestuous relationship with Museveni's government. He was given a number of high government positions including ministerial posts but was arrested for treason in April 1990. He was released in June 1992 after being cleared of the charges. Museveni brought him back into the cabinet and gave him other ministerial posts including that of deputy prime minister.

There was also a resurgence of the UNRF, that came be known as the Uganda National Rescue Front II, whose members broke away from the West Nile Bank Front in 1996. Some members of the first UNRF joined the group. The UNRF II did not sign a peace agreement with Museveni's NRM government.

The Uganda National Rescue Front II was led by Major-General Ali Bamuze and was supported by the Sudanese government in retaliation for Museveni's – NRM's – support for the Sudan People's Liberation Army (SPLA). The SPLA was led by Dr. John Garang, Museveni's friend. Museveni and Garang attended the University of Dar es Salaam in Tanzania during the same period and were active in revolutionary organisations on and off campus.

The UNRF II had its operational bases in Arua District in southern Sudan where its fighters retreated after launching attacks against government soldiers and other targets on Ugandan soil.

The conflict between the two ended in December 2002 when the Uganda National Rescue Front II signed a ceasefire agreement with Museveni's government in the town of Yumbe in the northwest. A battalion of the UNRF rebel fighters joined the national army. The group also got a monetary reward from the government for renouncing violence.

Another rebel group was the National Army for the Liberation of Uganda (NALU), formed in 1988, which was active in the northern and western parts of the country fighting the national army. NALU later merged with the Allied Defence Forces (ADF) and established operational bases in neighbouring Democratic Republic of Congo (DRC), especially in North Kivu province and in the border region of the Ruwenzori mountains.

When Museveni's government offered an amnesty to rebel groups in 2005, less than 50 members of NALU accepted the offer.

Museveni tried hard to achieve peace and stability after years of chaos and war and made a lot of progress in those areas.

He was also pragmatic enough to realise that the world had changed and abandoned his socialist beliefs. He became one of the most ardent advocates of free-market policies to rebuild the economy.

Although he won the war, there were still a number of rebel groups which continued to fight for various reasons including self-determination. And he made an effort to absorb them into the army and the National Resistance Movement to pacify the country. The insurgencies were mostly in the north, east and west, especially between the mid-eighties and early nineties.

They were mostly among the Langi, Obote's fellow tribesmen, and the Acholi in the central north; among the Teso – or Iteso – in the east; and among the Kakwa, Lugbara and Nubians in the northwest.

Among the Acholi, the Uganda People's Democratic Party (UPDA) led by Lieutenant-Colonel John Angelo Okello was the most active and prominent group. The Uganda People's Army (UPA) was active among the Teso from 1987 to 1992. It was led by Peter Otai who once served as minister of state for defence under President Obote during his second presidency.

The Citizen's Army for Multiparty Politics (CAMP)

led by Brigadier Smith Opon Acak was one of the groups active among the Langi.

A former army chief of staff under Obote, Brigadier Opon Acak also fought together with Langi rebels against Museveni's National resistance Army in Lira District, the home of former president Obote. He was killed in July 1999 near the town of Lira while fighting the NRA soldiers. He was 56.

All those rebel groups were no match for the National Resistance Army. But they waged prolonged fights.

The toughest fight was in northwestern Uganda, the regional and ethnic stronghold of former military ruler Idi Amin, because of the advantage the rebels had operating from across the border in southern Sudan.

Some of Museveni's major achievements in reconciliation were in 1988 when his government signed peace agreements with two rebel groups, the Uganda People's Democratic Army (UPDA) and the Uganda People's Army (UPA). In April that year, the government offered an amnesty to the UPA rebels and others.

They were mostly members of small rebel groups and agreed to surrender and support the government.

And in June 1988, the UPDA signed a peace agreement with the government.

A significant number of UPA and UPDA fighters and other rebels joined the government's National Resistance Army. But thousands of others refused to sign a peace agreement with Museveni's government and continued to fight.

However, Uganda under Museveni has been relatively stable. The stability the country has enjoyed is comparable to life in Uganda in the sixties after independence. Those were the early years of the post-colonial period under Obote when the country enjoyed peace and stability except for the conflict with the kabaka when he was violently ousted and forced to flee to Britain.

The country remained relatively peaceful until 1971

445

when Amin overthrew the government and instituted a reign of terror, killing countless innocent civilians as well as Acholi and Langi soldiers.

It was not until 1986 when Museveni rose to power that Uganda again started to enjoy relative peace and stability in spite of the continued violence in different parts of the country by rebel groups who were opposed to his rule. As Professor Frederick Byaruhanga states in his book, *Student Power in Africa's Higher Education: A Case of Makerere University*:

"President Museveni and his National Resistance Movement came into power surrounded by massive popular support, especially as a result of his army's demonstration of high-level discipline. For the first time in more than a generation, Ugandans felt secure in their own country, an aura that has buttressed President Museveni's popularity, especially, in the rural areas.

Threads of political, social, and economic initiatives across the spectrum have punctuated his almost twenty years of power. On the political arena, the Movement government maintained – until this year, 2005 – its no-party – Movement – umbrella political stance, arguing that political parties had only served to divide the people mainly along religious and tribal lines.

Instead, a new form of democracy, reflected in bottom-up grassroots governance, was introduced. This democratic triangle begins on grassroots local councils – Local Council I, II, III – to city mayoral council – LC IV – then district – LC V – and ultimately, the national parliament and the presidency. All these positions are elective based on individual merit.

A new constitution was promulgated in 1994 and in 1996 Yoweri Museveni was chosen – by universal suffrage – as the first constitutionally elected president (Mugaju, 1999).

The second presidential elections were held in March

2001, which gave Museveni the presidential mandate for a second and last constitutional five-year term (he remained in power after that and was still in office at this writing in July 2012 – comment by Godfrey Mwakikagile).

In both presidential elections, constituency-based parliamentary elections were held a few months later, forming a British-style constitutionally mandated legislative branch of government.

Despite occasional imbalance caused mainly by rebel incursions from the northern and western parts of the country, and most recently, political instability in neighbouring Rwanda and Democratic Republic of Congo, Uganda has enjoyed relative political stability.

In regard to the economy, the Movement government has since 1980s abandoned its near socialist stance, and embraced the World bank/IMF-mandated Structural Adjustment Policies (Programmes). The economy has for the most part been liberalized, resulting in considerable institutional privatisation....

Other reform highlights include decentralization of governance, allocating more power and resources to district leadership; educational reforms as exemplified by the introduction of free Universal Primary Education; various public civil service reforms; and the women's empowerment movement (Mugaju, 1999)....

Other challenges, however, remain. These include but are not limited to the alarming presence of corruption in high places; the need to forge a climate of lasting peace with neighbouring countries; the reality of poverty, especially in rural areas; and the HIV/AIDS epidemic, among other things."[13]

There is no question that Uganda has achieved economic success under Museveni. The country is not the same as it was under Idi Amin or during Obote's second presidency which is often identified as Obote II.

And the achievement is significant when one takes into

447

account the fact that the country was devastated by Amin's reign of terror and by civil war under Obote. It was hard to revive the economy.

It is this achievement which has earned Museveni credit and accolades from his fellow countrymen and from donor countries. He has also used it to justify his long tenure as if he is the only leader who can sustain peace and Uganda's economic growth. He has also used it to insulate himself from criticism by donor countries about his authoritarian leadership under which freedom is curtailed and the people are denied other human rights.

He also uses it as shield against criticism by his own people, reminding them, even if indirectly, that if it were not for him and his National Resistance Movement, Uganda would not be where it is today as a relatively prosperous country which is also stable and peaceful.

The danger is that, by using such achievements to claim credit for good leadership, Museveni and his colleagues in the National Resistance Movement seem to be saying that denial or curtailment of human rights is justified or is the price Ugandans have to pay in order to enjoy economic growth, peace and stability; human rights are not that important, or denying people their rights is not a problem at all.

People in Uganda do enjoy some rights, including freedom of movement which many critics of Museveni have used to flee the country. But no amount of economic progress, peace and stability can be used to justify violation of human rights or be used as a substitute for democracy. There is no substitute for democracy. And that includes appeasing political opponents or manipulating local systems to co-opt critics in order to perpetuate Museveni in power:

"A polarization between good political leadership and long-term political institutionalization is occurring (in Uganda). Museveni and his contemporaries are deriving

448

legitimacy from the international arena rather than by securing it internally through genuine political competition and participation.

Sophisticated manipulation of the political arena ensures a certain degree of compliance and stability. For example, Museveni has also developed a broad-based inclusionary system, bringing political leaders from all the political parties, regions and ethnic groups into the government by using both the 'carrot and the stick.' Increasingly, however, Museveni and the army have become less tolerant of criticism from members of parliament (MP) and the cabinet. Cabinet shuffles have become an effective way of silencing dissenting MPs and promoting loyal 'movementalists' and 'Musevenists'....

Uganda has achieved impressive economic growth and relative political stability – with the major exception of the instabilities in the North, the West and increased terrorism in Kampala. The LC (Local Council) system has allowed for limited participation and community self-help, but there are clear limits to popular participation. Economic liberalization is occurring at an accelerated pace, while political liberalization has encountered clear roadblocks. It seems as if Museveni still believes that he is the only one that can lead Uganda out of its difficult past. He has clear control over the military and clear support from the West, but decreasing control over the country.

It is, however, questionable how long he will be able to control the political process from above. Although political parties are divided, they are united in their resolve to bring back freedom of association, political pluralism and to rid Uganda of Museveni. The population may wish to avoid the turbulence of the past, but undermining the development of a viable opposition will only create more extrajudicial movements like the WNBF (West Nile Bank Front), the LRA (Lord's Resistance Army) and NALU (National Army for the Liberation of Uganda formed in 1988 and engaged in fighting the Uganda People's

Defence Force – UPDF – in the north and in the west).

Although one could argue that Museveni's 'no-party democracy' has allowed for significant economic and political stability, the degree of freedom in Uganda, measured by such indicators as freedom of association, elections, political participation, separation of power, respect for human rights and the rule of law indicates that Uganda is far from a transition to or consolidation of democracy."[14]

For a leader who talks so much about broad-based grassroots democracy, and who even established local councils whose legitimacy was derived from direct participation by the masses in elections at the village level, it is inconceivable that he would believe such democracy can be built and be consolidated from the top instead of starting at the bottom by letting the people decide what kind of political system and what form of government they want.

He dismisses such criticism by saying Westerners who believe that there is only one kind of democracy, or that it can only be patterned after Western democratic institutions, are wrong because they don't know Africa, a continent where the vast majority of the people live in traditional societies and don't have the slightest idea of what democracy is.

To most Africans, he contends, formation of political parties means consolidation of tribal divisions and rivalries because any political parties which are established will be formed on tribal basis. So he wants to control everything from the top, telling the people what to do instead of the people – whom he claims are "sovereign" – telling him what they want:

"Political participation is present in Uganda, in fact actively encouraged, but through the LC system. In other words, political participation is controlled and channeled through state establishment structures....Unfortunately for the NRM regime, however, its consensus from above cannot be successfully imposed throughout Uganda. The North, Northeast and Western portions of Uganda have been in a state of virtual civil war since 1986, although relatively speaking; Uganda is still considered one of the more stable countries in the Great Lakes Region.

Museveni has successfully implemented its ERP, receiving considerable accolades from the West and the IMF. A positive investment climate has been encouraged and substantial economic growth has occurred in Uganda, even though the gaps between the rich and the poor, the urban and the rural have been increasing rather than decreasing. All in all, Uganda is still considered a relative 'success' story, mainly because it is on the road to economic recovery.

The key to Museveni and the Movement's success in ensuring economic restructuring and limited political liberalization while securing Western support rests on their ability to control consensus from above. Similarly, Museveni's success and popularity are contingent to economic success, which is based on the whims of export prices, international aid and recognition, which are for the most part, beyond his control....

The regime still ensure(s) its continued position of power by...using intimidation when necessary and overall controlling the speed and timing of political liberalization. The whole issue of whether the Movement has been 'successful' and whether it is a 'durable' success story revisits the classic debate over whether strong-man rule is necessary in developing societies, and whether economic growth must precede competitive, political participation.

Exclusive Movement rule from 1986 – 1996 may have been necessary to stabilize the political and economic arena, but Museveni and the Movement have missed their window of opportunity to make Uganda a truly democratic nation....Uganda under Museveni can be characterized as a

451

'soft authoritarian' system which is increasingly resorting to not so soft methods of holding onto power.

Too much rests on one man as the messiah of Uganda. International donors and institutions may currently perceive Uganda as a successful story, but the long-term sustainability of Uganda as a success story to perhaps emulate, will depend on the institutionalization of power, the opening up of political competition, and the move away from glorifying one man as the savior or in contrast, the enemy of Uganda.

Ultimately, there are no 'quick fixes' for democracy and development in Africa. Uganda may well be stuck with an imperfect but reasonably effective and functioning alternative that is a compromise between dictatorship and democracy."[15]

Museveni has also been accused of dividing the very same country he fought so hard to free from tyranny and domination by northern tribes, the Langi and the Acholi, who controlled the army and the security forces.

It should be remembered that although he mobilised forces across ethnic lines when he started his rebellion against Obote, his focus was almost exclusively on the south inhabited by Bantu tribes, contrasted with the North which is Nilotic. Therefore he won support on ethnic and regional basis. The south became his stronghold even if it was for logistical reasons, as indeed was the case.

But even in the south, there were divisions along ethnic lines. Museveni may have consolidated those divisions after he assumed power.

It is a tragedy that ethnicity continues to play a major role in national life. It is an enduring phenomenon and a major problem.

Ethnicity fosters identity politics and makes the transition to democracy – under which people should be judged as individuals and not as members of a group – extremely difficult. Politicians use it to perpetuate themselves in power by exploiting ethnic and regional rivalries, thus weakening the opposition by indirectly encouraging members of different ethnic and regional groups not to work together.

A strong opposition can be established only if it cuts across tribal and regional lines, thus presenting a formidable challenge to the government.

Although Museveni is seen as a nationalist and as a Pan-Africanist, he has sometimes exploited ethnic sentiments to the detriment of other groups, probably northerners more than anybody else.

But there are complaints even among southerners. His critics contend that people from western Uganda, Museveni's home region, hold most of the key posts in the government and in other areas including the ruling National Resistance Movement (NRM). Thus, while the country was dominated by northerners, the Langi and the Acholi, when Obote was in power because they controlled the army and the security forces tipping scales in his favour; and by the people from the northwest, especially the Kakwa, the Lugbara and the Nubians when Amin was in power; under Museveni, it is his fellow westerners, especially from his home region of Ankole, who dominate the country:

"Museveni appointed a government broad-based politically and ethnically, although recently it has been accused of giving Ankole disproportionate jobs and influence.

Prominent members of the various political parties and the different regions and religions in the country gained positions in the administration, even if the balance favoured the Western and Central regions."[16]

Charges against Museveni that he favours members of his tribe, the Banyankole – or Ankole – have also come from some of his colleagues in the ruling National

Resistance Movement (NRM). According to a report, "NRM NEC: Museveni Accused of Tribalism," by Edris Kiggundu in a Ugandan newspaper, *The Observer*, Kampala, 13 January 2010:

"A member of the ruling NRM this week rattled the National Executive Committee (NEC) meeting, which concludes today at State House Entebbe, when she suggested that President Museveni had no moral authority to preach against tribalism yet he's wont to appoint largely tribe mates to senior government positions.

Sources have told us that Angella Kebba, a delegate from Adjumani known for her boldness, made her submission during a session that debated Museveni's opening speech.

'You are saying we should not be tribal but you have appointed many people from your region in government compared to other regions,' our sources quote her as having said candidly.

She was responding to Museveni who said in his opening speech that people pushing for the creation of new districts were being motivated by tribalism and other selfish reasons.

'As all of you know I rear cattle and I do not mind which tribe the people who buy my milk come from as long as they give me money,' Museveni, who is also the NRM chairman, had said.

Kebba's submission caused excitement among delegates, sources attending the meeting told us. Many stomped their feet and clapped their hands, momentarily bringing proceedings to a halt. For some time, Museveni who appeared to have been caught flat-footed, remained seated at the high table but shortly took the floor to respond.

'This is a small issue,' Museveni began his defence, as the hall fell silent. 'I have heard this for a long time but the problem with people is that when you appoint a Munyoro,

Mukiga and Mufimbira to Cabinet, they say they are from my place. Many people cannot tell the difference.'

Because of its delicate nature, Secretary General Amama Mbabazi cut short debate on the matter and pleaded with members to discuss other issues in Museveni's speech. Indeed, no other member appeared willing to further the debate. Kebba too did not push the issue.

Indeed this is not the first time the President has been accused of favouring people from a particular region by members of his own party.

A couple of years ago, Mike Mukula, a former minister of state for Health who is currently NRM vice chairman, eastern region, said in a Central Executive Committee (CEC) meeting that people in eastern Uganda were unhappy with NRM because the President had mainly appointed people from the western region to influential positions in government.

Outside the NRM, the opposition has always claimed that some regions are favoured when it comes to sharing the national cake.

Makindye West MP, Hussein Kyanjo, for instance, caused a stir in Parliament last year when he said that Army promotions were not fair. He claimed that some officers from a particular region were favoured for promotion. He gave an example of the five generals in the Army who all hail from Ankole sub-region."[17]

Other NRM members have raised the same issue on different occasions. According to a report by *In2EastAfrica*, 3 March 2012:

"The National Resistance Movement party National Vice Chairman for central region Hajj Abdul Nadduli has cautioned President Museveni and the party leadership against hypocrisy and tribalism, trends he said are growing and threatening to ruin the party.

'We as NRM members from the central region are increasingly getting concerned that a party that had national ideologies is now taking a direction that favours individual party members (on the basis of tribalism),' Hajj Naduli said.

'We are also aware that all the individuals singled out clearly pointed out that they were under instruction from the top man, who is the President. Why should our party be reduced to the level that highlights hypocrisy and favouritsm for particular individuals?' he asked.

Hajj Naduli was commenting on the Cabinet sub-committee decision and information that a section of NRM members have resolved not to fire Bank of Uganda Governor Emmanuel Tumusiime-Mutebile over his role in the compensation of businessman Hassan Basajjabalaba.

Two cabinet ministers, Syda Bbumba (Gender) and Khiddu Makubuya (General Duties) were forced to resign their ministerial positions over the role they played in the irregular payment of the money.

'Why has Basajjabalaba who allegedly received this money been left to walk free? Any actions taken on these national matters should be held transparently and in the interest of the nation and not of particular individuals,' Hajj Nadduli told the NRM Katikamu South party members at Nyimbwa Sub-county headquarters on Monday.

It is reported that party members were divided during the Wednesday caucus meeting whether Mr Mutebile should be fired or not and it spiralled into a tribal contest, forcing the leaders to end the meeting prematurely.

In the meeting, the Buganda contingent is said to have questioned why Ms Bbumba and Prof. Makubuya, who both represent constituencies in Nadduli's Luweero District, were summarily dumped from Cabinet for their role in the same transaction."[18]

Like President Museveni, the Bank of Uganda

governor, Emmanuel Tumusiime-Mutebile, came from western Uganda. But he did not come from Ankole, the home of Museveni. Still, pressure from the president to keep Tumusiime-Mutebile at his job as the nation's bank chief brought charges of tribalism – or call it sectarianism or regionalism – against the president for favouring someone from his home region: western Uganda.

The subject was addressed by other prominent Ugandan leaders including Ssemujju Ibrahim Nganda of the Forum for Democratic Change (FDC) political party and member of parliament for Kyadondo County East – Wakiso District, in his article, "Mutebile Saga Has Brought Out Real Museveni," in *The Observer*, Kampala, Uganda, 14 March 2012:

"I have taken long without writing about tribalism and nepotism, not because it ceased, but my relentless efforts almost reduced me into one.

In fact, towards the end of 2010, *The New Vision* named me the second worst person of the year on account of being 'tribalistic.' After sacking two ministers Hajjat Syda Bbumba and Prof Khiddu Makubuya, both from Buganda, *bonafide* NRM supporters from this region, thinking like I always do, realised their party chairman, Yoweri Museveni, is practising tribalism. This is because the same Museveni has convened at least three NRM parliamentary caucus meetings and at each one of them asked MPs to save Central Bank Governor, Emmanuel Tumusiime-Mutebile.

Mind you, the three are accused of the same crime – giving businessman Hassan Basajjabalaba, a whopping Shs 142bn in compensation. That is the reason Buganda caucus chairman, Godfrey Kiwanda, summoned us last week. His view was that there should be no selective justice in the fight against corruption, and I believe many of you agree with him. Former Buganda caucus chairman, Latif Ssebaggala, called a similar meeting when former

Vice President, Prof Gilbert Bukenya, was sent to Luzira after his committal to the High Court on charges related to abuse of office.

The reason Ssebaggala summoned Buganda MPs was because people accused with Gilbert Bukenya, including Sam Kutesa, John Nasasira and Mwesigwa Rukutana had not even been arraigned before the court by the Inspector General of Government. Eventually, the three ministers from Museveni's region were also arraigned and charged with some crimes. The government shockingly decided to bungle the Bukenya case and it was immediately and summarily dismissed. I think this was intended to pave way for the eventual acquittal of the three Ankole blue-eyed boys.

Already, the three have won round one against the IGG in the Constitutional Court, courtesy of the Attorney General. If I remember well, the court has already found some errors in their prosecution. Mutebile is not from Ankole, but from neighbouring Kigezi, from where Prime Minister Amama Mbabazi also hails. These two sub-regions compete, sometimes even recklessly, in giving Museveni votes. I personally think that although Museveni rigs elections and wins, in these two sub-regions, his support is about 55%.

Maybe this is the reason Museveni has never humiliated a senior leader from there. Dr Samson Kisekka who hailed from Buganda was sacked while away on an official trip. Prof Gilbert Bukenya was not only sacked, but made to suffer the worst humiliation of being sent to Luzira. But the bigger point many may have missed in this Mutebile saga is not the tribalism, but the contempt and arbitrariness of Museveni. First, Museveni appoints a ministerial sub-committee to look into the whole Basajjabalaba compensation saga. The committee is supposed to scrutinise the Public Accounts Committee report and advise government on what to do.

The committee is chaired by Defence Minister, Dr

Chrispus Kiyonga. Members of the committee include Gen Moses Ali, the Second Deputy Prime Minister and deputy Leader of Government Business in Parliament. Moses Ali, by virtue of his appointment, is Kiyonga's senior, but here is a situation where the junior is supposed to call a senior to order!

The institution that has suffered the worst humiliation is the military, and now the police under Lt Gen Kale Kayihura. What Ugandans need to know is that sometimes people are appointed to higher positions and deliberately denied authority. That is why the Security ministry has only functioned while Amama Mbabazi was there. The previous security ministers like Betty Akech and subsequent ones like Muruli Mukasa are just occupying shells. Real power and authority is transferred elsewhere before someone outside the ruling class is deployed there.

But most important is the issue of skills and capabilities. Dr Kiyonga is a decent person and many MPs will give him a hearing. In this case, he's appointed to head a sub-committee in order to give it a human face. Although senior, Kiyonga is not considered to be part of the 'eating clique.' He, therefore, attracts sympathy and respect from many MPs that Amama doesnít. If he's the only one who can deliver results in tricky missions like saving Mutebile, why not appoint him Prime Minister? Another such person is Dr Ruhakana Rugunda.

Three critical issues: tribalism, failure to appoint people according to their skills and refusing to elevate scandal-free personnel to higher offices are what the Mutebile saga has helped unmask about Museveni."[19]

Museveni has discussed the problem of tribalism in a broader context with regard to multiparty politics, although that has no deflected criticism directed at him that he favours people from his home region in western Uganda.

With regard to multiparty politics, his refusal to allow

party politics is justified – by him and by his colleagues in the National Resistance Movement – on the grounds that having political parties encourages sectarianism, tribalism and regionalism and could easily take the country back to its dark past when such divisions plunged the nation into chaos and civil wars.

His critics say he uses this argument to suffocate dissent, perpetuate himself in office and ensure that his National Resistance Movement (NRM) continues to have hegemonic control of the country to the total exclusion of other parties – even if he doesn't call the NRM a political party but a national movement.

In a country with intense regional rivalries, especially between the north and the south, Museveni seems to have a valid point.

But his argument is refuted by what he himself said when he assumed power that "the sovereign people must be the public, not the government."

And his "no-party" or "movement" system is no more than a poorly disguised excuse to justify and institutionalise one-party rule during his tenure and under his successors whom he hopes he will be able to choose or recommend to perpetuate the National Resistance Movement in power.

In that sense, he is no better than the other African leaders, the "big men" of the 1960s and 1970s, who became life presidents or instituted imperial presidencies to perpetuate themselves in office.

He has not shown much interest in broad-based democracy which embraces and accommodates divergent views including those which are in sharp contrast with his position and the policies of the National Resistance Movement. That is why no political parties can contest elections on equal footing, although they are now allowed to field candidates unlike before.

Even democracy within the National Resistance Movement itself is questionable. No-one can challenge

Museveni. That is why he has been in power for 26 years now and may still be at the helm for more than 30 if nothing is done to remove him from office.

His view of democracy as a system that can function only within the parameters or boundaries of the National Resistance Movement undermines the very basis of a democratic society in which everybody has equal say. And that includes opponents of the National Resistance Movement and people who belong to different political parties regardless of how repugnant their views may be. Let the people decide.

While his argument that political parties can divide the nation along tribal, religious and regional lines may have some merit, it is not valid in all contexts. Parties can transcend ethno-regional loyalties. Any party which does not do that should not be allowed to operate.

Also, to broaden support across ethnic and regional lines, there should be only a few parties – with significant membership in every part of the country – which are allowed to compete in elections on equal basis instead of having only Museveni's National Resistance Movement as the contestant – virtually against no other party.

If there are only a few truly nationalist parties, people who are interested in voting will be forced to join or support one of those parties because there won't be any others to join. Even historical or tribal enemies will end up joining the same party cutting across ethnic and regional lines. Any parties which are regionally entrenched, if they are not outlawed, should merge with other parties to broaden their support across the nation.

A broad-based consensus transcending ethnic and regional loyalties should be the basis for forming any political party. Museveni has not allowed that.

He thinks only the National Resistance Movement (NRM) is capable of bringing the people of all regions and ethnic groups together; a view shared by his colleague next door, President Paul Kagame of Rwanda, who also

461

thinks that only the Tutsi-dominated Rwandan Patriotic Front (RPF) should rule the country and is the only party – may be even "movement" – that is capable of maintaining peace and stability and uniting all Rwandans even if it means under Tutsi domination as has been the case since 1994 when the RPF seized power after ending the genocide by the Hutu-dominated government which ruled for 32 years at the expense of the Tutsi.

That is the case in many other African countries including my own, Tanzania, where the ruling Chama Cha Mapinduzi (CCM) – the Party of the Revolution – having ruled for decades, acts as if it has divine mandate to rule. It uses state resources and agencies including the police to frustrate the opposition in an an attempt to neutralise it. The primary target is Chama Cha Demokrasia na Maendeleo (Chadema) which means the Party for Democracy and Progress. It is the strongest opposition party in the country.

Chadema rallies and demonstrations are broken by the police for no apparent reason, using flimsy excuses to do so. Its leaders are harassed and arrested. The party is often denied permission to hold rallies and does not get equal time on state radio and television. And its victory at the polls has been nullified in a number of cases in an attempt to weaken it.

In some elections, voters in opposition strongholds were not allowed to vote or their names were not even on the voters' registry. Some ballots were destroyed or rejected by government agent overseeing the polls.

There were even some reports that Chadema won the 2010 presidential election but was denied victory by the electoral commission – whose members belong to the ruling party, are appointed by the president and are therefore beholden to him – and by some members of the Tanzania Intelligence and Security Service (TISS) specifically assigned to the task of changing the results in favour of the ruling party.

Some of those reports, that the election was rigged and and that the vote count was manipulated by some members of the intelligence service, reportedly came from some of the intelligence officers themselves who had inside knowledge of this nefarious scheme by the ruling party to give the president, Jakaya Kikwete, victory for a second term instead of Dr. Wilbrod Slaa who was the presidential candidate of the main opposition party, Chadema.

Voting in opposition strongholds was probably suppressed and the overall counting of the votes was also probably manipulated. But whether or not the main opposition presidential candidate, Wilbrod Slaa, really won the election is debatable. No credible evidence was provided to the public to show that he won.

However, there is no question that the ruling party, CCM, dominates the political landscape, scales are tipped in its favour, and Tanzania remains a *de facto* one-party state.

The opposition itself has played a major role in helping the ruling party to stay in power because it is hopelessly divided. There are many opposition parties which don't want to unite to form one strong opposition party which could pose a serious challenge to CCM.

Still, there is no question that CCM has used its formidable power to weaken and even neutralise the opposition, especially in the rural areas where it has had srong support for decades. It has also used undemocratic tactics to silence its opponents.

Therefore this phenomenon – of the ruling party denying the opposition equal opportunity to articulate its position and mobilise support, and of rigging elections and even arresting opposition leaders – is not peculiar to Uganda under Museveni or Rwanda under Kagame. It is common in most countries across Africa where even today leaders don't value democracy. They are afraid of it because they know they could lose elections.

In the case of Uganda, there is no question that

Museveni has had remarkable achievements through the years since he has been in power. But he also risks tarnishing his legacy by repeating the same mistakes his predecessors made. Obote was one of them.

Obote was accused of favouring and of being overly reliant on fellow northerners, the Langi and the Acholi. He was also accused of being a dictator. Amin favoured his fellow tribesmen and eliminated his ethnic rivals, especially the Langi and the Acholi. He was also a brutal dictator.

Museveni seems to have fallen into the same trap, with regard to his kinsmen from western Uganda, and of being an authoritarian ruler who has no respect for true democracy. As Ugandan journalist Andrew Mwenda states in "Personalizing Power in Uganda," in *Democratization in Africa: Progress and Retreat*:

"With Museveni...set to stay in office indefinitely, the future of democracy in Uganda looks bleak....

In 1996, he expanded his cabinet from the constitutionally prescribed 40 members to 67. Since most cabinet officers are Members of Parliament (MPs), and since the army has ten seats in the legislature, this meant that nearly a quarter of all MPs belong to the executive branch. More direct ways of keeping legislators in line exist as well: In October 2004, soldiers arrested and brutally beat four northern MPs for trying to hold a political rally in one of their constituencies....

On November 14 (2005), the government jailed (opposition leader Kizza) Besigye. When his supporters attempted a peaceful demonstration, soldiers crushed it with tanks and armored personnel carriers, leaving three people dead. Kampala looked like a war zone; newspaper headlines began comparing it to Baghdad.

Besigye was taken before the High Court and charged with treason plus a rape allegedly committed in 1997. When the High Court granted bail, the military accused

Besigye of terrorism and placed him in the custody of a court martial. Foreign diplomats whom the minister of internal affairs had accredited to attend the trial found themselves ejected and locked out of the courtroom by soldiers.

In one especially macabre incident, the government sent hooded gangs sporting sunglasses and brandishing automatic weapons into the High Court to kidnap 21 of Besigye's codefendants in the event that they received bail. Looking on the thugs waved their guns at jurists and diplomats, the terrified detainees decided to remain in custody. The courts later released Besigye himself, but only after almost two-thirds of the campaign period had gone by.

On election day, the *Daily Monitor* opened a tally center to monitor results, which the paper's radio affiliate KFM began to broadcast. As this independent effort was starting to make it clear that Museveni would not get the 50 percent required to avoid a runoff, the president's men moved in to close the tally center, jam its radio signal, and block its website. It was amid circumstances such as these that the Electoral Commission announced Museveni's first-round reelection with 59 percent of the vote."[20]

Although Museveni may have an instinctive aversion to democracy, his contempt for democratic institutions is sometimes attributed to his revolutionary past shaped by a strong belief in the imperative need for violence as an instrument for fundamental change. As Mwenda goes on state:

"Looking back over Museveni's career, it is fair to say that he has never been a friend of liberty. He scorns the rule of law, shuns due process, and is always willing to run roughshod over people's rights. He believes in violence as a legitimate instrument to bring about 'revolutionary' political change and in the army as an important pillar of political power. At the University of Dar es Salaam in Tanzania, Museveni wrote a bachelor's thesis defending Frantz Fanon's calls for the use of violence. Both before and since Museveni became president, the themes of violence and the military have played central roles in his speeches and writings.

After claiming that President Milton Obote had stolen the 1980 election from them, Museveni and his party took to the bush as the National Resistance Army (NRA). Their goal was always to seize power by force of arms. In order to keep itself in funds and supplies, the RNA robbed banks, looted stores, and raided hospitals. Nor did it shrink from terrorism, blowing up petrol stations and mining roads in order to destroy ambulances.

Impunity thus lies at the very foundation of its bid for power.

Can anyone seriously think that a group which seeks to rule by the gun and stoops to pillaging hospitals will, once it captures the state, stay its hand from plundering the public fisc or brutalizing political foes?

From its inception, Museveni's army-turned-party has been informed by the logic of authoritarianism. The leader wears all the hats and pulls all the strings.

During his time in the bush, Museveni was the chairman of the NRM as well as commander of the NRA, sitting atop both the Army Council and the High Command. He also presided over the legislative National Resistance Council, all the while acting as his movement's chief theoretician and philosopher. Checks and balances to guard against the abuse of power can mean but little when so many levers rest in one pair of hands. When in January 1986 Museveni's forces took Kampala and made him president, he gained the resources of a state to help him rent or if need be coerce political support from the distressed body of his wounded country."[21]

He goes on to state:

"At first, the authoritarianism did not seem so bad. Museveni's forcefulness helped to promote economic reform. The various organs of the shadow state that he had created as a guerrilla had the potential to become partners in an internal debate. Yet Museveni never truly tapped that potential. Instead, he adeptly manipulated these organs to project the illusion that consultation was occurring even as he was effectively ruling by decree.

A close look at what was happening could often reveal the sham. Many times in the late 1980s and early 1990s, for example, if Parliament was slow to pass some measure that Museveni saw as important, he would put on his uniform and chair a closed legislative session until his bill had been rammed through.

The desperate situation that Museveni inherited in 1986 required a strong and dynamic leader. Amin's depredations – he had killed somewhere between 80,000 and a half-million people and had expelled the country's Indo-Ugandan merchant class *en masse* in 1972 – were followed by seven years of savage infighting that came in the wake of his ouster. Uganda was on its knees, its government and economy alike in ruins. Iron-fisted tactics appeared necessary – and even legitimate – since the country needed a leader who could take quick and decisive decisions where institutions were too slow or inept. Thus did Parliament swiftly approve Museveni's plans to restore the traditional local monarchies, privatize state enterprises, allow Indo-Ugandans to return and reclaim their property, cut back on the civil service, and the like.

Yet as institutions recovered and fresh economic growth produced new interest groups, Museveni's penchant for informal methods and arbitrary decision making became increasingly counterproductive.

In 1986, not long after it seized power, Museveni's government restricted political-party activities on national-healing grounds. At the time, this sounded reasonable.

Museveni appeared magnanimous as he invited leaders of other parties to join him in a national-unity – or as the president called it, a 'broad-based' – government. Yet even as the situation improved, Museveni held fast to the ban on political parties, letting go of it only under considerable pressure in 2005.

With the benefit of hindsight, we can understand the subjective motives for his seeming magnanimity.

The NRA was the strongest armed force in the country by the mid-1980s. But Museveni's political vehicle, the NRM, was unseasoned and rested on a narrow, unsteady base. Museveni, a brilliant student of Uganda's politics, reasoned that the no-party, 'broad-based' approach offered several advantages, including: 1) a viable alternative to the counterproductive expedient of open military rule; 2) a boost to his own NRM's political appeal nationwide; and 3) the means to make rivals and potential rivals from other parties serve at his beck and call.

To improve his chances for success, Museveni not only used his soldiers, police, and security agents to stop other parties from organizing, but also exploited local councils to build the NRM's organizational infrastructure, cajoled leaders from other parties to join the NRM, and systematically rid official ranks of all those who remained loyal to their old parties.

The decentralization of the budget process gave local officials reason to work with the NRM; the continued use of armed coercion made them fear what would happen if they broke with the president's movement.

Evidence that Museveni never had any intention of building a democracy may be gleaned from the NRM regime's conspicuous refusal to repeal any of the many repressive laws – including some of the worst of Idi Amin's decrees – that remained on the books in 1986. in fact, Museveni's time in power has seen draconian statutes hampering freedoms of organization, expression, assembly, and publication not only retained, but

468

reinforced.

The only signs of nascent democratization appeared in the constitution-making process. Even there, however, enabling acts to give effect to many of the 1995 basic law's provisions were not forthcoming, and activists from opposition groups, civil society, and the media had to sue in court in order to have repressive laws struck down.

The worst obstacle to democratic development in Uganda has been the personalization of the state. Arms and money are essential to this malign process. The arms belong to the military and security services, which the regime deploys selectively in order to suppress dissent. The money sluices through a massive patronage machine that Museveni uses to recruit support, reward loyalty, and buy off actual and potential opponents.

In his efforts to personalize the state, Museveni has skilfully undermined formal institutions of governance, preferring as he does to use highly arbitrary and informal methods of recruiting and rewarding officials. The destruction of the Parliament's will and ability to check executive power has been a keystone of his approach. Not surprisingly, the personalization of the state has gone hand in hand with its increasing arbitrariness.

Museveni has always sought to use the army to build his personal – less so the NRM's – political base. He employs violence sparingly and selectively – as an instrument of last resort when the political process fails to yield before his requirements or the opposition appears to need whipping into submission. Patronage, typically in the form of government contracts, tenders, and jobs, is his preferred tool and the one that he used to render Parliament ineffective.

Museveni's success at consolidating his power and stifling democracy flows from his knack for integrating large chunks of the political class into his vast patronage empire."[22]

Like most African countries, Uganda has never developed strong democratic institutions during the post-colonial period. The institutions it inherited at independence from the departing British colonial rulers were for domination just as they had been during the colonial era.

Even the press, which is supposed to be the guardian of truth and the watchdog for human rights, was used by the colonial rulers to serve their own interests, not to serve the interests of colonial subjects.

The judiciary may have been the only institution inherited from the colonial rulers which could have been used effectively to dispense justice and protect human rights. But it was used by the new rulers to serve their own interests and lost its independence under the strong arm of the government. That also has been the case under Museveni.

Uganda has gone through a lot of changes since the sixties when it was led by Dr. Milton Obote who also earned a reputation as one of Africa's leading statesmen during the era of the "big men" who laid the foundation for the modern African state in the post-colonial era. Then came the reign of terror under Idi Amin when the law meant absolutely nothing. All institutions, except the military, were destroyed.

During Obote's second presidency, the civil war made the country virtually ungovernable. Chaos reigned, with both the national army and rebel groups wreaking havoc across the land.

Museveni, who himself was partly responsible for the chaos that reigned during Obote's second presidency since he is the one who started the civil war, closed that chapter after he assumed power.

Under his regime, chaos ended except for some insurgencies in the north, northwest, east and west. A combination of military might and diplomacy ended those rebel activities.

What did not end was suppression of human rights. Museveni's National Resistance Army and other security forces including the police and the intelligence service did not refrain from using torture, imprisonment and other tactics to suppress dissent and punish government opponents. As Mary Anne Fitzgerald stated from Kampala in her article, "With Chaos Ended, What About Rights?" in *The New York Times*, 9 October 1992:

"One of the National Resistance Movement's most notable achievements has been the restoration of order. For a decade and a half, Ugandans had experienced levels of state-authored persecution and chaos that were extraordinary even for a continent known for its unreliable rule of law.

Visitors to Uganda in earlier years recall nocturnal fusillades, routine roadblocks manned by not always courteous soldiers, deeply pockmarked streets and hotels bereft of running water. On at least two occasions during a period of interim government in 1980, Western diplomats engaged in gun battles with intruders to defend their homes.

Today, people walk the streets safely at night and drive along Kampala's resurfaced roads without fear of being harassed by armed men. And as a barometer of the new confidence, in the marbled lobby of the Sheraton Hotel businessmen and aid officials sip coffee while they watch CNN news. The five-star hotel opened in November 1987 after undergoing a $35 million restoration.

Last month, the hot item of conversation in Kampala was a report on Uganda by Amnesty International, the London-based human rights organization. It alleges torture and unlawful arrest, particularly by the National Resistance Army (NRA), and government failure to safeguard human rights.

Ominous as this sounds, officialdom's reaction to the publication of the report contradicts the picture of a decline in basic constitutional freedoms. Politicians and bureaucrats were open to frank discussion of the report. Many had a copy lying on their desks. In most other African countries, Amnesty publications are considered seditious literature and their contents hotly denied.

'It's in a way grossly unfair,' said Augustine Ruzindana, inspector general of government. 'It gives the impression the human rights condition is very bad and deteriorating, which is not true.'

The inspector general's office was created by the National Resistance Movement parliament to investigate human rights abuses and corruption under the present government. The office says that it was never consulted by the Amnesty authors when drafting the report. During a three-hour interview in Amnesty's London office on June 26, the existence of the report was not mentioned, Mr. Ruzindana said.

Politicians, bureaucrats and Western diplomats concur that while there have been recent incidents of violence and lawlessness perpetrated by NRA soldiers, Uganda's record is markedly better than it was some years ago. This year there has been a clear effort to correct abuses of the law. The Amnesty report contained only two instances of such abuse so far this year, in which seven suspected rebels were arrested by the army and executed without trial.

There have been further unsubstantiated allegations of mistreatment at the hands of government forces from lawyers based in Gulu, the seat of a rebel insurgency. At Palengo, 12 miles – 19 kilometers – south of Gulu, three suspected rebels were arrested by soldiers and buried from the neck down in holes they had been forced to dig themselves. All three died. Another three men were allegedly tortured to death while in custody, according to the lawyers.

Last month, 59 followers of the Uganda Democratic Christian Army (UDCA), led by Joseph Kony, were released. They had been awaiting trial for treason since

October last year. Treason charges, which preclude the possibility of bail for 480 days, have in the past been used as a mechanism for dampening rebel support.

On coming to power in 1986, the National Resistance Movement faced a rebel insurgency in the north from a group called the Uganda People's Democratic Army (UPDA). It consisted of soldiers who had served under previous regimes. After a 1988 peace agreement, the UPDA was disbanded and incorporated into the NRA. Some remnants joined Mr. Kony's less effective UDCA.

Meanwhile, in the east, the Uganda People's Army, another rebel movement, was blamed for hundreds of killings. Thousands subsequently took advantage of a 1987 amnesty and presidential pardon to join the NRA. This conciliatory move by the government effectively undid the rebellions. Following a major military operation last year, armed opposition has disintegrated into banditry by small groups.

Observers say arrests for treason have now abated. In many instances, treason cases have been dismissed in court for lack of evidence.

Rebel atrocities, however, continue to occur. Last year, followers of the Uganda Democratic Christian Army cut off the noses, ears and upper lips of several women suspected of being government sympathizers. Hacking victims to death or mutilating them is common among rebel forces.

Last March, treason charges were dropped against 18 northern leaders arrested the previous year. The accused included the state minister for foreign affairs, Daniel Omara Atubo. Prior allegations of assault were investigated by the inspector general's office. A report on the incident has yet to be released, but Major General David Tinyefuza, who ordered the arrests, was relieved of his northern command.

In August, President Yoweri Museveni ordered the release of more than 1,500 political prisoners. The majority had been rounded up by the army last year during a counterinsurgency operation in northern rebel areas. They were sentenced *en masse* to serve jail terms of five years or more for desertion from local units. The International Committee of the Red Cross claims that at least 500 detainees are still being held. By comparison, in 1988 the NRA admitted to the existence of over 4,000 detainees.

The improvement in legal procedure has, to some extent, resulted from pressure by international aid donors. The month before the release of Mr. Atubo and others accused with him, the United States and European Community members lodged an official protest with the government over their detention.

'If the government senses a real concern, it behaves more responsibly,' a diplomat said. 'There's no doubt about that. The arrests happened in the context of heightened insecurity, which should be taken into account.'

JUDGED against the background of its recent past, Uganda has made progress in instilling moral probity in the military and its political leaders. Both Idi Amin and Milton Obote, former heads of state, were responsible for some of the grossest violations of human rights in modern history. All told, more than half a million Ugandans died at their hands.

'There was abuse of power by all levels of public officials,' said Mr. Ruzindana. 'There were no limits to their authority so ordinary people were very much at their mercy.'

'We have replaced the vicious circle of violence by accommodating everyone,' said First Deputy Prime Minister Eriya Kategaya. 'No group should be hunted for its past deeds. We don't need the West to tell us how to safeguard our human rights. It's our duty to do it.'"[23]

So, while peace returned to Uganda, democracy did not. In fact, there has never been full democracy in

Uganda.

And that is the biggest challenge the country faces in its transition to a stable, vibrant and just society where every individual has equal rights without fear of being punished or killed by the authorities for simply speaking up and telling the truth.

Many problems Uganda continues to face can be attributed to lack of democracy. For example, one of the biggest problems the country faces even under Museveni is corruption. But corruption cannot be solved without transparency. And transparency is impossible without democracy to enable the people to tell the truth without fear and to expose those who do wrong.

There can be no accountability where there is no transparency. Laws mean nothing. Therefore the rule of law itself is impossible without democracy.

Therefore, the biggest challenge Uganda and the rest of Africa faces is the establishment of strong democratic institutions which guarantee transparency, accountability and good governance in order to achieve peace, stability, and development. And the people themselves must be full participants in the process in order to secure their rights and hold leaders accountable for their actions.

Dictatorship or authoritarian rule cannot guarantee prosperity for Africa because the people who should be the primary focus are not allowed to participate in making decisions which affect their lives. Dictatorship cannot last forever. It carries seeds of its own destruction.

Part III

Conclusion

THE SIXTIES was a decade of excitement as Africans celebrated the end of colonial rule in most countries across the continent.

But the excitement did not last very long. In every country, when Africans woke up the next day after independence, they knew that little had changed.

The people had indeed regained their dignity and the right to rule themselves after years of colonial rule. And they were highly optimistic of the future, riding on a wave of high expectations for the fruits of independence although they did not see any tangible benefits right away.

The only major change they witnessed, or were aware of, was the transfer of power from Europeans to Africans. And the most obvious difference was in the race and skin colour of the rulers.

In most cases, white rulers relinquished power to blacks and in some cases to other non-whites.

They were the people who led the struggle for

independence and were an integral part of the indigenous elite that assumed the leadership of the newly independent countries.

But in terms of power and institutional arrangements, and the relationship between the leaders and the led, things remained almost the same as they were under colonial rule.

The power structure instituted by the colonialists remained intact; only that this time it had new masters: the indigenous elite. To the new rulers, one of the most attractive features of the colonial power structure was centralization, or concentration of power in the hands of a few people at the centre, under a unitary state.

And in a way, the departing colonial rulers found many comfortable allies among the indigenous elite who admired European ways of life and institutions. It was clear where they got this influence.

Almost all the new African leaders were educated in schools which had been established by missionaries or by colonial governments. Like the colonial rulers, the missionaries themselves came from Western countries. The education they provided, as did the colonial authorities, was based on the Western intellectual tradition. And the values they instilled in their African students were also Western.

Many educated Africans became carbon copies of Europeans, although poor carbon copies. They could never be the same as the original.

Yet, in spite of all that, they still and quite often tried to be more European than the Europeans themselves. Among them were dedicated "nationalists" who led the struggle for independence.

Some of the best examples of this abjectly servile and despicable imitation of the imperial masters were the leaders of Francophone Africa who after independence remained beholden to France and were unabashedly Francophile.

Another good example is Dr. Hastings Kamuzu Banda of Malawi who was very British in his manners, values and attire.

He even established a school in Malawi named after himself, Kamuzu Academy, where he allowed only whites to teach in order to produce a generation of African Anglophiles who would follow in his footsteps to spread Western education and "civilization" in Malawi and, hopefully, in other African countries as well.

And as *The New York Times*, 27 November 1997, stated in its report, "Kamuzu Banda Dies: 'Big Man' Among Anticolonialists":

"Hastings Kamuzu Banda, a founding father in postcolonial Africa who led Malawi to independence in 1964 and then ruled it with a combination of caustic wit, eccentricity and cruelty for 30 years, died on Tuesday (25 November) night in a hospital here (in Johannesburg)....

After a revolt within his cabinet, he declared himself President for Life in 1971 and said his opponents would become "food for crocodiles." Hundreds were killed, tortured or forced into exile....

Dr. Banda was perhaps the most idiosyncratic of the "big men" who led their countries out of colonialism. He held degrees from American and Scottish universities and his London medical offices became a sort of anticolonialist salon frequented by Jomo Kenyatta of Kenya and Kwame Nkrumah of the Gold Coast (now Ghana).

But once in power, Dr. Banda simultaneously affected the lion-tail fly whisk of an African king, the dark suits and homburgs of a British businessman and the arms of a Scottish baron. He refused to make speeches in African languages and established a school modeled on Eton in his birthplace, Mtunthama, where penniless students were taught Latin, Greek and African history from the British point of view. He hired only white foreigners to teach at the school and to run the ministries and businesses that built his personal fortune.

Under his rule, Malawi spurned black nationalist movements and was the only African nation with diplomatic ties to apartheid South Africa and to Israel. He was the darling of cold warriors and big business, and amassed power in his own hands, keeping the Ministries of Justice, Foreign Affairs, Agriculture and Public works to himself, as well as the trusteeship of the state monopolies in tobacco farming, factories, oil and banking....

Victorian in his demands on public morality, he banned women from wearing pants or miniskirts. Long-haired male tourists arriving in Malawi either submitted to shearing by the airport barber or went home.

He also banned television, though he watched it himself by satellite, and prevented the Simon and Garfunkel song "Cecelia" from being played on local radio, considering it an affront to his consort (Cecilia Kadzamira). He referred to Malawi's 10 million citizens as "my children" and was said to be deeply embittered when they turned him out in 1994....

His sleek capital, Lilongwe, was built with South African money and South Africa underwrote and trained the red-shirted Young Pioneers, a paramilitary youth group that spied on citizens and terrorized dissidents. And in one of the world's smallest and poorest nations, where the per-capita income was $200 a year, Dr. Banda kept five residences, a fleet of British luxury cars and a private jet....

His first education was at a Church of Scotland mission, but he left at a young age to run away to South Africa....After eight years as a clerk at a Johannesburg gold mine, studying at night, he won help from a Methodist bishop to come to the United States. He studied at the Wilberforce Institute in Xenia, Ohio, and at Indiana University before becoming the only black to graduate from the University of Chicago in 1931.

He received an M.D. from Meharry Medical College in

480

Nashville, then moved to Britain to train at the Universities of Glasgow and Edinburgh and study tropical medicine in Liverpool.

He prospered as a physician in suburban London, but in 1953, furious that Britain had allowed the establishment of the Federation of Rhodesia and Nyasaland instead of taking power away from white expatriates, he moved to the Gold Coast, now Ghana, and railed against British treachery. Despite their fear of his firebrand tendencies, the colonial authorities let him return in 1958 to lead the Nyasaland African Congress.

He had apparently forgotten his native tongue, but got an uproarious welcome when he told his audience in English, borrowing from Patrick Henry, "In Nyasaland, we mean to be masters. And if that is treason, make the most of it."

Riots broke out, and he spent a year in prison in Rhodesia before being released to lead his new Malawi Congress party to victory in a 1961 election. He told white settlers to accept majority rule "or pack up"....

In 1994, under pressure from Western nations who cut off aid to enforce demands for democratic reforms, he called elections. He was defeated by Bakili Muluzi, a former protege who had resigned from the Cabinet in 1982 suspecting he was about to be killed. His replacement, Mr. Muluzi said, was murdered."[1]

Dr. Banda ended up being one of the worst dictators Africa has ever produced.

Soon after independence, he turned against his colleagues such as Kanyama Chiume and Henry Chipembere, the very same people who had invited him back to Nyasaland from Britain to help lead the struggle for independence.

By the time he was invited, he had lived in the United States and Britain for 40 years, mostly in Britain, and spent some time in Ghana after his friend Kwame

Nkrumah became the leader of that country, only to become a tyrant soon after he led Nyasaland to independence.

His former compatriots were forced to flee their homeland and sought refuge in neighbouring countries, especially Tanzania and Zambia.

Banda was just one among many African leaders who went on to establish authoritarian or despotic regimes soon after independence.

Therefore, while independence was supposed to have ushered in a new era of freedom, the people soon learned that the freedom they had been promised was more apparent than real. Yet, one of the most attractive slogans African leaders used in their campaign for independence was that they would establish democracy the people had been denied under colonial rule. But when independence came, it was an entirely different story.

In almost all African countries, the new African rulers had little respect for freedom. They justified curtailment of freedom on grounds of nation unity and security, contending that they could not afford the luxury of freedom which entails the establishment of opposition parties in pursuit of partisan interests to the detriment of national well-being.

Therefore multiparty democracy was out of the question, not only for the sake of national unity but for other reasons as well: nation building and consolidation of independence which could not be achieved without mass regimentation, according to this rationale.

Freedom of speech was curtailed and opposition parties were strongly discouraged or banned, ushering in what became a new era of one-party rule and dictatorship on a continent where the people had been promised freedom during the struggle for independence.

There were only a few exceptions, in countries such as Nigeria with its regionally entrenched parties dominated by the country's three main ethnic groups – the Hausa-

Fulani in the north, the Yoruba in the west and the Igbo in the east; Botswana, Gambia, and Senegal; also Zambia but where the ruling party (UNIP – United National Independence Party) remained dominant at the expense of two opposition parties which, unfortunately, thrived on ethnoregional loyalties in the western and southern regions.

Kenya is another example. The ruling party, KANU (Kenya African National Union), wanted a strong central government under a unitary state but virtually an ethnocracy dominated by the Kikuyu.

Soon after independence, it neutralized KADU (Kenya African Democratic Unity), the opposition party in parliament which wanted a federal constitution under which there would be devolution of power to the regions to safeguard the interests of smaller ethnic groups which were afraid of being dominated by the country's two main ones: the Kikuyu and the Luo.

The situation was basically the same in other countries on the continent which also had opposition parties. The opposition parties were neutralized or simply withered soon after independence. And in many cases they were banned.

But even in countries such as Tanganyika, where the opposition party, the African National Congress (ANC), was simply overwhelmed at the polls by the ruling party TANU (Tanganyika African National Union), and thus died a natural death in the early sixties, laws were passed to give legal status to one-party rule leading to the establishment of the one-party system.

Tanganyika became a *de jure* one-party state in 1965, within five years after independence in December 1961 when it was a *de facto* one-party state like most were, across the continent.

One-party states became the dominant feature of the African political landscape at the expense of freedom soon after independence. Tolerance of dissent was equated with

483

weakness and abdication of responsibility by the leaders.

Some people still spoke up, but at their own risk. They knew that criticism of government was tantamount to treason. And the authorities left no doubt in any one's mind how they would respond. They were ruthless in their suppression of dissent.

Thus, paradoxically, the new era of freedom led to denial of freedom. If the new nations could not be built into cohesive units because the people had the freedom to disagree on how to build those nations, then freedom had to go.

Therefore in most African countries, freedom became the first casualty under the new African leaders who felt that it was only they who knew what was best for the people and not the people themselves. It was a betrayal of trust and the people became increasingly distrustful of their own leaders who not long ago had led them to independence.

But freedom was not the only casualty. Nation building, which the new leaders argued could not be achieved if opposition parties were allowed to exist and if criticism of government even by individuals was allowed as well, also suffered because the people – besides the leaders – were not given the opportunity to examine and challenge government decisions.

Had they been allowed to do so, and had opposition parties which were truly national in character been allowed to exist, African countries would have had the chance to pursue alternative policies which in some and may be even in many cases would have been better than those pursued by the government.

But the people were not allowed to do that. They couldn't even freely discuss government policies and offer constructive criticism even among themselves without fear of being arrested. They were muzzled.

All that led to apathy with dire consequences for the new nations in terms of nation building and national development. For, without the people's involvement in decision making all the way down to the grassroots level, meaningful change including development is virtually impossible. It is the people themselves who know what is best for them. Yet the leaders turned a deaf ear to what they had to say except in a few cases. The result was pursuit of wrong policies, by the leaders, which led to stunted economic growth.

This was compounded by a lack of high-level manpower and necessary skills needed in many areas to implement development projects and provide efficient administration throughout the country.

At independence, almost all African countries lacked a critical mass of educated people and professionals as well as administrative skills not only in technical fields but in almost all the other areas as well. For example, when my home country, Tanganyika, won independence from Great Britain in December 1961, it had only two engineers and 12 doctors.

The situation was basically the same in most countries across the continent, except in countries such as Ghana and Nigeria which had a significant number of educated people compared with other African countries.

Without trained workers and needed skills, it was obvious that the young African nations would not be able to develop. The only place they could turn to for help to meet their needs was foreign countries including their former colonial rulers.

But foreign aid, which included financial and technical assistance, did not solve Africa's problems. In most cases, there were no trained people or well-established institutions to use the assistance effectively and on the right projects. In some cases, the wrong kind of aid was sought or provided, sadly demonstrated by rusted machinery which one could see in many countries on the continent. The equipment couldn't be used and was simply left out there to rust.

And in other cases, when the equipment arrived, there were no skilled people to use it. Or there were no spare parts or someone to fix it when it broke down. Sometimes it was the wrong kind of machinery that was sent; for example snow ploughs, instead of tractors, sent to Guinea from the Soviet Union.

Also, because the new governments lacked accountability since there was no organized or formal opposition to act as a watchdog over those in power, mismanagement of resources including outright theft became a major problem in the early days of independence.

Ethnic loyalties was also a major factor in the allocation of power and resources and, most of the time, those in power usually came from one or only a handful of ethnic groups, thus accentuating ethnic cleavages in multiethnic societies. People sought power to help themselves and "their people," members of their own "tribes," almost to the total exclusion of other ethnic groups.

Thus, while the leaders who led the struggle for independence also campaigned against tribalism, contending that the colonial rulers had used divide-and-rule tactics by keeping "tribes" separate from each other and sometimes even turning some against others, they did exactly the same thing themselves when they assumed power.

They used ethnic and regional loyalties to perpetuate themselves in office by keeping their opponents divided. They also outlawed opposition parties even if there were some prospects that some of those parties could have become truly national parties in character, transcending ethnic loyalties, regionalism and other forms of sectarianism militating against national unity.

Yet, there were some leaders who made genuine attempts to achieve national unity on the basis of equality for all regardless of race, class, ethnicity, national origin or religious affiliation: Nkrumah, Nyerere, Obote, and Kaunda among others.

They were also some of the most prominent Pan-Africanists and among the strongest advocates of African unity on a continental scale and on regional basis.

Nkrumah stood out alone among them as an opponent of regional federations or formation of any regional blocs which he described as "balkanization on a grand scale" and an obstacle to continental unification.

But in spite of the genuine attempts by a number of African leaders to create a sense of national unity and identity among their citizens, ethnoregional loyalties remained strong and an intractable problem in most African countries and one of the most devastating. And it was only one among many of the major problems the new African nations faced in their early days of independence in spite of the optimism the leaders and the people had for their future free from colonial rule.

Therefore, in the initial euphoria after independence, even the leaders themselves did not realize the scope and magnitude of the task that lay ahead especially in terms of nation building. And in many cases, it is a task that has yet to be accomplished. A large number of countries across the continent remain fractured along ethnic and regional lines, and most of them are still trapped in poverty, fifty years after independence.

The struggle for power among different ethnic and regional groups, mainly because many of them have been excluded from the decision-making process and allocation of resources, is a perennial problem. And it has been one of the major causes of conflict on the continent since independence.

Tragically, even after decades of independence, few African countries have seriously considered decentralisation, and devolution, as a viable alternative to concentration of power at the centre and as a practical solution to so many problems – including ethnic rivalries and conflicts – which plague the continent.

African countries, almost all of which are composed of diverse ethnic and racial groups, need to be innovative and devise means or formulate solutions relevant to African conditions in order to maintain unity in diversity without imposing uniformity in an attempt to create homogeneous societies and thereby risk civil conflicts and wars by members of different groups who don't want to be regimented into a monolithic whole under the oppressive machinery of the highly centralised state.

They must also redefine the concept of sovereignty – domestic and international legal sovereignty exercised by independent states – in order to reflect their own realities and without compromising their national identities. A number of countries around the world have done that and have survived and prospered without falling apart. There is no reason why African countries can not do the same thing to accommodate conflicting interests, defuse ethnic tensions, and neutralise secessionist tendencies and sentiments which are accentuated when different groups feel that they are excluded from the political process and from other areas of national life simply because of what they are.

Some of the most suitable candidates for this experiment in the reconfiguration of Africa include the so-called Democratic Republic of Congo (it is a mockery of democracy to call it democratic as is the case with most countries across the continent), Angola, and Rwanda and Burundi.

Somalia would be another prime candidate for such restructuring. But she is dead as a nation-state. However, the same approach may be tried in the case of Somalia as well, to see if the country can be put back together, although probably as a confederation – of Somaliland, Puntland, and the other components of the rest of Somalia – and may be as a loose federation.

A look around the world gives us a glimpse at what

some countries have done to share sovereignty with their people instead of having power concentrated in the hands of a highly centralised authority only to risk explosion. Details will have to be worked out by the African countries themselves which may want to use some of these arrangements to suit local circumstances. It is the underlying principles – not the mechanics – of these political systems which are most relevant in terms of application in the African context.

There is no question that after what we have witnessed on our continent during the past decades since independence, African countries – especially those which are torn by conflict or those which face chaos and instability – need to establish autonomous, federal or confederal systems to replace the highly centralised unitary state which tends to fuel strife by muzzling dissent and denying the people the opportunity, *and the right*, to manage their own affairs.

In deeply divided countries such as Congo, Somalia, Rwanda and Burundi (although in the last two, especially in Rwanda, the Hutu and the Tutsi don't live in separate ethnic enclaves), restive provinces should be given maximum freedom to rule themselves as domestic sovereign states, but without the international legal authority exercised by *bona fide* independent nations. In other words, they will be independent domestically without being independent internationally.

That may be one of the best ways to discourage secession – an aspiration that is, more often than not, inspired by oppression and marginalisation of groups which want to secede – and end civil conflicts in African countries; for example, the separatist insurgency in Casamance Province in Senegal, as I have explained in one of my other books, *Military Coups in West Africa Since The Sixties*.[2]

Another example is the insurgency among the Tuaregs in northern Mali who complain that they have been ignored by national leaders in the capital Bamako in the southern part of the country since independence. For decades, they have demanded autonomy for their homeland and even asked the French colonial rulers before independence to partition the country so that they could have their own independent state in the north.

Continuing to ignore them could radicalise them even further and rekindle secessionist demands in the future, backed by armed struggle as they did in 2012 until the French intervened in 2013 to neutralise them and keep Mali intact.

The uprising by the Tuaregs could have been defused – it could even have been avoided – had they been allowed to rule themselves as a *de facto* independent state while remaining an integral part of Mali. They have been fighting for their rights since 1916.

It is the same situation in neighbouring Niger where the Tuarges in the northern part of the country are marginalised and face the same fate as their brethren in Mali. Before the advent of colonial rule, the Tuarges in what is now northern Niger had their own form of government, confederation, that suited them well.

When the French colonised the region, they changed all that and centralised power. After independence, the new African leaders continued to rule the same way the French did, denying the people the right to make decisions for themselves as they had done in the past before they were conquered by Europeans.

But there is a way to avoid conflict. It's simple. Allow the people to rule themselves. Let them have their own form of government, their own "independent state." Devolution is not synonymous with national disintegration.

Such maximum freedom and capacity for self-rule is a form of self-determination which Biafra (Eastern Nigeria) could also have been accorded to keep it within Nigeria as a domestic sovereign entity or state without international recognition. It should have been done before the eruption of the conflict, but even in the midst of war to mitigate disaster.

Self-determination in a domestic context does not mean or imply independence in all cases, with full diplomatic recognition and all the attributes of sovereignty a legal sovereign entity such as Nigeria or Senegal has. It can be applied to *de facto* states such as Somaliland which seceded from the defunct state of Somalia in 1991. It can be applied to Casamance Province if the restive region is accorded such status – as a *de facto* state like Somaliland or even Puntland.

And it could have been applied to Biafra had the Nigerian federal government chosen to resolve the conflict peacefully, while keeping the federation intact, with the secessionist Eastern Region as an integral part of it – but without secessionist aspirations which would have been neutralised through compromise. Or the Nigerian federation could have been restructured and reconstituted to form a confederation to accommodate conflicting ethno-regional interests and loyalties and end domination of other ethnic groups by the three major ones: Hausa-Fulani, Igbo, and Yoruba.

There are many precedents for extensive devolution of power, although not necessarily based on the model presented above. The main point here is that maximum self-determination (which *must* include equitable revenue sharing to satisfy the demands of local communities where resources such as minerals are extracted by the state and whose income is channelled into national coffers) – synonymous with full domestic sovereign status – for constituent units of nation-states is a practical proposition with a lot of benefits including preservation of national integrity.

In Africa itself, post-apartheid South Africa has achieved a degree of devolution or decentralisation rare on the continent for a unitary state; and by doing so, has not only reduced the danger of national disintegration but also of civil war caused by provinces which may opt for violence to secede from the union as the predominantly KwaZulu-Natal Province threatened to do in the early nineties.

KwaZulu-Natal, the homeland of the country's 10 million Zulus who constitute the largest ethnic group in South Africa (the Xhosa in the Eastern Cape being the second-largest), enjoys a large degree of autonomy virtually as a *de facto* domestic sovereign entity – an ethnostate (overwhelmingly Zulu); so does the Western Cape dominated by whites and Coloureds.

In 1994 and 1998 the ruling African National Congress (ANC), which enjoys a high degree of popularity across the country because of its unrivalled status and credentials as a liberation movement which freed South Africa from white domination, lost elections in KwaZulu-Natal to the Zulu Inkatha Freedom Party (IFP) whose ethnic composition is reminiscent of the Kabaka Yekka, a party – led by Kabaka (King) Mutesa – composed of the Baganda of the Buganda kingdom in Uganda.

In both cases, ethnonationalism prevailed in the formation of those parties, and in the case of KwaZulu-Natal, even at the polls.

But ethnonationalism can be a threat to national unity if it is not properly managed as an expression of local aspirations and sentiments. Equally dangerous is suffocation of local dissent and aspirations which can lead to instability if the people are not allowed to ventilate their grievances and pursue their goals for the benefit of their own communities.

In Uganda, secessionist threats by the Buganda kingdom were neutralized by force when soldiers from the Ugandan army led by Idi Amin on orders from President Milton Obote stormed Kabaka's palace on Mengo Hill to oust him and preserve national unity under a unitary state.

In South Africa, KwaZulu-Natal remained an integral

part of the nation, although at a cost of thousands of lives in the early nineties, after it achieved a high degree of autonomy and at the expense of the ruling African National Congress at the polls in the province which is overwhelmingly Zulu.

The African National Congress also lost in 1994 in Western Cape to the old apartheid National Party dominated by whites and supported by the vast majority of Coloureds who were apprehensive of black majority rule which became a reality after apartheid formally ended in May that year with the establishment of the first democratically elected government in the history of the country, with Nelson Mandela as the first black president.

In the 1998 general election, the ANC won in Western Cape but was frozen out of power in the province by a coalition of parties supported by whites and Coloureds.

But also in both provinces – KwaZulu-Natal and Western Cape – it was a case of self-determination and curtailment of national sovereignty in a domestic context, yet without compromising national unity and state authority and the essence of the democratic tradition.

Another example is Tanzania where Zanzibar enjoys a high degree of autonomy, although there are strong secessionist sentiments in the former island nation which need to be addressed and defused through dialogue, especially by granting more autonomy to the isles or by holding a referendum for the people of Zanzibar to decide whether or not they want to remain in the union and under what kind of political arrangement.

But a referendum should be the last resort. Before that, the two sides, the former nation of Tanganyika and the former nation of Zanzibar, should try to form a confederation in which both will regain their sovereignties but continue to be under one government with limited powers responsible for only a few things such as defence, national security, monetary policy and immigration.

A confederation may be the best system for Tanzania

because the people of Zanzibar have been complaining since the union was formed in April 1964 that they have been "swallowed up" by Tanganyika; and that they are junior partners in the union and are not treated fairly by the union government ("dominated by Tanganyikans") which also serves as the government for the mainland. Zanzibar has its own government.

Zanzibaris are so conscious and so protective of their identity as Zanzibaris that nothing is going to stop them from identifying themselves as Zanzibaris and from saying they are different from the people of Tanzania mainland or what they like to call Tanganyika, although Tanganyika no longer exists as a country; it does not even exist as a geographical entity let alone as a political region.

Most Zanzibaris don't even call themselves Tanzanians. They call themselves Zanzibaris, mainly because that is what they are, but also as a protest against the union. It is also an assertion of their identity. They claim a separate identity which sets them apart from their counterparts on the mainland whom they continue to call Tanganyikans, deliberately, to make a point that the two peoples are different, have nothing in common, and have only been forced to be together in a union they don't like.

They even call the people on Tanzania mainland, the former Tanganyika, "Wadanganyika," instead of "Watanganyika."

"Watanganyika" is a Swahili term which means "Tanganyikans," and "Wadanganyika" is "Danganyikans" in English.

"Wadanganyika" is a derogatory term derived from Kiswahili meaning "gullible ones," deliberately coined to rhyme with "Watanganyika," implying the people on Tanzania mainland, or in Tanganyika (although the country no longer exists), are "gullible."

In Kiswahili or Swahili, "danganya" means "cheat, dupe or deceive."

"Amenidanganya" means "He or she has cheated me."

"Ametudanganya," singular form, means "He or she has cheated us."

"Umenidanganya," singular form, means "You (an individual) have cheated me."

"Mumenidanganya," plural form, means "You (as a people or as a group) have cheated me."

"Mumetudanganya," plural form, means "You (people) have cheated us."

"Wametudanganya," plural form, means "They have chaeated us."

"Umedanganywa," singular form, means "You have been cheated."

"Mumedanganywa," plural form, means "You (as a people or as a group) have been cheated"; for example, the people of Tanganyika or Zanzibar or both have been cheated.

"Wamedanganywa" means "They have been cheated."

"Tumedanganywa" means "We have been cheated."

I know all this because I am a native speaker of Swahili which we call Kiswahili.

Zanzibaris emphasise that it is "Tanganyikans" who are "gullible" because they are the ones who believe that President Julius Nyerere of Tanganyika was right when he united the two countries. Hence the designation "Wadanganyika": "gullible ones."

Nyerere was the driving force behind the unification of the two countries, together with Abeid Karume, the president of Zanzibar.

Although the union of Tanganyika and Zanzibar has survived, it also has come under a lot of strain through the decades. There are many people on Tanzania mainland who don't want the union just like many Zanzibaris don't. The main argument advanced by Tanzanians on the mainland is that Zanzibar is an economic burden on them; which it is. It is Tanzania mainland which pays for almost all the expenses incurred by Zanzibar.

The former island nation has virtually nothing in terms

of natural resources besides cloves. Even one former cabinet member in the union government, Hassan Diria, a Zanzibari who also served as Tanzania's ambassador in a number of countries and as minister of information and broadcasting and as minister of foreign affairs at different times, among other posts, bluntly stated that Zanzibar can not survive and prosper without the union.

But ways must be found to allay the fears of Zanzibaris that they have been "swallowed up" by "Tanganyika" and that they are being dominated and exploited by "Tanganyikans" although there really is nothing for "Tanganyikans" to exploit in Zanzibar.

One of those ways has been to let Zanzibar continue to exist as a political entity with its own government, enjoying extensive autonomy, and to let Zanzibaris retain their identity as Zanzibaris, while denying former Tanganyikans the same right. There is no Tanganyika, and there are no Tanganyikans anymore. They are the ones who were swallowed up by the union when the two countries united in 1964.

Restructuring the union to form a confederation may allays the fears of many Zanzibaris and may help to contain or even neutralise secessionist sentiments.

If a confederation fails, dissolution of the union of Tanganyika and Zanzibar which led to the creation of Tanzania will be the only option left. But the dissolution must be confirmed by the people in a referendum to make sure that is what the majority of them – on both sides – want.

Technically, and constitutionally, Zanzibar is semi-autonomous. But for all practical purposes, it is really autonomous despite professions to the contrary by Zanzibaris.

There is also the case of Nigeria, a federation of 36 states whose federal constitution is being continually challenged by the people to achieve maximum self-rule; a challenge the government sees as a threat to its authority and national unity.

But if carefully managed, the result of such devolution of power will be exactly the opposite, instead of being the beginning of the end of the Nigerian federation. It will not lead to dissolution of the federation or to the disintegration of Nigeria as a nation or as a single political entity.

The conflict between the states or the people and the the federal government is best exemplified and clearly illustrated by the case of Zamfara, a state in the northern part of the country.

Located in northwestern Nigeria, Zamfara is an overwhelmingly Muslim state. It is mostly inhabited by the Hausa and by the Fulani, two ethnic groups which are close allies and which share the same culture including language (Hausa); hence the designation Hausa-Fulani, since they are identified as one group. They have so much in common that they are virtually the same people.

Members of smaller ethnic groups also are among the indigenous people of Zamfara. Like the Hausa-Fulani, they are also overwhelmingly Muslim.

But Zamfara also has some Christians, mostly Igbos and some Yorubas as well as others from the southern part of the country, especially in the state capital Gusau. There are also other people from other parts of Nigeria.

In October 1999, the newly-elected governor of Zamfara, Ahmed Sani (his whole name is Ahmed Rufai Sani Yerima but is simply called Ahmed Sani), an economist and former civil servant in the federal government, introduced *sharia*, or Islamic law. The announcement was significant in another respect because Sokoto, the country's Muslim spiritual centre, is also located in Zamfara.

Sokoto was also the home of the late Sir Ahmadu Bello who controlled the Nigerian federation in the sixties when he was the premier of Northern Nigeria. He controlled the federation because the largest number of the members of the Nigerian parliament were northerners who were under his rule since he was the the premier of the region they came from. The federal prime minister himself, Abubakar Tafawa Balewa, also came from the north and was controlled by the northern premier.

Also, the largest number of soldiers in the national army, the most powerful institution in the country, were northerners. A large number of the army officers were also northerners.

Almost all the Nigerian rulers since independence, including military heads of state, were northerners. The exceptions were Nnamdi Azikiwe who served as governor-general and then as the country's first president from October 1960 to January 1966 when the government was overthrown in a military coup.

Northerners dominated the Nigerian federation from independence in 1960 until 1999 when a southerner, Olusegun Obasanjo, was elected president. He became the second southerner, after Azikiwe, to serve as president.

Ahmadu Bello, also known the Sardauna of Sokoto, dominated the federation until he was assassinated on 15 January 1966 during the coup. And he was the unchallenged head of the northern Muslim aristocracy.

The introduction of *sharia* in Zamfara, a Muslim stronghold, amounted to a *de facto* declaration of independence from the federal government and to an assertion of domestic sovereignty as a Muslim state.

Nigerian President Olusegun Obasanjo declared the adoption of the rigid Islamic code to be unconstitutional. And the draconian nature of an Islamic fundamentalist theocracy – one is reminded of Saudi Arabia, Afghanistan under the Taliban, and Iran under the Ayatollah Khomeini and his fanatical successors – alarmed many Nigerians; the potential for the establishment of such a theocratic state in a country that was under a secular constitution could not be ignored. According to a report from Gusau, Zamfara, by *The Economist*:

"Mr. Sani says he intends to enforce the (Islamic) law strictly, as in Saudi Arabia, which means that thieves could have their hands amputated and people caught drinking could be flogged....Zamfara's Christians, he says, will not be affected, but will remain under the jurisdiction of the existing legal code.

The Christians do not agree. 'The *sharia* will surely affect us, because we are part and parcel of the state,' says...the Reverend Olu Joseph (of) a small Christian church in Gusau, the capital of Zamfara....

Zamfara, a rural and hitherto obscure state, is now at the centre of a controversy with much wider ramifications. Africa's religious fault-line, between a predominantly Muslim north and a more pluralist but largely Christian south, cuts across the Sahel, dividing several countries.

Sudan has suffered decades of religion-based civil war. In Nigeria, the massacre of thousands (at least 30,000) of Christian Igbos in Kano and other northern cities in 1966 was one of the factors that led to the Biafran civil war.

In recent years, relations between Nigeria's north and south have been relatively calm but, even so, they remain delicate, all the more so since religious and ethnic divisions tend to overlap."[3]

Governor-elect Ahmed Sani's announcement inflamed passions among Christian leaders across Nigeria who saw the introduction of Islamic law in Zamfara state as a violation of the country's secular constitution whose strict interpretation demands separation of church and state. Therefore adoption of *sharia* by a secular government – which, by doing so, is invoking religious authority and illegally transforming itself into a theocratic regime – upsets the uneasy religious balance in a country deeply divided along ethnoregional and religious lines between Muslims in the north and Christians in the south.

When Sani made the announcement, Muslim leaders, especially in the north where they predominate, either supported the change or said nothing publicly. As one northern politician said: "People in the north can't come out and oppose this thing in public. If you do, you open yourself to the accusation that you are unIslamic."[4]

President Obasanjo himself said nothing at first in public. As a Christian, any public criticism of the introduction of Islamic law by him would have infuriated many Muslims. And as a southerner, from southwestern Nigeria, he was already being criticised by northerners who claimed – although without any credible evidence – that he was favouring his own people, the Yoruba, at the expense of other ethnic groups.

The new governor of Zamfara tried to exploit the situation to advance his Islamic cause. But he was wrong thinking that the Nigerian president would remain passive or silent on this highly volatile issue. And when he spoke, he made made it clear that the introduction of Islamic law in Zamfara state – or anywhere else – violated the Nigerian constitution.

However, Governor Ahmed Sani was adept at invoking and at manipulating the same constitution to promote his Islamic agenda. It is true that the Nigerian constitution – as a concession to the country's large Islamic population, which is probably the country's largest religious group – has a provision that allows the introduction of *sharia* but only in the area of family law dealing with divorce, inheritance and other related matters.

In response to that, Sani – and here, he was on solid ground – contended that the fundamental right to freedom of worship, which is also enshrined in the federal constitution, justifies the introduction of Islamic law, although he did not explicitly acknowledge the prescribed limits mandated by federal law. So, he proceeded to introduce the measure, with immediate impact:

"The new policies are already beginning to show. It is now virtually impossible to buy alcohol in Gusau. Boys and girls are soon to be educated in separate schools, and men and women are starting to travel in separate buses. Mr. Sani has even said that only men with beards will be awarded government contracts."[5]

In December 1999, Kano state said, it too, like Zamfara, would adopt Islamic law.[6] By January 2000, three northern states had adopted *sharia* and three more were getting ready to do so. According to *The Economist*:

"Islamic law – *sharia* – came into force in Zamfara state in Nigeria. Two other state legislatures have passed laws adopting *sharia* and three have committees studying it."[7]

But the introduction of *sharia* did not proceed well. It sparked ethnoreligious violence between northern Muslims, mostly Hausa-Fulani, and southern Christians living in Northern Nigeria.

In February 2000, more than 100 people were killed in the city of Kaduna following clashes between the two sides as a result of protests by Christians opposed to the proposed introduction of Islamic law in the northern state of Kaduna, named after its major and capital city, which is also the second-largest in the north after Kano.

The city's population is equally divided between Muslims and Christians (mostly from the south), providing a potent mix of an ethnoreligious cauldron. According to a report from Kaduna:

"HUNDREDS of Christians burst into the offices of the governor of the northern Nigerian state of Kaduna this week to protest at the demand by local Muslims for the imposition of the *sharia*, or Islamic law. An office was smashed, several civil servants were beaten and slogans ranging from "Jesus is Lord" to "Sharia is not Y2K compliant" were daubed on the wall....

Over 100 people were killed, shops and houses were destroyed, and cars and trucks set on fire, in a terrifying outbreak of communal and religious violence. On February 23rd, an indefinite curfew was declared in the city and surrounding towns. Troops and heavily armed paramilitary police struggled to separate the armed gangs of militant Christian and Muslim youths responsible for the killing."[8]

The conflict took another dimension when it became regionalised, with other Muslims in the north expressing solidarity with their Islamic brethren in the midst of crisis, and with more northern states adopting *sharia*:

"By unhappy coincidence, the authorities in two other states, Niger and Sokoto, chose this week to sign bills that declared the *sharia* to be the law in their states. Last month, Zamfara, which had announced its intention of imposing Islamic law in October, began implementing it with the public flogging of a man found guilty of drinking alcohol. At least three more states – Kaduna, Kano and Yobe – are now thinking of introducing the law.

Of all the states, Kaduna and Kano present the greatest potential for trouble. Unlike other cities in the Muslim-dominated north, Kaduna has a population that is split roughly equally between Muslims and Christians. Kano, by far the largest city in the region, has a sizeable Christian minority and a history of religious violence.

Muslims in northern Nigeria are drawn to the idea of the Islamic code, partly because they are disillusioned by years of corrupt military rule, but also because they are alarmed by ever-rising crime figures. The Muslim governors of the northern states that have introduced the *sharia* try to reassure Christians by saying repeatedly that it will not affect non-Muslims.

But Nigeria's Christians are not reassured. "They are saying that anyone who is a Christian should act like a

Muslim. They ban drink. They ban men seeing their wives," said Wajoba Bhaturi inaccurately. He is a blanket-maker in Kaduna, and he was sporting a bandage over a deep cut in his forehead after the fighting this week.

For many Nigerians, the issue is more political than religious. Islamic law has existed in Nigeria for centuries, but under British and military rule it was restricted (as in several Arab countries) to family matters. Now, in a new era of elective politics, it is seen as a winning policy for governors in states with strong Muslim majorities. Parliament this week said it would start to investigate whether imposing the *sharia* is legal under the 1999 constitution.

All this leaves President Olusegun Obasanjo, a committed Christian, in an extremely difficult position. All he could do, this week, was to appeal rather helplessly to all sides to settle their religious differences peacefully. His critics say his difficulties are partly of his own making: he has been too weak on the issue."[9]

But the introduction of *sharia* was not mainly for religious purposes. The religious issue was politicised because it resonated well among northern voters. Such deep resonance proved to be a powerful platform for northern politicians to articulate their grievances against the federal government and promote their agenda – which naturally took on a religious character – in states that are predominantly Muslim and where, because of the dominance of Islam as a way of life, many issues assume a religious dimension.

Leading Islamic candidates for gubernatorial office easily coasted to victory on a wave of religious sentiment, sending panic among minority Christians living in the north and even raising the spectre of a civil war between northerners and southerners which could split Nigeria along religious and ethnoregional lines. As Minabere Ibelema, a Nigerian professor at the University of

Alabama, Birmingham, in the United States, stated in his article, "Nigeria: The Politics of Marginalization," in *Current History: A Journal of Contemporary World Affairs*:

"These ethnoreligious tensions are reminiscent of the events in 1966 and 1967 that precipitated Nigeria's civil war in which more than 1 million Nigerians died when the Igbos created the secessionist state of Biafra.

Emeka Odumegwu Ojukwu, who led the 30-month secession, has been blamed by some northern leaders for fomenting this year's Kaduna crisis. Ojukwu has responded by calling the accusation a halluciation and by suggesting psychiatric examination for the accusers. But he has also said of the Igbos that 'we have to get prepared, be on our toes and wait.' Leaders used similar language directly preceding the declaration of secession in 1967."[10]

Nigerian President Olusegun Obasanjo who was elected in February 1999 and inaugurated in May the same year vowed to keep Nigeria one; the same vow he made during the Nigerian civil war (1967 – 1970) when he spearheaded the final military offensive against the secessionist Biafran forces as a senior officer in the Nigerian federal army, forcing the secessionist to surrender.

But northerners were equally adamant, determined to pursue their agenda of Islamisation of the northern states in the secular spheres of law and government to virtually separate themselves from other Nigerians. And some of them implemented the measures in a highly defiant manner to snub the president who remained resolute in his commitment to uphold a secular constitution:

"In a pointed snub, Sokoto has said it will start implementing Islamic law on May 29th, the first anniversary of the president's coming to power."[11]

Many northerners and other Nigerians also misinterpreted the president's initial response to the promulgation of *sharia* as indecisiveness in the midst of what could have escalated into a national crisis. He didn't say much about it at the beginning. However, what was perceived as a tepid response by Obasanjo was a calculated move on his part to seek a diplomatic solution to the crisis and avert escalation of the ethnoreligious conflict.

Those who had underestimated him or misconstrued his muted response also had a rude awakening when he responded forcefully with federal might. More than once, he sent federal troops to Kaduna to end the violence between Christians and Muslims and maintained that federal law was paramount. The president was also able to exert enough pressure on the governors of northern Nigeria, enabling the federal government to secure substantial concessions from them by the end of February 2000. According to a report from Nigeria by *The Christian Science Monitor*:

"Governors of northern Nigeria had the task of explaining to their mostly Muslim people why the decision had been made to abandon the idea of adopting strict Islamic law.

The agreement earlier this week with President Olusegun Obasanjo also calls for states that already have *sharia* to stop enforcing it. The deal followed three days of rioting between Muslims and resentful Christians that killed at least 400 people.

Analysts said the retreat from *sharia* could pose a problem for the governors, who made the strict code the basis of their platform in Nigeria's elections last year."[12]

Some reports said probably as many as 2,000 people were killed in the violence in Kaduna in February.[13] And the suspension of *sharia* did not end the violence or the demand for the enforcement of Islamic law; nor did it stop the adoption of the rigid Islamic code in other parts of Northern Nigeria. It only fuelled discontent in the Islamic population whose members overwhelmingly voted for the adoption of the strict law based on the interpretation of the Koran by their fundamentalist clerics.

Enforcement of *sharia* brought even more publicity to the theocratic state authorities in Northern Nigeria when on 24 March 2000, a man in Zamfara who was sentenced under Islamic law for stealing cows had his right hand amputated in what was reportedly the first case to be adjudicated under *sharia* since the law was adopted by the predominantly Muslim state at the beginning of the year.[14]

There was widespread criticism of *sharia* and this kind of punishment, with many critics in other parts of Nigeria, especially in the south, invoking the sanctity of the country's secular constitution. One such critic was Steve U. Nwabuzor who stated in *Niger World*, 24 March 2000:

"Again, we are called upon to raise our voices, dip our pens and scrutinize the very basis of our existence as a nation. Zamfara state government, despite the recent undertaking to put on hold implementation of the Sharia penal code, has been quoted to amputate a man said to be notorious for stealing cows. In this pursuit of amputation, we are told that a medical professional was party to it.

One is forced to ask, when will this madness stop? Common sense has shown that sanity produces peace, while madness begets anarchy and intolerance. This latest show of insanity by the Zamfara State government should not go unchallenged. It was barely a month ago that President Obasanjo informed the whole world of the criminality of stoning and amputation of any individual, as these were against the provisions of the Nigerian constitution.

Sharia activists are not willing to abate their struggle,

at least in Zamfara. What does Zamfara State government want? Why decimate Nigerian citizens in order to score cheap political points? This latest act occurring at a time when the constitutionality of the Sharia penal code is being challenged by some indigenes of Zamfara only points to one fact, that the Zamfara government is ready to bite the hand that feeds her and I hope that hand would smack the mouth, and if possible snuff the life out of it.

My hypothesis on Sharia being a tool for intermittently causing unrest for the Nigerian nation still holds. We should not forget that Zamfara is the arrowhead of the Sharia for testing the waters of the Federal government. Zamfara was the first state to declare Sharia criminal law, and now it has effected the first amputation.

Other sharianized states are watching if the federal government is just a toothless bulldog.

I hope our leaders are not going to say this is just a flash in the pan and wish this incident away.

Apparently, Zamfara government is determined to continuously generate controversy within the Nigerian polity.

Saddening to note that a state that is the poorest in Nigeria has decided to be the rate-determining step in our progress. While efforts should be geared in Zamfara to improve the lots of the numerous beggars and jobless charlatans roaming the streets, more handicaps are being manufactured for the system. There are right now enough beggars and physically disabled people in Nigeria. We do not need more of these.

This latest act was meted out to a Moslem and so we might be tempted to say who cares? After all, it is their Sharia. We are further told that the amputation received applause from a sizable crowd within the precincts of a government hospital where the amputation took place. If there is any way to define sadism, this latest incident is more than a perfect example.

The Federal government continues to palliate the

507

proponents of the Sharia penal code by making ambiguous statements to the effect of seeking a political solution, rather than judicial. Why can't the federal government pursue the legal and political in tandem? One is disappointed at the Nigerian Bar Association for supporting only the political option. Are we being told that we do not have good cause to challenge this illegality and barbaric act that has further tarnished our image in the civilized world?

A trend is emerging in this unfolding drama, it is the game of the 'father of all lies,' which is to cause confusion in the minds of those opposed to the wiles of these agents of destabilization. When there appears to be a lull, the Sharia dragon is unleashed and goes berserk.

We need to put on our girdles, for this Sharia penal code is a spiritual battle. The plan has been made in the spiritual domain of darkness to obfuscate the progress of the Obasanjo regime. Now we (those opposed to the Sharia penal code) have to go back to the drawing board and invoke our spiritual armor in Christ. It is only then can we be assured of victory.

Meanwhile, let the Obasanjo government confront this dragon with all the might it can muster. It is only then will the true message cut deep into the 'Sardauna of Zamfara."[15]

If the criticism above is indicative of anything, it was a passionate plea to respect Nigeria's secular constitution which prohibits the establishment of a theocracy anywhere in the country. But by invoking the spiritual guidance of Jesus Christ, as Steve Nwabuzor did in his commentary above obviously because he was a Christian, his criticism also had a religious dimension and reflected a collective sentiment prevalent among southern Nigerians the majority of whom are Christian, thus showing that there is a very real divide between the north and the south that is defined along religious lines.

Although other northern states, all overwhelmingly Muslim, agreed (at least in theory) to suspend enforcement of *sharia* in criminal proceedings until the matter was resolved constitutionally by the federal authorities, the governor of Zamfara refused to do so until the Nigerian federal government agreed to settle the dispute without compromising the essence of Islamic law and the interests of his Muslim subjects who supported the measure.

Many people in Nigeria including the federal government wanted civil and criminal statutes – as stipulated by the constitution in what is essentially a secular nation – to take precedence over Islamic law invoked by the theocratic regimes in the northern states.

In May 2000, more violence erupted in Kaduna, claiming more lives and fuelled by religious intolerance:

"Renewed sectarian violence has killed more than 100 people in northern Nigeria, reports said. Heavily armed soldiers and police were patrolling the city of Kaduna after two days of fighting between Christians and Muslims, a revival of the clashes in February in which hundreds – and perhaps as many as 2,000 people – died. The violence was inspired by the proposed imposition of *sharia*, the rigid Islamic legal code, which prescribes such punishments as amputation."[16]

And that was not the last of it. Violence continued to erupt, now and then, here and there, between northern Muslims and southern Christians in Northern Nigeria. There was religious-inspired violence even in some parts of Southern Nigeria, for example, in Lagos in the heart of Yorubaland in the southwest, where the Hausa and other northerners lived in large numbers.

The Hausa have interacted with the Yoruba as traders for hundreds of years. But an increasing number of them also settled in southern Nigeria when the country was under military rule dominated by northern generals for almost 40 years since independence in 1960. The ethnoregional crisis in the north only exacerbated tensions between northerners and southerners in Southern Nigeria. As Minabere Ibelema pointed out:

"The recent institution of planned introduction of shariah – the Islamic penal code – by several Muslim-populated states in northern Nigeria has aggravated the already complex political atmosphere. Since October 1999, at least 5 northern states have passed laws in favor of implementing the code, and one – Zamfara – has signed it into law.

Tension over imposing shariah climaxed in February in a bloody clash in the northern city of Kaduna between northern Muslims and southern Christians residing in the north. As many as 400 people were killed, most of them southerners. Reprisal killings of resident northerners soon followed in the southeastern city of Aba.

The ensuing insecurity precipitated an exodus of southerners (reminiscent of the mass exodus of southerners from Northern Nigeria just before the outbreak of the Nigerian civil war, 1967 – 1970) – especially Igbos who are mainly Christian – from northern cities, and of northern Hausa-Fulani, who are mainly Muslim, from the south....

Radical members of the Yoruba group Oodua People's Congress have...attacked non-Yorubas in Lagos at the slightest pretext. In November 1999, a Yoruba and Hausa merchant skirmish over control of a food market spiraled into a conflict that killed nearly 100 people....

Following a February 29 meeting of the Council of States – attended by state governors and former heads of state – the federal government ordered the suspension of shariah as a criminal code. Its long-standing application to civil cases, which is acknowledged in the constitution, was allowed to continue.

The responses of the affected states have been mixed.

A few, such as Jigawa and Zamfara, seem intent on defying the federal government; Zamfara demonstrated its resolve in late March by amputating a convicted thief's right hand, as required under shariah.

Other states, such as Niger and Yobe, have formally shelved the code, and Kwara has declared it will never implement it. Several states, including Kaduna and Plateau, appear ambivalent about their intent."[17]

But even such ambivalence was more than enough to send confusing signals to southern Christians and other southerners living in Northern Nigeria that they were not welcome in the north; which partly explains the departure of many of them from all parts of the region, their exit facilitated by the violence that erupted in Kaduna.

It was reminiscent of the sixties when more than 2 million Eastern Nigerians were forced to flee the north just before and after the outbreak of the civil war. It was one of the largest mass migrations in modern history precipitated by an ethnoregional conflict. Almost the same kind of conflict again threatened to split the country 30 years later in the nineties and beyond. Religion was one of the factors in the massacre of Igbos in the north in 1966; it was a factor again in the 1990s and beyond when southern Christians were forced to flee Northern Nigeria.

The prospect for such an outcome, fragmentation or dissolution of the federation, seemed real to many Nigerians in the 1990s – as much as it was in the 1960s during the civil war – especially after the military head of state, General Ibrahim Babangida, a northerner who seized power in 1985 from Major-General Muhammadu Buhari, a fellow northerner, annulled the results of the 1993 general elections to prevent a southerner, Moshood Abiola who had won the electoral contest, from becoming president. One of the Nigerians who felt that Nigeria could collapse anytime during that period was prominent author Wole Soyinka. As he stated in his book, *The Open Sore of A*

Continent: A Personal Narrative of the Nigerian Crisis:

"When I listen therefore to some pontificating voice declaring that the unity of Nigeria is non-negotiable, I detect only woolly or opportunistic thinking....There is absolutely no foundation in the absolute for such a declaration....

We did not shy from the probability of a civil war and the possible disintegration of the country as a consequence....With all the imponderables that confronted the nation, with all the variables of sectarian interests, some of them overlapping, others canceling one another, I frankly could not advance any invulnerable reason for my preference for a solution that did not involve disintegration.

I had been involved in discussions with countless numbers of people...businessmen, intellectuals, students, traders, professionals, clergymen. The mood for them was this: Let us prepare for the inevitable separation or, at best, the loosest arrangement possible, such as confederation.

During the most violent day of the anti-Babangida riots, trapped within the tumult of thousands that submerged my car, sat, drummed, or danced on it, voices would ring out with shouts of 'Lead us out of this mess called Nigeria!' 'I am ready, recruit me. Let's go our own way'....

All highly emotive, born out of deep frustration, but one must be careful not to dismiss such voices as products of an abnormal moment, of a temporary phase. They were outbursts that conveyed a summation of positions argued in offices, marketplaces, bus stops, factories, palace courtyards and more secretive recesses of traditional enclaves, classrooms and debating halls. They were a continuation of discourses begun in 1960, and even long before then.

We heard them during the various Leaders of Thought meetings after the countercoup of July 1966, we heard the then head of state, Yakubu Gowon, declare loud and clear that there was no longer any basis for Nigerian unity.

We were deafened by the apotheothis of such sentiment in the roar of guns during the Biafran war....

Every day still reminds us that the factors that led to Biafra neither were ephemeral nor can be held to be permanently exorcised."[18]

While northern domination of the federation helped precipitate the Nigerian civil war during the sixties, it was the north again – the end of its domination of Nigeria – which threatened to destroy the country this time because northerners sill wanted to assert their dominance, at least in the north, without or with very little federal control over them.

The problem was compounded by complaints from other ethnic groups in different parts of Nigeria that they were marginalised in the federation, prompting some of them to threaten secession or seek a new political arrangement including confederation – which President Obasanjo flatly rejected, saying it was tantamount to treason. As Professor Ibelema states:

"That 36 smaller states rather than four powerful regions now constitute federal Nigeria would seem to militate against secession (Nigeria in 1966 was composed of the North, the East, the West, and the Midwest regions). Regional coordination among states has, however, created powerful alliances.

Since the shariah crisis, political and religious leaders from northern, western, eastern, and southern minority states have met as discrete blocs to formulate unified positions or to discuss Nigeria's political future. Youths from the middle-belt states have also called for a separate leadership meeting of their states. Still, differences among the states within each bloc makes regional cohesion and secession unlikely.

513

As in 1967, claims have been made that some military personnel have supplied weapons to and otherwise aided civilians in the communal attacks....

In an address in the wake of the Kaduna riots, the chief of defense staff, Rear Admiral Ibrahim Ogohi, admonished them to eschew partisanship and to remain loyal to federal civilian authority. He pledged to defend Nigeria's nascent democracy.

Similar statements of commitment to a united and democratic Nigeria have been made by political and religious leaders on all sides. Yet these statements have been countered by others advocating confederation, dissolution, or even secession. Thus, the danger remains that Nigeria could splinter violently.

Although the present crisis is veiled in religious differences, it is at root political. The causes of tension and instability in Nigeria remain the same as in the (1967 – 1970) civil war: the fear of domination."[19]

The election of Olusegun Obasanjo in 1999 as president ended almost 40 years of northern domination of the Nigerian federation. And many northerners were painfully aware of that when power was transferred to a southerner, who was also a Christian, for the first time after an entire generation.

The campaign to introduce *sharia* in the northern states was a very important part of an effort by northern leaders to regain some of the power they had lost in the federation and reassert their authority as the only rulers at least of the northern states where they felt the federal government could be challenged and obstructed from exercising full control by introducing and enforcing Islamic law.

They used Islamic law in an attempt to "nullify" the federal constitution in their states by invoking religious freedom enshrined in the same secular constitution they did not want to uphold when it clashed with their interests, ignoring the fact that federal law is paramount: when state law conflicts with federal law, federal law must prevail.

It was obvious that northern Muslims were not going to abandon *sharia*. And the violence it spawned underscored the imperative need to forge a national consensus on the matter in order to balance – within constitutionally prescribed limits – the interests of the vast majority of the people in the northern states who supported Islamic law and the rest of the Nigerians who wanted to uphold a secular constitution as the paramount law of the land because of the country's religious and ethnic diversity.

We have had similar experiences in my home country, Tanzania, where for the sake of national unity and respect for the right of the Muslim majority in Zanzibar to live under Islamic law, the union constitution allows the enforcement of the Islamic legal code in well-defined areas involving civil matters without compromising the interests of Christians and other non-Muslim minorities in the isles (of Pemba and Unguja – the latter also known as Zanzibar – which together constitute the autonomous political entity known as Zanzibar); a subject I discuss in a chapter entitled, "Tanzania: Union of Two Independent States – Challenge to Unity and Ideology," in one of my books, *Economic Development in Africa*.[20]

The constitution unequivocally states that Tanzania is a secular state, a stipulation that acknowledges the country's religious and ethnic diversity in order to protect the rights of all of its citizens which would be impossible under a theocracy.

Similarly in Nigeria, there is a need for a secular constitution, which the country already has, in order to accommodate different religious and ethnic groups. And where there is a clash between state and federal law, the latter must prevail. Unity in diversity is possible only when federal law is paramount. And protection of the rights of all Nigerians is possible only when state law is superseded by federal law.

If the doctrine of nullification – prevalence of state law

515

over federal law – is to be applied, it must be only when the majority of the states in the federation decide to nullify federal law in specific areas. It can not be nullified by unilateral action – taken by one state or by only a few states – or by violence.

However, what the violence that was sparked by the introduction of *sharia* helped to do, although in a very tragic way, was to highlight local grievances and the urgent need for devolution of power but without undermining federal authority. It also underscored the fragile nature of African countries, in general, which inherited the highly centralised state at independence without restructuring it to reflect African realities and accommodate conflicting interests.

One of those realities should have been, right after independence, a concerted effort to build unity in diversity under a strong central government necessary to maintain national unity and neutralise secessionist threats but without stifling dissent. And that would have entailed decentralisation and devolution of power to achieve true democracy all the way to the grassroots level.

The northern Nigerian states could not legitimately claim that they were denied freedom of expression by the federal government especially after the end of military rule. It was precisely because they had such freedom that they were able to openly campaign for the adoption of Islamic law and even succeeded in introducing it. But the violence that erupted as a result of those efforts to introduce and enforce *sharia* was not protected by the constitution and justified federal intervention. According to a report by *The Christian Science Monitor*:

"Nigerian security forces intensified efforts yesterday (25 May 2000) to halt renewed religious violence in the northern city of Kaduna, in which more than 200 people have died. Hundreds of buildings – including mosques and churches – have been burned to the ground since fighting broke out Monday (22 May)....

Since the turn of the 20th century, when the British conquered the Sokoto caliphate and extended colonial rule into what is now northern Nigeria, the application of *sharia* in Muslim communities has been restricted largely to civil and customary law. But popular demand for its extension into other areas of life – including criminal law – has spread rapidly across the mainly Muslim north of the country since October (1999). It was then that the governor of the rural state of Zamfara unilaterally declared it the governing legal system of his state."[21]

The escalation of violence continued to demand and provoked an even tougher response from the federal authorities. Also, opposition to Islamic law in the northern states by many Nigerians including some Muslims who wanted Nigeria to remain a secular state found forceful expression in the national media which articulated a collective sentiment that resonated across the country, especially among Christians who were some of the most vocal and ardent supporters of secularisation of authority at the state and federal levels.

Some people openly talked about the possibility of a civil war that could engulf the whole country if the matter was not resolved amicably and if Muslims continued to enforce or adopt Islamic law in the north. And there were those who said a civil war was already going on in Nigeria. As Joe Igbokwe, an author and social commentator, stated in an interview published in the weekly *Tempo*:

"We just had a war in Kaduna, a civil war....
Let nobody describe this as a religious upheaval. What is happening now has been designed because they [northern leaders] can no longer go to their friends in Saudi Arabia and Libya and tell them that Nigeria is an Islamic state....They no longer have easy access to the

national treasury...(and) government contracts."[22]

And in the same edition, *Tempo* stated in an editorial: "The proponents of Sharia are intent on implementing a political agenda."[23]

Another Nigerian newspaper, the *Guardian*, expressed similar sentiments:

"We recognize the right of Muslims to fulfill the tenets of Islam to the letter, but the carnage that the Sharia has brought is indefensible. Now Christians in Kaduna are demanding their own portion of the state."[24]

Such demands only fuelled the conflict in a country that already had to contend with secessionist threats especially in the Niger Delta. But similar rumblings calling for secession and dissolution of the federation during the 1990s and thereafter were heard in other parts of the country: among the Yoruba in the West, the Igbo in the East, and some groups in the North and in the mid-regions. For example, Ojukwu, who led Biafra's secession and who was still seen as an embodiment of the ideals and aspirations of his people, expressed a sentiment shared by many Igbos when he said:

"(The) problem is that we are in Nigeria and we are finding it extremely difficult to find accommodation in Nigeria."[25]

The introduction of Islamic law in the northern states, in addition to widespread discontent among Nigeria's different ethnic groups, is another potent force that can lead to serious political instability in the future and even fragmentation of Africa's largest nation. The adoption of *sharia* is, in fact, tantamount to *de facto* secession of the northern states from the federation since they are trying to evade and defy federal control. And it may be the biggest threat to the continued existence of Nigeria as a nation and as a single political entity unless a consensus is reached on how to maintain a delicate balance between the interests of the states and of the federation.

How Nigeria reacts to this challenge – which may trigger a chain reaction in the rest of the overwhelmingly Muslim northern states and in other predominantly Muslim communities elsewhere in the country which may follow suit and adopt Islamic law – will have profound implications for the future of Africa's largest federation. Clamping down on Islamic fundamentalists will not solve the problem of conflicting interests between secular authorities and theocratic elements. Algeria learned the hard way during the 1990s.

Nigerian leaders may say Nigeria is not Algeria. That is true. But Islamic fundamentalism is Islamic fundamentalism regardless of how distorted its image is, when refracted through secular lenses, and regardless of where it is practised – Algeria or Nigeria, Egypt or Somalia, Mali or Mauritania, Kenya or Tanzania. It is an enduring phenomenon. And it provides spiritual sustenance to a large number of people.

The key to conflict resolution lies in making maximum concessions to the states which constitute the Nigerian federation – virtually granting independence from the central government in all matters that can be administered and resolved locally – yet without compromising national sovereignty. Devolution of power does not mean dissolution of national sovereignty or national unity.

An autonomous state is still subject to central authority and national laws as long as the laws do not deny the state the right to choose and decide what is best for its people but without sacrificing the rights of minority groups living under its jurisdiction: for example, Christians in Zamfara, Kano or Kaduna, or the Hausa-Fulani in Oyo state of the Yoruba people in the southwest or in Imo state of the Igbo in the southeast.

If the majority of the people in a given state are denied – by the national government – the right to choose how they want to live and how they want to be governed, as long they don't violate the rights of the minorities amongst them, then the national government can not honestly say that it is protecting all its citizens. And the constitution it is invoking to exercise power over them would be unconstitutional since it does not embody the will of the governed even if a majority of the states conspired against a few states to deny them the right to choose. There is no stronger case for self-determination for the oppressed group, whether a state or states, or ethnic groups such as the oppressed Hutu majority in Rwanda and Burundi or the Tutsi minority who fear extermination at the hands of the Hutu.

Let's take Rwanda as an example.

The Tutsi-dominated government of Rwanda (of the Rwandan Patriotic Front – RPF), afraid of extermination of its Tutsi minority, can guarantee the safety of its people by allowing the oppressed Hutu majority to rule themselves. This form of self-determination may not amount to statehood – of domestic sovereign status – in the Rwandan context because the two groups do not live in separate ethnic enclaves. They live on same hills, in the same villages, share the same land as neighbours as much as they share deep mistrust of each other especially after the 1994 genocide.

But such self-determination will allow maximum self-rule for the Hutu which they have been denied throughout Rwanda's history, for hundreds of years, except for the 32 years they were in power since independence in 1962, a position they maintained with ruthlessness at the expense of the Tutsi minority until they were ousted in July 1994 by the predominantly Tutsi Rwandan Patriotic Front (RPF).

Unless such extensive devolution of power takes place – short of complete separation of the two groups into fully sovereign ethnostates as some African leaders such as former Kenyan President Daniel arap Moi have suggested – there will be no peace in Rwanda. There will also be no peace in Rwanda if the Tutsi are not guaranteed security and if they continue to fear they are going to be exterminated by the Hutu.

A similar situation exists in Nigeria where the survival and stability of this large federation hinges on maximum devolution of power to the states to enable them to enjoy self-determination, not as independent states but as domestic sovereign entities whose sovereign status is superseded in only a few areas – such as national defence, foreign affairs, immigration, international trade, and monetary policy – by federal authority; which is not the case today.

Even if such extensive devolution of power leads to the establishment of a confederation – a move President Obasanjo equated with treason – and to more loss of power for the central government, it should be embraced as a positive change because it is better than the disintegration of Nigeria into independent tribal homelands. Such fragmentation would be a disaster for Nigeria and for Africa as a whole.

Decentralisation is not abdication of responsibility by the central government; nor is it encouragement of secession. It's simply sharing power with the people: allowing the people to rule themselves, allowing them to manage their own affairs.

Even the United States which has a strong central government at the federal level has a constitution which allows states to exercise a lot of freedom in many areas. States are allowed to enact their own laws. They are allowed to have their own judicial systems all the way up to the highest court in each state. They elect their own leaders, including governors who are the "heads of state" of those states. They even conduct trade with foreign countries as if they were independent states, but within prescribed limits restricted and guided by federal laws.

They even have their own legislatures, or parliaments, their own constitutions, their own flags, and their own anthems: official state songs.

That does not mean they are independent nations. It does not mean they are not integral parts of the United States of America; nor does it mean that they have been given or have been allowed that kind of freedom to rule themselves so that they can secede.

There is no reason why African countries can not do the same thing: allow their constituent parts – regions or provinces – to manage their own affairs without interference or guidance from the national government as long as they don't violate national laws which are vital to keep the regions and provinces united to maintain national unity and territorial integrity of the countries on the continent.

If the people don't want to have federations, because federations are too restrictive in some matters, they can have confederations of the constituent parts which collectively constitute African countries. It's not going to be the end of African countries as we know them.

Paradoxically, a confederation – despite its potential for encouraging secession – can neutralise separatist tendencies precisely because it allows its component units to enjoy maximum freedom in the management of their own affairs as if they were *de facto* sovereign states. And benefits of membership in a larger body, such as a confederation, will also discourage secession because the advantages of such membership far outweigh its disadvantages especially in terms of security and economic viability. Also, it can be a form of confederation with a strong central government that does not allow secession but more devolution of power to accommodate conflicting interests and contain secessionist sentiments.

Therefore a confederation could serve Nigeria well, unless the current federation wants to avoid that by taking further steps to give more power and freedom to the states to manage their own affairs but without trampling on the rights of minority groups – in which case the central government would have the right to intervene to protect them. Any government that can not protect minority groups does not have the moral authority to rule even if it has the electoral mandate to do so.

Unfortunately, despite having a federal constitution which guarantees decentralisation – hence devolution of power to the states – Nigeria has, more often than not, functioned as a highly centralised state especially under military regimes which have no respect for the constitution. But even under civilian leadership, it has functioned the same way although without being draconian as is the case when soldiers are in power.

The objectives, for example maintaining national unity and stability under a highly centralised state, may be noble. But such concentration of power at the centre has had tragic consequences – oppression, suppression of freedom, exploitation which can not be challenged because people are muzzled – which could have been avoided had power been decentralised even under a unitary state. It has thus achieved exactly what it intended to avoid, including instability, chaos and even threats to national unity.

Zamfara's promulgation and enforcement of Islamic law – that of other northern states as well – may have been a quest for such extensive autonomy, but only if it was done within well-prescribed constitutional limits. It may also have been a major part of a hidden agenda by the northern Islamic rulers to destabilise and possibly destroy the Nigerian federation while invoking the constitution which allows devolution of power and implementation of Islamic law in some areas of life – because they resented the loss of power to southern leaders since Obasanjo was elected president in 1999.

After Zamfara adopted the rigid Islamic legal code,

other northern states followed suit as if they had formulated a common strategy to pursue a common agenda for northern "salvation" from southern "domination."

Besides the quest for freedom and self-rule, equally important is diversity within African countries as a matter of paramount concern to the people who make up these heterogeneous societies. It is in the context of unity in diversity – and not unity in uniformity as if Africa's different ethnic groups constitute a monolithic whole – that the quest for devolution of power must be seen, including the introduction of Islamic law in Zamfara and other states in Northern Nigeria.

However, such unity – in diversity – is impossible if the people are not free to choose the kind of political system under which they they want to live. If they are allowed to choose, there is no question they are going to choose a system that allows them maximum freedom to manage their own affairs and which accommodates conflicting interests and loyalties without compromising national unity and identity.

That is the only way the people in different countries can work together to build and develop their multiethnic societies. Governments can force them to live together within the same national boundaries. But they can't force them to work together productively. They have a way of life they want to preserve, and they should be allowed to do so, as long as they don't impede national progress, and as long as they don't interfere with the lives of others who are equally entitled to theirs and to maximum local expression in all areas – social and cultural, economic and political, as well as religious.

What happened in Zamfara was an expression of collective will in the quest for maximum self-rule, hence domestic sovereignty, within constitutional limits critics of the state's theocratic regime contend the governor overstepped, as he probably did, by invoking a secular constitution – of the Federal Republic of Nigeria – to establish a theocracy. But what should not be overlooked is the will of the people of Zamfara – and of the other predominantly Muslim states in Northern Nigeria – regardless of how much one may disagree with them on the adoption and enforcement of Islamic law.

Yet the majority of the people of Zamfara and other northern states can not legitimately claim they have the right to enforce Islamic law while ignoring the rights of the minorities amongst them. That is a violation of the federal constitution which guarantees equal rights for all.

Still, since Muslims constitute the vast majority in each of those states, they are automatically entitled to majority rule (so are the Hutu, of course, in both Rwanda and Burundi). That is democracy. And you can't have peace and stability without them (the majority) even if you bring in tanks. There can be peace and stability, hence harmony and progress, only if they get what they are entitled to, as they did when they introduced *sharia*, although violation of the country's secular constitution – which supersedes state law – is a matter of concern for the entire nation.

But if the constitution does not accommodate the interests of the northern Islamic states (and there are several of them, with tens of millions of people), it losses its legitimacy which is derived from the consent of the governed who include probably no fewer than 70 million Muslims in Northern Nigeria. No one can pretend they don't exist; and there's no one who claims they don't. They are there. They are going nowhere. And they support Islamic law. As Tajudeen Suleiman stated about the support for sharia in Zamfara in his article, "The Man Behind Sharia," in the Nigerian independent weekly, *Tempo*:

"The official notice preceding the declaration of Islamic law, or Sharia, by the government of Zamfara, a state in northern Nigeria, came as a surprise only to people outside the area. The groundwork for the establishment of Islamic law was laid before the election of Governor Ahmed Sani.

Sani, as a secretary in the state's Ministry of Lands and Housing, promoted the renovation and construction of several mosques and Islamic schools in Zamfara. These were said to have prepared for him a fertile ground when he decided to go into politics.

The indigenous peoples of the predominantly Muslim state simply drooled over him, seeing him as a pious person who would promote the cause of Islam in the state....

With the support of moneybags such as All People's Party (APP) official Alhaji Ruwan Dorowa, he had enough resources to oil his political machine. He also had sufficient mass appeal with his Islamic bent. Sani's campaign rallies kicked off with vigorous shouts of 'Allahu Akbar,' three times before any speech. This, it was gathered, greatly endeared him to the masses, who thronged his rallies.

During the All People's Party primaries, Sani defeated Ezed Anka, who was regarded as a more cosmopolitan figure. While campaigning, Sani courted clerics and village heads whom he felt would have sympathy for his envisaged Islamic revolution. Wherever he went during his campaign, Sani visited imams and village heads before going to see the political leaders. He was said to have sought their support and that of the congregation with a promise of the adoption of the Sharia. Sani's campaign slogan was openly tilted toward his promise: '[Sani] Yerima for Islam' worked instant wonders, culminating in his electoral victory.

The governor has become both a political and spiritual hero among ordinary folk. According to Sambo Gusau, a local official, Sani 'is a God-sent man doing what we want. In fact, we are lucky to have him as governor'....Alhaji Ahmed A. Ladan Gusau, an All People's Party chieftain in the state, agrees with this view....'Sani,' he says, 'is a boy who is blessed with foresight. We all know him. He did not enter politics to amass wealth. He is always thinking of the people.' Ladan further argues that since Christianity abhors prostitution, drunkenness, and other vile practices which the Sharia would eliminate, there was no reason for Christians to fear.

Sani was born 40 years ago, is married to four wives, and has many children. He holds a master's degree in economics and has been a civil servant all his life. Sani began his career at the (Federal) Ministry of Finance and Economic Planning, where he rose to become the director of budget. He worked with the National Directorate of Employment in Lagos (the former federal capital) and the Central Bank of Nigeria. He later returned to Sokoto. On the creation of Zamfara state, Sani was named permanent secretary in the Ministry of Land and Housing, from where he resigned to join politics."[26]

Ahmed Sani will go down in Nigerian history as the first elected governor of a state to seriously challenge the constitutionality of the country's secular constitution, one of whose bedrock principles is the separation of church and state. However, his theocratic agenda was equally challenged on constitutional grounds by invoking the same principle: there shall be no state religion. Yet, by introducing Islamic law, he also attempted to achieve maximum self-rule within constitutionally prescribed limits by citing a constitutional provision that allows the adoption of such a law, although only in a few areas unlike the mandate he sought from the Islamic electorate in Zamfara to institute a theocratic state.

Zamfara became Nigeria's first theocracy, although without explicitly saying so, and pushed the federal constitution to the limit as a blueprint for extensive devolution of power to the states. Cameron Duodu, a Ghanaian and one of Africa's most seasoned journalists,

527

expressed some concern over the adoption of *sharia*:

"Ahmed Sani's declaration to adopt Islamic law, or Sharia, in his state is a frontal attack on the Nigerian constitution, which designates Nigeria as a secular state. Scores of alarmed organizations and prominent citizens called on President Obasanjo to intervene and prevent Nigeria from becoming a country in which there is one law for some citizens and a different law for others....

Apart from ethnicity, religion is the most explosive issue in Nigerian politics....Some areas of the north already practice the Sharia through traditional rulers, known as emirs, and their underlings. But the emirs' courts are restricted in what they can do.

Governor Sani and other advocates of Sharia have tried to explain that it will be applied only to Muslims. But this has not reassured non-Muslims, who know from experience that Sharia, in practice, will also affect them. Advocates of the Islamic law argue that Nigeria's 'superior' courts, which operate under secular laws, can protect individuals. In practice, however, these superior courts may not be able to intervene to help non-Muslims enforce their rights under the Nigerian constitution, because once an establishment has been marked 'sinful,' every Muslim will feel obliged to ensure that it ceases to operate.

Another bone of contention, which even Muslims are worried about, is the severity of Sharia punishments....The (federal) constitution forbids the imposition of inhuman or barbaric punishment, which may leave some Sharia punishments (such as amputations) open to challenge. Many fear that the clash of laws can bring about a nasty constitutional confrontation between the state governments of the north and the federal government.

Nigeria has already experienced one extremely costly attempt at secession (Biafra's)....Clearly, Obasanjo does not want any such eventuality."[27]

Compromise solutions should be found to resolve the conflict between Islamic law and Nigeria's secular constitution while enabling Muslims in the predominantly Islamic states of Northern Nigeria to live under *sharia*. They should include the following:

Cases involving only Muslims should be adjudicated under Islamic law. Those involving Christians and Muslims should be tried in secular courts under state and federal. No Christian should appear in any Islamic court to testify for the prosecution or for the defence. If his or her testimony is needed, the case – even if it involves only Muslims – must be tried in federal court or in a secular state court under state and federal law.

Cruel punishments such as amputations and flogging imposed by Islamic courts should be challenged in secular courts under federal law. Islamic courts should also, under federal law, be compelled to take into account mitigating factors – and accept plea bargains – to reduce the severity of cruel punishments and to temper the rigidity of the Islamic code with pragmatic considerations. Anybody convicted in an Islamic court should have the right to appeal the decision in a federal court.

There should be no discrimination against Christians and other non-Muslims in areas of employment which have nothing to do with Islamic law or the Islamic way of life involving only Muslims. And all establishments owned by non-Muslims, including bars and businesses which sell pork and other items offensive to Muslims, should be exclusively under federal law.

Probably one of the best things to come out of this controversy over *sharia* is the constitutional debate on the clash between state and federal laws which may clarify matters and increase, rather than reduce, prospects for extensive devolution of power currently severely limited by the Nigerian federal government which functions as a highly centralised unitary state.

It is a debate that will resonate across the continent and

may contribute to conflict resolution in different contexts; for example, the war in Sudan – between the south which is predominantly black and Christian and the north which is mostly Arab and Muslim – that was routinely described by pundits as just another political conflict in spite of its racial overtones and religious nature even after the south seceded in July 2011 following a referendum in which more than 98 per cent southerners voted to secede.

Another major example is the conflict between the Hutu and the Tutsi in Rwanda and Burundi that also calls for dynamic compromise between the two groups to achieve peace, enable the Hutu enjoy their rights commensurate with their status as the democratic majority, and guarantee security for the dominant Tutsi minority if the Hutu come to power.

There are many other examples. Almost in every African country where violence has erupted – in the quest for power, fighting over resources – ethnicity has always played a role. Politicians stir up and fuel ethnic conflicts and exploit ethnic differences, loyalties and rivalries in the quest for power. The people themselves compete on ethnic basis. And in many cases, there is always the desire to exclude members of other ethnic groups in favour of one's own, and for personal gain, even if there is no threat from other groups. It is raw-naked tribalism.

Conflict in the quest for power with tribal or ethnic overtones has been a prominent feature of African politics since independence. And complaints by smaller or weaker groups is a perennial problem in every African country where there are dominant groups which routinely discriminate against other groups.

In Kenya, there are complaints against the Kikuyu and the Luo by smaller ethnic groups. As far back as the sixties even before independence, members of other groups feared they would be dominated by the Kikuyu and the Luo after the country attained sovereign status. They formed political parties to protect the interests of smaller tribes. One of those parties was the Kenya African National Union (KADU), formed in 1960. It was led by Ronald Ngala, a former teacher from the Coast Province and one of Kenya's most prominent politicians.

KADU called for the establishment of a federation, instead of a unitary state, as a safeguard against domination of the smaller tribes by the larger ones. It advocated devolution of power to the regions, enabling smaller tribes in those regions to rule themselves under a federal system – granting regional autonomy – which would have circumscribed the powers of the central government, something that could not be done under a unitary state.

Bloody ethnic conflicts have also been an integral part of political campaigns in Kenya, as happened in the 1990s in the Rift Valley Province where many Kikuyus and other people were killed by the Kalenjins. Their property including land was confiscated and they were forced to flee the region. The Luo and the Luhya were also expelled from the province. But the primary target were the Kikuyu.

Those who survived the attacks were forced to return to their original tribal homelands, making a mockery of their common Kenyan citizenship which gives them the right to live anywhere they want to live. It was a case of ethnic cleansing. As Professor Michael Chege, a Kenyan who was teaching at Harvard University during that time, stated:

"As in Rwanda (in 1994), Kenya in 1992 – 93 witnessed state-sponsored violence directed against ethnic Kikuyu, Luo and Luhya farmers who had migrated to the Rift Valley – President Moi's home province – and then voted for parties opposed to his KANU (Kenya African National Union) Party, which is associated in the main with Moi's own Kalenjin tribe and its allies.

The perpetrators of the violence – window-dressed as

'Kalenjin warriors' – attacked wearing uniform T-shirts and shorts. They conducted Klan-style night rallies and vowed to cleanse the Rift Valley of the baleful 'Kukes' (Kikuyus). Use of guns, bows and arrows, and nighttime firebombing of homestead, Christian churches, and Kikuyu businesses were standard procedures....Some fifteen hundred people – mainly Kikuyus – perished in these pogroms, while about three hundred thousand others became, and remain, internal refugees."[28]

Only a few years later before the presidential election in 1997, the Coast Province was the scene of the same kind of violence: ethnic cleansing. The people who were targeted and killed were mostly "outsiders" who came from other parts of Kenya and settled in the Coast Province.

The violence was indigenous in inspiration. It was also partly inspired by politicians who exploited and fuelled the animosity and visceral hatred some people in the Coast Province had for the non-indigenes from other parts of Kenya.

Leaflets written in Kiswahili were distributed in the Coast Province urging the people native to the region to drive out the "invaders" from other provinces. They were regarded as "foreigners" who had settled in the region to exploit the indigenes and deprive them of economic opportunities and take their land. According to the *International Herald* Tribune, 18 August 1997, some of the leaflets stated:

"The time has come for us original inhabitants of the coast to claim what is rightfully ours. We must remove these invaders from our land."[29]

The ruling Kenya African National Union (KANU) under President Moi – which was dominated by the Kalenjins (who are a collection of different groups of people who speak the Nandi language) and their allies who were also mainly members of "smaller" groups like the Kalenjins themselves – was accused of instigating the violence.

The main target were members of tribes opposed to Moi's despotic rule. They were mostly Kikuyu, Luo, Luhya, and Kamba, Kenya's major and most influential ethnic groups. But others were targeted as well.

The attacks were reminiscent of what had taken place in other African countries where members of ethnic groups who were not considered to be original inhabitants of the regions they had migrated to were killed or expelled from those regions where many of them had lived for decades.

The attacks in the Rift Valley and Coast Provinces in Kenya and the inflammatory language used by the instigators of this kind of violence to inflame passions among the indigenous people in those areas had strong similarities to what happened in Nigeria in the sixties and in Zaire in the early nineties.

The language had striking parallels to what Northern Nigerian leaders said about the Igbo who had settled in their region. As Representative Mallam Mukhtar Bello stated in the Northern House of Assembly during the February-March 1964 session just two years before the massacre of the Igbos in that region:

"I would like to say something very important that the Minister should take my appeal to the Federal Government (controlled by Northerners) about the Igbos....I wish the number of these Igbos be reduced....There are too many of them in the North. They are just like sardines and I think they are just too dangerous to the Region."[30]

The rest of the representatives in the Northern Regional Assembly expressed the same sentiment, including the Northern Premier himself, Sir Ahmadu Bello.

The Premier, Alhaji The Honourable Sir Ahmadu Bello, K.B.E., Sardauna of Sokoto:

"It is my most earnest desire that every post in the Region, however small it is, be filled by a Northerner (Applause)."[31]

Representative Mallam Muhammadu Mustapha Maude Gyari:

"On the allocation of plots to the Ibos, or the allocation of stalls, I would like to advise the Minister that these people know how to make money and we do not know the way and manner of getting about this business.... We do not want Ibos to be allocated plots, I do not want them to be given plots."[32]

Mallam Bashari Umaru:

"I would like (you), as the Minister of Land and Survey, to revoke forthwith all Certificates of Occupancy from the hands of the Ibos resident in the Region (Applause)."[33]

Mr. A. A. Abogede (Representative of Igala East):

"I am very glad that we are in Moslem country, and the Government of Northern Nigeria allowed some few Christians in the Region to enjoy themselves according to the belief of their Religion, but building of hotels should be taken away from the Ibos and even if we find some Christians who are interested in building hotels and have no money to do so, the Government should aid them, instead of allowing Ibos to continue with the hotels."[34]

Dr. Iya Abubakar (Special Member: Lecturer, Ahmadu Bello University, Zaria):

534

"I am one of the strong believers in Nigerian Unity and I have hoped for our having a United Nigeria, but certainly if the present trend of affairs continues, then I hope the Government will investigate first the desirability and secondly the possibility of extending Northernization policy to the petty traders (Applause)."[35]

Mallam Ibrahim Muse (Representative of Igala North-West):

"Mr. Chairman, Sir, well, first and foremost, what I have to say before this honourable House is that we should send a delegate to meet our honourable Premier to move a Motion in this very Budget Session that all Ibos working in the Civil Service of Northern Nigeria, including the Native Authorities, whether they are contractors, or not, should be repatriated at once."[36]

Mallam Bashari Umaru:

"There should be no contracts either from the Government, Native Authorities, or private enterprises given to Ibo Contractors. (Government Bench: 'Good talk' and shouts of 'Fire southerners'). Again, Mr. Chairman, the Foreign Firms too should be given time limit to replace all Ibos in their firms by some other people."[37]

Alhaji Usman Liman (Representative of Sarkin Musawa):

"What brought the Ibos into this Region? They were here since the Colonial days. Had it not been for the Colonial Rule there would hardly have been any Ibo in this Region. Now that there is no Colonial Rule the Ibos should go back to their Region. There should be no hesitation about this matter. Mr. Chairman, North is for

Northerners, East for Easterners, West for Westerners, and the Federation for us all (Applause)."[38]

The Minister of Land and Survey, Alhaji The Honourable Ibrahim Musa Gashash, O.B.E.:

"Mr. Chairman, Sir, I do not like to take up much of the time of this House in making explanations, but I would like to assure Members that having heard their demands about Ibos holding land in Northern Nigeria, my Ministry will do all it can to see that the demands of (the) members are met. How to do this, when to do it, all this should not be disclosed. In due course, you will see what will happen (Applause)."[39]

This hostility exploded into violence almost exactly two years later against the Igbos who had settled in Northern Nigeria. Most of them had lived there for decades.

And almost exactly 30 years later, the same thing happened in the Coast Province of Kenya against the people who came from the interior; and in Zaire (now the Democratic Republic of Congo) in 1993 when President Mobutu Sese Seko employed the same tactic against his opponents, igniting tribal violence which led to the massacre of thousands of people from Kasai Province who had settled in Shaba Province (formerly Katanga Province).

They also had lived there for decades. And their home province, Kasai, was also the home region of Mobutu's most powerful and influential rival, Etienne Tshisekedi.

Like the Igbos in Northern Nigeria, and the Kikuyu, the Luo, the Luhya, the Kamba and members of other tribes from inland who had settled in Kenya's Coast Province, the people from Kasai Province were also expelled *en masse* from Shaba Province.

And in all these cases, murder was the primary weapon

used to facilitate the expulsion of these "outsiders" and "invaders."

Kenyan newspapers were quick to report the violence in the Coast Province and stated that the attacks in that region appeared to be similar to those which took place in the Rift Valley Province before and after the general election in 1992.

There was unmistakable evidence of ethnic hostility which ignited and fuelled the violence. At least 1,500 Kikuyus and members of other tribes – but mostly Kikuyus – who had settled in the Rift Valley Province were killed. Their property was also destroyed. As Gibson Kuria, a renowned human rights lawyer who was active in the movement for constitutional reforms, stated:

"This looks too much like 1992. The violence is aimed at certain ethnic communities, the government response has been lukewarm, and the violence we're seeing has had the same kind of brutality."[40]

When the attacks were launched, no one knew what the outcome would be. There were tens of thousands of Kikuyus, Luos, Kambas, Merus, Luhyas and members of other inland tribes who had lived in the Coast Province for decades and knew no other place as home. They were well-established in the region and no one would have expected them to pack up and leave just like that. And it seemed that the majority of them were going to stay. But that is not what happened in many cases.

Marauding gangs of between 200 and 500 indigenous people, native to the Coast, attacked these "foreigners" and "invaders" indiscriminately, determined to force them to go back where they came from. And they succeeded in driving them out of many areas.

They used all kinds of weapons including guns, clubs with nails, machetes, and bows and arrows. They also used arson as a major weapon. According to the *International*

Herald Tribune:

"They burned homes and businesses and hacked off people's limbs....Signs of tension are everywhere. Trucks bounce along, stuffed with fleeing families' belongings (going back upcountry)."[41]

The government denied involvement but there was incontrovertible evidence showing that it was indeed behind the violence.

In fact, some of the irrefutable evidence came from the government itself and its ruling party officials based on what they said in public on different occasions before this politically motivated ethnic violence – fuelled by xenophobia – erupted. Even the police, to fool and impress the public, arrested one KANU activist involved in the violence – yet did nothing to stop it:

"Thus far, police have arrested at least one KANU activist in connection with the unrest....

In recent months several ruling party politicians have exhorted indigenous Mombasans to force outside groups back up country."[42]

The fears opponents of Moi's regime had expressed were now justified. They accused the ruling party, KANU, of using violence to consolidate the president's position just before the general election and burnish his image in the Coast Province by expelling from the region members of ethnic groups such as the Kikuyu and Luo opposed to his tribalistic and autocratic rule. As Richard Leakey, a Kenyan of British origin born in Kenya who was one of Moi's most vocal critics, bluntly stated:

"There is no doubt that there is a political agenda in scaring the hell out of the upcountry people."[43]

The Luo and the Kikuyu, who are main rivals, have also clashed at different times during Kenya's turbulent post-colonial history. They are the dominant groups in the country and have been rivals for decades since the sixties when they first dominated Kenyan politics.

When Tom Mboya, a prominent politician who was a Luo and who was considered to be Jomo Keyatta's heir apparent, was assassinated in July 1969, the Luo directed their wrath against the Kikuyu. Mboya's assassination was seen by many Luos and others as an effort by the Kikuyu to prevent a Luo from becoming the president of Kenya. He was said to have been killed by the Kiambu Mafia composed of Kenyatta himself and other Kikuyu leaders including cabinet members from Kiambu, Kenyatta's home district.

Another prominent Luo, Oginga Odinga, who once served as vice president under Jomo Kenyatta, had his political career ruined by Kenyatta who even detained him without trial. He differed with Kenyatta politically and resigned as vice president in 1966. He formed an opposition party in the same year and was arrested in 1969 following disturbances in the town of Kisumu, a Luo stronghold and Odinga's operational base in western Kenya, where President Kenyatta was almost killed by a mob of angry Luo men and women who blamed him for Mboya's assassination in July. Oginga Odinga was detained for two years after his arrest. The Kenyan authorities blamed him for the disturbances.

In fact, it was Oginga Odinga who was the most prominent African leader in Kenya during the struggle for independence when Kenyatta was in prison and even led the Kenyan delegation to the constitutional talks in London on the transfer of power from the colonial rulers to Africans. He also spearheaded the campaign to release Kenyatta from prison and would have become Kenya's first president had he wanted to. Some people encouraged him to seek the presidency and sideline Kenyatta but he refused to do so. Instead, he stepped aside to let Kenyatta lead Kenya to independence after Kenyatta was released. But only a few years after independence, Kenyatta undermined Odinga and went on to favour his fellow tribesmen, the Kikuyu, who became the dominant group in the government.

Relations between the Luo and the Kikuyu got worse after that. And inter-ethnic warfare between them remains a strong possibility as they continue to compete for power on the basis of ethnic loyalties, including mobilising support from their ethnic and regional allies with whom they can share power.

When Vice President Daniel arap Moi, a Kalenjin from the Rift Valley Province, succeeded Kenyatta in 1978 following Kenyatta's death, it was his fellow tribesmen who became the most powerful leaders in the country. They came to be known as the Kalenjin Mafia and went on to marginalise the Kikuyu and the Luo as well as other groups, thus fuelling tribal sentiments, and as Moi went on exploit ethnic rivalries to consolidate his political base, a tactic typical of most leaders across the continent who have not yet transcended ethnic loyalties for the sake of national unity.

Here are other examples:

In Uganda, rivalries and conflicts have assumed ethno-regional dimensions since the sixties, especially between the north and the south, and between Nilotic tribes in the north and Bantu tribes in the south.

In Guinea, the Fula (or Fulani) and other groups have complained about discrimination by the Mandinka, especially when Sekou Toure, a Mandinka, led Guinea for 26 years since independence in 1958 – until his death in 1984. He was a great-grandson of the legendary Samori Toure who resisted French colonisation of West Africa for about 16 years until he was captured in 1898 and sent into exile in Gabon where he died two years later in 1900.

In spite of their large numbers, the Fula feel they have

been marginalised. No Fula has ever served as president of Guinea.

In Togo, members of the Kabye tribe have dominated the country since Gnassingbé Eyadéma (formerly Étienne Eyadéma) became president after seizing power in a military coup in 1967.

In Malawi under Dr. Hastings Kamuzu Banda, members of his tribe, the Chewa, dominated the country.

In most cases, members of the tribes which have produced presidents and other national leaders are the biggest beneficiaries, as those who have been left out continue to demand their share of the national cake usually through violence since there are no other ways for them to get what they are entitled to. And that is a continental phenomenon.

Opportunity in almost all countries across the continent is virtually synonymous with ethnicity. The result is conflict among ethnic groups most of which are on the periphery of the mainstream because of discrimination by the members of the tribes which are in control of the country or many areas of national life.

None of those conflicts can be resolved without providing equal opportunity to all. The alternative is to grant autonomous status to different groups so that they can control their own areas including resources on the basis of a formula that enables them to get a fair share of the resources while at the same time contributing to the national economy.

Autonomy in their home districts and regions or provinces must also be in well-defined areas such as local government, police control, taxation, revenue allocation, the judiciary, health and education.

The national government should exercise power only in areas which affect the whole country including enforcing the right of all citizens to live anywhere they want to live, not just in their home districts and provinces or regions.

None of these groups can work together, as a nation, to achieve unity and progress unless their concerns are addressed. And in most cases, they do have legitimate grievances.

There is no better way to address their grievances than to allow them maximum local expression through their own institutions without any interference by the national leaders in some distant capital who hardly know anything about local circumstances, problems, interests and needs. How such self-determination is achieved will depend on the history and circumstances – and demographic composition – of each country.

In Africa itself, there are examples of political entities – during precolonial times – in which the people made decisions on what to do with their lives, in their own communities, without interference by the "national" leaders. Power was decentralised. For example, in what is Ghana today, there was the Ashanti confederation formed in the 17th century. It was one of the most powerful on the continent and fought the British in one of the most bitter conflicts in the history of colonial Africa.

There was also the Fanti confederation. The Fanti, who are members of the Akan stock like the Ashanti, formed the confederation in the early 1700s primarily as a means of protection against Ashanti invasions but also, like the Ashanti, to allow a maximum degree of independence for component units of the union. It was, like the Ashanti confederation, one of the most well-known and most successful confederations in precolonial and colonial Africa.

The existence of these powerful confederacies in Ghana (even before it became a British colony known as the Gold Coast), as well as in other parts of Africa such as Zimbabwe and Congo, shows that Africans in different parts of the continent were able to forge unity in diversity, maintained the territorial integrity of their nations, and enjoyed maximum self-rule until colonial rulers came and imposed on them alien institutions which evolved into the highly centralised modern African state that we know today and which is notorious for its instinctive aversion to democracy and devolution of power.

African countries can do better than what they are doing now if they do one thing: return to roots for better governance. If they are ashamed of their traditional institutions (which can be modified to conform to modern realities) because they think these social and political structures are "primitive," then they should look elsewhere, for example, Switzerland, for inspiration; only to find out that "what you are trying to learn from others is already within you."

Even the political systems inherited from colonial rulers can be restructured to satisfy the demands of the people, maintain stable political entities, and provide an environment in which freedom – as perceived by the leaders – is no longer seen as a threat to national unity, peace and stability.

Look at the United Kingdom which had colonies in Africa. It has embraced devolution, prompted by Scottish nationalism and by a resurgence of the Welsh language and culture which has fostered a strong national identity among the Welsh.

In 1999, with strong support from Britain's prime minister, Tony Blair, Wales opened the Welsh National Assembly, the first real self-government Wales has had in more than 600 years. And in the same year, the people of Scotland elected their first separate parliament in 300 years.

Yet, such devolution of power by the British government has not led to the disintegration of the United Kingdom.

The Scottish National Party (SNP) wants full independence. But it does not have majority support among the voters in Scotland. Even some of the most ardent micro-nationalists remain loyal to the larger nation of which they are an integral part and resolutely oppose secession. Yet when denied autonomy, they can become some of the most rabid secessionists. Respect their identity, you have patriots on your side who can also serve as a catalyst in the pursuit of a larger union on a supranational scale. Welsh writer, Bobi Jones, made some pertinent remarks on the subject of devolution when he talked about Celtic resurgence:

"The 'Celtic resurgence'...is part of a worldwide phenomenon. It belongs to the whole anti-colonial movement. Wherever there has been 'empire,' there has been...an attempt to win freedom....

The pattern, as I see it, is what we would call 'diversity within unity.' The unity in this equation is now becoming wider – for us, Europe is becoming more and more significant. As Europe becomes more important as a unit – both political and economic – the smaller units, too, are becoming more important.

So you have this 'diversity' increasing and becoming politically more essential. At the same time, people are forfeiting some of their personal power. It's already happening, but in a new way. Europe unconsciously encourages Welsh people to look over the head of London. For Wales that's a good thing, because it's always been a bad thing for us to be centrally directed from London.

Since the 16th century, the center of gravity – the center of economic, political, cultural and linguistic gravity – has been outside Wales. Wales has played toward the center, to a point outside of itself. That has been where the heart of things has been, anyway. Our blood leaks toward the center. Our population has gone in that direction. Our economy, too, has shifted; our unemployment is always worse than at the center. The energies of production, of some cultural riches, drift that way.

Wherever you have centralization, you tend to have uniformity. Whenever you have movement toward revival or resurrection, there's a different kind of energy going on – toward more fruitfulness or variety."[44]

In the African context, Nigeria provides one good example where the leaders attempted to accommodate conflicting interests of different ethnic and regional groups by trying to restructure the federation.

One of the country's main leaders, Chief Obafemi Awolowo, came up with some ideas to decentralise power, maintain national unity and stability and protect the interests of minority groups in Africa's giant federation dominated by three ethnic groups: the Hausa-Fulani in the north, the Igbo in the east, and the Yoruba in the West. In 1947, Awolowo, a Yoruba from Western Nigeria, proposed in his book, *Path to Nigerian Freedom*,[45] that the country should be divided into 40 states, with cultural and linguistic affinity as the basis of division.

Nigeria was then a federation of three massive regions – North, East and West – formed in August 1946 by the British colonial government and remained so until 5 May 1967 when the country was divided into 12 states not long before the outbreak of the civil war (2 July 1967 – 15 January 1970) which was triggered by the declaration of independence for the Eastern Region as the Republic of Biafra on 30 May 1967. The federation also included the smaller Mid-West Region carved out of the Western Region in 1963. The Mid-West was mostly composed of the Edo who wanted their own region separate from the Western Region dominated by the Yoruba. After the Mid-West was carved out, the federation was restructured again a few years later in April 1967:

"A communique issued after the meeting of the (ruling) Supreme Military Council on April 22nd, stated that it had adopted a political and administrative 'programme of action' for preserving the Federation of Nigeria as one country. The main items in the approved programme, according to the communique, included: 'creation of States as the basis of political stability in Nigeria.'"[46]

Long before then, the division of Nigeria was also suggested along similar lines (as Awolowo's) by the National Council of Nigeria and the Cameroons (NCNC) – renamed in 1960 the National Council of Nigerian Citizens (NCNC) – led by Nnamdi Azikiwe, an Igbo from Eastern Nigeria, who became Nigeria's first president when the country won independence on 1 October 1960; he first served as governor-general (1960 - 1963) before becoming president (1963 – 1966).

The party issued a Freedom Charter in 1948 advocating a federal form of government with the new states based on ethnic and linguistic affinity. Earlier, Azikiwe advocated in his book, *The Political Blueprint of Nigeria*[47] published in 1943, a federal form of government and the division of the federation into eight states.

Then in 1953, Awolowo proposed the division of Nigeria into nine states. In 1959, his party, the Action Group, called for the creation of more states. And everywhere across the country, minority groups demanded their own states as a safeguard against domination by the three major groups – the Hausa-Fulani, the Igbo and the Yoruba – who dominated the three massive regions of the federation.

It was therefore clear from the beginning when the Nigerian federation was formed that creation of more states to protect minority groups was critical to national unity and stability.

In 1967, the federation was divided into 12 states. The number went up to 19, 21, 30, and finally to 36. But more states may be created in the future.

That is what other African countries, especially those wracked by ethnic conflicts – including Rwanda and Burundi despite their identity primarily as biethnic states of Hutus and Tutsis, with a small minority of the Twa who constitute about 1% of the population – need to do to resolve these conflicts and maintain national unity and stability.

Create more states or provinces and grant maximum self-rule to disgruntled and oppressed groups. Otherwise expect perpetual conflict and even disintegration of these countries into non-viable entities dominated by warlords, looters, smugglers, kidnappers, rapists and cold-blooded murderers as happened in Somalia, Sierra Leone and Liberia where bandits treated these failed states as their personal fiefdoms.

The key to conflict resolution in Africa is consensus building by different ethnic groups and political parties as well as other interest groups including regional alliances in order to form governments which allow extensive devolution of power.

Besides granting extensive autonomy to ethnoregional groups – while maintaining a strong national government for the sake of national unity in spite of such diversity – much smaller and weaker groups such as the Twa in Rwanda and Burundi and the Mbuti in neighbouring Congo, collectively known as Pygmies, need extra protection from larger groups. Other groups which need such protection and access to the political process as well as inclusion in the government include the San and the Khoikhoi (so-called Bushmen) in the countries of southern Africa especially in Botswana and Namibia where they are on the periphery of the mainstream.

Almost none of the African countries across the continent provide this kind of protection, let alone extra-protection, for smaller and weaker minorities.

Multiethnic India is one of the countries which has this kind of guarantee of group rights for its weaker citizens embodied in the law, although, frankly speaking, her performance has been less than stellar with regard to the untouchables.

But a constitutional guarantee is necessary. It is a vital

step towards equality for oppressed minorities. Without such a guarantee, they may never be able to win their rights in many areas if they try to go through conventional channels whose authority for such preferential treatment is derived from a constitutional text. Without such constitutional authority, the government can not legitimately claim to have the mandate to formulate and implement such a policy unless laws are passed to justify preferential treatment as happened in the United States where affirmative action is upheld by federal laws and regulations and by the courts.

In India, the constitution forbids the practice of "untouchability," and legislation has been used to reserve quotas for former untouchables – and also for tribal peoples – in the legislatures, education, and in public services. But the caste system remains a fact of life, as it has been for centuries, although somewhat eroded nowadays. In Africa, it has a rough but functional equivalence to tribalism – and to racism in the United States especially before the civil rights movement and the civil rights laws which were passed in the sixties to guarantee racial equality – especially in Rwanda and Burundi where the Tutsi aristocracy would be analogous to the Brahmans and other Indians of the upper castes.

But the Indian caste system is much more rigid. For example, marriage outside the caste is prohibited, while the Hutu and the Tutsi have intermarried for so long, through the centuries, that it is sometimes very difficult to tell the difference between a Hutu and a Tutsi from physical features alone: you could be right or wrong 6 times out of 10, may be even more than that. Yet, there are some parallels between the Indians of the upper castes and the Tutsi, as underscored by this statement from Tutsi leaders:

"The relations between we (Batutsi) and they (Bahutu) have always until the present been based on servitude.

There is, therefore, between we and they no foundation for brotherhood....Since it was our kings who conquered the Bahutu country and killed their petty little kings and thus subjugated the Bahutu, how can they now pretend to be our brothers?"[48]

As things turned out, the Hutu did not even try to pretend to be their brothers during the 1994 Rwandan genocide. Yet, they continue to live together because they have to. They have no choice. They must share the land. And they must live under the same government. But they don't have to be denied maximum self-rule, preferably in their own ethnic enclaves, if they continue to kill each other and oppress one another.

And Rwanda (or Burundi) does not have to be a unitary state in order to remain united as one country, especially when the unitary state is used by one group to dominate others. It should be decentralised.

Decentralisation in Rwanda and Burundi will probably work best if power is shifted from the centre to the periphery – at the grassroots level in the villages – to create autonomous entities linked together in some kind of confederation as a safeguard against oppression of one ethnic group by the other if one group is dominant at the centre. This will also enable the people – both the Hutu and the Tutsi as well as the Twa, a tiny minority – to manage their own affairs without undue interference from their leaders whether local or national.

There are many other cases in different parts of the world where devolution of power has not led to national disintegration but has, instead, helped to foster and maintain national unity and stability.

Also, in Africa, each country has its own unifying institutions – even if they are intangible, such as common cultural values, language, and history – which can be used to forge and strengthen national ties in spite of the fact that Africans are divided along ethnic and regional lines. But a concerted effort can be made to institutionalise cultural values and other things shared by different ethnic groups across the nation and strengthen those institutions in order to use them as the basis for unity across ethnoregional lines.

One example is Kenya and Tanzania where language, Kiswahili, has served as a unifying factor. Extensive decentralisation along ethnoregional lines has not been used as the basis for unity and stability in those two countries, although it is valid in other contexts on the continent, probably even in Kenya, given the nation's history of ethnic rivalries.

In Tanzania during Nyerere's presidency, decentralisation was pursued along political lines, only coincidentally on ethnic basis for no other reason than that administrative boundaries in most districts and regions happen to coincide with ethnic identity, yet without assuming the attributes or character of ethnostates – political entities which may be necessary in some African countries to maintain national unity. For example, Ethiopia, a country of about 80 different ethnic groups, is a federation of provinces which are virtually ethnostates. Although autonomous only in theory since power is still concentrated at the centre, the provinces were created on ethnic basis as stipulated by the federal constitution – based on ethnic confederalism – which even allows them to secede.

This kind of federal structure was instituted in recognition of a people's right to self-determination, in fulfillment of a fundamental natural right of every people to rule themselves, and as a safeguard against domination and oppression by other groups. However, Ethiopia's national leaders have shown little tolerance for secessionist sentiments.

Nigeria is another country which also has, through the years since the civil war (1967 – 1970), gradually evolved towards a federation of ethnostates as a durable basis for national unity.

Congo, former Zaire, may follow the same path as the only way of saving the country form breaking up. And probably that is the only way it can be saved, if it's not already too late to do so.

There may never be one Congo again other than being an area that is frozen indefinitely as a patchwork of *de facto* independent states which may only be brought together as an organic whole under a federal system or even a confederation to replace the highly centralised state whose power is not even felt in many remote parts of this vast country – the size of Western Europe – which has the unenviable distinction of being the bleeding heart of Africa.

One of the biggest advantages of decentralisation, or devolution, is the freedom and inspiration people have in finding solutions to their own problems without interference by the central government.

The people become more energetic under a decentralised system of government. They become more engaged, more creative and more dynamic because there is no one telling them what to do and what not to do. They are free to use their own skills and talents without waiting for instructions from some bureaucrats usually hundreds of miles away in the nation's capital.

It is these bureaucrats and national leaders who impede progress. They stifle individual initiative by directing virtually everything from the centre, thus ruining lives which could have been more productive in a variety of ways had the people been left alone to come up with their own solutions to their own problems instead of those solutions being provided by the central government without even knowing they will be suited to local circumstances which only the local people know best. They are the ones who are in the best position to know what they want and what kind of solutions will work for them.

Bureaucracy not only stifles individual initiative; it stunts growth at the local and national levels across the spectrum. And it thrives best under centralisation or centralised systems of government which are usually under bad leadership because leaders have nothing to fear in terms of accountability. There is no one to hold them accountable for their actions because power is concentrated in their hands.

Africa has been plagued by bad leadership for decades. But the problems of poor governance and lack of accountability, which have institutionalised corruption that has become synonymous with Africa, are not going to be tackled without strong institutions, the most prominent being democratic institutions and an independent judiciary. Democratic institutions demand transparency.

However, these institutions can not be built, and they can not function, under a political system which enables a few individuals to monopolise power, concentrated in their hands for their own benefit, thus blocking change which will reduce their power and even force them out of office. The system which enables them to abuse power and perpetuate themselves in office, and which insulates them from accountability including prosecution for the crimes they commit – especially corruption and trampling on human rights – is fostered by the centralised state.

Once power is decentralised and spread out all the way down to the grassroots level, it will be very difficult and in many cases even impossible for leaders to abuse their power. Most of the power will be in the hands of the people, not in the hands of their leaders. It will enable the people to rule themselves.

Under a decentralised system, leaders are going to have less power; the system will enable the people to manage their own affairs; it will also make power less attractive to aspiring dictators and other unscrupulous elements seeking office.

Leaders are also going to be held accountable for their

actions because of transparency under a decentralised system, exposing wrongdoing, and punishing culprits, without fear of retribution from the leaders because they will no longer have the kind of power they had under a highly centralised state.

Africa can not even start to sort things out unless power is decentralised or devolved. That is because there is a need to get the people involved in sorting things out. But they can not get actively involved without having power in their hands. They can get it only under devolution or under a decentralised system of government.

That is one of the main issues, and one of the major challenges, Africa will have to address in the twentieth-first century in her quest for peace, stability and progress.

Even some of the strongest supporters of African unity who built their nations under highly centralised states which they justified on the grounds that African countries would break up along ethnic and regional lines if they did not have strong central governments support decentralisation or at least acknowledge its advantages. Although very few practise it, they see no contradiction between decentralisation and unity. As President Julius Nyerere of Tanzania stated in his work, *Decentralisation*:

"The purpose of both the *Arusha Declaration* and of *Mwongozo* was to give the people power over their own lives and their development....To the mass of the people, power is still something wielded by others....

The planning and control of development...must be exercised at the local level....Our nation is too large for the people at the centre in Dar es Salaam always to understand local problems or to sense their urgency. When all the power remains at the centre, therefore, local problems can remain, and fester, while local people who are aware of them are prevented from using their initiative in finding solutions. Similarly, it is sometimes difficult for local people to respond with enthusiasm to a call for development work which may be to their benefit, but which has been decided upon and planned by an authority hundreds of miles away....

We have to work out a system which gives more local freedom for both decision and action on matters which are primarily of local impact....The system must...reduce the amount of red tape and bureaucracy which is at present in danger of strangling our people's enthusiasm....(But) projects which are of national importance must remain under national control, even though they may be situated in one particular area – a decision which does not preclude greater delegation of authority to the responsible officers on the spot....

Regions and districts should plan and implement local development activities as well as administer local affairs with the very minimum of interference from Dar es Salaam. This will mean, for example, that a very large proportion of agricultural programmes will be made the direct responsibility of the Districts and Regions. Small industrial and commercial developments will be a local responsibility where these fall outside the programmes of...national parastatal organisations. Local roads, water supplies, health and primary education will also be dealt with at the local level....The Regions and Districts will be free to make their own decisions about priorities and methods of work....

We have to decentralise the control and decision-making now exercised from Dar es Salaam, and also centralise local control, decision-making and responsibility....

The present system of rural local government will be abolished, as will the present practice of each Ministry having its own officers working in Regions and Districts....The abolition of the present system of local government does not mean the abolition of local representation. On the contrary, the purpose of the new system is to increase the people's participation in decision-making, and it will therefore demand that the powers and responsibilities of local representatives are increased....

The new District Development Councils will be...responsible to the people for the use of the new powers at District level. It will be their job to lead the work of direct consultation with the people, so that this decentralisation really does result in the people themselves having a say in their own development and in their own affairs....One of the major purposes of this reorganisation is to ensure that future economic planning stems from the people and serves the people directly....

The transfer of power to the Regions and Districts must not also mean a transfer of a rigid and bureaucratic system from Dar es Salaam to the lower levels. Not is it the intention of these proposals to create new local tyrants in the persons of the Regional and District Development Directors....

Decentralisation...is based on the principle that more and more people must be trusted with responsibility – that is its whole purpose."[49]

No one would accuse President Nyerere of pursuing a policy – decentralisation – that would lead to the fragmentation of Tanzania or any other African country. His nationalist and Pan-African credentials were beyond dispute.

Decentralisation in Tanzania took place under a unitary state. Therefore, it is possible even for devolution – not just decentralisation – to take place under a strong central government which may still be good for the sake of national unity if African leaders make it more democratic instead of using it as an oppressive machinery as has been the case in most countries across the continent since independence.

Under devolution, regional governments and other component units of the state including local jurisdictions have the statutory power to make laws. Under decentralisation, such power remains at the centre – which is a unitary state – but is dispersed all the way to the grassroos level; for example, in Tanzania where there were ten-cell units each comprising ten households under its own leader.

Although the unitary system has many disadvantages, resulting mainly from abuse of power because power is concentrated in the hands of a few people at the centre, it also has its advantages which must be looked at in their proper historical context, especially in post-colonial Africa.

Therefore its benefits can not be ignored. Kwame Nkrumah used the unitary – centralised – state effectively in Ghana to contain separatist threats among the Ashanti in the central province, the Dagomba and others in the north (what was once known as the Northern Territories), and an irredentist movement among the Ewe in the Volta region in the east who wanted to unite with their kinsmen in neighbouring Togo. In Tanzania, Nyerere used it to build one of the most cohesive and most stable countries on the continent.

Unfortunately, most African leaders refuse to share power with their people and have tarnished the image of the centralised state even when it has proved to be useful in some cases. Hence the need for devolution.

Devolution of power can also be implemented in different ways depending on the circumstances of each country that is trying to pursue it. For example, African countries threatened by secession could grant non-sovereign independent status to restive regions and enable them to be freely associated with the national government as a way of satisfying disgruntled populations in those areas and neutralising separatist sentiments.

Equatorial Guinea could loosen its grip on the independence-prone island of Bioko, formerly known as Fernando Po, and even allow it to fly its own flag as a symbol of domestic sovereignty – short of international recognition – in addition to having its own government and its own president, premier or prime minister the way it has been done in Tanzania where Zanzibar has its own government, its own president and its own flag although subordinate to the union government of the United Republic of which Zanzibar remains an integral part.

The island nation of the Comoros can take the same approach towards resolving its conflict with the secessionist islands of Anjouan and Moheli; so can Senegal with regard to the separatist Casamance Province, and Namibia towards Caprivi Strip where separatists also want to establish their own independent state.

Cabinda Province which is separated from the rest of Angola by a strip of land which is a part of the Democratic Republic of Congo (DRC) is another major contender for full autonomy and domestic sovereignty for historical and geographical reasons as well, not just because of its unique identity as an ethnic and cultural entity.

Its demand for independence is one of the most stubborn cases on the continent because of strong separatist elements in the province.

But its quest for full sovereign status is also partly, if not largely, motivated by a desire to have full control of the region's resources instead of sharing them with the rest of Angola. Cabinda has some of the largest oil fields in the world. Most of Angola's oil revenues come from those oil fields. Cabinda is also rich in other resources. If the region did not have such abundant resources, the demand for independence would not have been as strong as it is now. It may not even have existed if Cabinda were a barren, desperately poor territory.

The secessionist movement in the province can be weakened or neutralised by granting extensive autonomy to the province, with a self-government that has all the attributes of sovereignty in all areas except defence, national security, foreign policy, immigration, monetary policy, and without international recognition as a sovereign state.

Besides its geography as a territory separate from the rest of Angola, which reinforces its unique identity, Cabinda's history also differs in some fundamental respects from the history of the rest of Angola in spite of the colonial ties which bind both as one colony once ruled by Portugal. But it is also a fact that Cabinda was once ruled separately by Portugal, as a protectorate, separate from the rest of Angola until it was later incorporated into the larger colony to create a single colonial entity.

Even the Berlin conference conceded the status of Cabinda as a separate territory, distinct from the rest of Angola which was known as Portuguese West Africa.

It was as if there were two distinct colonies in the region ruled by Portugal: Portuguese West Africa (Angola), and Portuguese Congo as Cabinda was known when it was a protectorate.

The Organisation of African Unity (OAU) itself once considered Cabinda to be a separate Portuguese colony, distinct from Angola. But it also refused to recognise the separatist movement in Cabinda, fearing that it would encourage secession in other countries on the continent.

So, Cabinda's history has reinforced the region's unique identity in a very significant way. And it has been one of the major factors fuelling the independence movement in the province. It can also be used by Cabindans to demand even more concessions - for greater autonomy - from the Angolan government, some of which should be granted, provided the people of the province also agree to remain an integral part of Angola – a concession, and a sacrifice, they should be prepared to make in order to win extensive autonomy from the central government in Luanda.

The fundamental aspiration among disgruntled groups, encompassing whole regions and tribes or ethnic groups – is the desire to rule themselves. They are disgruntled because they do not have the freedom to be what they are and to do what they want to do. They are also disgruntled because they are marginalised by the central government.

But even if they are not marginalised, they want to rule themselves because they have their own identities, aspirations and desires, and their own cultural values and traditions and traditional institutions which are not allowed to flourish or are deliberately suppressed by the highly centralised state which abhors unity in diversity and wants to mould the people into a monolithic whole under mass regimentation ostensibly for the sake of national unity. In many cases, the result is mass discontent and civil strife including civil wars.

The biggest fear among African governments is that if the demands of these groups are fulfilled, such a concession will have a domino effect and African countries are going to break up along ethnic and regional lines.

But both sides can have their wishes satisfied if they use dynamic compromise which entails acknowledging the legitimacy of both quests: separatist regions should be accorded "sovereign" status but without their own personality as full-fledged independent states in the international arena. They must remain within their present national boundaries as a part of the compromise with the countries from which they want to separate. Such an offer by national governments confronted with separatist threats will help to ward off secession and placate even some of the most uncompromising secessionists.

Separatist regions should also be allowed to fly their own flags, have their own anthems, and celebrate their own holidays – along with those of the larger nation of which they remain an integral part. They should have their own governments responsible for all aspects of administration within their regional boundaries – without any interference, none whatsoever, from the central government unless there is anarchy and violence which the region's security forces can not handle, or if they want to secede.

Each separatist region should also have its own constitution, its own regional parliament and local assemblies.

Those are usually the basic demands separatists expect to fulfill if they secede. They are also the basic demands of practically every government in the world; they are the attributes of national sovereignty. Once these demands are met in restive regions, the secessionist movement in those areas will be robbed of its momentum.

The only thing that disgruntled ethnoregions – such as Cabinda in Angola, Casamance in Senegal, Bioko Island in Equatorial Guinea, and Caprivi Strip in Namibia, all of which want to secede – will not have is an international personality of their own and recognition as independent nations. But most of their basic demands will have been fulfilled under this compromise formula. Not only will secessionist movements in those regions lose momentum; they will also lose their legitimacy and appeal among many – if not among the majority – of their supporters who may see the leaders of these movements as sheer opportunists and power-hungry individuals if they continue to demand secession after the national government has acceded to their basic demands as outlined above.

Once such a compromise formula is applied, African countries will no longer have to worry about splitting along ethnoregional lines, one of the main reasons most African leaders refuse to grant autonomy to the regions, besides their inordinate ambition for power.

But if African leaders really want to save their countries from degenerating into chaos and anarchy and from disintegrating into tribal independent states, they must be willing to share power and make major concessions to the regions agitating for independence, along the lines of the compromise formula outlined here. Denying them maximum self-rule will not solve the problem; it will only inflame passions among the people in the restive regions and fuel secessionist sentiments. And what African leaders have always feared – national disintegration – will become a self-fulfilling prophecy.

One of the most troubled countries which can benefit from such devolution of power through shared sovereignty – the nation sharing sovereignty with the regions – is Rwanda whose northwestern provinces of Gisenyi and Ruhengenri constitute traditionally Hutu strongholds which have never been totally subdued by the Tutsi rulers throughout the country's history.

Maximum self-rule for regions and ethnic enclaves in Rwanda will achieve several things:

It will ease ethnic tensions. It will ventilate grievances of individual citizens and ethnic groups who feel that they are dominated and oppressed by the central government which is controlled by the members of one ethnic group.

Maximum self-rule will guarantee justice and equality for all – Hutu, Tutsi, Twa, and others. It will help to promote peace and stability and maintain national unity.

It will encourage productivity by removing government control which stifles individual initiative and robs the people of the incentive to work.

It will also maximise performance in all areas and foster regional cooperation at the macronational level (East-central African), with the border districts and provinces of Rwanda bordering Congo, Uganda, Burundi and Tanzania functioning as vital links to these neighbouring countries once they are allowed to trade freely and even integrate their economies with them.

No restrictions should be imposed on currency flow across borders even if this creates havoc for weaker economies. It will be a blessing in disguise since a neighbouring country with a weaker currency and economy will be forced to be more competitive, hence more productive, and will be forced to devalue its inflated currency. The countries involved will also be encouraged by potential benefits of regional integration and will be

561

compelled by need to institute a common currency.

What is proposed here for Rwanda should also be applied to Burundi, the two being twin states in terms of history and ethnic composition.

Extensive decentralisation will save many African countries from economic ruin, political chaos and anarchy and from disintegration – restive regions which have been denied autonomy opt for secession.

In the case of Rwanda and Burundi, already embroiled in conflict, the alternative to devolution of power is chronic instability – and civil war neither the Hutu nor the Tutsi can win, in absolute terms, although odds are in favour of the Hutu after a long war of attrition because of their superiority in numbers.

If the two countries can not end wars within their borders, then the international community should help to implement a radical solution to this perennial conflict between the Hutu and the Tutsi. The solution entails the partition of both Rwanda and Burundi into Hutuland and Tutsiland, but only if the people of both countries agree to do so in an internationally supervised referendum.

The partition will inevitably involve massive relocation of populations to create viable, independent ethnostates which will become safe havens for the members of their ethnic groups and which may even be compelled by economic needs and political circumstances to form a confederation in spite of the hostility between the two.

Otherwise the Hutu and the Tutsi will be locked in perpetual conflict. The rest of the world can't do anything about it if the people who are fighting don't want to stop fighting. Peace is possible only if the people involved in conflict want peace.

The goal should be peace at any price even if it means separation of the two groups – unless they accept war as a better alternative.

The conflict in Rwanda and Burundi, a microcosm of a tragic continental phenomenon, is but one aspect of what

Africa has failed to be, an entire generation after independence. The African continent has not done much to end its wars and solve other problems which have turned Africans into international beggars – not only begging for food but also for help to end their conflicts and even to maintain peace in conflict zones. And prospects are bleak the world's poorest yet richest continent will do better in the future after decades of rotten leadership, oppression, institutional decay and economic ruin unless the modern African state is restructured to reflect African realities and to make it responsive to the needs and aspirations of the people; a process that entails a complete overhaul of the system in most parts of the continent in order to replace it with a better one through creative destruction. Nothing short of revolution is going to change Africa and improve her condition.

Therefore, there may be some prospects, however dim, even in some of the most hopeless cases. And there are examples to vindicate this position.

Out of the ashes of Somalia, a wasteland, emerged a stable Somaliland which separated from the rest of the country and went on to become a viable state although no country has recognised it as a legal sovereign entity. But it has continued to function as a *de facto* state (so has its neighbour, Puntland, another stable enclave in northern Somalia) and is in better shape than the rest of Somali which has been ravaged by war. In fact, Somaliland is governed far better than many African countries are. They are failed states. Yet they enjoy international recognition. Why shouldn't Somaliland be accorded the same status? It deserves full recognition as a legal sovereign entity.

There are other examples. After being battered by war for years, Liberia and Sierra Leone returned to peace, staggering, and may even slide back into anarchy, especially in the case of Sierra Leone, a country that enjoyed only intermittent peace until the the former colonial power, Great Britain, intervened.

But they, at least, tried to end their conflicts with the help of the international community although it was not enough and it came too late in the case of Sierra Leone. It was not until 2000 that the United Nations intervened in Sierra Leone on a somewhat significant scale, almost 10 years after the war started in that country.

In the case of Liberia, the country showed that in spite of several failures during the course of its conflict, peace could be achieved. Out of the ruins of this old republic emerged a stable nation, although under a brutal despot, former warlord Charles Taylor who terrorised his fellow countrymen into voting for him to be president. They feared that if they did not elect him, he would go back to the bush and plunge the country into another civil war and shoot his way into office as he tried to do earlier until he was blocked by the Nigerian-led West African peacekeeping forces (ECOMOG) from seizing power. He wanted to rule without electoral mandate.

Durable and just peace in Africa is possible but not through intimidation. It can be achieved and sustained only when African countries adopt a system of power sharing to allay fears among different groups – especially ethnic groups, and not just political parties – which feel, and in most cases rightly so, that they have been deliberately excluded from meaningful participation in the political process and representation in the government. And that means the winner-take-all system, an alien institution brought to Africa by Europeans and based on Western political traditions, must be abolished.

Losers in elections should, together with the winners, form a coalition government to rule by consensus; an accommodation and reconciliation of conflicting views that has been the hallmark of African traditional institutions of governance.

It is a travesty of justice and a mockery of true representative government to claim that only the party that wins the election is entitled to rule because it has the mandate from the electorate to do so. Which electorate?

What about those who did not vote for it but instead voted for the candidates of the other party or parties? Are they not part of the electorate? If they are, why are they excluded from the government of their country?

If the winning party has the right to form a government whose legitimacy is derived from the consent of the governed, it has the right to govern only those who voted for it since it is they who have given it such consent. The other voters have given the other party or parties the mandate to govern them and implement their policies.

A party that wins only 48% - 50% or even 55% - 60% of the votes does not have the right to have 100% of the power to rule the country, excluding the 50% - 52% or 40% - 45% who did not vote for it and who do not support its policies. That is discriminatory and divisive especially in African countries where exclusion of some groups from power is a way of life.

Yet almost all African governments derive their legitimacy from such politics of exclusion while claiming to represent all the people.

Only rule by consensus, which mandates inclusion of all groups, can guarantee fair representation, justice and equality for all.

In addition to power sharing and rule by consensus typical of traditional Africa, there is also an imperative need to reduce the power of the central government. Le the people decide for themselves. They know what they want.

Extensive devolution of power will enable the people not only to release their creative potential; it will enable them to solve their own problems and incorporate into the modern political system an array of traditional institutions and values which served Africa well for centuries before the advent of colonial rule which led to the imposition of alien institutions on the continent, wreaking havoc.

In many cases, imperial rule distorted and destroyed traditional institutions without which African societies could not have survived and functioned as viable entities in precolonial times. It is these same institutions, values and traditions which can help Africa to survive and thrive without rejecting all aspects of modern life in this global village.

Africa needs to reclaim her past. Africa must also recognise the enormous potential of her people, the vast majority of whom still live in traditional societies across the continent. But their potential can not be fully harnessed if they remain powerless. Power in African countries must be shared all the way down to the grassroots level instead of being concentrated in the hands of a few people at the top.

That is one of the challenges Africa faces in the twentieth-first century: to let the people determine their own destiny without interference by anybody, especially national leaders, most of whom oppress and exploit their own people and even collude with foreign interests to plunder the continent.

If the people start to have control over their lives and make decisions which affect them instead of being told what to do; if the leaders are held accountable for their actions including well-meaning incompetence; and if the people start to control their resources which are being ruthlessly exploited by unscrupulous elements in power together with external forces, then there is hope for Africa. Otherwise, all talk of an African renaissance is no more than empty rhetoric.

But enabling the people to have power – the power to make decisions for themselves and even to rule themselves – does not mean they are being encouraged to break up their countries and establish their own independent states.

The future of African lies *not* in secession but in regional integration and in the creation of federations or confederations, especially federations with strong federal institutions to achieve and maintain unity in diversity, and stability.

Formation of such large political units will inevitably lead to the abolition of national borders as we know them today. And the map of Africa will have to be redrawn to reflect the changes.

We may need our own Berlin conference not only to legitimise new borders resulting from unification but also from disintegration of some countries where entire populations of particular groups may be justified to have their own independent states. Again, Somaliland stands out as a classic example of such a group of people in this contetx.

Therefore, in some parts of the continent, the reconfiguration may result from secession. But the focus should be on the creation of larger political entities or macronations.

However, there are extreme – but very few – cases which may justify secession; the secession of South Sudan being a prime example. Another example is Eritrea when the people of that country voted for separation from Ethiopia although even before then, Eritrea, a former Italian colony, was a separate territorial entity forcibly incorporated into Ethiopia.

Western Sahara is another territorial entity which has a legitimate claim to independence denied by Morocco which has forcibly annexed the territory.

And where anarchy is endemic as in the case of Somalia, the breakaway region of Somaliland which has been able to function as a stable and prosperous *de facto* state – and whose boundaries are the same the territory had when it was a colonial entity known as British Somaliland – such a region may be a strong candidate for recognition although African countries and the rest of the international community have refused to recognise Somaliland as an independent state.

Another extreme case was the secession of the predominantly Igbo Eastern Region of Nigeria which declared independence as the Republic of Biafra. It was recognised by four African countries: Tanzania, Zambia, Ivory Coast and Gabon. It was also recognised by Haiti. Another country that came close to recognising Biafra was Uganda under the leadership of President Milton Obote. But Obote did not do so because he hosted peace talks in Uganda's capital Kampala between the Nigerian federal government and the secessionist leaders.

Ghanaian military head of state, Lieutenant-General Joseph Ankrah, was also sympathetic towards Biafra and reluctantly supported Federal Nigeria before and after his country hosted peace talks between the two sides.

President Habib Bourguiba of Tunisia also said he understood the position of the countries which recognised Biafra as "a protest against massacre."

Sierra Leone, Dahomey, Senegal, Rwanda and Burundi were also very sympathetic towards Biafra and acknowledged the merits of its cause although they did not formally recognise the secessionist region.

Fortunately, Africa has not had many cases which have justified secession. The few cited above are extreme, and justified, unlike the secession of Katanga Province in the former Belgian Congo which was externally engineered.

The rest of the secessionist movements or threats on the continent – there are hardly any credible ones in terms of legitimacy and military power – can be contained and neutralised by extensive devolution of power to let the people in restive or secessionist regions manage their own affairs as autonomous entities.

Highly centralised states which are in most cases intolerant of dissent, suffocate the opposition, and even discourage cross-fertilisation of ideas – however potentially fruitful – have been a major source of instability in many countries across the continent. And they have contributed to retarded growth across the spectrum precisely because they don't allow robust, vigorous debate and local input and discourage the people from finding solutions to their own problems, solutions suited to local circumstances.

Extensive devolution or decentralisation will not only contribute to growth and development but to peace and stability, all of which have been elusive in many countries across the continent since independence. Without peace and stability, any kind of progress, including regional integration, is impossible.

Already, there are regions with great potential for integration. In East Africa, the countries of Kenya, Uganda and Tanzania have been close for many years, culturally and historically including their shared colonial experience of being ruled by Britain. Rwanda and Burundi have historical and cultural ties to Tanzania and Uganda and even constituted one colony together with Tanganyika (now mainland Tanzania) known as Deutsch-Ostafrika – German East Africa – ruled by Germany.

Neighbouring Congo, once ruled by Belgium, has political, cultural and historical ties to East Africa, especially Tanzania, more than it does to its other neighbours such as the Central African Republic.

Swahili, Tanzania's national language also spoken in Kenya, Uganda, Rwanda and Burundi, is the *lingua franca* of the entire eastern Congo. It is also widely spoken in the southern part of Congo, in Katanga Province, and even as far west as the capital Kinshasa and elsewhere in the country. And Congolese music is as popular in Tanzania as it is in Congo itself, and to a smaller degree in Kenya, Uganda, Rwanda and Burundi.

With all those ties, Congo has the attributes to become an integral part of a large federation composed of Kenya, Uganda, Tanzania, Rwanda and Burundi.

Cong's ties to East Africa are also enhanced by the fact that during colonial rule, the country was ruled by the same colonial masters who ruled Rwanda and Burundi, what was then a single territory known as Ruanda-Urundi. And its capital Leopoldville (now Kinshasa) was also the colonial capital of Ruanda-Urundi.

The Belgian colonial rulers ruled Ruanda-Urundi from Leopoldville, far away, because they considered the territory to be a minor colonial possession unlike Congo.

Before then, Rwanda-Urundi was ruled by Germany. Before the Germans lost the territory in World War I, they also considered Ruanda-Urundi to be a minor possession and made it an integral part of Tanganyika.

Another region which has great potential for unification is what was once known as the Central African Federation or the Federation of Rhodesia and Nyasaland which broke up into what are now the countries of Zambia (formerly Northern Rhodesia), Zimbabwe (the former Southern Rhodesia), and Malawi (formely Nyasaland). The three countries have many political, cultural and historical ties and could form a strong federation.

The dissolution of the federation in 1963 was even opposed by President Milton Obote of Uganda who argued that had the federation survived and emerged from colonial rule as a single political entity under one leadership, it would have had the potential to become a strong nation and would have been a step towards African unity and continental unification.

In East Africa during British colonial rule, African leaders in Kenya, Uganda and Tanganyika were resolutely opposed to formation of an East African federation by the colonialists.

They argued that if such a federation were formed, it would, together with the federation of Rhodesia and Nyasaland, and apartheid South Africa, have constituted a vast belt of white-ruled territory – from Kenya, Uganda and Tanganyika all the way down to the Cape – which would have helped to consolidate and perpetuate white rule and domination on the continent.

In his book *Towards A Pax Africana: A Study of Ideology and Ambition*,[50] Professor Ali Mazrui states that Obote was the only African leader who was opposed to the dissolution of the Federation of Rhodesia and Nyasaland because he felt that dissolving the federation was a step backwards in the quest for continental unity.

But there is still great potential for its revival, only in a different form as a vehicle for regional integration and continental unification instead of being an instrument of racial domination as it once was during British colonial rule.

Farther south, colonial ties could also facilitate formation of a federation comprising Botswana (once known as Bechuanaland during British colonial rule), Swaziland, Lesotho (known Basutoland when it was under the British) and South Africa.

Namibia, formerly known as South West Africa and once ruled by apartheid South Africa, could join the federation, as would Mozambique.

The people of all those countries also have had extensive historical, cultural and political ties for a long time as is the case with the people of the former Federation of Rhodesia and Nyasaland and of East Africa.

In the western part of the continent, there is also great potential for formation of a West African federation or smaller federations; for example, a federation of the countries of the Mano River Basin: Guinea, Sierra Leone and Liberia.

Ivory Coast can also join the federation whose nucleus is the Mano River Union, an association for economic cooperation formed by Liberia and Sierra Leone in 1973. Guinea joined the union in 1980.

The people of the four countries have extensive historical, ethno-cultural and linguistic ties predating colonialism.

The confederation of Senegal and The Gambia, known as Senegambia, can be revived. It was formed in 1982 and collapsed in 1989. The people of the two countries are the same in terms of historical, cultural, ethnic and linguistic ties.

Those are only a few examples of possible federations

on the continent. Anything short of that will be a tragedy for Africa.

Africans can not even begin to think seriously in terms of sustained development, peace and security, without regional integration which can eventually lead to formation of federations, or confederations, across the continent. That is one of the challenges Africa is going to face in the twentieth-first century.

Prospects are dim that national boundaries will be completely erased. That is because of "the sanctity of borders," a cardinal principal that has been upheld by most African leaders since independence.

Unfortunately, many Africans invoke the sanctity of borders – to maintain their territorial integrity and national identities – to their detriment because they have not transcended their differences for the sake of African unity. Therefore it is unlikely that borders will be changed.

But something may still happen that will facilitate continental or subcontinental unity. Instead of national boundaries being abolished, what will probably happen is the loosening of borders through regional integration which may eventually lead to formation of federations or confederations in different parts of Africa.

Therefore, there may come a time when national boundaries will be rendered meaningless by the imperative need for regional integration when Africans realise that their countries can not develop, and can not survive and thrive as viable political and economic entities, without full cooperation with their neighbours and others on the continent.

Such cooperation will require the establishment of institutions and infrastructures which transcend national boundaries and sovereignties, leading to the creation of larger political and economic units in which national identities will be virtually submerged eventually leading to unification of the countries involved.

But this will require Africans to realise that they are

Africans first, before anything else, and that all their other identities – ethnic, national, regional or subregional and so on – are secondary to that. Then and only then will they give concrete expression to the professed belief that "We are all Africans."

Chapter notes:

Chapter One

1. Ahmadu Bello, quoted by Odumegwu Ojukwu in his speech to the Organization of African Unity (OAU), seeking recognition of the secessionist region of Eastern Nigeria as the independent Republic of Biafra, in Addis Ababa, Ethiopia, August 5, 1968, in Colin Legum and John Drysdale, *Africa Contemporary Record: Annual Survey and Documents 1968 - 1969* (London: Africa Research Ltd., 1969), p. 670.

2. Northern Nigerian delegation to the Ad Hoc Conference on the Nigerian Constitution, Lagos, Nigeria, September 1966, in *Africa Contemporary Record*, ibid.

3. Odumegwu Ojukwu, ibid., p. 652.

4. Obafemi Awolowo, *Path to Nigerian Freedom* (London: Faber & Faber, 1947), chap.5. See also George Padmore, *Pan-Africanism or Communism?: The Coming Struggle for Africa* (London: Dennis Dobson, 1956), p. 276.

5. Kenneth Kaunda, quoted in *Africa Contemporary*

Record, op. cit., p. 245. See also Kenneth Kaunda, in *Times of Zambia*, Lusaka, Zambia, February 1968.

6. Obafemi Awolowo, *Path to Nigerian Freedom*, op. cit.

7. Julius Nyerere, quoted by James C. McKinley Jr., "Many Failures, and One Big Success," in the *International Herald Tribune*, September 2, 1996, p. 2.

8. Ibid.

9. Julius Nyerere, quoted in *Sunday Independent*, Johannesburg, South Africa, October 17, 1999; and by R.W. Johnson, "Nyerere: A Flawed Hero," in *The National Interest*, Washington, D.C., No. 60, Summer 2000, p. 73.

On Tanzania's achievements under his leadership despite many failures, see Nyerere in R.W. Johnson, "Nyerere: A Flawed Hero," ibid. As Johnson stated: "Until the end Nyerere was proud about how well he had served Tanzanians. As he told the World Bank: 'We took over a country with 85 percent of its adults illiterate. The British ruled us for 43 years. When they left, there were two trained engineers and 12 doctors. When I stepped down there was 91 percent literacy and nearly every child was in school. We trained thousands of engineers, doctors and teachers.'"

10. Nyerere, in his radio broadcast to the nation on the seventh anniversary of Tanzania's independence, Radio Tanzania, Dar es Salaam (RTD), December 9, 1968, quoted in *Africa Contemporary Record*, op. cit., pp. 216 - 217. See also full text of the speech released in Kiswahili, and translated into English, by the Tanzania Ministry of Information and Broadcasting, Dar es Salaam, Tanzania, December 10, 1968.

11. Nicephore D. Soglo, "Benin's Election Was A Victory for Democracy and the People," in *The Washington Post*, reprinted in the *International Herald Tribune*, August 24 - 25, 1996, p. 6.

12. Godfrey Mwakikagile, *Military Coups in West Africa since the Sixties* (Huntington, New York: Nova

Science Publishers, Inc., 2001), pp. 7 - 13. See also, pp. 211 - 232.

13. Crawford Young, "The Impossible Necessity of Nigeria: A Struggle for Nationhood," in *Foreign Affairs*, November/December 1996, p. 142. See also, Wole Soyinka, *The Open Sore of A Continent: A Personal Narrative of the Nigerian Crisis* (New York: Oxford University Press, 1996).

14. Wole Soyinka, *The Open Sore of A Continent*, op. cit., p. 8; George B.N. Ayittey, *Africa in Chaos* (New York: St. Martin's Press, 1998), p. 171.

15. Soyinka, ibid. See also, "Soyinka at SOAS (Schoo of Oriental and African Studies, University of London), in *Africa Analysis: Fortnightly Bulletin of Financial and Political Trends*, London, No. 259, 1 November, 1996, p. 5.

16. Ibid.

17. Crawford Young, "The Impossible Necessity of Nigeria: A Struggle for Nationhood," in *Foreign Affairs*, op. cit., p. 143.

18. Sekou Toure, quoted in *West Africa*, July 22, 1961, p. 799. See also Julius Nyerere, "One-Party Rule," in *Spreahead*, Dar es Salaam, Tanganyika, November 1961; Nyerere, "The Role of African Trade Unions," in *Labour*, Accra, Ghana, June 1961; Gwendolen M. Carter, editor, *African One-Party States* (Ithaca, New York: Cornell University Press, 1962); Thomas Hodgkin, *African Political Parties* (Baltimore, Maryland: Penguin Books, 1961); Immanuel Wallerstein, *Africa: The Politics of Independence* (New York: Random House, 1961); Herbert J. Spiro, *Politics in Africa: Prospects South of the Sahara* (Englewood Cliffs, New Jersey: Prentice-Hall, 1962).

See also, in his analysis of the creation of a new nation, David Apter, *The Gold Coast in Transition* (Princeton, New Jersey: Princeton University Press, 1955). And for a distinction between "mobilization" and "consociational" regimes, see David Apter, *The Political*

Kingdom of Uganda (Princeton, New Jersey: Princeton University Press, 1961). See also Thomas Hodgkin, "A Note on the Language of African Nationalism," in *African Affairs*, Carbondale, Illinois, No. 1, 1961, pp. 22 - 40.

For a general comparison between Africa and other developing regions of the world, see Gabriel Almond and James S. Coleman, *The Politics of the Developing Areas* (Princeton, New Jersey: Princeton University Press, 1960); Rupert Emerson, >*From Empire to Nation* (Cambridge, Massachusetts: Harvard University Press, 1960); Vera Micheles Dean, *Builders of Emerging Nations* (New York: Holt, Rinehart and Winston, 1961); Max F. Millikan and Donald L.M. Blackmer, editors, *The Emerging Nations* (Boston: Little, Brown & Co., 1961); John H. Kautsky, editor, *Political Change in Underdeveloped Countries* (New York: John Wiley & Sons, 1962); Barbara Ward, *The Rich Nations and the Poor Nations* (New York: W.W. Norton & Co., 1962).

19. Sekou Toure, in *La Lutte du Parti Democratique de Guinee pour l'Emancipation Africaine* (Conakry, Guinea: Imprimerie National, 1959), pp. 58, and 149; translated in Sekou Toure, "African Emancipation," in Paul E. Sigmund, Jr., editor, *The Ideologies of the Developing Nations* (New York: Frederick A. Praeger, 1963), pp. 154 - 169.

For an opposing view on the one-party system, see Nnamdi Azikiwe, "Parliament and Parties," and "Parliamentary Democracy," in Nnamdi Azikiwe, *Zik: A Selection from Speeches of Nnamdi Azikiwe* (New York: Cambridge University Press, 1961); Obafemi Awolowo, "A Critique of One-Party Systems," in *Awo: The Autobiography of Chief Obafemi Awolowo* (New York: Cambridge University Press, 1961); James S. Wunsch and Dele Olowu, editors, *The Failure of the Centralized State: Institutions and Self-Governance in Africa* (Boulder, Colorado: West View Press, 1996).

20. Robert S. Greenberger, "Africa Ascendant: New

Leaders Replace Yesteryear's 'Big Men,' and Tanzania Benefits," in *The Wall Street Journal*, December 10, 1996, pp. A1, and A5.

21. Thomas Sowell, *Race and Culture: A World View* (New York: Basic Books, 1994).

22. Godfrey Mwakikagile, *Africa and the West* (Huntington, New York: Nova Science Publishers, Inc., 2000).

23. Harold Cruse, *The Crisis of the Negro Intellectual* (New York: William Morrow, 1967).

24. Harold Cruse, *Rebellion or Revolution?* (New York: William Morrow, 1968), pp. 240 - 241. See also, Cornel West, *Race Matters* (Boston, Massachusetts: Beacon Press, 1993); Andrew Hacker, *Two Nations: Black and White, Hostile, Unequal* (New York: Ballantine, 1992).

25. Bailey Wyat, a former slave, quoted by Hugh Pearson, "The Birth of the New South," in *The Wall Street Journal*, June 24, 1996.

26. Ali A. Mazrui, *Towards A Pax Africana* (London: Weidenfeld & Nicolson, 1967), p. 97.

27. Kwame Nkrumah, *Ghana: The Autobiography of Kwame Nkrumah* (New York: Thomas Nelson and Sons, 1957). See also Julius Nyerere, "The Rational Choice," in Andrew Caulson, editor, *African Socialism in Practice* (Nottingham: Russel Press, 1979), pp. 19 - 26; "False Starts: Capitalist and Socialist," in Richard Sandbrook, *The Politics of Africa's Economic Recovery* (Cambridge: Cambridge University Press, 1993), chap. 2; Nigel Dower, "Is the Idea of Development Eurocentric?," in Richard Auty and John Toye, editors, *Challenging the Orthodoxies* (New York: St. Martin's Press, 1996), pp. 85 - 102.

The asymmetrical relationship between African countries and the former colonial powers and other industrialized nations, which is inherently exploitative, is analogous to the situation in the United States where African-Americans (black Americans), constituting a

579

virtual colony within, are at the mercy of white Americans because of racism, an in-built component of the American political socio-economic system; an argument rejected by black American conservatives such as Thomas Sowell, and others, without any empirical evidence.

See, for example, Thomas Sowell, *Race and Economics* (New York: Longman, 1975), and *Markets and Minorities* (New York: Basic Books, 1981), in which he dismisses the significance of racism in the American context, contending that it is overcome by market forces in a capitalist economy because of the nature of the system which is driven by competition in the quest for profit.

This is a very myopic view, and deeply flawed analysis, which ignores the racist practices of many white business owners and employers who simply refuse to patronize or hire blacks even if it means losing them as customers or as prospective and highly productive employees. They don't need blacks because most of their customers and employees are white in a predominantly white nation. Otherwise there would have been no need for civil rights laws to open up opportunities for blacks and try to level the playing field, if market forces by themselves were enough to eliminate or effectively contain racism. They had not done that in 300 years, a simple historical fact black conservatives, for some inexplicable reason, fail to grasp.

Whites also view with apprehension the fact that they are going to be a minority within a few decades; which partly explains their siege mentality, hence their belief that they are being overwhelmed - swamped - by hordes of non-whites who must be kept at bay. Therefore they must help only their own kind in terms of employment, housing and whatever else; nothing but feeble attempts to justify racism.

28. Tom Mboya, in *Transition*, Kampala, Uganda, Vol. 3, No. 8, March 1963, p. 17. See also Tom Mboya, *Challenge of Nationhood* (London: Heinemann, 1970);

Julius Nyerere, *Freedom and Socialism: A Selection from Writings and Speeches 1965 - 1967* (Dar es Salaam, Tanzania: Oxford University Press, 1968).

29. Nnamdi Azikiwe, *Zik: A Selection from the Speeches of Nnamdi Azikiwe* (Cambridge: Cambridge University Press, 1961), p. 102.

30. Charity Ngilu, speaking in Bokoli village, Bungoma, Kenya, January 8, 2000. Quoted by Kenyan Professor Kivutha Kibwana, "Ethnic Politics: Curse or Blessing," Nairobi, Kenya, July 2001. As Kibwana states in his paper:

"I cannot resist joining debate with both Kwendo Opanga (The tribal card in the succession game plan) and Murungi Kiraitu (Gema and the politics of tribal solidarity). The question both writers were addressing is: Is it the tribe or the political party which matters in Kenya's politics and society?....

Kwendo Opanga bluntly concluded his piece by stating that he rather a political party told him what to do and not his tribe through a proxy political party. Kiraitu on the other hand concluded that tribal alliances have a key role in Kenya's politics.

If we organize politics through tribes, are we not conceding either poverty of ideas and issues or opting for a deliberate strategy of concealing our political vision or ideology? Or are we saying political parties will always be eclipsed by tribe? Should we then search for a new vehicle for our African democracy? Is President Yoweri Museveni's no-party system one of the viable alternatives? Or should we go back to the one-party model?

I think two dangerous trends are emerging in Kenya currently. We are entrenching the ethnic principle to such an extent that we shall have to live with it for many decades to come. Do we want to? All sectors of the elite including the media elite are popularizing ethnic politics. Secondly, those who attempt to shift Kenya's politics to the plane of issue politics are not encouraged and are often vilified. It would therefore seem to me that a conspiracy to banish issue politics is afoot.

Interestingly, however, GEMA is not one tribe. If one can bring several tribes together through GEMA, why not do so through broad issues and a party?....

Tribal alliances are another form of trying to recreate new political parties. Frankly, Kenya needs about three or even two political parties i.e. a conservative party, a liberal party and a radical party. We have to work on reducing the 40 or so registered political parties into two or three.

If we organize on the basis of tribal alliances, we could easily encounter a stalemate if one alliance does not put together most tribes together (sic). We would be fanning secession fires. What do tribes that lose do? How are the expectations of their people to be satisfied?

Where an ethnic group comes into power after mobilizing on ethnic basis, it must satisfy its ethnic following. Can it do so and equally satisfy all other ethnic groupings?....

My personal dream - and I agree with Kwendo Opanga - is that Kenyans should develop parties of issues. We must venture beyond tribe."

The question is, how is that going to be done, in the midst of such intense ethnoregional loyalties, not only in Kenya but in other African countries as well? People talk about issues, yet mobilize forces on ethnic basis.

See also one of my books in which I address the subject, suggesting, among other things, formation of coalition governments, and reduction of the number of political parties to two or three to broaden the base of support that cuts across ethnoregional lines. With only two or three parties allowed, members of different tribes - including enemies - will have to work together as members of the only political parties they can join in the country. After all, when we talk about a multi-party system for functional purposes, we are really talking about a two-party system, *not* a system of 5, 10, 20, or 40 parties.

That's nothing but chaos. And it is used to justify dictatorship or military intervention in government. Even third parties don't win elections; it's extremely rare. When was the last time the Liberal Party won a general election in Britain? Just remember that.

See Godfrey Mwakikagile, *Ethnic Politics in Kenya and Nigeria* (Huntington, New York: Nova Science Publishers, Inc., 2001).

See also, "Kenyan MPs Seeks End to Political Parties," in "BBC News: Africa," 7 December, 2000:

"A Kenyan opposition legislator has moved a motion in parliament seeking the abolishment of political parties and the creation of a partyless state.

Social Democratic Party (SDP) member for Juja, Stephen Ndicho, wants all political party activities in the country to be suspended for at least 10 years to curb tribalism.

Kenya, which has 47 (sic) tribes, ended its single party rule in 1991 and has since held two multi-party general elections.

Mr. Ndicho insisted that his motion did not advocate for a return to a single party political system but seeks to provide a stopgap measure in the country's politics to heal tribal and political divisons.

'Since the advent of multi-partism in this country in 1991, tribalism has really taken a tall order on this country,' Mr. Ndicho told the BBC. 'Every tribe in Kenya seems to be owning a political party,' he said, adding that 'if this trend continues, you can imagine Kenya will be a disintegrated country.'

The member said Kenya should borrow a leaf from Uganda where President Museveni banned political parties when he took power in 1986 in order to restore stability in a country that had been ravaged by war.

Mr. Ndicho said there was political enmity among Kenya's different party members, adding that during the 1992 and 1997 general elections, results showed that voting was done along tribal or regional lines."

Chapter Two

1. Julius K. Nyerere, in a speech delivered to the Second Pan-African Seminar, World Assembly of Youth, Dar es Salaam, Tanganyika, August 1961, in *WAY* (World Assemby of Youth) *Forum*, No. 40, September 1961; reprinted in Paul E. Sigmund, Jr., editor, *The Ideologies of the Developing Nations* (New York: Frederick A. Praeger, 1963), pp. 205, 208, and 209. See also *Tanganyika Standard*, Dar es Salaam, Tanganyika, August and September 1961.

2. Godfrey Mwakikagile, *Africa after Independence: Realities of Nationhood* (Atlanta, Georgia: Protea Publishing, 2002).

3. John Reader, *Africa: A Biography of the Continent* (New York: Alfred A. Knopf, 1998), pp. 659, 660, and 662.

4. Ibid., p. 662; Catherine Hoskyns, *The Congo since Independence: January 1960 - December 1961* (Oxford: Oxford University Press, 1965), p. 308; M. Meredith, *The First Dance of Freedom* (London: Hamish Hamilton, 1984), p. 150. See also Patrice Lumumba, *Congo: My Country* (London, 1962).

5. Quoted in Madeleine G. Kalb, *The Congo Cables: The Cold War in Africa: From Eisenhower to Kennedy* (New York: Macmillan, 1982), p. 27; J. Reader, *Africa: A Biography of the Continent*, op. cit., p. 659.

6. Adam Hochschild, *King Leopold's Ghost: A Story of Greed, Terror, and Heroism in Colonial Africa* (New York: Houghton Mifflin Co., 1998), pp. 301 - 302; Sean Kelly, *America's Tyrant: The CIA and Mobutu of Zaire* (Washington, D.C.: American University Press, 1993), pp. 57 - 60, 71, and 178.

7. Ibid. See also John Ranelagh, *The Agency: The Rise and Decline of the CIA* (New York: Simon & Schuster,

1986), p. 342; John Stockwell, *In Search of Enemies* (New York: W.W. Norton, 1978), p. 105; Report from the US Senate investigation, headed by Democratic Senator Frank Church of Idaho, into CIA covert activities against foreign leaders and governments, *Alleged Assassination Plots Involving Foreign Leaders: An Interim Report of the Select Committee to Study (US) Governmental Operations with Respect to Intelligence Activities*, Washington, D.C., November 20, 1975.

8. Ludo de Witte, *The Assassination of Lumumba* (New York: Verso, 1999).

9. Allen Dulles, quoted by Kevin Whitelaw, "A Killing in Congo: Lumumba's Death...," in *U.S. News & World Report*, July 24, 2000, p. 63.

10. "A Killing in Congo," in *U.S. News & World Report*, ibid.; Ludo de Witte, *The Assassination of Lumumba*, op. cit. See also (US) National Security Archive: "It is possible to kill a man with bare hands, but very few are skillful enough to do it well," reads a declassified 1954 CIA "Study of Assassination" on covert activities in Guatemala. And "persons who are morally squeamish" make bad assassins. This and other CIA documents can be seen at www.gwu.edu/-nsarchiv. Choose Electronic Briefing Books, and click on "CIA and Assassinations."

11. Zaire, in *1997 Almanac: Information Please* (Boston: Houghton Mifflin Co., 1996), p. 295.

12. Government of Tanganyika, in a message to UN Secretary-General U Thant, on the assassination of President Sylvanus Olympio of Togo, in *Tanganyika Standard*, Dar es Salaam, Tanganyika, January 26, 1963; quoted by Ali A. Mazrui, *Towards A Pax Africana* (London: Weidenfeld & Nicolson, 1967), p. 123.

13. Ronald Ngala, in *Uganda Argus*, Kampala, Uganda, April 25, 1964; A.A. Mazrui, *Towards A Pax Africana*, op.cit., p. 270.

14. Julius Nyerere, "The Honour of Africa," address to

the Tanzania National Assembly, December 14, 1965, before Tanzania broke off diplomatic relations with Britain the following day, the first African country to do so (followed by Ghana under Nkrumah), in J.K. Nyerere, *Freedom and Socialism: A Selection from Writings and Speeches 1965 - 1967* (Dar es Salaam, Tanzania: Oxford University Press, 1968), pp. 123 - 124.

15. *Sunday Times*, Johannesburg, October 3, 1999; R.W. Johnson, "Nyerere: A Flawed Hero," in *The National Interest*, No. 60, Washington, D.C., Summer 2000, p. 76.

16. *The Mercury*, Durban, South Africa, October 5, 1999; R.W. Johnson, "Nyerere: A Flawed Hero," ibid., pp. 67 - 68.

17. Julius Nyerere, quoted in *Sunday Times*, London, October 3, 1999; R.W. Johnson, "Nyerere: A Flawed Hero," ibid., p. 73. See also, "Farewell to the Father of Tanzania," in the *Mail and Guardian*, Johannesburg, October 15, 1999; "Julius Nyerere of Tanzania Dies; Preached African Socialism to the World," in *The New York Times*, October 15, 1999, p. B10; "Former Tanzanian President Julius Nyerere Dies at 77; African leader Led Independence Movement and Worked to Unify Nation, Continent," in *The Washington Post*, October 15, 1999, p. B-06; "Julius Nyerere: Former President of Tanzania Led Country to Independence," in the *Los Angeles Times*, October 15, 1999, p. 30.

18. Hackman Owusu-Agyemang, "Tribute to Dr. Julius Nyerere: Death Has Robbed Africa of A Leading Light," in *The Independent*, Accra, Ghana, October 27, 1999. See also "Tanzania Mourns Its 'Teacher'; Nyerere Remembered as A Leader Who Unified the Nation, " in *The Washington Post*, October 22, 1999, p. A-25.

586

Chapter Three

1. "Sekou Toure," in Paul E. Sigmund, Jr., editor, *The Ideologies of the Developing Countries* (New York: Frederick A. Praeger, 1963), p. 154.

2. Fred Greene, *Dynamics of International Relations*: *Power, Security, and Order* (New York: Holt, Rinehart and Winston, 1964), p. 676.

3. Okon Udokang, "The Third World as A Political Force," in *The Black Scholar*, Sausalito, California, May 1975, p. 12. See also Okon Udokang, editor and contributor, *African Politics and Foreign Relations* (Toronto: University of Toronto Press, 1975); and Julius Nyerere, on the Cold War and Africa, cited by *The New York Times*, April 1, 1964, p. 2.

4. Julius Nyerere, quoted by *The New York Times*, December 19, 1961; and Ali A. Mazrui, *Towards A Pax Africana* (London: Weidenfeld & Nicolson, 1968), p. 77. See also Nyerere, in *Tanganyika Standard*, Dar es Salaam, Tanganyika, December 18, 1961.

5. Julius Nyerere, *Freedom and Socialism*: *A Selection from Writings and Speeches 1965 - 1967* (Dar es Salaam, Tanzania: Oxford University Press, 1968), pp. 189, and 190.

6. Ibid., pp. 190, and 202.

7. Ibid., pp. 190 - 191.

8. "Sekou Toure," in Paul E. Sigmund, *The Ideologies of the Developing Nations*, op. cit., p. 154.

9. Julius Nyerere, *Freedom and Socialism*, ibid., p. 202. Kwame Nkrumah also discusses attempts by the CIA to overthrow Nyerere in the mid-sixties and how the American intelligence agency succeeded in overthrowing his Ghanaian government on February 24, 1966. See

Kwame Nkrumah, *Dark Days in Ghana* (New York: Monthly Review Press, 1966).

10. John F. Kennedy, quoted by Richard Reeves, *President Kennedy: Profile of Power* (New York: Simon & Schuster, 1993), pp. 227 - 228.

11. Richard Reeves, *President Kennedy*, op. cit., p. 227.

12. Oran R. Young, *The Politics of Force: Bargaining During International Crises* (Princeton, New Jersey: Princeton University press, 1968), pp. 132 - 133, 159 - 160. For analyses of the proceedings of the Belgrade Conference, see Paul Hoffman in *The New York Times*, September 3, 1961, Sect. IV, p. 4; and Harry Schwartz in *The New York Times*, September 10, 1961, Sect. IV, p. 3. And for a general analysis of the Belgrade Conference, see Peter Lyon, *Neutralism* (Leicester, England: Leicester University Press, 1963), Chap. VI.

13. Kwame Nkrumah, in his speech to the United Nations General Assembly, March 7, 1961. See also the full text issued by the Ghana Ministry of Information, Accra, Ghana, p. 8; and *Ghanaian Times*, Accra, Ghana, March 8, 1961.

14. John F. Kennedy, quoted by Ernest R. May and Philip D. Zelikow, editors, *The Kennedy Tapes: Inside the White House During the Cuban Missile Crisis* (Cambridge, Massachusetts: Harvard University Press, 1997), pp. 144, 150, 175, 176, 179, 183, 256, 272, and 275.

15. Jorge G. Castaneda, *Companero: The Life and Death of Che Guevara* (New York: Alfred A. Knopf, 1997), pp. 228 - 229.

16. Henry Tanner, reporting from Abidjan, Ivory Coast, in *The New York Times*, March 25, 1962. For contrast, see Victor D. DuBois, "The Role of the Army in Guinea," in *Africa Report*, Vol. 8, No. 1, January 1963. See also George Weeks, "The Armies of Africa," in *Africa Report*, Vol. 9, No. 1, January 1963.

For comparative analysis of military strength in Africa vis-a-vis white-minority-regime military preparedness during the sixties, see "Military Strength in Southern Africa" in *Central Africa Research*, London, August 10, 1968; and Colin Legum and John Drysdale, *Africa Contemporary Record: Annual Survey and Documents 1968 - 1969* (London: Africa Research Ltd., 1969), pp. 716 - 717.

17. "Declaration of Federation by the Governments of East Africa," signed by the President of the Republic of Tanganyika, Dr. Julius Nyerere; the Prime Minister of Uganda, Mr. Milton A. Obote; and the Prime Minister of Kenya, Mr. Jomo Kenyatta, in Nairobi, Kenya, June 5, 1963.

See full text in Anthony J. Hughes, *East Africa: The Search for Unity: Kenya, Yanganyika, and Uganda* (Baltimore, Maryland, USA: Penguin Books, 1963), Appendix pp. 265 - 269. The full text of the declaration is also found in Godfrey Mwakikagile, *Ethnic Politics in Kenya and Nigeria* (Huntington, New York: Nova Science Publishers, Inc., 2001), pp. 218 - 220.

18. Nnamdi Azikiwe, "African Unity," in Paul Sigmund, *The Ideologies of the Developing Nations*, op. cit., pp. 216 - 217, and 218 - 219. See also Nnamdi Azikiwe, *Zik: A Selection from Speeches of Nnamdi Azikiwe* (New York: Cambridge University Press, 1961).

19. Jorge Castaneda, *Companero: The Life and Death of Che Guevara*, op. cit., p. 277.

20. Nelson Mandela, his speech to the Pan-African Freedom Movement for East and Central Africa (PAFMECA), Addis Ababa, Ethiopia, February 1962.

21. Nelson Mandela, *Long Walk to Freedom: The Autobiography of Nelson Mandela* (New York: Little, Brown and Co., 1994), pp. 250, 251, 252, and 253.

22. Mamadou Dia, *The African Nations and World Solidarity* (New York: Frederick A. Praeger, 1961); Mamadou Dia, "Independence and Neocolonialism," in

Paul E. Sigmund, *The Ideologies of the Developing Countries*, op. cit., pp. 232, 235 - 236.

23. Kaye Whiteman, "France's Year in Africa," in *Africa Contemporary Record*, op. cit., pp. 29 - 30.

24. Ali Mazrui, *Towards A Pax Africana*, op. cit., p. 253.

25. Julius Nyerere, cited by James C. McKinley, "Tanzania's Nyerere Looks Back: Many Failures, and One Big Success: Bringing a Nation to Life," in *The New York Times*, September 2, 1996; and the *International Herald Tribune*, September 2, 1996, p. 2.

26. "Declaration of Federation by the Governments of East Africa," in Anthony J. Hughes, *East Africa: The Search for Unity*, op. cit., pp. 265 - 266; and Godfrey Mwakikagile, *Ethnic Politics in Kenya and Nigeria*, op. cit., pp. 218 - 220.

27. George Bennett, "Settlers and Politics in Kenya," in Vincent Harlow, E.M. Chilver, and Alison Smith, editors, *History of East Africa*, *II* (Oxford: Oxford University Press, 1965), pp. 304 - 305; see also p. 578.

28. "Uganda," in *Africa Contemporary Record*, op. cit., p. 230. See also "Dr. Obote's Decade - Ten Years in Parliament" (Kampala, Uganda: Milton Obote Foundation, 1968).

29. James C. McKinley, "Tanzania's Nyerere Looks Back," ibid.

30. Ronald Ngala, quoted in *Uganda Argus*, Kampala, Uganda, April 25, 1964.

31. "Declaration of Federation by the Governments of East Africa," Anthony J. Hughes, *East Africa: The Search for Unity*, op. cit., p. 266; and Godfrey Mwakikagile, *Ethnic Politics in Kenya and Nigeria*, op.cit., p. 219.

32. Ahmed Ben Bella, "The Future of Algeria," an interview with Maria Macciochi, *L'Unita*, an Italian newspaper, in Algiers, August 13, 1962; reprinted in Paul Sigmund, *The Ideologies of the Developing Nations*, op. cit., pp. 147 - 148.

33. Julius Nyerere, "The Stress is Now on Dignity," in *Sunday News*, Dar es Salaam, Tanganyika, September 8, 1963, p. 9.

34. Kwame Nkrumah, in *Ghana Today*, Vol. 8, No. 21, Accra, Ghana, December 16, 1964; and Ali Mazrui, *Towards A Pax Africana*, op. cit., p. 73.

35. Paul Lee, "Documents Expose US Role in Nkrumah Overthrow," ghanaweb.com, March 7, 2001.

36. Adebayo Adedeji, interviewed by Margaret A. Novicki, in *Africa Report*, September - October 1983, p. 14.

37. Ali Mazrui, *Towards A Pax Africana*, op. cit., pp. 65 - 66. See also *West African Pilot*, May 18, 1961, and *West Africa*, May 6, 1961.

38. Ali A. Mazrui, *Towards A Pax Africana*, ibid., p. 251. See also Ali A. Mazrui, "African Attitudes to the EEC," in *International Affairs*, Vol. 38, No. 1, London, January 1963. For a report on the Pan-African militancy of the Nigerian youth, see *The New York Times*, March 3, 1962.

39. *Ghanaian Times*, Accra, Ghana, April 27, 1965.

40. "Guinea," in *Africa Contemporary Record*, op. cit., pp. 505 - 506.

41. Julius Nyerere, "Nationalism and Pan-Africanism," speech to the Second Pan-African Seminar, World Assembly of Youth (WAY), Dar es Salaam, Tanganyika, August 1961. Published in *WAY Forum*, No. 40, September 1961; and Paul Sigmund, *The Ideologies of the Developing Nations*, op. cit., pp. 208 - 209. See also Nyerere, text of the same speech, in the *Standard*, Dar es Salaam, Tanganyika, August 1961.

Chapter Four

1. Julius Nyerere, quoted in Colin Legum and John Drysdale, eds., *Africa Contemporary Record: Annual*

Survey and Documents 1968 – 1969, London: Africa Research Limited, 1969, p. 233.

2. Saadia Touval, *The Boundary Politics of Independent Africa*, Cambridge, Massachusetts, USA: Harvard College, 1972, 1999, p. 30.

3. James Minahan, *Encyclopedia of The Stateless Nations: Ethnic and National Groups Around the World*, Westport, Connecticut, USA: Greenwood Publishing Group, 2002, p. 1429.

See also, cited by James Minahan, V.W. Nyakatura, *Anatomy of an African Kingdom: A History of Bunyoro-Kitara*, 1973; Clarence Apuuli, *A Thousand Years of the Bunyoro-Kitara Kingdom*, 1981; and Phares Mutibwa, Lawrenceville, New Jersey, USA: *Uganda Since Independence: A Story of Unfulfilled Hopes*, Africa World Press, 1992.

4. J. Minahan, *Encyclopedia of the Stateless Nations*, ibid., pp. 1429 – 1430.

5. J. Minahan, *Encyclopedia of the Stateless Nations*, ibid., p. 1912.

6. Ibid., p. 1913.

7. Ibid., pp. 1913 – 1914. See also Kenneth Ingham, *The Kingdom of Toro in Uganda*, 1975; Emmanuel K. Twesigye, *African Monarchies and Kingdoms of Uganda*, 1995; Thomas P. Ofcansky, *Uganda: Tarnished Pearl of Africa*, 1996.

8. W. J. Argyle, in P. H. Gulliver, ed., *Tradition & Transition in East Africa: Studies of the Tribal Element in the Modern Era*, London: Routledge and Kegan Paul Ltd., 1969, pp. 52 – 53.

9. Ibid., p. 53 – 54.

10. Edward Kannyo, Chapter 18, "Uganda," in Jack Donnelly and Rhoda E. Howard-Hassmann, eds., *International Handbook of Human Rights*, Westport, Connecticut, USA, 1987, pp. 386 – 387.

See also, cited by E. Kannyo: 4. The *Kabaka* (king) of Buganda was the only ruler accorded the honorific 'His

Highness.' See D. Anthony Low and R. Cranford Pratt, *Buganda and British Overrule*, London: Oxford University Press, 1960; 5. Cf. Ali A. Mazrui, 'Privilege and Protest as Integrative Factors: The Case of Buganda's Status in Uganda,' in *Protest and Power in Black Africa*, ed. Robert I. Rotberg and Ali A. Mazrui, New York: Oxford University Press, 1970, pp. 1072 – 87; David E. Apter, *The Political Kingdom in Uganda*, Princeton, New Jersey: Princeton University Press, 1967; Tarsis B. Kabwegyere, *The Politics of State Formation*, Nairobi, Kenya: East African Literature Bureau, 1974; Nelson Kasfir, *The Shrinking Political Arena*, Berkeley: University of California Press, 1976; Samwiri R. Karugire, *A Political History of Uganda*, Nairobi, Kenya: East African Literature Bureau, 1980; Grace S. Ibingira, *The Forging of an African Nation*, New York: viking Press, 1973.

11. E. Kannyo, ibid., pp. 387 – 389.

See also, cited by E. Kannyo, in his chapter notes: 6. Cf. Mahmood Mamdani, *Politics and Class Formation in Uganda*, New York: Monthly Review Press, 1976, pp. 189 – 227; 7. George W. Kanyeihamba, *Constitutional Law and Government in Uganda*, Nairobi, Kenya: East African Literature Bureau, 1975, p. 67; 8. Ibid., p. 68.

12. Joshua B. Forrest, *Subnationalism in Africa: Ethnicity, Alliances, and Politics*, Boulder, Colorado, USA: Lynne Rienner Publishers, Inc., 2004, p. 220.

See also, cited by Joshua B. Forrest: 22. Crawford Young, *The Politics of Cultural Pluralism*, Madison, Wisconsin, USA: University of Wisconsin Press, 1976, p. 227; 23. Frank van Acker, "Ethnicity and Institutional Reform: A Case of Ugandan Exceptionalism?" in *Politics of Identity and Economics of Conflict in the Great Lakes Region*, ed. Ruddy Doom and Jan Gorus, Brussels: VUB University Press, 2000, p. 165; Donald Rothchild, *Managing Ethnic Conflict in Africa: Pressures and Incentives for Cooperation*, Washington, D.C.: Brookings

Institution, 1997, p.68; 24. Young, *Politics of Cultural Pluralism*, pp. 150, 265; 25. Ibid., pp. 264 – 266; 26. van Acker, "Ethnicity and Institutional Reform," p. 152.

13. Ibid., pp. 221 – 222. See also, cited by Joshua B. Forrest: 28. van Acker, "Ethnicity and Institutional Reform," p. 151; 29. Rothchild, *Managing Ethnic Conflict*, p. 90; 30. Ibid.; 31. van Acker, "Ethnicity and Institutional Reform," p. 165.

14. Ibid., pp. 224.

15. BBC, "Mali Tuareg Rebels Declare Independence in the North," 6 April 2012.

16. Saadia Souval, *The Boundary Politics of Independent Africa*, op.cit., pp. 30 and 31.

Chapter Five

1. Milton Obote, in an interview with Andrew Mwenda, *Daily Monitor*, Kampala, Uganda, in April 2005.

2. King Freddie, *Desecration of My Kingdom*, quoted by Crawford Young, *The Politics of Cultural Pluralism*, Madison, Wisconsin, USA: The University of Wisconsin Press, 1976, p. 151. See also King Freddie, *Desecration of My Kingdom*, London: Constable & Co., Ltd. 1967, pp. 1 – 3.

3. Godfrey Mwakikagile, *Africa is in A Mess: What Went Wrong and What Should Be Done*, Pretoria: New Africa Press, 2006, pp. 12 – 13; 19 – 20.

See also "Africa's Democratic Despots," in *The Economist*, January 3, 1998; Reginald Dale, "Finally, Some Good News From Africa," in the *International Herald Tribune*, December 13, 1996, p. 15; Yoweri Museveni, in a speech to the UN General Assembly, February 1997, cited by Tom Stacey, "African Realities," in *National Review*, May 19, 1997, p. 30; Godfrey Mwakikagile, *Economic Development in Africa*

(Commack, New York: Nova Science Publishers, Inc., 1999), pp. 3, and 99.

See also Yoweri Museveni, in a speech to the UN General Assembly, February 1997, cited by Tom Stacey, "African Realities," in *National Review*, May 19, 1997, p. 30).

4. Juma Anthony Okuku, "Ethnicity, State Power and The Democratisation Process in Uganda," Discussion Paper 17, University Printers, Uppsala, Sweden, 2002, p. 15.

5. Colin Legum and John Drysdale, eds., *Africa Contemporary Record: Annual Survey and Documents 1968 – 1969*, London: Africa Research Limited, 1969, p. 230. See also, cited above: 1. A commemorative pamphlet, *Dr. Obote's Decade – Ten Years in Parliament* was published by the Milton Obote Foundation, Kampala. It contains his speech to parliament on 6 May 1958 quoted above.

6. J. A. Okuku, "Ethnicity, State Power and The Democratisation Process in Uganda," op. cit., pp. 15 – 16.

7. Colin Legum and John Drysdale, *Africa Contemporary Record*, op. cit., pp. 230 – 231.

8. J.A. Okuku, "Ethnicity, State Power and The Democratisation Process in Uganda," op.cit., pp. 18, 19 – 20.

9. Colin Legum and John Drysdale, *Africa Contemporary Record*, op.cit., p. 235.

10. Ibid., pp. 231 – 232.

11. Ibid., pp. 234 – 235.

Chapter Six

1. Godfrey Mwakikagile, *Nyerere and Africa: End of an Era*, Pretoria, South Africa: New Africa Press, 2010, pp. 306 – 312.

See also, cited above by G. Mwakikagile, 1. Idi Amin,

on Radio Uganda, Kampala, Uganda, January 25, 1971; *Uganda Argus*, Kampala, Uganda, January 26, 1971. See also *The Nationalist*, and the *Standard*, Dar es Salaam, Tanzania, January 26, 1971; *Daily Nation*, and *The East African Standard*, Nairobi, Kenya, January 26, 1971; 2. Linda de Hoyos, "Idi Amin: London Stooge Against Sudan," in the *Executive Intelligence Review*, June 9, 1995, pp. 52 - 53. See also George Ivan Smith, *Ghosts of Kampala: The Rise and Fall of Idi Amin* (New York: HarperCollins, 1980). 3. Milton Obote, quoted in *Executive Intelligence Review*, ibid.; 4. Ali A. Mazrui, "Nyerere and I," in *Voices*, Africa Resource Center, October 1999; 5. Henry Kyemba, quoted by Wairagala Wakabi, "Idi Amin Just Won't Go Away," in *The Black World Today*, Maryland, USA, April 30, 1999. See also Henry Kyemba, *A State of Blood: The Inside Story of Idi Amin* (New York: Putnam, 1977); 6. Brigadier Moses Ali, quoted by Wairagala Wakabi, "Idi Amin Just Won't Go Away," ibid.; 7. Edward Heath's remarks to Obote, Nyerere, and Kaunda, during the Commonwealth conference in Singapore, January 1971, quoted in "The Making of Idi Amin," in *New African*, London, February 2001; 8. *The Daily Express*, London, January 1971.*The Daily Express*, London, January 1971.*The Daily Express*, London, January 1971; 9. *The Daily Telegraph*, London, January 1971; 10. *The Times*, London, January 1971; 11. Quoted in *New African*, op. Cit.; 12. Pat Hutton and Jonathan Bloch, "The Making of Idi Amin," People's News Service, 1979; *New African*, ibid. British gvernment documents, declassified at the end of the 1990s under the 30-year rule, verify earlier accounts by journalists Pat Hutton and Jonathan Bloch which said the coup by Idi Amin against Dr. Milton Obote was engineered by outside powers - Britain, Israel, and the United States. Sky News, the London-based satellite TV channel, also quoted from one of the British documents in which the Foreign Office in London had said, "Amin was reliable."; 13. *The*

Economist, August 1972. See also Ralph Uwechue, editor, *Africa Today* (London: Africa Books Ltd., 1996), pp. 1554 - 1557; Jeffrey T. Strate, *Post-Military Coup Strategy in Uganda: Amin's Early Attempts to Consolidate Political Support in Africa* (1973); Phares Mutibwa, *Uganda since Independence: A Story of Unfulfilled Hopes* (Lawrenceville, New Jersey: Africa World Press, 1992).

2. Phares Mukasa Mutibwa, *Uganda Since Independence*, op.cit., p. 112.

3. Anthony Appiah and Henry Lou Gates, Jr., *Encyclopedia of Africa, Volume 1*, Fifth Edition, New York: Oxford University Press, 2010, p. 25.

4. P.M. Mutibwa, *Uganda Since Independence*, op. cit., pp. 100 – 101.

See also, cited by P. M. Mutibwa above: 27. Grace S. Ibingira, *African Upheavals Since Independence*, Boulder, Colorado, USA: Westview Press, 1980, pp. 288 – 289; 28. A prominent politician, who was a minister under Amin and who is serving the NRM – National Resistance Movement – Administration in a high office, is suspected by many Ugandans of having been involved in the death of Chief Justice Kiwanuka. This may eventually be investigated by the Ugandan Human Rights Commission sitting in Kampala at the time of writing (comment by P.M. Mutibwa).

See also Richard Muscat, *A Short History of the Democratic Party, 1954 – 1984*, Kampala: Foundation for African Development, 1984, p. 88.

5. Phares Mukasa Mutibwa, *Uganda Since Independence: A Story of Unfulfilled Hopes*, London, England: C. Hurst & Co. (Publishers) Ltd.; Trenton, New Jersey, USA: Africa World Press, Inc., 1992, pp. 106 – 108.

6. Donald L. Horowitz, *Ethnic Groups in Conflict*, Berkeley, Los Angeles, London: University of California Press, 1985, p. 487 – 488.

See also, cited by D.L. Horowitz in the preceding

quotation: 28. A special correspondent, "The Uganda Army: Nexus of Power," *Africa Report*, December 1966, p. 39; cf. Michael Lofchie, "The Uganda Coup: Class Action by the Military," *Journal of Modern African Studies* 10 (1972): pp. 19 – 25, and 21 – 23; 29. Ali A. Mazrui, *Soldiers and Kinsmen in Uganda*, Beverly Hills: Sage, 1975, p. 113; David Martin, *General Amin*, London: Faber & Faber, 1974, p. 105, says the Acholi share (in the army) may have been closer to three-fifths. Later, Martin claimed the army was only about half Langi and Acholi. *Boston Globe*, 15 August 1976; 30. A special correspondent, "The Uganda Army: Nexus of Power," *Africa Report*, December 1966, p. 38; 31. After the shooting, twenty-six people were arrested, twenty-one of them Baganda. The total number of people detained, according to an official list, was sixty-six. Of these, fifty-one were Baganda, fifteen other Southerners. No Northerners were on the list. These were signs of the extent to which conflict had polarized along North-South lines. *Africa Report*, March 1970, pp. 6 – 8.

7. D.L. Horowitz, *Ethnic Groups in Conflict*, ibid., pp. 488 – 489. See also, cited above by Horowitz: 32. Another cousin (of Obote) headed one of two Muslim organizations, the one friendly to the regime. A younger brother (of Obote) served in the Ministry of Home Affairs. Other Langi headed the Public Service Commission, with its important power over appointment and promotion, and the Immigration Department; 34. David Martin, *General Amin*, op. cit., p. 14, says Amin's father was a Kakwa who lived many years in Southern Sudan. According to Martin, Amin's mother was a Lugbara; 35. Ibid., pp. 138 – 139; Henry Kyemba, *A State of Blood: The Inside Story of Idi Amin*, New York: Ace Books, 1977, p. 28; 36. A correspondent, "Uganda After the Coup," *Swiss Review of World Affairs 20*, March 1971, pp. 9 – 10; 37. Nelson Kasfir, *The Shrinking Political Arena: Participation and Ethnicity in African Politics*, Berkeley and Los Angeles:

University of California Press, 1976, p. 220; 38. David Martin, *General Amin*, p. 89; 39. Ibid., p 59; 40. Ibid., pp. 25 – 61.

8. D.L. Horowitz, *Ethnic Groups in Conflict*, ibid., pp. 489 – 490.

See also, cited above by Horowitz: 41. David Martin, *General Amin*, op.cit., pp. 59 – 61; 42. Amin said later that he had moved against Obote only after Obote had ordered Acholi and Langi troops to disarm the rest of the army and kill Amin. Whether intended as such or not, this statement proved to be a signal to Amin's own supporters to take violent action against Acholi and Langi soldiers. A final purge and slaughter of all remaining Acholi and Langi soldiers was reported six years later. *The Washington Post*, 3 March 1977; 43. David Martin, *General Amin*, ibid., 137; 44. Ibid., p. 240. Of the twenty-three top officers in army service at the time of the coup, only four were still on duty three years later; at least thirteen of them had been murdered. Ibid., p. 154. See also Holger Bernt Hansen, *Ethnicity and Military Rule in Uganda*, Uppsala: Scandinavian Institute of African Studies, 1977, p. 108; 45. See David Martin, *General Amin*, pp. 182, 230, 238 – 239; Colin Legum, ed., *Africa Contemporary Record, 1973 – 1974*, p. B310. Compare Henry Kyemba, *A State of Blood,* op. cit., pp. 134 – 136.

9. D.L. Horowitz, *Ethnic Groups in Conflict*, ibid., pp. 490 – 492.

See also, cited above by Horowitz: 47. David Martin, *General Amin*, op.cit., pp. 168, 213, 234 – 235; Colin Legum, ed., *Africa contemporary Record, 1973 – 1974*, op. cit., pp. B294 – 295; 48. C. Legum, ed., *Africa Contemporary Record, 1974 – 1975*, p. B311; 49. Ibid., p. B309. On the various terror units and their commanders, see Henry Kyemba, *A State of Blood*, op.cit., pp. 111 – 114; 50. Some estimates put the Kakwa at less than 1 percent of the Uganda population. See Kasfir, *The Shrinking Political Arena*, op. cit., p. 110. Muslims, all told, are probably 10 percent or less of the population. See also C. Legum, ed., *Africa Contemporary Record, 1973 – 1974*, pp. B294 – 297.

10. Charles Harrison, "Uganda: The Expulsion of the Asians," in Willem Adriaan Veenhoven, Vinifred Crum Ewing, Stichting Plurate Samenlevingen, *Case Studies on Human Rights and Fundamental Freedoms: A World Survey, Volume 1*, eds., Martinus Nijhoff, The Hague, Netherlands, 1976, p. 304. See also David P. Forsythe, ed., *Encyclopedia of Human Rights: Volume 1*, New York: Oxford University Press, 2009, p. 58.

11. Charles Harrison, "Uganda: The Expulsion of the Asians," in Willem Adriaan Veenhoven, Vinifred Crum Ewing, Stichting Plurate Samenlevingen, *Case Studies on Human Rights and Fundamental Freedoms: A World Survey, Volume 1*, op.cit., pp. 296 – 303; Jean-Marie Henckaerts, "A Catalogue of Grievances: Speech of President Amin to a Meeting of Leaders of the Asian community in Uganda, December 6, 1971," *Mass Expulsion in Modern International Law and Practice*, The Hague, The Netherlands: Martinus Nijhoff Publishers, 1995, pp. 210 – 215.

12. Godfrey Mwakikagile, *Nyerere and Africa: End of an Era*, op. cit., pp. 65.

13. David P. Forsythe, editor, *Encyclopedia Human Rights, volume 1*, New York: Oxford University Press, 2009, p. 58.

14. Nina Lakhani, "After the Exodus: 40 years on From Amin's Terror Offensive Against Asians in Uganda," in *The Independent*, London, 24 June 2012.

Chapter Seven

1. John Kato, "Julius Nyerere, the Godfather of Uganda's Political Set-up," *New Vision*, Kampala, Uganda, 4 April 2012.

2. Frederick Kamuhanda Byaruhanga, *Student Power in Africa's Higher Education: A Case of Makerere University*, New York: Routledge, Taylor & Francis Group, 2006, p. 11.

3. Jeni Klugman, Bilin Neyapti and Frances Stewart, *Conflict and Growth in Africa, Vol. 2: Kenya, Tanzania and Uganda*, Paris: Development Centre Studies, OECD Publications Service, 1999, p. 24.

4. George W. Lugalambi, *An Assessment of Democratic Deliberation in Uganda: A Case Study of The Framing of Key Issues in The Press* (A Thesis in Mass Communication submitted in partial fulfillment of the requirements for the degree of Doctor of Philosophy, Pennsylvania State University, December 2006) UMI Microform, Ann Arbor, Michigan, 2009, p. 39.

5. Kefa M. Otiso, *Culture and Customs of Uganda*, Westport, Connecticut, USA: Greenwood Press, 2006, p. 18.

6. Edward Khiddu-Makubuya, "Violence and Conflict Resolution in Uganda," in Kumar Rupesinghe and Marcial C. Rubio, eds., *The Culture of Violence, Vol. 81*, Tokyo: United Nations University Press, 1994, p. 152.

7. Devra C. Moehler, *Distrusting Democrats: Outcomes of Participatory Constitution Making*, Ann Arbor, Michigan, USA: The University of Michigan Press, 2008, p. 46.

8. F.K. Byaruhanga, *Student Power in Africa's Higher Education: A Case of Makerere University*, op.cit., p. 11.

9. Joshua B. Rubongoya, *Regime Hegemony in Museveni's Uganda: Pax Musevenica*, New York: Palgrave Macmillan, 2007, p. 53.

10. Ibid., p. 54.

11. Ibid., pp. 54 – 55.

12. Milton Obote, in an interview with Andrew Mwenda, *The Monitor*, April 2005. The interview, which was a part of a series of interviews by Mwenda with the former Uganda president, took place in Lusaka, Zambia,

where Obote was living in exile together with his wife Miriam.

13. Frederick Golooba-Mutebi, "Economic Liberalization and Politics in Uganda," in Francisco Gutiérrez, Gerd Schönwälder , eds., *Economic Liberalization and Political Violence: Utopia or Dystopia?*, New York: Pluto Press, 2010, pp. 94 – 95.

14. Ibid., pp. 95 – 96.

15. Ibid., pp. 96 – 97.

16. Ibid., p. 97.

17. D.C. Moehler, *Distrusting Democrats: Outcomes of Participatory Constitution Making*, op.cit., p. 46.

18. Obote, in an interview with Andrew Mwenda, "Liberation from Colonialism Was My Greatest Contribution," *The Monitor*, Kampala, Uganda, 16 April 2005.

19. Human Rights Watch/Africa, *The Scars of Death: Children Abducted by the Lord's Resistance Army in Uganda*, New York, Washington, London, Brussels: Human Rights Watch, September 1997, p. 63.

20. Robert Barlas, *Uganda: Cultures of the World*, Times Books International, 2002, p. 35.

21. A.B. K. Kasozi, *The Social Origins of Violence in Uganda 1964 - 1985*, Montreal, Canada: McGill-Queen's University Press, 1994, p. 172.

22. Obote, in an interview with Andrew Mwenda, "Museveni is Responsible for Most of the Killings in Luweero," *The Monitor*, 15 April 2005, Kampala, Uganda.

23. Jacob J. Akol, *Burden of Nationality: Memoirs of an African Aidworker/Journalist 1970s – 1990s*, Nairobi, Kenya: Paulines Publications Africa, 2006, p. 249.

24. F.K. Byaruhanga, *Power in Africa's Higher Education*, op.cit., pp. 11 – 12.

25. D.C. Moehler, *Distrusting Democrats: Outcomes of Participatory Constitution Making*, op. cit., pp. 46 – 47.

26. Jacob J. Akol, *Burden of Nationality*, op. cit., pp.

249 – 250.

27. Ibid., pp. 250 – 251.

28. Ibid. p. 251.

29. David Kibirige, "Who Killed Kayiira?," *The Monitor*, Kampala, Uganda, 6 March 2004.

30. Ugandan journalist, Rodney Muhumuza, talked to one of the NRA soldiers sent to kill Andrew Kayiira. His article, quoting the killer, was entitled, "I Took Part in Kayiira Murder," published in *The Monitor*, Kampala, Uganda, 13 January 2007.

31. Aaron Griffiths and James Katalikawe, "The Reformulation of Ugandan Democracy" in Sunil Bastian and Robin Luckham, eds., *Can Democracy Be Designed? The Politics of Institutional Choice in Conflict-torn Societies*, London: Zed Books, 2003, pp. 94 – 95.

32. Phares Mukasa Mutibwa, *Uganda Since Independence: A Story of Unfulfilled Hopes*, op. cit., pp. 149 – 150.

33. Ibid., pp. 150 – 151.

Chapter Eight

1. Joshua B. Rubongoya, *Regime Hegemony in Museveni's Uganda: Pax Musevenica*, New York: Palgrave Macmillan, 2007, pp. 61 – 62.

2. Ibid., pp. 62 – 63.

3. Ibid., pp. 63 – 64.

4. "Outrage at Ugandan President's Plan to Buy Himself £25 million Private Jet," subtitled, "Under Fire: Yoweri Museveni Wants to Blow Millions of Pounds on a Jet," in the *Daily Mail*, London, 19 December 2007.

5. Regina Jere-Malanda, "Special delivery--the VIP baby: President Museveni has been trying hard to rebuff critics who have denounced his grandchild's costly birth at a German private clinic. But why did it happen?," *New African*, November 2003.

6. James Mpinga, "With Mwalimu Gone, Free Bread for Butiama Children Goes Too," *The East African*, Nairobi, Kenya, November 3, 1999.

7. Ali A. Mazrui in Ali. A. Mazrui, ed., *General History of Africa VIII: Africa Since 1935*, Berkeley, California, USA: University of California Press, 1993, p. 674.

8. Ali A. Mazrui in Alamin M. Mazrui and Willy M. Mutunga, eds., *Governance and Leadership: Debating the African Condition: Mazrui and His Critics, Volume Two*, Trenton, New Jersey, USA: Africa World Press, 2003, p. 85.

Ali Mazrui's assessment of Nyerere and his policies, cited here, was first published as an article, "Tanzaphilia: A Diagnosis," in *Transition: A Journal of The Arts, Culture and Society*, Vol. 6, No. 31, June – July 1967, Kampala, Uganda, pp. 20 – 26. The article was also republished in Ali Mazrui's book, *Violence and Thought: Essays on Social Tensions in Africa*, London: Longmans, 1969. See also Ali A. Mazrui, *On Heroes and Uhuru-Worship: Essays on Independent Africa*, London: Longmans, 1967.

9. Ali A. Mazrui, in an interview with Seifudein Adem, *The Gambia Echo*, 25 July 2008.

10. Ali A. Mazrui, "Towards Re-Africanizing African Universities: Who Killed Intellectualism in the Post Colonial Era?", Nairobi, Kenya, 14 September 2003.

11. Jonathan Power, TFF Jonathan Power Columns, "Lament for Independent Africa's Greatest Leader," TFF Jonathan Power Columns, London, 8 October, 1999.

12. Philip Ochieng', "Africa's Greatest Leader Was A Heroic Failure, " *The East African*, Nairobi, Kenya, 19 October 2009.

13. Frederick Kamuhanda Byaruhanga, *Student Power in Africa's Higher Education: A Case of Makerere University*, New York: Routledge, Taylor & Francis Group, 2006, pp. 12 – 13.

14. Robert A. Dibie in Robert A. Dibie, ed., *The Politics and Policies of sub-Saharan Africa*, Lanham, Maryland, USA: University Press of America, 2001, pp. 181 – 182.

15. Ibid., pp. 182 – 183.

16. Jeni Klugman, Bilin Neyapti and Frances Stewart, *Conflict and Growth in Africa, Vol 2: Kenya, Tanzania and Uganda*, Paris: Development Centre Studies, OECD Publications Service, 1999, p. 25.

17. Edris Kiggundu, "NRM NEC: Museveni Accused of Tribalism," *The Observer*, Kampala, 13 January 2010.

18. *In2EastAfrica*, 3 March 2012.

19. Ssemujju Ibrahim Nganda, "Mutebile Saga Has Brought Out Real Museveni," *The Observer*, Kampala, Uganda, 14 March 2012.

20. Andrew M. Mwenda, "Personalizing Power in Uganda," in Larry Diamond, Marc F. Plattner, eds., *Democratization in Africa: Progress and Retreat*, Baltimore, Maryland, USA: Johns Hopkins University Press, 2010, pp. 234, 236.

21. Ibid., pp. 236 – 237.

22. Ibid., pp. 237 – 239.

23. Mary Anne Fitzgerald, "With Chaos Ended, What About Rights?", *The New York Times*, 9 October 1992.

Conclusion

1. "Kamuzu Banda Dies: 'Big Man' Among Anticolonialists, " *The New York Times*, 27 November 1997.

2. Godfrey Mwakikagile, *Military Coups in West Africa Since the Sixties* (Huntington, New York: Nova Science Publishers, Inc., 2002).

3."Nigeria: Islamist Push," in *The Economist*, 6 November 1999, pp. 48 and 49. See also Minabere Ibelema, "Nigeria: The Politics of Marginalization," in

Current History: A Journal of Contemporary World Affairs, May 2000, p. 211:

"These ethnoreligious tensions are reminiscent of the events in 1966 and 1967 that precipitated Nigeria's civil war in which more than 1 million Nigerians died when the Igbos created the secessionist state of Biafra.

Emeka Odumegwu Ojukwu, who led the 30-month secession, has been blamed by some northern leaders for fomenting this year's Kaduna crisis. Ojukwu has responded by calling the accusation a hallucination, and by suggesting psychiatric examination for the accusers. But he has also said of the Igbos that 'we have to get prepared, be on our toes and wait.'

Leaders used similar language directly preceding the declaration of secession in 1967."

4. Northern Nigerian politician, quoted in "Nigeria: Islamist Push," *The Economist*, ibid.

5. *The Economist*, 6 November 1999, p. ibid., p. 49.

6. "A Survey of Nigeria – Here's Hoping: Fissiparous Folk," in *The Economist*, 15 January 2000, p. 14 of the survey. See also David L. Bevan, Paul Collier and Jan Willem Gunning, *Nigeria and Indonesia: The Political Economy of Poverty, Equity and Growth* (Oxford: Oxford University Press, 1999).

7. *The Economist*, 29 January 2000, p. 4.

8. "Nigeria: Religious Blood," in *The Economist*, 26 February 2000, p. 55.

9. Ibid.

10. Minabere Ibelema, op. cit.

11. "Nigeria: Religious Blood," *The Economist*, ibid.

12. *The Christian Science Monitor*, 2 March 2000, p. 24. See also Nigeria in *The Economist*, 4 March 2000, p. 6: "Some 400 people...were killed in ethnic and religious violence after fighting between Christians and Muslims in the north. Troops eventually brought order. The

government said that northern Muslim states had suspended plans to introduce full *sharia* law."

13. *The Christian Science Monitor*, 25 May 2000, p. 24.

14. "Africa News: Africa Nightline," voice of America (VOA), Washington, D.C., 25 March 2000.

15. *The Christian Science Monitor*, 25 May 2000, p. 24; *The Wall Street Journal*, 23 May 2000, p. A-1.

16. Steve U. Nwabuzor, in *Niger World*, 24 March 2000.

17. Minabere Ibelema, "Nigeria: The Politics of Marginalization," *Current History: A Journal of Contemporary World Affairs*, op. cit., p. 211.

18. Wole Soyinka, *The Open Sore of a Continent: A Personal Narrative of the Nigerian Crisis* (New York: Oxford University Press, 1996), pp. 31 – 32.

19. Minabere Ibelema, "Nigeria: The Politics of Marginalization," *Current History: A Journal of Contemporary World Affairs*, op. cit., pp. 211 – 212.

20. Godfrey Mwakikagile, *Economic Development in Africa*, op. cit.

21. *The Christian Science Monitor*, 26 May 2000, p. 20.

22. Joe Igbokwe, in *Tempo,* Lagos, Nigeria, 9 March 2000; *World Press Review*, May 2000, p. 28.

23. *Tempo*, and *World Press Review*, ibid.

24. *Guardian*, Lagos, Nigeria, 28 February 2000; *World Press Review*, ibid.

25. Odumegwu Ojukwu, quoted by M. Ibelema, *Current History: A Journal of Contemporary World Affairs*, op. cit., p. 213.

26. Tajudeen Suleiman, "The Man Behind the Sharia," in *Tempo*, Lagos, Nigeria, 11 November 1999; *World Press Review*, January 2000, pp. 31 – 32.

27. Cameron Duodu, Gemini News Service, London, 29 October 1999 in *World Press Review*, ibid., p. 31.

28. Michael Chege, "Africa's Murderous Professors,"

The National Interest, No. 46, Washington, D.C., Winter 1996/97, pp. 33 – 34; also quoted by Godfrey Mwakikagile, *The Modern African State: Quest for Transformation* (Huntington, New York: Nova Science Publishers, Inc., 2001), p. 190.

29. Quoted in "Kenyan Strongman Blames Political Foes for Surge in Violence," in the *International Herald Tribune,* 18 August 1997, p. 1. Also quoted by Godfrey Mwakikagile, *Ethnic Politics in Kenya and Nigeria*, Huntington, New York: Nova Science Publishers, Inc., 2001, p. 120.

30. Mallam Mukhtar Bello, quoted by Colin Legum and John Drysdale, eds., *Africa Contemporary Record: Annual Survey and Documents 1968 - 1969* (London: Africa Research Ltd., 1969), p. 664.

31. Ahmadu Bello, quoted in *Africa Contemporary Record,* ibid.

32. Mallam Muhammadu Mustapha Maude Gyari, ibid.

33. Mallam Bashari Umaru, ibid.

34. A. A. Abogede, ibid.

35. Iya Abubakar, ibid.

36. Mallam Ibrahim Muse, ibid.

37. Mallam Bashari Umaru, ibid.

38. Alhaji Usman Liman, ibid.

39. Alhaji Ibrahim Musa Gashash, ibid.

40. Gibson Kuria, quoted in "Explosion of Violence in Kenya Stirs Fears of Electoral Mayhem," in the *International Herald Tribune,* 21 August 1997, p. 6. Also quoted by Godfrey Mwakikagile, *Ethnic Politics in Kenya and Nigeria*, ibid., p. 121.

41. *International Herald Tribune,* ibid. G. Mwakikagile, ibid.

42. Ibid.

43. Richard Leakey, quoted by the *International Herald Tribune*, 21 August 1997, p. 6, and by Godfrey Mwakikagile, *Ethnic Politics in Kenya and Nigeria*, op. cit, p. 122.

44. "A Celtic Resurgence: A Conversation with Welsh writer Bobi Jones," in *The Bloomsbury Review*, Denver, Colorado, May/June 2000, pp. 3, and 25.

45. Obafemi Awolowo, *Path to Nigerian Freedom*, Faber & Faber, London, 1947.

46. "Nigerian Civil War: Aburi Conference and Subsequent Developments, January - July 1967," in *Africa Research Bulletin, Vol. 4, Nos. 1 - 7, 1967; Africa Contemporary Record: Annual Survey and Documents 1968 - 1969,* Africa Research Limited, 1969, p. 648.

47. Nnamdi Azikiwe, *The Political Blueprint of Nigeria,* African Book Co., 1943.

48. Quoted in Jack David Eller, *From Culture to Ethnicity to Conflict: An Anthropological Perspective on International Ethnic Conflict*, University of Michigan Press, Ann Arbor, 1999, p. 221. See also Neil Jeffrey Kressel, *Mass Hate: The Global Rise of Genocide and Terror,* Plenum Press, New York, 1996, pp. 87 – 118.

49. Julius K. Nyerere, *Decentralisation*, National Printing Co., Ltd., 1972, Dar es Salaam, Tanzania, pp. 1, 2, 3, 5, and 10.

50. Ali A. Mazrui, *Towards A Pax Africana: A Study of Ideology and Ambition*, (London: Weidenfeld & Nicolson, 1967).

See also Juan Enriquez, "Too Many Flags," *Foreign Policy*, Washington, D.C., Fall 1999, pp. 30 - 48; George F. Will, "The Poor Are Unwanted in the 'Secessionist Age'," *The Washington Post*, June 24, 1998, and in the *Internatuinal Herald Tribune*, June 25, 1998, p. 5; Pascal Boniface, "The Proliferation of States," *The Washington Quarterly*, 1998; Francis Deng and Terrence Lyons, eds., *African Reckoning: A Quest for Good Governance* (Washington, D.C.: Brookings Institution Press, 1998); Carol Lancaster, *Aid to Africa: So Much to Do, So Little Done* (Chicago: university of Chicago Press, 1999).

Gidon Gottlieb, *Nation Against State: A New Approach to Ethnic Conflicts and the Decline of Sovereignty* (New

York: Council on Foreign Relations, 1993); Robert Jackson, *Quasi-States: Sovereignty, International Relations and the Third World* (Cambridge: Cambridge University Press, 1990); Kenichi Ohmae, *The End of the Nation-State: The Rise of Economic Regional Powers* (New York: Free Press, 1995); David Elkin, *Beyond Sovereignty: Territory and Political Economy in the Twentieth-First Century* (Toronto: University of Toronto Press, 1995).

Saskia Sassen, *Losing Control? Sovereignty in an Age of Globalization* (New York: Columbia University Press, 1996); James Minahan, *Nations Without States: A Historical Dictionary of Contemporary National Movements* (Westport, Connecticut: Greenwood Press, 1996); Joseph Nye Jr., "In Government We Don't Trust," in *Foreign Policy*, Washington, D.C., Fall 1997; "The World Economy: The Future of the State," in *The Economist*, 20 September 1997; Ted Robert Gurr, "Ethnic Warfare on the Wane," in *Foreign Affairs*, May/June 2000, pp. 52 – 64.

See also Obiora C. Okafor, "After Martydom: International Law, Substitute Groups, and the Construction of Legitimate Statehood in Africa," in *Harvard International Law Journal: International Law and the Developing World - A Millennial Analysis*, Harvard Law School, Cambridge, Massachusetts, Spring 2000; Stephen Ellis, *The Mask of Anarchy: The Destruction of Liberia and the Religious Dimension of an African Civil War* (New York: New York University Press, 2000).

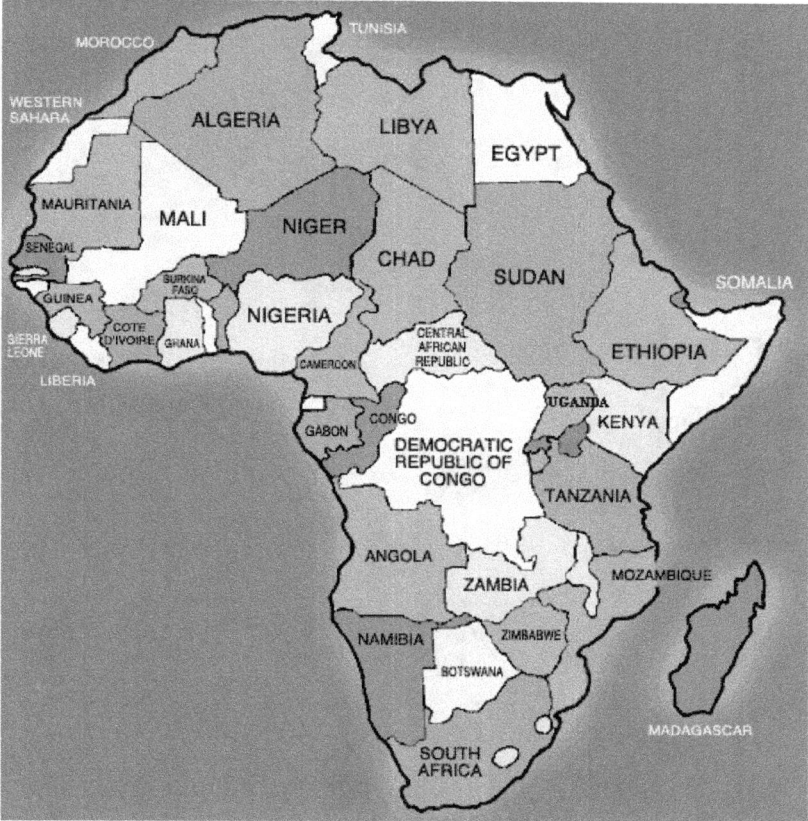

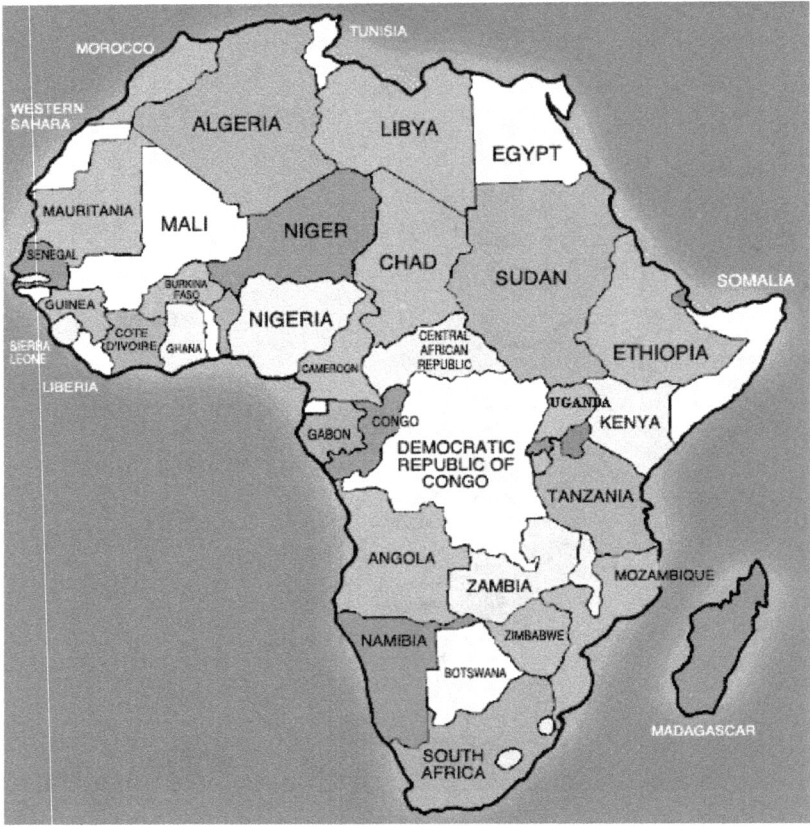

www.ingramcontent.com/pod-product-compliance
Lightning Source LLC
Chambersburg PA
CBHW071947270326
41928CB00009B/1371